lonely planet

Seoul

**Ann Babe, Esther Carlstone, Jennifer Chang,
Simon Richmond, Phillip Tang, Charles Usher**

FROM LEFT: JOHN W. BANAGAN/GETTY IMAGES, FRANKVANDENBERGH/GETTY IMAGES

Changing of the guards, Deoksugung (p82)

CONTENTS

Plan Your Trip

The Guide

Painted wooden ceiling, Changdeokgung (p60)

Toolkit

Storybook

OZONE FOTO/SHUTTERSTOCK

Seoul skyline and N Seoul Tower (p78)

SEOUL

THE JOURNEY BEGINS HERE

Seoul is my favourite city. Maybe it's because so many of my memories come from here. Maybe it's because of its familiarities and comforts – the taste of *pajeon* and *makgeolli* on rainy days, the scent of cherry blossoms come spring – or because of its surprises. One of my most vivid memories is from when I was 22, wobbly and bleary-eyed after a marathon night out in Itaewon. It's cold. As I'm wandering, trying to work out which way to go, a grandmother comes up behind me. Just as I'm wondering what she's about to do – feeling slightly worried, mildly embarrassed – she reaches her hand to my coat neck and gently tucks the tag back inside, then flashes a small smile and disappears. Maybe I love Seoul the way I do because, as the world hurtles forward, with this city often leading the way, there will forever be some part of it that's lost, dreamlike, somewhere else. This is the feeling I hope you get to experience, too.

Ann Babe

@ann_e_babe

Ann is a Korean-American writer who covers Korea and beyond. She wrote the introductory chapters, Gwanghwamun & Jongno-gu, Itaewon & Yongsan-gu and Toolkit chapters.

My favourite experience is going to **Gwangjang Market** (p72) at night, and people-watching while eating *bindatteok*.

WHO GOES WHERE

Our writers and experts choose the places that, for them, define Seoul.

GALITSKAYA/GETTY IMAGES

I arrived in Seoul for the first time just days before the restored **Cheonggye-cheon** (pictured; p94) reopened, so my relationship with the city has always been tied to its most famous urban-regeneration project. The stream encapsulates everything I love about Seoul – its ambition, its commitment to public life, its self-reinvention. I also love the Cheonggye-cheon's multifaceted nature. At its headwaters, you have art, crowds and skyscrapers, but move downstream and you're in quiet, locals-only territory.

Charles Usher

@charlesreclausher

Charles is a writer and editor, who lived in Seoul for a decade. He wrote the Myeong-dong & Jung-gu, Western Seoul, Gangnam & Southern Seoul and Day Trips chapters.

CHANOO8/SHUTTERSTOCK

There's something amazing to see around nearly every corner in Seoul, but when I need to take in the broader picture, get some exercise and enjoy a quick burst of nature, I follow **Seoul City Wall** (pictured; p181) up to the summit of one of the four guardian mountains. From the exposed granite peaks of **Inwangsan** (p190), I have a bird's-eye view of it all – the Joseon-dynasty palaces, the pixelated patchwork of modern buildings and the iconic N Seoul Tower.

Simon Richmond

@simonrichmond

An award-winning travel writer, Simon has contributed to many Lonely Planet guidebooks. He wrote the Dongdaemun & Eastern Seoul and Northern Seoul chapters.

HALLYU!

Get hyped for *hallyu* (the Korean Wave), the global cultural force that is Korean pop music, dramas, fashion and beauty products. Seoul is the epicentre of interactive K-Pop experiences and famous locations from K-Drama series and films. It has the flash of Apgujeong and Cheongdam, the neon of Myeong-dong and the flair of Hannam, all places where you can ride the wave of that K-Style way of life.

K-Pop

Gangnam is the home of K-Pop record labels such as SM, JYP and Cube, while HYBE is in Yongsan and YG is in Hapjeong.

K-Drama

From palaces serving as sets for period dramas, to the vibrant nightlife of Itaewon and bright lights of N Seoul Tower backdropping contemporary series, all of Seoul's a stage.

K-Beauty

Seoul is cosmetics heaven, selling top-quality, inexpensive products, many made famous by K-Pop and K-Drama idols. Apgujeong is ritzy, while the young congregate in Hongdae and Myeong-dong.

FROM LEFT: IMBC/IMAZINS VIA GETTY IMAGES, ALBUM/ALAMY, SORBIS/SHUTTERSTOCK

Olive Young brand, which organises the Olive Young Festa (p131)

BEST HALLYU EXPERIENCES

Hold a K-Pop video shoot in a filming zone at ❶ **HiKR Ground** (p95), where you can adjust the lighting and choose the soundtrack.

Take a dance or voice class at the ❷ **Ktown4u Academy** (p143), or just pick up merch to support your favourite idol.

Trace the history of Korean cinema at the ❸ **Korean Film Museum** (p109) from early silent features to international blockbusters like *Parasite* and *Train to Busan*.

Experience the zenith of K-Design and retail at ❹ **Haus Nowhere** (p171), a futuristic department store that's like exploring a contemporary-art hall.

Go bonkers for K-beauty products at the annual ❺ **Olive Young Festa** (p131), a bonanza of cosmetic classes, shopping and samples.

KIMCHI, K-BBQ & MORE

Everywhere you go in Seoul, tasty treats await, from sticky snacks at budget street stalls to sumptuous royal banquets with a seemingly endless array of *banchan* side dishes at full-course *hanjeongsik* (banquet) restaurants. Join Seoulites taste-testing fusion food in trending eateries, or dive into the market buzz where cooks prepare time-honoured favourites before your eyes (and nose). You can try your hand at cooking by joining a class or two.

FROM LEFT: URVASHI9/GETTY IMAGES, TOP PHOTO CORPORATION/ALAMY, RAYTAN/SHUTTERSTOCK

Market & Street Stalls

If you can stick it on a skewer, you'll find it in Seoul. Thrills include *tteokbokki* (spicy rice cakes), *odeng* (fish cakes; pictured) and Korean takes on corndogs and fried chicken.

Michelin Spots

From classic and contemporary Korean to international cuisines, there are 197 restaurants in the Seoul capital area recommended in the Michelin Guide.

Restaurant Reservations

While unnecessary for casual joints, reservations are recommended (and sometimes required) for top-end or trending restaurants. RSVP on Korea's No 1 restaurant-reservation app, CATCHTABLE.

Gwangjang Market (p72)

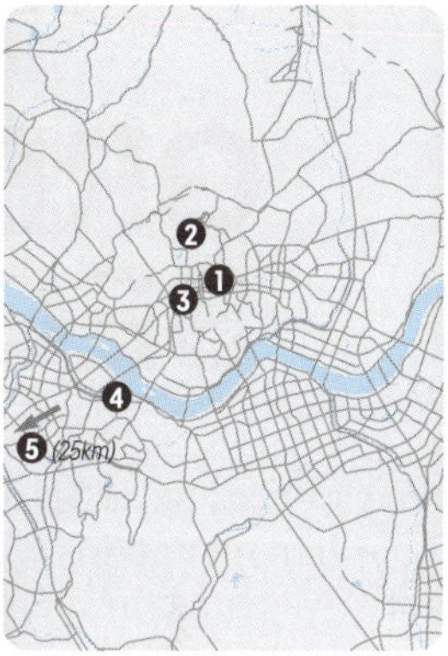

BEST CULINARY EXPERIENCES

Eat *jokbal* (pig trotters), *bindaetteok* (mung-bean pancakes) and *yukhoe* (raw beef) while sitting shoulder-to-shoulder with locals at ❶ **Gwangjang Market** (p72).

Learn how to make kimchi, *jeon* (savoury pancakes) or other classic Korean foods at a cooking class at ❷ **O'ngo** (p73).

Join locals bellying up to the bar for bowls of noodles or braised hairtail in the atmospheric food alleys of ❸ **Namdaemun Market** (p90).

Pick your dinner from the hundreds of stalls at ❹ **Noryangjin Fisheries Wholesale Market** (p116), Seoul's largest seafood market, and have it sliced up on site.

Slurp up some *jajangmyeon*, Korea's favourite Chinese food, and then learn about its history at the ❺ **Jajangmyeon Museum** (p196) in Incheon's Chinatown.

GREEN SEOUL

Green space is never far away in Seoul, where four guardian mountains watch over the city and a mighty river runs through it. The metropolis weaves narrow parks through its streets. The sound of birdcall has come back to a stream that once was a highway, industrial spaces have been returned to the land, and when you really want to escape the city, there are spectacular hikes for all levels of fitness in easy reach.

The Han River

Flowing west-east through Seoul, Hangang is Korea's most important river. It may not be the country's longest, but it is the biggest by volume and flow rate.

Capital Parks

With 26 city-run parks and hundreds of local neighbourhood parks and municipal gardens, Seoul is a public-parkland paradise.

Restored Spaces

From the Cheonggye-cheon to Oil Tank Culture Park to Seoullo 7017, the city has renovated many former highways and industrial spaces into lush green spaces.

Baegundae (p194)

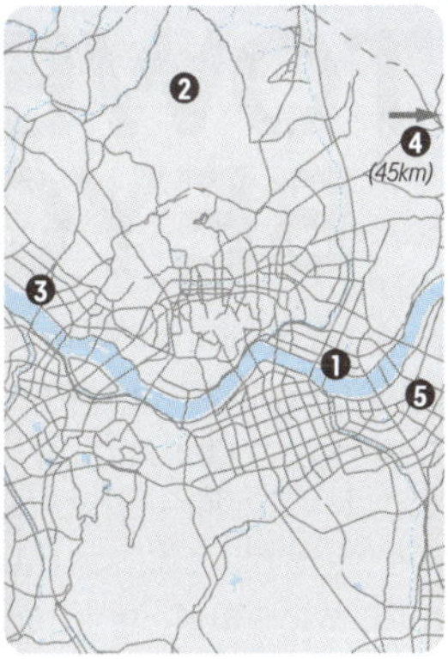

BEST OUTDOORS EXPERIENCES

Head to ❶ **Ttukseom Hangang Park** (p171) to join a guided kayak paddle along the river at sunset run by Koa Travel.

Challenge yourself to reach Bukhansan's 836.5m summit of ❷ **Baegundae** (p194), Seoul's highest peak, or hike myriad other trails.

Fly a kite, stroll through silver grass and look for wetland wildlife at ❸ **World Cup Park** (p108), a collection of five interconnected green spaces.

Fill your phone's camera roll at the ❹ **Garden of Morning Calm** (p212), an incredible assemblage of themed gardens, which range from English to traditional Korean.

Walk the walls of an ancient earthen fortress at ❺ **Olympic Park** (p158), or just picnic on the grass of this sprawling green space.

TEMPLES, TOWERS & BEYOND

Korea's form of feng shui and geomancy is called *pungsu*, a practice that harmonises architecture with nature by balancing the flow of energy from wind and water. It's why, looking back, palaces and temples were placed so strategically near mountains and waterways and, looking forward, glass and steel appear to be forged into such natural curves. Seoul's buildings of the past, present and future tell the story of what happens when architecture meets nature.

Hanok Villages

Bukchon may be the most famous (and overtouristed), but it's just one of Seoul's neighbourhoods known for beautiful *hanok*. Others include Eunpyeong (pictured; p111), Namsangol, Seochon and Ikseon-dong.

Royal Palaces

Seoul's five main royal palaces are Gyeongbokgung, Changdeokgung (pictured; p60), Changgyeonggung, Deoksugung and Gyeonghuigung.

Buddhist Temples

From Jogye-sa to Bongeun-sa, Seoul is home to 60 temples, best appreciated when slowing down for a Templestay programme.

FROM LEFT: FRANCESCO RICCARDO IACOMINO/GETTY IMAGES, MESAMONG/SHUTTERSTOCK, POPOVA TETIANA/SHUTTERSTOCK

Hanbok traditional clothing, Gyeongbokgung (p50)

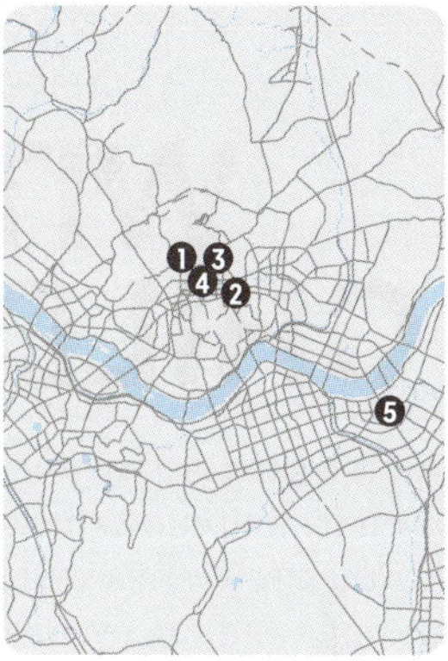

BEST ARCHITECTURAL EXPERIENCES

Dress up in *hanbok* (traditional clothing) and pretend you're Joseon royalty walking the grounds of ❶ **Gyeongbokgung** (p50), Seoul's largest royal palace.

Marvel at ❷ **Dongdaemun Design Plaza** (DDP, p166), a dazzling spaceship-like complex showcasing Seoul design and fashion with exhibition halls, museums and shops.

Be awed at ❸ **Won Buddhism Wonnam Temple** (p180), a unique Seoul temple designed by acclaimed Korean architect Minsok Cho that turns concrete walls into a thing of beauty.

Take a picture of Korea's longest wooden building at UNESCO-listed ❹ **Jongmyo** (p66), a Confucian shrine housing the spirits of Joseon royalty.

See the city from ❺ **Lotte World Tower** (p160), Korea's tallest building, or join a tour to walk across an exterior bridge 124 floors up.

WITH CHILDREN

Seoul is a safe, family-friendly city with lots of kid-friendly museums (including several devoted to kids themselves), as well as amusement parks, playgrounds and fun events that will appeal to all age groups. From Haechi, Seoul's big pink mascot often accompanied by his four guardian pals, to Kakao Friends, the emoticons of the messaging app KakaoTalk, lots of cute surprises await the little ones around the city.

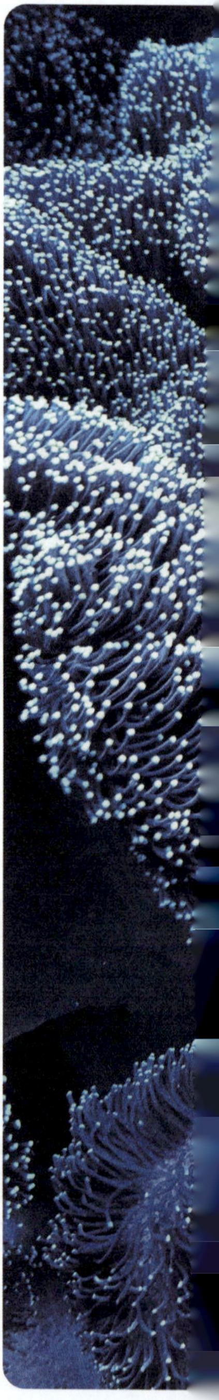

Children's Day

Korea celebrates Children's Day (pictured) every 5 May, which sees special events for kids across Seoul.

Eating & Sleeping

Korean-style guesthouse rooms are family-friendly, as everyone sleeps together on *yo* (mattresses) on *ondol* (heated floors). Children are welcome in restaurants, though few will have kids menus. High chairs aren't common.

Public Transport

Children under six years of age travel free. Child fares apply to kids under 13.

SEA LIFE COEX, Seoul Aquarium (p143)

BEST FOR KIDS EXPERIENCES

Pilot aircraft, work as an air traffic controller, or ride in a stunt plane at a ❶ **National Aviation Museum of Korea** (p117) virtual-reality experience.

Watch sharks and rays glide past and catch one of the mermaid shows or otter feedings at ❷ **SEA LIFE COEX, Seoul Aquarium** (p143).

Join a tour of the hands-on ❸ **Robot and AI Museum** (p192), where robots play soccer, draw portraits and talk to you.

Take a spin on the amusement rides at ❹ **Seoul Children's Grand Park** (p175) and glimpse elephants, tigers and lions at its zoo.

Press your face to the window of ❺ **Namsan Cable Car** (p79) as it soars over the city on its way up Namsan.

FOR FREE

You don't need a wallet packed with won to enjoy Seoul. Many of the best things you can do – hiking around ancient fortress walls, enjoying the pomp of the changing-of-the-guard ceremonies at the palaces, attending a Korean culture festival, watching busking, dance and other street performances on Hongdae St – cost nothing at all. Don't miss the opportunity to simply wander, either. It's one of the best ways to experience the city and there are plenty of free things to see.

Free Museums

The list of museums with no entrance fee is pretty extensive and includes heavy hitters like the **Seoul Museum of History** (p52), **War Memorial of Korea** (p128) and **Seoul Museum of Craft Art** (pictured; p68).

Festivals & Events

Not a week goes by without a free festival or event happening somewhere in the city. Keep tabs on the Korea Tourism Organization website for listings.

Culture Day

The last Wednesday of the month is Culture Day, with many museums, such as **MMCA Seoul** (p62), offering free admission.

FROM LEFT: JAMES TALALAY/ALAMY, JULY7TH/GETTY IMAGES, MLENNY/GETTY IMAGES

Cheonggye-cheon (p94)

BEST FREE EXPERIENCES

Sift through centuries of history and culture at the country's most visited museum, the ❶ **National Museum of Korea** (p124) in Yongsan.

Spot herons, enjoy light shows or just people-watch while strolling along the ❷ **Cheonggye-cheon** (p94), then learn all about the revived stream at its museum.

Pack a picnic and watch the ❸ **Moonlight Rainbow Fountain** (p152), a nightly water-and-light show pouring off a bridge over the Han River.

Traverse the street-art-painted alleys of the 'moon village' of ❹ **Ihwa Maeul** (p178) and rest at a cafe with a glorious view across Seoul.

Explore the gates, guard towers and secret entrances of Suwon's fortress of ❺ **Hwaseong** (p206), representing the peak of Joseon accomplishment.

UNDER THE RADAR

Done touring Gyeongbokgung, going to the *hanok* cafes of Bukchon, shopping in Myeong-dong and COEX and partying in Hongdae? Lucky for you, that's only the beginning of all there is to do in Seoul. Among the city's endless diversions are many that are hidden away, distant to reach and harder to photograph. But sometimes that's part of what makes something special. And often, it's what you don't expect that ends up being most memorable. So go ahead – get out there!

A Tourist's Footprint

Some places in Seoul are iconic for a reason, such as the *hanok* in Bukchon, but searching for alternative sights (Namsangol, pictured; p80) can help ease their overtourism.

Winter Holiday

For fewer crowds and lower prices on flights and hotels, consider visiting Seoul in winter. It'll be cold, but it'll be fun.

Stay on the Outskirts

It's fun to stay where the action is – and it can be equally rewarding to stay where the action is not, in out-of-the-way places where only the locals go.

FROM LEFT: AARONCHOI/GETTY IMAGES, JULY7TH/GETTY IMAGES, ONGI/SHUTTERSTOCK

Mullae Arts Village (p115)

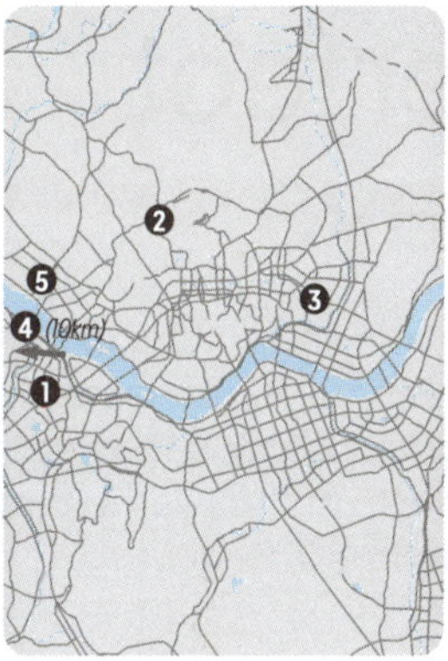

BEST UNDER-THE-RADAR EXPERIENCES

Embrace the unexpected at ❶ **Mullae Arts Village** (p115), a neighbourhood where galleries and street art share alleys with old factories and machine shops.

Stroll through the beautiful hillside gardens surrounding ❷ **Seokpajeong Seoul Museum of Art** (p186), an elegant late-Joseon villa secreted behind a top-drawer art museum.

Find unique pieces among the younger vendors offering a curated selection of antiques and retro treasures at ❸ **Dapsimni Antiques Market** (p170).

Navigate pipes and peer into dark corners to find boundary-pushing art at ❹ **Bucheon Art Bunker B39** (p205), which was once a rubbish incinerator.

Check out an art exhibition or snap some postindustrial pics at ❺ **Oil Tank Culture Park** (p107), an oil-storage facility turned cultural complex.

Perfect Days

From arts and culture to temples and teahouses, there are plenty of sights, history, shows and food venues to enthral you in three super days in Seoul.

Jungsik (p152)

TOP PHOTO CORPORATION/SHUTTERSTOCK

DAY 1

Gwanghwamun & Jongno-gu

Start with a tour through **Gyeongbokgung** (p50), being sure to return to the palace's beautiful main gate, **Gwanghwamun**, at 10am to watch the pageantry of the changing of the guard. Walk the winding streets of **Bukchon Hanok Village** (p70) and **Insa-dong** (p64), pausing for refreshments at a teahouse in between browsing the art galleries and craft stores.

Lunch Stop at **Koong** (p52) to try the legendary meat dumplings.

Gwanghwamun & Jongno-gu

Go on an afternoon tour of **Changdeokgung** (p60) and its serene Secret Garden, **Huwon** (p61). Explore the wooded grounds of the venerable **Jongmyo** (p66) shrine, housing the spirit tablets of Joseon kings and queens. If you finish early, continue on to the cool converted *hanok* cafes and shops of **Ikseon-dong** (p54).

Dinner Sample *bindaetteok*, *yukhoe* or *sundae* at the stalls of **Gwangjang Market** (p72).

Myeong-dong & Jung-gu

Take your seat at an engaging nonverbal show such as **Nanta** (p80) or **Jump** (p80). Be dazzled by the bright lights and retail overload of **Myeong-dong** (p74), stopping to graze on street food, as well as neighbouring **Namdaemun Market** (p90). Stroll along the **Cheonggye-cheon** (p94), stopping in **Euljiro** (p97) for a drink at a neon-lit bar.

DAY 2

Northern Seoul

Shadow the **Seoul City Wall** (p181) down to Buam-dong, over **Bukaksan** (p181) and to Seongbuk-dong, a hike of around two hours. Catch your breath and rest your feet in the beautiful **Suyeonsanbang** (p185) teahouse, and the equally serene surrounds of the temple **Gilsang-sa** (p183).

Lunch Stuff yourself with cheap and tasty rice cake at **I Love Sindang-dong** (p169).

Dongdaemun & Eastern Seoul

Admire the 21st-century architectural styling of **Dongdaemun Design Plaza** (p166), where you can get up close on a guided tour, or walk across its gently curving roof. Head over to **Seoul Forest** (p173) for some time in nature, before going to **Seongsu** (p174) to search out the latest fashions in its boutiques and pop-ups.

Dinner South of the river, treat yourself to neo-Korean cuisine with a booking at **Jungsik** (p152)

Gangnam & Southern Seoul

Catch a concert at **Seoul Arts Center** (p152) or the next-door **National Gugak Center** (p152), or see the day's final floodlit flourish of the **Moonlight Rainbow Fountain** (p152) off the Banpo Bridge. Finish at the flash cocktail bars of **Apgujeong** (p149) and **Cheongdam** (p149).

DAY 3

Western Seoul

Enjoy the horticultural environments of a dozen countries at the **Seoul Botanic Park** (p118). Rent a bicycle and take a spin around the island of **Seonyudo Park** (p115), a former water-treatment plant, before cycling on to the island of **Yeouido** (p114), home to Korea's **National Assembly Building** (p112).

Lunch Select your own seafood for cooking at **Noryangjin Fisheries Wholesale Market** (p116).

Itaewon & Yongsan-gu

Go east to the **National Museum of Korea** (p124) for a sampling of its centuries of Korean history, then on to the **Leeum Museum of Art** (p136) for its splendid collection of traditional and contemporary pieces. Shop around the haute hood of **Hannam-dong** (p134), the stomping ground of many a celebrity Seoulite.

Dinner Head to Haebangchon for dinner and drinks in buzzy **Sinheung Market** (p131).

Western Seoul

Back west, check out the hip quarters of **Mangwon-dong** (p104) and its trending street **Mangnidan-gil** (p104). Round out the day in **Hongdae** (p100), Seoul's youth-culture district, seeing a show at a bar or a busking or dance crew performance along Hongdae St (aka Red Road). If you feel inclined, put on a performance of your own inside one of the private karaoke rooms at **Luxury Su Noraebang** (p100).

WHEN TO GO

Think twice before coming to Seoul in the humid height of summer. The ideal times are spring and autumn.

Koreans are proud of their four seasons – and indeed each one bestows its own beauties. Spring brings the candy-floss froths of delicate pink and white cherry blossoms, at their height in late March and early April, along with comfortable climes for viewing them. Summer, from June through August, though at times stifling, is lush and verdant, particularly in the city's many expansive parks that travail mountain passes and hug the Han River. Come autumn, the landscape is an explosion of burnished foliage, a prime time for hiking. And December through February is a wintry wonderland, when a walk amongst snow-dusted palaces and *hanok* (traditional houses) is nothing short of magical.

Seasonal Rates on Lodging

Reserve accommodation well in advance if you're visiting in spring or autumn and you wish to stay in popular neighbourhoods in centrally located Jung-gu and Jongno-gu. Boutique *hanok* stays fill up fast. January and February are the cheapest months.

I LIVE HERE

SUMMER NIGHTS

Benjamin Coz is a bboy, singer-songwriter and proud Korean-American adoptee who cherishes community.

Seoul summer nights unravel next to the Han River through crowds of people, rows of scattered street-food stands and square foam picnic mats. The heavy, humid air is electric with banter, musicians and entertainers busking. Make sure to look both ways before crossing running paths as it's not uncommon to have a bike (and occasionally, a skateboard or two) zip right by you.

Yellow dust, Seoul

FROM LEFT: TTLSC/SHUTTERSTOCK, MAREMAGNUM/GETTY IMAGES

YELLOW DUST

In spring, fine sand can come to town, blowing in from the Gobi Desert and reducing visibility. The phenomenon, called *hwangsa*, can carry industrial pollutants such as heavy metals, pesticides and other ultrafine particles. Pay attention to government-issued warnings and wear a face mask.

Weather through the Year

JANUARY	FEBRUARY	MARCH	APRIL	MAY	JUNE
Avg. daytime max: **1°C**	Avg. daytime max: **4.5°C**	Avg. daytime max: **10°C**	Avg. daytime max: **19°C**	Avg. daytime max: **23°C**	Avg. daytime max: **27°C**
Days of rainfall: **7**	Days of rainfall: **6**	Days of rainfall: **6**	Days of rainfall: **7**	Days of rainfall: **7**	Days of rainfall: **10**

MONSOON SEASON

Known as *jangma* season in Korea, the end of June through July (and sometimes August) brings heavy and frequent rains that last for over a month. Low-lying areas of Seoul, in particular, are at risk of flash flooding and landslides, so always stay informed.

Blockbuster Events

One of the best places to experience the blossoming trees and flowers is Yeouido for the **Yeongdeungpo Yeouido Spring Flower Festival** (p109).
April

In celebration of Buddha's Birthday, the UNESCO-listed **Yeon Deung Hoe** (p70), or Lotus Lantern Festival, sees the city's temples and Gwanghwamun Sq festooned in colourful paper lanterns. The climax is a nighttime parade of giant illuminated floats that snakes its way through the city from Dongdaemun to Jogye-sa.
April or May

Jongmyo Daeje (p67) reenacts a solemn Confucian ceremony involving ritual music, song, dance and lavish offerings of food and alcohol. It begins with a procession from Gwanghwamun Sq to Jongmyo, culminating in front of the main shrine Jeongjeon.
May

The Cheonggye-cheon is aglow with lights during the **Seoul Lantern Festival** (p70), when gigantic, fantastic lanterns made by expert craftspeople wow spectators.
November

Hangang, Fireworks & Fringe

Held according to the lunar calendar (on the fifth day of the fifth month), **Dano** features shamanist rituals and mask dances at several locales, including Namsangol Hanok Village and the National Folk Museum of Korea.
May

The month-long **Hangang Summer Festival** is focused along Seoul's main river. In summer, outdoor swimming pools are also open in parks along the Han River.
July and August

One of Seoul's best performing-arts festivals, running since 1998, the **Seoul Fringe Festival** brings together experimental and trailblazing local and international artists who converge on Hongdae.
July and August

The city's night skies come alive for the **Seoul International Fireworks Festival** (p109). Best viewed from Yeouido Hangang Park, this event sees dazzling fireworks displays by Korean and international teams
October

I LIVE HERE

AUTUMN COLOURS

Eunjeong Lee is a freelancer who works as a barista, Airbnb host and more.

When summer has passed, the hot weather finally cools off. When autumn comes, I like to walk around my neighbourhood of Hongdae to see the leaves changing colours. It's a good time to hike the mountains in the city, to cycle by the riverside and spend time there with delivery food. It's a beautiful time to be in Seoul.

Hongdae (p100)

SWELTERING SUMMER

Seoul's stickiest time of year typically comes at the end of monsoon season, when the city's atmosphere is left in subtropical conditions. The high humidity makes the soaring temperatures feel even hotter. Remember to keep hydrated.

JULY	AUGUST	SEPTEMBER	OCTOBER	NOVEMBER	DECEMBER
Avg. daytime max: **29°C**	Avg. daytime max: **30°C**	Avg. daytime max: **25°C**	Avg. daytime max: **20°C**	Avg. daytime max: **12°C**	Avg. daytime max: **3°C**
Days of rainfall: **15**	Days of rainfall: **13**	Days of rainfall: **9**	Days of rainfall: **6**	Days of rainfall: **7**	Days of rainfall: **6**

FROM LEFT: THE CHOSUNILBO JNS/IMAZINS VIA GETTY IMAGES, TCD/PROD.DB/ALAMY

Dokyeom, Seungkwan and Hoshi of K-Pop group Seventeen

GET PREPARED FOR SEOUL

Useful things to load in your bag, your ears and your brain.

Clothes

Warm layers Wrap up for Seoul's snowy, cold winters. Spring days can be warm with big drops in temperature at night, so a light jacket comes in handy.

Sun protection Summer is oppressively hot and humid, so dressing in light, loose-fitting clothing and using a hat, parasol or umbrella to shield from the sun, as well as a hand fan, is common. Wearing tank tops and flip-flops is not.

Waterproofs In June and July come the heavy rains of monsoon season; be prepared with waterproof shoes.

Hiking gear Any kind of outdoor activity, even walking up Namsan, sees many Koreans outfitted in full hiking gear. Join them by donning your own (or not).

Muted colors Young Seoulites are fashion-conscious but usually stick to current trends and mostly muted colors, so as not to stand out.

Manners

A quick, short bow is most respectful for meetings and departures.

Use both hands to give and receive any object, especially name cards (an essential feature of doing business in Korea), money, gifts and drinks.

Remove your shoes upon entering a Korean home, guesthouse, temple or Korean-style restaurant.

Avoid arguments and other situations that cause embarrassment, and quickly smooth over potentially awkward scenes.

READ

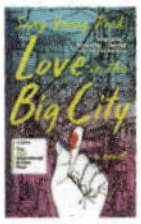

Love in the Big City (Sang Young Park; 2019) The story of a young gay man facing loneliness and love in Seoul (also adapted into a film in 2024).

Kim Jiyoung, Born 1982 (Cho Nam-joo; 2020) Fictional account of a woman's mental breakdown living in a misogynistic society.

The Plotters (Un-su Kim; 2010) A fantastical thriller about a criminal underworld of assassins jockeying for control of an alternate Seoul.

I Want to Die But I Want to Eat Tteokbokki (Baek Se-hee; 2018) Memoir that helped normalise mental-health conversations in Korea.

Words

An·nyong·ha·se·yo (안녕하세요) Hello.

An·nyong·he·gye·se·yo (안녕히 계세요) Goodbye (if leaving).

An·nyong·hee·ga·se·yo (안녕히 가세요) Goodbye (if staying).

Ne/Ye (네/예) Yes. (Both words mean yes and both are commonly used.)

A·ni·yo (아니요) No.

Yo·bo·se·yo? (여보세요?) Hello? (on the phone)

Shil·le·ham·ni·da (실례합니다) Excuse me.

Jway·song·ham·ni·da (죄송합니다) Sorry.

Gam·sa·ham·ni·da (감사합니다) Thank you.

Go·map·seum·ni·da (고맙습니다) Thank you.

Gwaen-cha-na-yo (괜찮아요) It's fine/It's alright/It's no problem

Ne. An·nyong·ha·se·yo? (네. 안녕하세요?) Fine, thanks. And you?

Song-ha-mul ot-to-ke dway-se-yo? (성함이 어떻게 되세요) What is your name?

Je i·ru·mun ...·im·ni·da (제 이름은 ...입니다) My name is ...

Yong·uh hal su iss·seum·ni·kka? (영어 할 수 있습니까?) Can you speak English?

Mot a·ra du·ross·o·yo (못 알아 들었어요) I didn't understand.

Gwaen·cha·na·yo (괜찮아요) It's OK.

Jam·kkan·man·yo (잠깐만요) Just a moment, please.

Ot·to·ke? (어떻게) How?

On·je (언제) When

O·di (어디) Where

Wae (왜) Why

WATCH

House of Hummingbird (Kim Bora; 2018) Coming-of-age story set in 1990s Seoul, as the city reels from a deadly bridge collapse.

The Housemaid (Kim Ki-young; 1960; pictured) A seductive maid terrorises an upper-middle-class family in this cinema classic.

Burning (Lee Chang-dong; 2018) A psychological drama about a mysterious woman, an insecure, indignant man and obsessive love.

Kpop Demon Hunters (Maggie Kang & Chris Appelhans; 2025) A runaway hit animated musical on Netflix.

Parasite (Bong Joon-ho; 2019) Oscar-winning thriller about a poor family infiltrating the life of a wealthy family.

LISTEN

Sugungga (Leenalchi; 2020) Debut album of the acclaimed genre-crossing band who blend *pansori* (musical storytelling) with pop-funk.

Born Pink (BLACKPINK; 2022) The K-Pop quartet's definitive international breakthrough album, cementing their global superstardom.

FML (Seventeen; 2023) South Korea's best-selling album of all time, with more than 6.2 million copies sold.

The Dark Side of Seoul Podcast Episodes exploring the hidden histories and stories of the city.

CHINTUNG LEE/SHUTTERSTOCK

A'REX station, Incheon International Airport

GETTING THERE

Most likely you'll arrive at Incheon International Airport, Seoul's primary global entry point, about 40km west of Seoul, though it's also possible to land at Gimpo International Airport, especially if your connecting flight has come through Asia (or if you're flying from within Korea).

Airport Train & Tmoney Card

The A'REX train connects Incheon and Gimpo airports to Seoul. From Incheon, there are two types of A'REX trains available: the all-stop train, which makes all stops along the route to Seoul station, departing every 20 to 40 minutes and taking about an hour; and the express train, which goes directly to Seoul station, departing every five to 10 minutes and taking about 40 minutes. From Gimpo, there is only an all-stop train.

For the express train, you buy a ticket for a specific seat using credit card, cash or South Korea's main transport card, called a Tmoney card (which can be purchased and loaded with cash at kiosks). For the all-stop train, which has subway bench-style seating, tap your Tmoney card at the fare gate as you would for the subway.

Airport Buses

Airport buses service all major parts of Seoul, taking between 60 and 80 minutes. Timetables and fares vary depending on your destination, and tickets can be bought at ticket booths at the airport, payable by cash, credit card or Tmoney. Most depart about every 10 to 20 minutes.

By Taxi

Taxis can easily be called at the taxi rank, and vary in price, depending on your destination. From Incheon to Myeong-dong, for example, a standard taxi costs around ₩60,000 (not including the additional expressway toll) and takes about 85 minutes. However, fancier deluxe taxis and jumbo van taxis will cost up to 50% more.

Another option is to book a ride on the Kakao T app, but you'll need a Kakao account to set it up.

FROM THE AIRPORTS TO CENTRAL SEOUL

From Incheon International Airport (ICN)

A'REX express	43min (from T1)/ adult/child ₩13,000/9500
A'REX all-stop	59min (from T1)/ from ₩4150/2400
Airport bus	60-80min/from ₩16,000/12,000
Taxi rank or Kakao Taxi	80-90min/from ₩60,000

From Gimpo International Airport (GMP)

A'REX all-stop	22min/from ₩4150/2400
Airport bus	30-50min/from ₩8000/6000
Lines 5 or 9	70-80min/from ₩1750/750
Taxi rank or Kakao Taxi	35-40min/from ₩30,000

TIP

Naver Map and Kakao Map are essential apps for navigating and trip planning in Seoul, with up-to-date information on departures and delays.

Scan the QR code for the Naver Map app

Scan the QR code for the Kakao Map app

SIM Cards

SIM cards can be easily bought at mobile-network counters in the airport, or purchased online in advance and picked up on site.

Wi-fi

Free wi-fi is available at the airports, as well as on airport buses, public transport and in other public areas such as pedestrian zones, parks, markets and libraries.

OTHER POINTS OF ENTRY

Incheon International Ferry Terminal

International ferries connect Incheon, west of Seoul, with 10 port cities in China, including Dalian, Qingdao and Dandong.

KTX Stations

If coming to Seoul from within Korea by high-speed rail, you will most likely alight at Seoul station, the city's primary KTX hub, but could also arrive at Yongsan, Cheongnyangni or Yeongdeungpo stations.

Express Bus Terminals

Long-distance buses arrive at one of five terminals around the city: Seoul Express Bus Terminal, Central City Terminal, Nambu Terminal, Dong Seoul Terminal or Sangbong Intercity Bus Terminal.

Subway, Seoul

GETTING AROUND

Seoul's subway is usually the best way to get around. The network is extensive, with frequent services and inexpensive fares. Buses are also very handy. Taxis, bike shares and e-scooters fill in the gaps.

Tmoney Card

Subway, bus and taxi fares can all be paid using a rechargeable touch-and-go transport card, the most common being Tmoney. It reduces subway fares (by ₩100) and bus fares (by varying amounts) for adults, and also provides discounts on transfers within 30 minutes.

Physical Tmoney cards can be bought with cash for a nonrefundable ₩3000 to ₩4000 from machines at subway stations, bus kiosks and convenience stores and can be reloaded with cash at any of these places, too.

As of the time of research, most stations are now equipped with the new machines that accept international credit cards, but be aware that these incur a 3.7% service fee.

Now there is also the option to download the Tmoney app, add it to your mobile wallet and tap in and out with your phone.

CREDIT CARDS AS TRANSIT CARDS

Seoul has begun rolling out a new open-loop system of machines that support tapping in and out of transport using international credit cards. It's a slow process, so still plan on getting a dedicated transport card.

Subway

The metro consists of nine colour-coded subway lines, which are integrated with urban railway lines, and the hours of operation are generally from about 5.30am to midnight. It's an efficient way to get around that avoids the city's often heavy traffic. All subway stations are signposted in English and on-board taped announcements of stops are also in English.

Bus

Buses are colour-coded. Most are blue mainline buses that go between districts along major roads. There are also red rapid buses, green village buses and yellow circular buses. The bus system generally runs from about 5.30am to midnight, with additional night routes marked 'N'. Most bus stops have route maps at least partially in English. On board, taped announcements are in English.

AVOID RUSH HOUR

Rush hour is typically from 7am to 9am and 6pm to 7pm Monday through Friday. At subway stations, long boarding queues mean you might have to wait several trains to board, and once you do, the cars will be packed like sardine cans.

Taxi

Taxis are metered and tipping is not required. Few drivers speak English, but you can call 1330 to reach a free interpretation service. It's also easy to use the Kakao T app, which allows you to set pick-up and drop-off locations on a mostly English interface.

Walking

Seoul is by and large a very walkable city, with many pedestrian zones, such as Myeong-dong and Insa-dong, and a focus on urban-

PUBLIC TRANSPORT ESSENTIALS

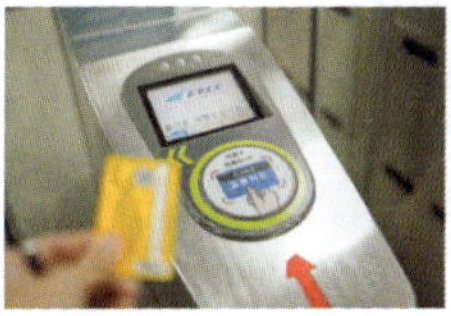

Rules & Etiquette

Open beverages aren't allowed on public transport. Eating is frowned upon and wrapped-up takeaway that emits a strong odour can attract negative attention. Be mindful of your volume while speaking. Keep your phone quiet. And always respect the rules of seats reserved for pregnant people.

Special Transit Cards

In addition to Tmoney, there are several speciality cards that may be worth the investment.

MPASS Foreigner-exclusive transport card, available in one-, two-, three-, five- and seven-day increments, that covers use of all the city's public transport network plus A'REX trains up to 20 times per day. It can be bought at Tmoney Town (starting from ₩15,000).

WOWPASS Foreigner transport card that also functions as a service-fee-free debit card at participating stores. It's available for online purchase and airport pickup, or you can buy it from a WOWPASS kiosk at major subway stations, then top it up with a credit card, cash or mobile pay (via the app).

NAMANE Another transport card that functions as a debit card. It can be bought from a kiosk and topped up by credit card, cash or mobile pay (via the app).

Discover Seoul Card Pass Gives free or discounted entry to dozens of attractions across the city, while doubling as a rechargeable transport card. Available as a three-day (₩90,000) and five-day version (₩130,000), it also includes an A'REX or Airport Bus ticket and use of Ttareungi and the Seoul City Tour Bus. Purchase it online, then pick it up at Incheon airport or select tourist centres.

Climate Card An unlimited transport card, available in varying durations. Its usage is restricted to Seoul, meaning it doesn't cover routes such as intercity buses or the A'REX from Incheon, and it's not accepted by taxis. The 30-day version (from ₩62,000) has the option to add unlimited Ttareungi and Hangang River Bus rides for an additional fee. Purchase the card at the Seoul Metro Information Center.

Maps & Apps

Navigate using Korean apps like Naver Map (p27) and Kakao Map (p27), which are better integrated with local transport and show more accurate walking routes, particularly through Seoul's many narrow alleys. These apps also help plan your journey, even displaying the crowdedness level of buses and the exact subway cars to board for the quickest transfer time.

CSTRIKE/SHUTTERSTOCK

Hangang River Bus

TRAVEL COSTS

Subway
From **₩1550** per ride with Tmoney card

Bus
₩1500 per ride on mainline buses

Taxi
Daytime starting fare **₩4800** for first 1.6km

regeneration projects that promote walkability such as Cheonggye-cheon and the Seoullo 7017.

Bikes & Scooters

Ttareungi, Seoul's bike-sharing scheme, can be found at more than 150 locations across the city. Rental is via bikeseoul.com or its app – you'll be given a code, which is then keyed in on the bike itself to unlock it. The website and app have a live map of all docking stations and available bikes. The Kakao T app also has a bike-rental service. E-scooters such as GCOO, Swing and Beam are also widely available.

Boats & Ferries

The Hangang River Bus runs from 7am to 10.30pm Monday to Friday and 9.30am to 10.30pm on weekends and holidays. It stops at seven stations along the river from Magok in the northwest to Jamsil in the southeast. Services run every 15 to 30 minutes, depending on the time of day.

Driving

Driving is on the right. To rent a car, you must be over 21 and have both a driving licence from your own country and an International Driving Permit. However, driving in Seoul is not recommended, as there are frequent traffic jams, impatient road users and an occasional lack of signage and parking.

ACCESSIBILITY

Escalators, lifts and ramps are in almost all subway stations, along with accessible turnstiles and bathrooms, and train carriages offer priority seating and wheelchair spaces. Buses have ramps or floors that can be lowered, as well as priority seating. On the streets, the city is implementing low kerb heights.

NOONBUSIN/SHUTTERSTOCK

Kimchi

DINING OUT

Sampling the many varied delights of Korean cuisine is one of Seoul's greatest pleasures.

Think Korean cuisine is mainly about kimchi and barbecued beef? A few days in Seoul will swiftly bring you up to speed.

Restaurants, cafes and street stalls are scattered throughout every neighbourhood, with options to suit all budgets and tastes. Prepare to be blown away by the incredible diversity and spicy deliciousness of the city's food landscape, ranging from homey stews and comforting street snacks, to glorious royal banquets involving elaborate preparation and presentation, to Korean and international contemporary fine dining. The result is a restaurant scene that rivals the best of them, having become one of the most international and dynamic on the planet.

So whether you're sitting down to a simple meal of white rice and seasonal vegetables, a KFC (Korean fried chicken) extravaganza, the procession of *banchan* (side dishes) that make up a banquet, or a Michelin-starred menu starring the freshest, most local ingredients, you're in for a true culinary treat.

Have You Eaten?

In Korean, a common way to greet someone is *'bap meogeosseoyo?'* It's taken to mean 'how are you?', but literally translates to 'have you eaten?', a way to express care for another's wellbeing in a culture where food is deeply connected with love.

A Korean traditional meal (breakfast, lunch and dinner) typically consists of meat or seafood served with soup, rice and a collection of *banchan*, Korea's ubiquitous side dishes. The most popular *banchan* is, of course, Korea's quintessential fermented

SEOUL FOOD WEBSITES

ZENKIMCHI
(zenkimchi.com) For booking K-Food tours and learning K-Food 101.

SEOUL EATS
(seouleats.com) A resource run by a local food expert and tour operator.

MAANGCHI
(maangchi.com) The ultimate guide to Korean cooking.

DOOBYDOBAP
(doobydobap.com) Recipes and recommendations from a Korean food influencer.

cabbage or radish – kimchi – but there are many others, such as bean sprouts, eggplant, black beans, dried anchovy, spinach, lotus root, quail eggs, shellfish, zucchini, acorn jelly, tofu – the list goes on and on. It's a healthy approach to eating that emphasises a balance in saltiness, spiciness, temperature and colour.

The pinnacle of Korean dining is *hanjeongsik*, a traditional royal banquet spread that covers the table with 12 or more dishes, typically using *bangjja* (bronze) tableware. Try to experience it at least once while you're in town at a place such as **Korea House** (p81) in Jung-gu.

Solo Diners

Going out to eat is customarily a communal experience in Korea, and whether solo diners are welcomed will depend on the type of eatery. Fast-food franchises and food courts will, of course, permit diners sitting alone, as will Gimbap Cheonguk or Gimbap Nara chains – small, casual restaurants serving basic meals such as *gimbap* (rice and fillings wrapped in seaweed paper), soups, stews, rice dishes and the like. Korean barbecue restaurants, however, most often won't, turning away solo diners even if they promise to order two or more portions.

Going Viral

Though Korean tastebuds typically lean towards their own highly developed cuisine, young Seoulites gobble up global food trends with gusto, often adding their own localised flair.

Ongoing trends include anything Americana (the more regional the better), whether that's Texas brisket, Maine lobster or New York–, Chicago- or Detroit-style pizza. Spanish tapas, French fare and Italian flavours are perennially popular – sometimes putting a European spin on Korean favourites such as *minari* (water dropwort) pasta or rosé *tteokbokki* (rice cakes) – as are burgers, of which the variations are endless. Thai and Vietnamese are hot, and Mexican along with Korean-Mexican fusion continue to do well with *birria ramyeon*, kimchi tacos and tostadas and other hybrid dishes.

Pastries and baked goods are always a hit, including *sogeum-ppang* (salt bread), castella cake, bagels, donuts, waffles,

Handling *ssam*

RULES OF KOREAN DINING

Traditional restaurants Remove your shoes in traditional restaurants, where diners sit on floor cushions at low tables. When foods are placed in the centre of the table for communal eating, help yourself from each common dish, placing it in your own small dish.

Check your chopsticks Don't leave your chopsticks or spoon sticking up out of your rice bowl, as this is only done during ancestral ceremonies where food is being offered to the deceased.

Other manners Don't use your fingers to touch food, except when handling *ssam* (lettuce and other leaves used as edible wrappers for meat and other fillings). Don't blow your nose at the table.

Paying the bill When it's time to pay, go to the cashier counter. Tipping is neither required nor expected.

Best Seoul Foods

SEOLLEONGTANG Seoul's speciality soup made from beef bones and eaten with rice.

KOREAN FRIED CHICKEN The ultimate fried chicken, best enjoyed with beer.

YUKGAEJANG Fiery shredded-beef soup with spring onions, bean sprouts and bracken.

PYEONSU Seoul's square-shaped beef dumplings originate from a royal-court dish.

croissants or any mash-up of these (for example, cronuts and croffles).

Diners are prepared to queue for hours for the chance to eat at (and post pictures of) the hottest new restaurants. Social media is one reason why presentation is all-important – in Seoul, food has to look as good as it tastes.

Download Korea's No 1 reservation app CATCHTABLE to easily book tables at trending and fine-dining restaurants.

Street Snacking

Some of the best food you'll find in Seoul is off the street – from snack stalls set up in market alleyways, food carts on roadsides, or late-night *pojangmacha* (tent bars) on footpaths – and the wonders and delights of tasting it all cannot be overstated.

Go to Myeong-dong, Insa-dong, Hongdae or any concentrated pedestrian zone and the sheer variety of what's on offer is truly a sight to behold: French-fry-battered hot dogs and tornado potatoes; spicy-sweet *tteokbokki* (rice cakes) paired with *twigim* (deep-fried vegetables, squid, shrimp and more); *dakkochi* (chicken skewers), fish-cake skewers and other meats on sticks; sweet treats such as *hotteok* (dough pancakes filled with sugar, cinnamon and nuts), *bungeoppang* (fish-shaped waffles stuffed with sweet red-bean-paste) and *kkwabaegi* (twisted doughnuts). Street stalls are a fun way to try a smorgasbord of different foods throughout the day and night.

Head to marketplace food alleys to dig in shoulder-to-shoulder with locals – Gwangjang Market for *bindaetteok* (mung bean pancakes), *yukhoe* (beef tartare) or *sundae* (blood sausage), and Namdaemun Market for *galchi* (hairtail) or *kalguksu* (knife-cut noodles).

Pojangmacha are another great option for inexpensive meals, and some of them stay open long after other restaurants close. The best *pojangmacha* are around

Tosokchon (p52)

TOP KOREAN EATERIES

Hadongkwan (p80) Keeping it simple for nearly nine decades, this Myeong-dong spot specialises in *gomtang* (beef and rice soup).

Jaha Sonmandoo (p187) Dumplings don't get much better than those served at this long-running restaurant in Buam-dong.

Samwon Garden (p142) In Gangnam, top-class *galbi* (beef ribs) and a traditional garden take Korean barbecue upscale.

Tosokchon (p52) A longtime favourite in Seochon near Gyeongbokgung, serving different variations of *samgyetang* (ginseng chicken soup; pictured).

Woori Yeah Sool (p167) At the restaurant of this craft *makgeolli* brewer, dig into succulent pork ribs in a spicy sauce.

Grandmother's Recipe (p175) It's worth lining up for the delicious and great-value meals at this family-run Seoul Forest restaurant.

Oilje (p135) Michelin-recommended perilla *miyeok-guk* (seaweed soup) in trending Yongnidan.

FROM LEFT: 9919/SHUTTERSTOCK, LEANDRO MARASIGAN/SHUTTERSTOCK

TTEOKBOKKI
Chewy rice cakes in a sticky, spicy *gochujang*-based sauce.

SEOUL-STYLE BULGOGI
The capital's take on bulgogi simmers sliced beef in a special pot with broth.

BARBECUE
From *galbi* (beef ribs) to *samgyeopsal* (pork belly), perfectly grilled meat morsels.

CHUTANG
Seoul-style *chutang* boils loach with beef bones and intestines.

Jongno 3-ga and Euljiro 3-ga, where the streets are overflowing with plastic chairs and tables piled with dishes such as chicken feet, chicken gizzard and rolled omelettes.

Convenience Store Steals

For cheap eats on the go and around the clock, *pyeonuijeom*, or convenience stores, such as CU, GS25, EMart 24, Family Mart, 7-Eleven and Mini Mart can be found on nearly every block in Seoul. These shops sell items such as *gimbap, dosirak* lunch boxes containing a main served with *banchan* and rice, *ramyeon* and other instant noodles, packaged sandwiches, fruits, chips and other snacks.

Vegetarians & Vegans

While vegetarians and vegans generally have a tougher time travelling elsewhere in Korea, they'll be greeted by much greater choice in Seoul. From Korean vegetable dishes and 100% vegetarian Buddhist temple food, to non-Korean vegetarian and vegan options at Indian, Middle Eastern and other international eateries, there's a lot on offer.

Just make sure to confirm that what you're ordering fits your criteria, as many even seemingly vegetarian dishes may contain small amounts of meat or seafood in their recipes. This is true of kimchi, which is often made with fermented shrimp, anchovies or fish sauce, as well as many tofu stews, which may use meat or seafood in their stock. As a general guide, vegetarian-safe dishes include bibimbap (order it without meat or egg), vegetable *jeon* (savoury fried pancakes) and pumpkin *juk* (porridge).

Check Happy Cow *(happycow.net/asia/south_korea/seoul)* for a handy directory of Seoul's vegetarian and vegan-friendly restaurants.

K-Cooking

Don't stop at only tasting Korean cuisine; play chef for a day and try your hand at preparing and cooking it, too. Courses at culinary centres across the city give a primer on how to make Korea's most popular foods, including kimchi and dishes such as *japchae* (glass noodles), bulgogi (marinated thinly sliced beef), and *jeon*.

Other classes teach about ingredients essential to the Korean kitchen, such as its trio of *jang* – *gochujang* (red-pepper paste), *ganjang* (soy sauce) and *doenjang* (fermented soy-bean paste).

SUNGSU HAN/GETTY IMAGES

Japchae

AFLO CO. LTD./ALAMY

Pojangmacha, Ikseon-dong (p54)

BAR OPEN

From teahouses and coffee shops to beer pubs and cocktail bars, Seoul offers an unbelievable number of places to relax with a drink.

Ready to do the cha cha? Not dancing, but drinking. In South Korea, *cha* refers to each successive round of revelry in a night, beginning with *il-cha* (round one), moving to *ee-cha* (round two), on to *sam-cha* (round three), and then...well, you get the idea.

Among all these *cha*, the city's no-frills *hof* (pubs) are fun for trying Korea's customary food-and-drink pairings, and its upscale bars are poised to impress with their creatively constructed cocktails and mocktails. Don't miss, either, the quintessential Seoul nightlife experiences of soju and snacks at a *pojangmacha* (food-and-drink tent), and songs at a *noraebang* (private singing room), which is often the last *cha* of the night.

Then there's always another type of *cha*, which in Korean also means tea. At atmospheric cafes across the city, sit down to savour soothing traditional herbal infusions, along with artisanal coffees.

Cafe Craze

To say that Koreans love cafes is an understatement. From home-grown chains such as Terarosa, Paik's and Ediya, to independent third-wave roasters, to international franchises such as Starbucks (first opening in 1999 near Ewha Womans University), coffee shops are *everywhere* here.

In 2024, in fact, there were more than 100,000 coffee shops across Korea, the equivalent of one cafe per every 500-or-so people.

SEOUL DRINK WEBSITES

THE SOOL COMPANY
(thesoolcompany.com) Korean traditional alcohol classes, tours and other experiences.

KOREA CRAFT BREWERS ASSOCIATION
(en-craftbrewers.imweb.me) A directory of member breweries and other craft-beer resources.

SEOUL PUB CRAWL
(seoulpubcrawl.kr) For booking a night out on the town, with bar-hopping happening every weekend.

SEOUL NIGHTLIFE
(seoulnightlife.co) Information about Seoul's nightlife districts, as well as pub crawls to book.

Ranging from the very expensive to the ultra cheap (eg Mega Coffee and Compose), you're never far away from a caffeine hit.

Long before coffee, there was tea. Korea's centuries-old tea culture can be appreciated in quaint teahouses in Seoul's traditional neighbourhoods such as Insa-dong. These places major in herbal, fruit, roasted rice and barley teas, many of which have medicinal properties and don't actually contain tea leaves, though it is of course possible to find and sip green, black and fermented varieties, too.

While a cup of coffee or tea can cost the equivalent of a budget Korean meal, you're also paying for the ambience – Seoul has some of the most beautifully designed cafes in the world, many of them set in traditional wooden *hanok* or modern architectural spaces. There are art cafes packed with contemporary showpieces, book cafes with reading materials, music cafes with personal record players, and more.

Fresh Takes on Old Favourites

In line with the recent revival of Korean traditional culture among the younger generations, nostalgic drinks such as *makgeolli*, an old-time farmer's brew, have become trendy. An unrefined fermented rice wine, *makgeolli* has a milky appearance and a sweetish flavour, clocking about 5% to 8% ABV.

The *makgeolli* movement is a trend worth exploring, where local brewers strive for chemical-free, top-quality, artisanal drops, and craft *makgeolli* bars offer a range of varieties to sample and savour. Try **Mr Ahn's Craft Makgeolli** (p133) and **Namsan Sool Club** (p133) in Gyeongnidan. *Makgeolli* features, too, at upscale cocktail lounges, such as those in Euljiro, Seochon, Cheongdam and Mangwon, where mixologists stir and shake up innovative concoctions highlighting Korean traditional ingredients.

Similarly, the craft-beer revolution has firmly made itself known in Seoul, with microbreweries and brewpubs all over the city (and country) producing and pouring high-quality *maekju*. Regionally inspired, and often award-winning, brews from the likes of Magpie Brewing Co, Amazing Brewing Company, Euljiro Brewing and Ggeek Beer Company now share the market with Cass, Max, Hite and Korea's other old cheap local lagers.

Drinking etiquette in Korea

NEED TO KNOW

Hours Bars stay open late, usually until at least 2am; some much later. Clubs don't close until 5am or later.

Cover charge At clubs, the entry fee of around ₩10,000 to ₩30,000 sometimes operates on a graduated system, such as free before 10pm, ₩10,000 before 11pm and so forth. Sometimes entry includes a free drink.

Dress code Clubs in Hongdae and Itaewon are generally not too strict, though some will turn away those in sandals or sportswear. Dress up for swankier venues in Gangnam.

Tipping Neither required nor expected.

Drinking etiquette Drinking with Koreans, the custom is to always pour for your elders (using both hands – your right hand on the bottle and your left hand on your wrist), to never pour for yourself and to hold your glass with both hands while it's being filled.

Best Bars in Seoul

BAR CHAM
Artful drinks showcasing Korean traditional spirits and ingredients.

ZEST
Innovative, eco-friendly cocktails have put this stylish spot on the world's best lists.

GOPCHANG JEONGOL
DJs playing retro pop songs sometimes inspire singalongs.

OKBA
Try a highball at this *hanok* cafe-bar near Seodaemun Independence Park.

Soju Still King

There may be a *makgeolli* movement and craft-beer revolution, but soju still reigns supreme. Koreans drink so much soju – a mix of ethanol and water, with an ABV that ranges from about 12% to 24% – that the Jinro brand has been the world's top-selling spirit by volume for the past 24 years straight. You'll see the green bottles (and advertisements) everywhere, from restaurants and bars to *pojangmacha*, convenience stores and beyond.

While soju can go down easy (particularly the fruit-flavoured varieties), it can also leave you with a monstrous hangover the next day – and it's part of the reason why there are so many hangover remedies in Korea, too. These include hangover soup *(haejangguk)* and hangover drinks and pills from brands such as Condition and Dawn808, which contain ingredients like oriental raisin, Asian pear and other natural herbs intended to ease the aftermath of soju.

In Korean, 'cheers!' is *'konbae!'* or, more casually, *'jjan!'*

Cocktails & Clubs

Intimate speakeasy-style cocktail bars are what's hot these days, such as **Jean Frigo** (p170) in Dongdaemun, **Zoo Sindang** (p170) and **Myeongdong Sookhee** (p81).

For clubbing, head to the neighbourhoods of Hongdae, Itaewon and Gangnam, where most nightclubs don't get busy until midnight and only really start pumping after 2am.

Seoul's LGBTIQ+ Scene

LGBTIQ+-friendly areas include Itaewon (mainly gay and trans bars and clubs), Nakwon-dong near Insa-dong (gay bars) and Hongdae and Edae (mainly lesbian bars).

Coffee Hanyakbang (p95)

TOP CAFES

Suyeonsanbang (p185) Savour warming drinks and traditional sweets in Northern Seoul at one of Seoul's most charming *hanok* teahouses.

Conhas (p167) Sip your hand-dripped coffee while enjoying a view of Dongdaemun Design Plaza.

Coffee Hanyakbang (p95) Coffee with a side of century-old aesthetics: ornate tile floors, medicine chests and lots of mother-of-pearl.

Conflict Store (p151) Brews up great drinks in Gangnam and offers coffee tasting menus for the serious beanhead.

Green Mile Coffee (p73) Relax with a latte in its warm-wood interior, or up on the roof with a view onto Bukchon.

Leesar (p81) Cannoli, cantucci and espresso to be taken at the bar in Jung-gu. *Nonno* would approve.

Hay Coffee and Bar (p139) In a rustic *hanok* in Hangangno-dong, with premium coffee, cocktails and tiramisu.

GU SEOUL
Mixologist Chris Jang's quaffable drinks are made with ingredients from nearby Jungang Market.

TABACCHI
How many other bars do you know that serve wine and gelato sets?

BAR POMME
Beautiful seasonal cocktails, such as the Crimson Foliage with rum, peanut and Aperol.

VILLA RECORDS
Order your drink 'molecular', then watch the suited mad scientists go to work.

FROM LEFT: TIBOR BOGNAR/GETTY IMAGES, JUSTIN SHIN/GETTY IMAGES

Korean fan dance, Korea House (p81)

SHOWTIME

From Korean traditional music, K-Pop and K-Indie, to theatre, sports and more, you're sure to stay entertained in Seoul.

Seoul is a city of endless entertainment, from morning to night, in every district, in every season. Whatever you enjoy watching, hearing or spectating, there's a good chance you'll find it here. Feel the rhythm of Seoul at musical performances that range from time-honoured *gugak* (traditional music) to *hallyu*-headlining K-Pop. See decidedly local shows, such as *Nanta*, or hit Broadway musicals, touring international DJs, visiting orchestras and EDM and rock festivals.

Don't worry about the language barrier, either: Seoul offers a surprisingly accessible selection of theatre, drama, dance, opera and even nonverbal shows at performing-arts centres and venues across the capital.

Or go out to a baseball game, basketball showdown or soccer match for an only-in-Korea spectating experience you're sure to remember long after the game.

Sometimes in Korea, too, it's not even about attending an event; it's about creating your own fun. *Bang* (literally 'rooms') are facilities you can rent by the hour to make your own entertainment in a variety of ways, including playing computer games at PC bang, watching movies at DVD bang and singing karaoke in private *noraebang*.

Best Venues

JAMSIL BASEBALL STADIUM
Raucous cheers, squid jerky, epic bat flips – there's nothing like a day at the Korean ballpark (p161).

KOREA HOUSE
Enjoy dinner and a show, Joseon-style, with Korean table d'hôte and a traditional performance (p81).

NATIONAL GUGAK CENTER
Weekly Saturday concerts offer a good overview of traditional musical genres (p152).

ROLLING HALL
This live-music venue hosts big names in Korea's indie scene, from rock to hip-hop (p100).

Traditional Sounds of Seoul

For enjoying Korean traditional music and dance performances, such as *pansori* (dramas sung by a solo singer) and *nong-ak* (farmers' songs), the best places to go are the **National Gugak Center** (p152), **Seoul Donhwamun Traditional Theater** (p73) and **Namsan Gugakdang** (p81). The Seoul Gugak Festival *(seoulgugak.com)* also takes centre stage every June, celebrating Korean traditional music in front of Gwanghwamun, while traditional, classical and contemporary drumming shines at the Seoul Drum Festival *(seouldrumfestival.com)*, held on Nodeul Island each May.

Other classical music can be found at the **Sejong Center for the Performing Arts** (p54), **Seoul Arts Center** (p152), **National Theater of Korea** (p81) and Lotte Concert Hall, where you can expect a broad range of international offerings, too, from world-class visiting orchestras to contemporary dance troupes.

From K-Pop to K-Indie

If you're looking to attend a K-Pop show, major venues include KSPO Dome at **Olympic Park** (p158), Jamsil Arena, **Gocheok SkyDome** (p115) in southwestern Seoul and YES24 Live Hall in eastern Seoul.

Aside from the glossy, manufactured K-Pop industry, Seoul offers an eclectic assortment of live music. Hongdae is the place for Seoul's K-Indie scene, where the Zandari Festa *(zandarifesta.com)* is held every autumn, and intimate venues host local indie, punk, metal and hip-hop acts year-round. Live jazz venues of all sizes can be found throughout the city, particularly in Itaewon, and the Seoul Jazz Festival *(seouljazz.co.kr)* comes to Olympic Park every late May or early June.

The Greater Seoul Area plays host to a number of other music festivals throughout the year, including Pentaport Rock Festival *(pentaport.co.kr)* in Incheon in late July or early August, Ultra Korea *(umfkorea.com)* electronic-music festival in summer or autumn, Seoul World DJ Festival *(wdjfest.com)* in Gwacheon in summer and HBC Music Festival *(facebook.com/HBCFest)* in Haebangchon in autumn.

Theatre & More

While theatre is usually performed in Korean, some venues offer English subtitles, including **Myeongdong Theater** (p80), home to the National Theater Company of Korea, the **National Jeongdong Theater of Korea** (p80) and various theatres in the **Daehangno theatre district** (p178), home to Arts Council Korea.

Major Broadway musicals touring in Seoul, such as *Wicked* or *Phantom of the Opera*, will often be in English and can be seen at venues such as **Blue Square** (p129). There are also nonverbal performance shows such as *Jump* at **Myeongbo Art Hall** (p80), *The Painters* at NH Arthall and the long-running *Nanta* at the **Myeongdong Nanta Theater** (p80).

Pentaport Rock Festival

DAEHANGNO THEATRES
Take your pick from scores of theatre shows, including some with subtitles or performed in English (p178).

SEJONG CENTER FOR THE PERFORMING ARTS
Showcasing ballet, opera, orchestra and more, this is Seoul's largest performing-arts centre (p54).

ALL THAT JAZZ
Seoul's oldest jazz club, running since 1976, has gotten a fresh look in a new location in Itaewon (p139).

SHOWFLIX
Enjoy songs from musical theatre at this performance venue and dining bar in Sindang (p164).

NEED TO KNOW

Booking
Buy theatre, concert and sporting-event tickets on **Interpark Global** *(world.nol.com)* and **YES24** *(ticket.yes24.com)*.

Listings
Useful websites for finding shows include **Korea Gig Guide** *(koreagigguide.com)* and **10 Magazine** *(10mag.com)*.

Costs
Prices vary widely, with baseball games starting at ₩10,000 and K-Pop concerts at ₩120,000.

ENTERTAINMENT BY NEIGHBOURHOOD	
Gwanghwamun & Jongno-gu	District of the Sejong Center for the Performing Arts and Donhwamun Traditional Theater.
Myeong-dong & Jung-gu	Nonverbal theatre is king here; see traditional shows at the Korea House and Myeongdong Nanta Theater.
Hongdae & Western Seoul	Hongdae is the hub of Seoul's vibrant indie-music scene, and the Seoul World Cup Stadium hosts soccer.
Itaewon & Yongsan-gu	Seoul's most international 'hood is a great place for live jazz, and there's Blue Square for Broadway.
Gangnam & Southern Seoul	Baseball is at Jamsil, while the performing arts are at the National Gugak Center and Seoul Arts Center.
Dongdaemun & Eastern Seoul	Sindang is home to the popular musical bar Showflix.
Northern Seoul	Daehangno is a performing-arts district with scores of venues.

Korea's Most Popular Sport

Introduced in 1905 by American missionaries, baseball has entrenched itself in Korean popular culture, becoming by far the country's most watched sport. There are three Seoul teams in the 10-team Korean Baseball Organization *(KBO; eng.koreabaseball.com)* and two of them – the Doosan Bears *(doosanbears.com)* and LG Twins *(lgtwins.com)* – play at **Jamsil Baseball Stadium** (p161) in Seoul Sports Complex; its third team, the Kiwoom Heroes *(heroesbaseball.co.kr)*, plays at Gocheok Sky Dome.

The KBO season runs from March to October and games are well attended with a lively, boozy atmosphere and plenty of off-field entertainment. Purchase tickets on the teams' websites, or at the stadium up to 90 minutes before games.

Basketball & Football

Seoul's two professional basketball teams, the Samsung Thunders and SK Knights, play in the 10-team Korean Basketball League *(KBL; kbl.or.kr)* from October to April. The Thunders play at Jamsil Arena, while the Knights are at Jamsil Students' Gymnasium, both in Seoul Sports Complex. (Korea also has a women's professional basketball league, but Seoul doesn't have a team.)

For football (soccer), FC Seoul plays in the 12-team K-League *(kleague.com)* Division 1 from February to November at **Seoul World Cup Stadium** (p107).

LEONID ANDRONOV/SHUTTERSTOCK

Hongdae (p100)

SHOP

You'll never run out of places to shop in South Korea's capital, which is chock-full of traditional markets, modern malls and more.

Shopping is an endless pursuit in ultra-consumerist Seoul, with its multiblock underground centres, multistorey malls, round-the-clock markets and bounty of boutiques. Whether it's for *bojagi* (wrapping cloths) or *buchae* (handheld fans), art-and-design pieces, cutting-edge cosmetics or K-Pop merch, chances are slim that you'll go home empty-handed.

Some Seoul-inspired souvenirs to be on the lookout for include handmade paper *(hanji)*, chopsticks, *bangjja* bronzeware, stone bowls, tea sets, *gim* (dried seaweed), ginseng and more. There's celadon pottery in Icheon and antique furniture in Itaewon.

Aside from souvenirs, there are the Korean fashions, which run the gamut from luxury labels to cheap youth-centric brands. From here-today-gone-tomorrow trends to timeless traditional dress *(hanbok)*, it's all here in Seoul. Revived vintage wear makes an appearance, too, throughout shops in Hongdae and Seongsu, as well as the treasure-packed stalls of Dongmyo Flea Market and the upstairs levels of Gwangjang Market.

Fashion Forward

Dongdaemun Market (p164) and its sprawling surrounding area of high-rise malls offer a huge selection of clothing, shoes and accessories, though a lot of it is geared toward wholesale and fabrics. In Myeong-dong, the underground shopping centre and narrow, brightly lit streets stock plenty of local brands, as do the neighbourhoods of Hongdae and Seongsu. Additional underground shopping can be found at Gangnam and Express Bus Terminal stations, while other malls throughout the city include **Starfield COEX** (p143), Starfield Hannam, Lotte, I'Park, IFC, Times Square – the list goes on and on.

High-end fashion is best sourced from major department stores or the boutiques of Hannam, Apgujeong and Cheongdam, where luxury K-designers like Lie Sang Bong and big-name glam brands such as Louis Vuitton, Gucci and Prada are located.

Hanbok Renaissance

Modern takes on Korean traditional clothing, *hanbok*, are sweeping the city, with many designers creating reasonably priced looks that appeal to everyday wear. Some brands to check out include **Leesle** (p68) in Insa-dong and Hongdae, and **Teterot Salon** (p55) in Ikseon-dong, which sell contemporary styles of *jeogori* (tops), *chima* (skirts) and *baji* (trousers). These range from cotton (most affordable and traditionally worn by commoners) to more expensive silk and *ramie* (cloth made from pounded bark), once reserved for the upper class.

The most formal *hanbok*, naturally dyed and intricately embroidered, are objects of wonder that can cost a fortune.

K-Beauty

Korea's world-class cosmetics and skincare are a big draw for shoppers visiting Seoul. Myeong-dong is ground zero for local brands such as Etude House, Innisfree, Nature Republic, Tony Moly and 3CE, selling good-quality, inexpensive products. Some items that prove particularly popular include sheet masks, snail mucin, PDRN serums and BB (blemish balm) cream, a two-in-one moisturiser and makeup.

Medical tourism, too, is a booming industry in Seoul. While the focus might be on cosmetic surgery – Korea has the highest rate of procedures per capita in the world – medical tourism can include anything from cutting-edge cancer treatments to dermatological care to simple checkups. The industry is heavily promoted by the Korea Tourism Organization, with specialised information booths in Seoul, such as the **Gangnam Medical Tour Center** (p149).

Folk Crafts & Antiques

For Korean traditional craft arts, head to Insa-dong – the city's best shopping area for such items as *hanbok*, embroidery, calligraphy materials, wooden masks *(talchum)*, handmade paper *(hanji)*, painted wooden carvings and lacquerware boxes inlaid with mother-of-pearl *(najeon chilgi)* – as well as **Namdaemun Market** (p90).

More expensive items include reproduction Joseon-dynasty furniture and contemporary art from Seoul's multitude of commercial galleries. One of the best places to buy pale-green celadon pottery is **Ye's Park** (p210) ceramic village in Icheon.

Antique-lovers should seek out the **Dapsimni** (p170) arcades, which specialise mainly in Joseon-era items such as pottery, Buddhist statues and furniture. **Itaewon Antique Furniture Street** (p129) is lined with beautiful shops selling mostly Western furniture and objets d'art, while the **Seoul Folk Flea Market** (p167) has mountains of mid-century ephemera, old cameras and instruments and other retro finds.

Tal **(p68), Insa-dong**

Top Shops

DDP DESIGN STORE
A showcase for some of the best design products from the city and around Korea (p166).

GUIROE
Contemporary hanbok so beautiful it's been displayed at London's V&A museum (p64).

KT&G SANGSANG-MADANG
The shop in this cultural centre stocks lots of quirky goods by Korean creatives (p110).

POINT OF VIEW
Standout stationery store with a beautifully curated selection of products from Korea and overseas (p175).

NEED TO KNOW

Opening Hours

Stores are generally open from 10am to 9pm, though hours vary. Traditional market hours also vary, with some stalls staying open even when the rest of the market is closed.

Bargaining

Asking for a discount is acceptable at traditional market stalls and some independent shops, particularly if you're buying more than one item. Use your best judgement.

Tax Refunds

Spending more than ₩30,000 at participating tax-free shops yields a partial refund (between 5% and 7%) of the 10% value-added tax (VAT), either on the spot (present your passport) or at the airport (scan the special receipt).

SHOPPING BY NEIGHBOURHOOD

Gwanghwamun & Jongno-gu	Insa-dong, Bukchon and Seochon are packed with art galleries, crafts shops and boutiques.
Myeong-dong & Jung-gu	Best for department stores, fashion outlets and cosmetics, with all-night shopping at Namdaemun Market.
Hongdae & Western Seoul	Youth fashion trends are serviced in Hongdae and Yeonnam-dong.
Itaewon & Yongsan-gu	Itaewon is handy for larger-sized clothing, shoes and tailors, while Hannam-dong is flush with designer boutiques.
Gangnam & Southern Seoul	Luxe retail in Apgujeong and Cheongdam; more affordable boutiques west of Garosu-gil; one-stop shopping megamalls COEX and D Cube City.
Dongdaemun & Eastern Seoul	Sprawling markets and high-rise malls for serious shopaholics and bulk buyers. Local fashion in Seongsu.
Northern Seoul	Contemporary art and design stores.

Soju, Seaweed & More

For food souvenirs, *gim* (dried seaweed) is a popular purchase – get it in larger sheets from traditional markets to have a go at rolling your own *gimbap* back home. Ginseng, the miracle root, turns up everywhere, too – buy it raw, dried, steamed or as an ingredient in other products, and eat it, drink it or bathe in it to benefit from its health-giving properties.

The many varieties of Korean *cha* (tea) are another good buy, as are *sool* (alcohol), including rice wines such as *makgeolli* and *baekseju* and local liquors such as *soju*. The **Sool Gallery** (p70) in Jongno-gu is your one-stop shop.

KCDF GALLERY
Gorgeous design emporium embracing traditional crafts with a contemporary slant (p68).

VINYL & PLASTIC
Listen to your pick of thousands of LPs, then buy your favourites to take home (p131).

GENTLE MONSTER
This global eyewear fave sells frames ranging from the coolly classic to the extremely avant (p149).

DONGMYO FLEA MARKET
Bag a new look at Seoul's best sorting house for cast-off and hand-me-down fashions (p167).

SEOUL

THE GUIDE

Chapters in this section are organised by neighbourhood. Neighbourhoods are delineated by a specific local character or identity, where you'll find unique specific experiences, local insights, insider tips and expert recommendations.

Gyeongbokgung (p50)
JACKTAMRONG/SHUTTERSTOCK

NEIGHBOURHOODS AT A GLANCE

Find the neighbourhoods that tick all your boxes.

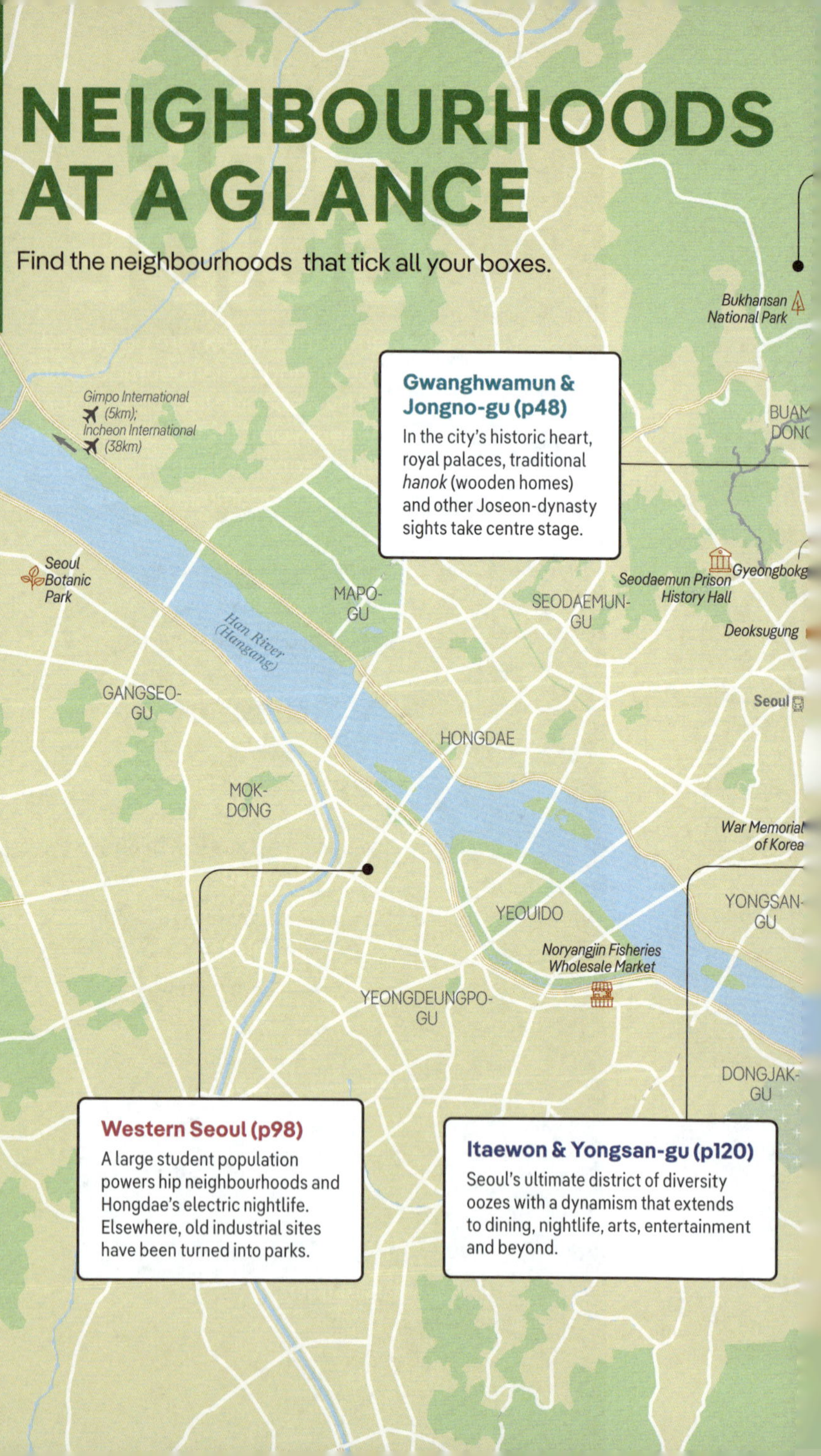

Gwanghwamun & Jongno-gu (p48)

In the city's historic heart, royal palaces, traditional *hanok* (wooden homes) and other Joseon-dynasty sights take centre stage.

Western Seoul (p98)

A large student population powers hip neighbourhoods and Hongdae's electric nightlife. Elsewhere, old industrial sites have been turned into parks.

Itaewon & Yongsan-gu (p120)

Seoul's ultimate district of diversity oozes with a dynamism that extends to dining, nightlife, arts, entertainment and beyond.

Northern Seoul (p176)

Stride along the Seoul City Wall to access amazing vistas across Seoul, then hike some more in a national park.

Myeong-dong & Jung-gu (p74)

Historic sites, urban escapes, adventurous art, late-night shopping and an eclectic bar scene – they all meet here, in Seoul's middle.

Dongdaemun & Eastern Seoul (p162)

Head here to shop at markets for clothing, food, traditional medicine and antiques, and to marvel at the architecture of Dongdaemun Plaza & Park (DDP).

Gangnam & Southern Seoul (p140)

Designer fashion and statement architecture announce this as Seoul's wealthiest quarter, while galleries and green spaces add substance to style.

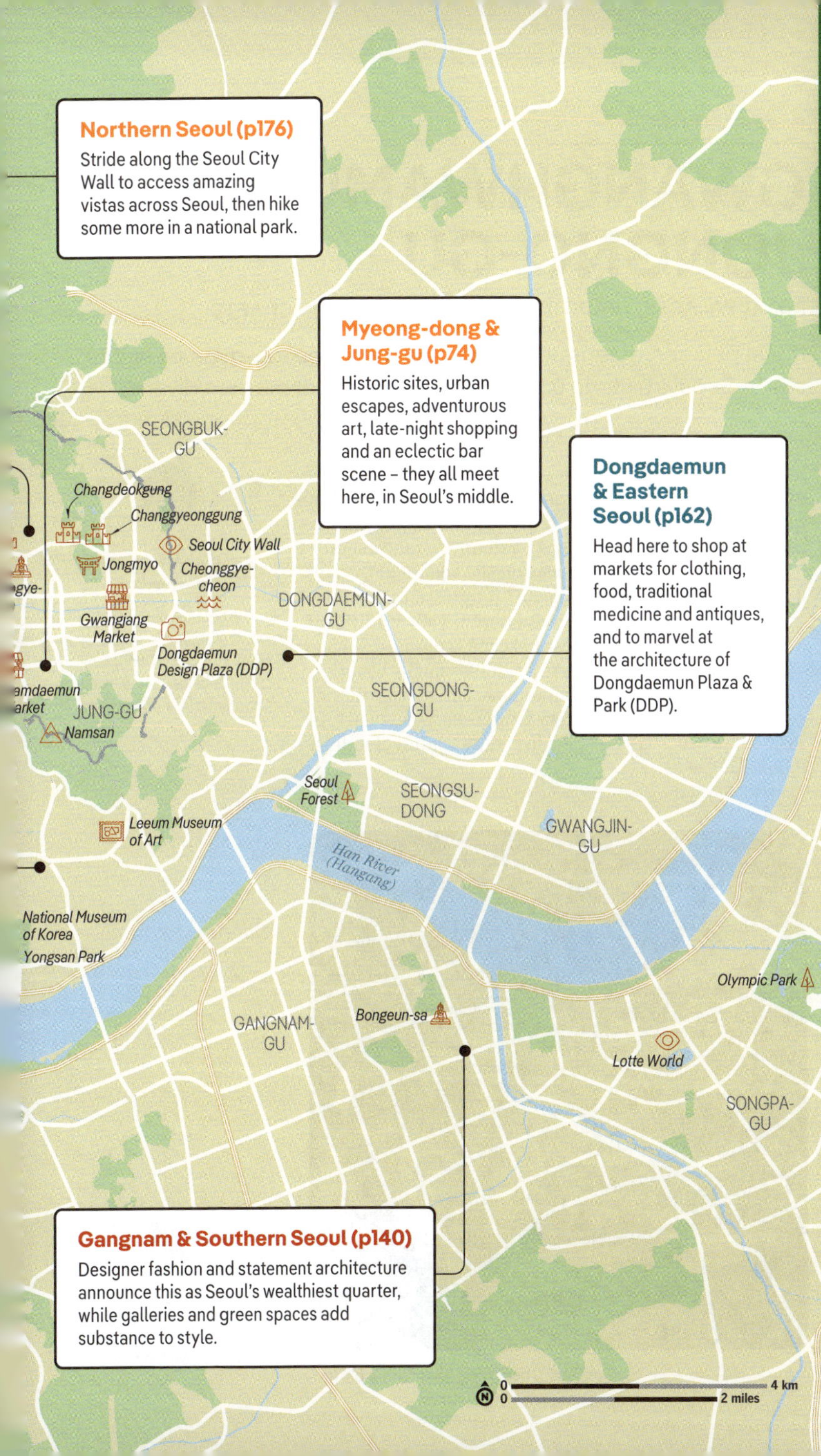

Researched by Ann Babe

GWANGHWAMUN & JONGNO-GU

ROYAL PALACES, TRADITIONAL HOUSES, ARTS AND CRAFTS

Royal palaces, celebrated *hanok* and other Joseon-dynasty sights star in Seoul's historic core, along with a host of modern diversions.

Seoul's regal heart is Jongno-gu, a district defined by two major palaces: Gyeongbokgung and Changdeokgung, with its magical Secret Garden. The area by Gyeongbokgung is commonly referred to as Gwanghwamun after the majestic gate to the main Joseon palace and the square in front of it, which has long served as Seoul's quintessential gathering place. Jongno-gu is the best place to view traditional *hanok* (Korean wooden homes). Bukchon is the most famous – and overtouristed – but there are some equally beautiful *hanok* in Seochon and Ikseon-dong. Many art galleries and craft shops can be found in Jongno-gu, particularly in Insa-dong, which is also home to Seoul's leading Buddhist temple, Jogye-sa.

TIP

Slurp up Seoul's speciality ox-bone soup, *seolleongtang*, simmered for 17 hours at Imun Seolleongtang, the Michelin-listed restaurant and time-honoured Insa-dong staple.

Secret Garden, Changdeokgung (p60)

See page 215 for places to stay in Gwanghwamun & Jongno-gu

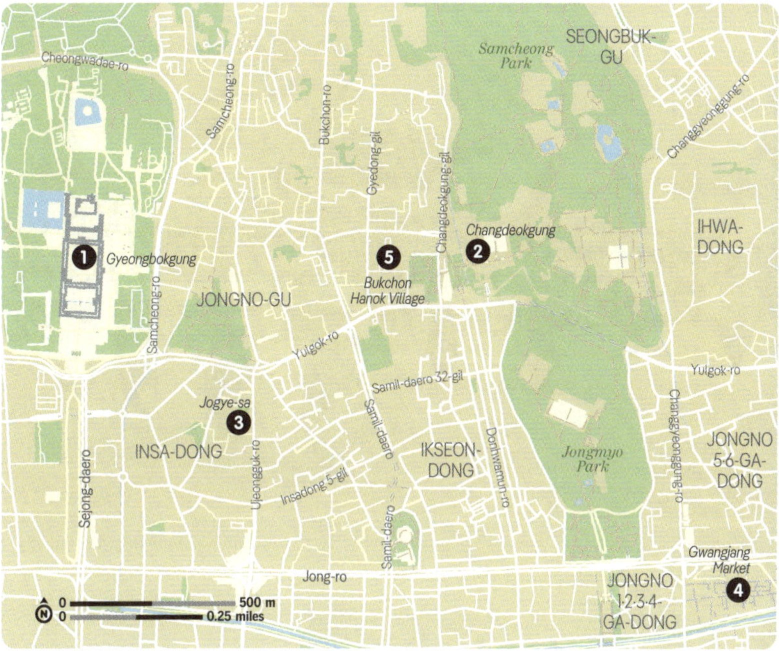

Highlights

❶ Gyeongbokgung
Admire the scale and artistry of Seoul's largest palace. **p50**

❷ Changdeokgung
Discover Huwon, the serene traditional garden behind the most beautiful of Seoul's palaces. **p60**

❸ Jogye-sa
Learn about Buddhism at this temple at the epicentre of the spectacular Lotus Lantern Festival. **p58**

❹ Gwangjang Market
Gorge on a sea of Seoul food in the city's busiest snack alleys. **p72**

▲ **❺ Bukchon Hanok Village**
Roam the picturesque maze of the city's densest cluster of traditional-style homes. **p70**

Getting Around

Subway
Lines 1, 3 and 5 all have stations in this area. Anguk is the best for Insa-dong and Bukchon; Jongno 3-ga exit 4 for Ikseon-dong. Gyeongbokgung is best for the palace and Seochon.

Walking
The only way to truly explore the densely packed streets of Bukchon, Seochon, Insa-dong and Ikseon-dong is on foot.

Tour Bus
The hop-on hop-off Seoul City Tour Bus is a handy way to reach some of Jongno-gu's star sights, starting and ending at Gwanghwamun Sq and stopping at Insa-dong, palaces and more.

VICTOR JIANG/SHUTTERSTOCK

Changing of the Guard ceremony

TOP EXPERIENCE

Gyeongbokgung

Set aside the better part of a day to do justice to Gyeongbokgung, the hub around which Seoul has revolved since 1395. Much altered over its history, the largest and oldest of the city's royal palaces also offers two great museums and spectacular changing-of-the-guard ceremonies.

DON'T MISS

- Gwanghwamun
- Geunjeongjeon
- Gyeonghoeru
- Changing of the Guard
- National Folk Museum
- National Palace Museum of Korea

Palace History

Meaning 'palace of brilliance and fortune', Gyeongbokgung was the principal royal residence until 1592, when it was destroyed by fire during the Japanese invasion. It lay in ruins until the 1860s, when it was rebuilt at enormous expense for King Gojong, who moved in during 1868. Japanese assassins broke into the palace on 8 October 1895 to assassinate his wife, Queen Min, one of the most powerful figures at that time in Korea.

PRACTICALITIES

- *royal.khs.go.kr*
- adult/youth/child ₩3000/1500/free
- 9am-6pm Mon & Wed-Sun (to 6.30pm Jun-Aug, to 5pm Nov-Feb)

The Japanese demolished more than 90% of the palace, including Gwanghwamun, to make way for the enormous Japanese Government General Building. This was pulled down in the 1990s to enable Gwanghwamun to be rebuilt in its original location.

Palace Layout

Moving across the palace's broad front courtyard, you pass through a second gate, **Heungnyemun**, to face the ornate two-storey **Geunjeongjeon**. In this impressive throne hall, kings were crowned, met foreign envoys and conducted affairs of state. West of Geunjeongjeon is **Gyeonghoeru**, a large pavilion resting on 48 pillars that stand in an artificial lake with two small islands. State banquets were held inside and royals went boating on the pond.

A series of smaller meeting halls precede the king's living quarters, **Gangnyeongjeon**, near which are **Gyotaejeon**, those of the queen. Next you'll come to the terraced garden, **Amisan** – the red-brick chimneys decorated with longevity symbols on the garden's top terrace were used to release smoke from the *ondol* (underfloor heating) system.

Symbolically located on the eastern side of the grounds (where the sun rises) is **Donggung**, the living quarters of the crown prince. Here you can see one of the palace's newest additions – the **Gyejodang** building, reconstructed in 2023. North of Donggung is the main kitchen, **Sojubang**.

At the palace ground's far-north end are more halls for King Gojong's personal use and an ornamental pond with **Hyangwonjeong**, an attractive hexagonal pavilion on an island.

Palace Museum

To gain insights into what life was like within the palace walls, it's worth spending some time exploring the **National Palace Museum of Korea** *(gogung.go.kr; free)*, to the left just inside Gwanghwamun. (Note that the museum is not accessible from within Gyeongbokgung's grounds.) Its comprehensive exhibitions highlight the artistic skills of the Joseon dynasty and come right up to date with the Digital Library for Cultural Heritage, which includes a multisided video zone as well as interactive virtual-reality experiences.

Folk Museum

Plan at least an hour at the superb **National Folk Museum of Korea** *(nfm.go.kr; free)*. It has three main exhibition halls, covering Korean culture through the perspectives of daily life, a year in Korea and significant moments in a Korean's life from birth to death. Among the many interesting exhibits is an amazingly colourful funeral bier. Don't miss exploring the open-air exhibition of historic buildings and structures, including an atmospheric street of buildings styled as they would have been in the 1970s and '80s. There's a separate **Children's Museum of National Folk Museum of Korea**, for which advance reservations are necessary.

RENTING HANBOK

Anyone wearing *hanbok* (Korean traditional clothing) is granted free entry to Gyeongbokgung (as well as the other main palaces and Jongmyo). It's an incredibly popular way to visit and you'll see loads of rental shops offering a wide range of outfits. Rentals start at ₩15,000 for four hours, but it's worth paying more for locally made high-quality *hanbok*.

TOP TIPS

- Time your visit to catch the highly recommended Changing of the Guard ceremony, which takes place at 10am and 2pm daily, except Tuesday. The guard dispatch is at 11am and 1pm.
- In spring and autumn, Gyeongbokgung has nighttime hours, from 7pm to 9.30pm (last entry at 8.30pm). Standard-admission tickets are sold on site, but *hanbok* wearers can get in for free.
- Also in spring and autumn, there are special guided starlight tours. Tickets for these are extremely hard to get and are sold through a lottery system via Ticketlink, or – only for foreigners – on a first-come, first-served basis on Creatrip.com.

WHEN SEOUL WAS HANYANG

Seoul, meaning 'capital' in Korean, has only been the official name of the city since 1945. Before the Joseon dynasty, it was known as Hanyang, and during the Joseon dynasty (1392–1910) it was named Hanseong – and both Hanyang and Hanseong were used interchangeably. (Later, during Japanese rule, Seoul was also called Gyeongseong.)

The centre of administration, arts and culture, Jongno district was the historic heart of Hanyang. Its name comes from the major east–west street Jong-no, which means 'Bell St', where the **Bosingak** bell pavilion is located, from which the opening and closing of the city wall gates were signalled. Today Bosingak is a popular gathering spot to ring in the New Year, with the bell (a replica) tolled 33 times to wish prosperity.

Delve into Seoul's History

MAP P53

From Joseon-dynasty Hanyang to modern megacity

For a comprehensive overview of the Korean capital's trajectory, from the dawn of the Joseon dynasty to the present day, spend some time at the excellent **Seoul Museum of History** *(museum.seoul.go.kr; free)*. The museum, closed Mondays, charts the city's journey from when it was called Hanyang, through the Korean Empire, Japanese occupation and post-liberation. One highlight is the scale model of Seoul brought to life with lights and projected videos. Guided tours in English take place Tuesday at 2pm, Wednesday at 11am and Thursday through Saturday at both 11am and 2pm.

Outside is one of the old tram cars that used to run in the city in the 1930s, as well as a section of the old **Gwanghwamun** gate. Note that at the time of research, the museum was still operating in this spot, but there have been ongoing considerations to relocate it as part of the city's broader plan to renovate the surrounding area into an expansive history and culture park.

Over at the **National Museum of Korean Contemporary History** *(much.go.kr; free)*, get more context about the country from 1894 onwards. The museum offers engaging exhibitions on how far the Korean people have come in the decades since their fight for freedom from Imperial Japan, navigating the tumult of the Korean War, the democracy movement and ultra-rapid modernisation. There's also an interactive gallery about intergenerational communication, imaginative art pieces and a rooftop that provides beautiful views of **Gwanghwamun Sq** and Gyeongbokgung (p50). Guided English tours depart from the 5th floor every Thursday at 2.30pm.

Gather at Gwanghwamun Square

MAP P53

Seoul's quintessential meeting place

The city's most iconic public plaza, **Gwanghwamun Sq** provides a grand approach to Gyeongbokgung (p50). A historic gathering space, it's the site of everything from protests and demonstrations to K-Pop concerts. It's also the

BOSINGAK
To see the original city bell, forged in 1468, head to the garden of the **National Museum of Korea** (p124).

EATING IN JONGNO-GU: KOREAN CLASSICS

MAPS P53, P56 & P63

Tosokchon: (토속촌) Renowned for its *samgyetang* (ginseng chicken soup). Try the black chicken version. *10am-10pm* **WW**

Gwanghwamun Jip: (광화문집) Warming bowls of *kimchi jiggae*, a spicy kimchi stew with fatty pork, at a humble place in Seochon. *11.30am-9pm* **WW**

Koong: (궁) Order Kaesong-style dumplings in a flavourful soup with a side of spring-onion pancakes. *11.30am-9pm* **WW**

Anam: Its mouthwatering *gukpab* (pork and rice soup) is topped with spicy chilli and kale oil. *11.30am-9pm Tue-Sun* **WW**

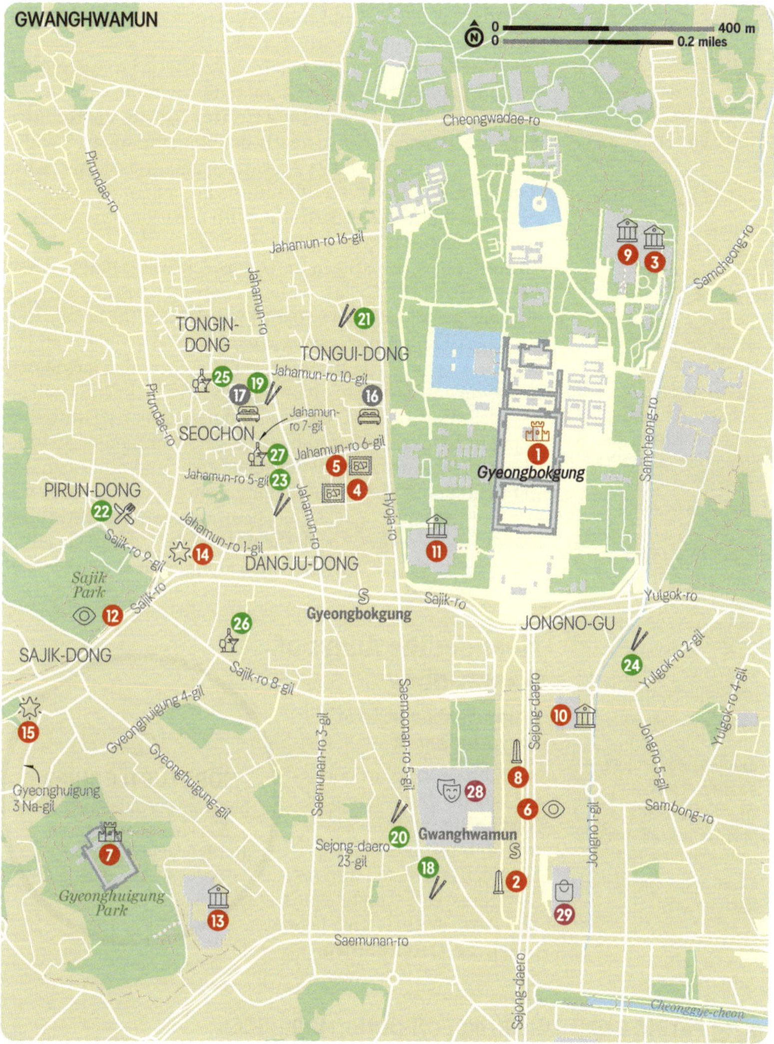

HIGHLIGHTS

1 Gyeongbokgung

SIGHTS

2 Admiral Yi Sun-sin Statue
3 Children's Museum of National Folk Museum of Korea
4 Daelim Museum
5 GROUNDSEESAW Seochon
6 Gwanghwamun Square
7 Gyeonghuigung
8 King Sejong Statue
9 National Folk Museum of Korea
10 National Museum of Korean Contemporary History
11 National Palace Museum of Korea
12 Sajikdan
13 Seoul Museum of History

ACTIVITIES, COURSES & TOURS

14 Food & Culture Korea
15 Seoul Kimchi Academy

SLEEPING

16 Boan Stay
17 Seochon Guesthouse

EATING

18 Gwanghwamun Jip
19 Horapa
20 Ogawa
21 Onjium
22 Rogpa Tea Stall
23 Tosokchon
24 Wooara

DRINKING & NIGHTLIFE

25 Bar Cham
see 25 Bar Pomme
26 Cobbler
27 Mutual Sound Club

ENTERTAINMENT

28 Sejong Center for the Performing Arts

SHOPPING

29 Kyobo Bookshop

NATIONAL HEROES

King Sejong (1397–1450) sponsored many cultural projects, consolidated border defences and served as a model of Confucian probity. At his direction, court scholars devised the phonetic *hangeul* alphabet, a simple system of writing the Korean language that made it possible for anyone to learn to read. *Hangeul* is one reason why Korea enjoys near-universal literacy today.

Admiral Yi Sun-sin (1545–98) designed innovative types of metal-clad warships called *geobukseon* (turtle ships), using them to help achieve a series of stunning victories over the much larger Japanese navy that attacked Korea at the end of the 16th century.

starting line of the Seoul International Marathon and a part of the Seoul Lantern Festival (p70).

Gwanghwamun Sq reopened in 2022 after a large-scale renovation that absorbed a five-lane roadway to its west to connect the plaza with the **Sejong Center for the Performing Arts** *(sejongpac.or.kr)*. In nearly doubling the square's width, the makeover increased its pedestrian and green space, while also installing new water fountains and expanding the memorial to **Admiral Yi Sun-sin**, with additional monuments near his statue.

Another bronze statue in the square celebrates national hero **King Sejong the Great**, while an entrance behind his enormous likeness leads down to the lower level of the Sejong Center, where exhibitions *(sejongstory.or.kr; free)* tell the stories of both the icons. The space, closed Mondays, also includes an experience zone offering hands-on activities the kids will enjoy, including a free 4D battle simulation (free), writing their name in *hangeul* calligraphy (free) and workshops (₩2000) to create their own keychains, popsockets and other trinkets.

On the floors above, the Sejong Center encompasses several performance spaces that host musical, orchestral, opera and other shows; check the website for the full schedule. There are also two art museums, along with several restaurants and a cafe.

Meander the Alleys of Ikseon-dong

MAP P53

A hip neighbourhood of converted *hanok*

Spend half a day in popular Ikseon-dong, north of Jongno 3-ga station, where a neighbourhood of *hanok* has been converted into retail stores, cafes, restaurants and bars. Begin with a hearty lunch at **Oncheonjip**, known

MORE TURTLE SHIPS
See more *geobukseon* at the **War Memorial of Korea** (p128), where a huge replica occupies the 1st floor.

EATING & DRINKING IN IKSEON-DONG: MORE PICKS

MAP P56

Ikseon Banju: Fresh Korean takes on carpaccios, pastas and other dishes, plus an excellent selection of *makgeolli* and *soju*. *noon-10pm* ₩₩	**Bogle House:** Top-notch pizzas (get the bacon mac and cheese) served alongside craft beers and highballs. *3pm-midnight* ₩₩	**Ikseon Dimibang:** A chic Korean-European bistro in a converted *hanok* cooking fusion risottos, pastas and more. *11am-3pm & 5-10pm* ₩₩	**Brew 3.14:** Along with sibling pub Brew 3.15 across the road, this place serves delicious pizza and craft beer. *6pm-midnight Mon-Thu, from 5pm Fri & Sat* ₩₩
Craft Roo: Pouring a wonderful selection of Korean craft beers, including the award-winning Sokcho IPA. *4-11.30pm Mon-Fri, from noon Sat & Sun*	**Cheongsudang:** Swaying bamboo marks the entrance to this trendy *hanok* cafe with signature items such as castella sponge. *10.30am-9pm*	**Sikmul:** Popular *hanok* cafe-bar with rustic decor and contemporary art. Come for croffles (croissant-waffles) and coffee – or cocktails and wine. *noon-11pm*	**Shortbus:** Welcoming gay bar mixing up a wide range of cocktails. Attracts an older clientele. *7.30pm-5am*

LEGOCAMERA/SHUTTERSTOCK

Ikseon-dong

for its *shabu shabu* (hot pot), or **Zio Cucina** for Italian. Grab dessert and coffee from one of the area's many picture-perfect *hanok* cafes – **Jayeondo Sogeumbang** and **Soha Salt Pond** are two viral salt-bread spots.

Afterwards, shop for modern *hanbok* (Korean clothing) at **Teterot Salon** *(teterot.kr)*, a boutique store that sells updated takes on classic *chima* skirts and *jeogori* tops, ranging from casual everyday wear to more dressed-up and formal. Head over to **Ikseon Shooting Club** for a bit of target practice, before stopping for dinner along **Galmaegisal Alley**, a string of pork-skirt BBQ joints with seating that flows out onto the street, and a pint at a craft-beer pub such as **Art Monster** or **Aledang**.

Check out **Saeseoul Com Com Play** for retro arcade games, and finish up with late-night street snacks and drinks at a *pojangmacha* (dining tent) along Donhwamun-ro.

WHAT ARE HANOK?

Vessels of Korean architectural tradition, *hanok* are single-storey wooden homes, insulated with mud and straw and topped with clay-tiled roofs. They are typically left unpainted, their earthy tones providing a warm, intimate feel. All rooms have sliding doors and *ondol* (underfloor heating), and face onto a *madang* (central courtyard).

In recent years, many of the *hanok* of Bukchon, Seochon and Ikseon-dong have been adapted to become guesthouses, restaurants, cafes, bars and boutiques, making it easy to appreciate this unique form of architecture. A few, such as Baek In-je House (p70), have been preserved in their original form.

EATING IN JONGNO-GU: CONTEMPORARY KOREAN

MAPS P53 & P56

Wooara: Near Gwanghwamun, *omakase* (chef's choice) meals are served in private rooms with impeccable presentation. *11am-3pm & 5-10pm* ₩₩₩

A Flower Blossom on Rice: Only organic, farm-fresh ingredients appear on the menu of this classy restaurant on an Insa-dong alley. *11.30am-3pm & 5.30-9pm* ₩₩₩

Onjium: Contemporary fine dining in a smart setting. Open kitchen with counter seating and views of Gyeongbokgung. *noon-3pm & 6-10pm Tue-Fri* ₩₩₩

Mishmash: Delicious set lunches and dinners at this Korean-Danish fusion restaurant in a modern *hanok* with a view over Changdeokgung. *11am-3pm & 6-9pm* ₩₩₩

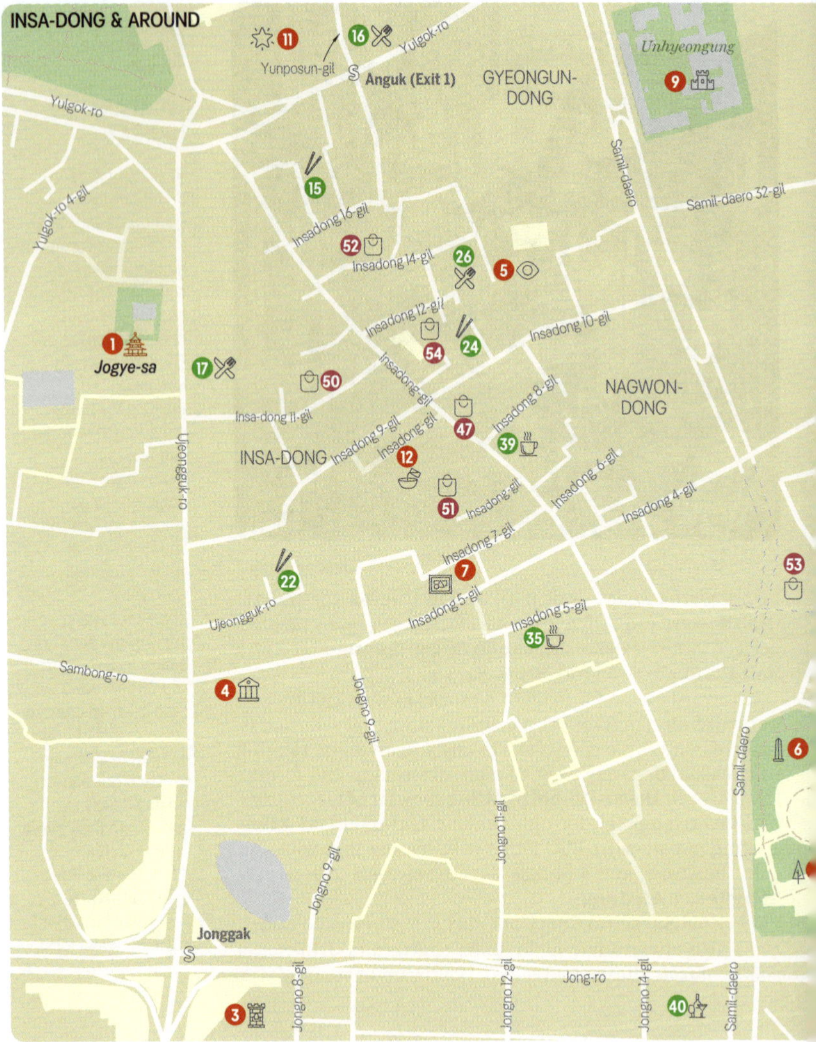

HIGHLIGHTS
1 Jogye-sa
2 Jongmyo

SIGHTS
3 Bosingak
4 Gongpyeong Historic Sites Museum
5 Kyungin Museum of Fine Art
6 Stone Pagoda of Wongak-sa
7 Sun Gallery
8 Tapgol Park
9 Unhyeongung

ACTIVITIES, COURSES & TOURS
10 Insadong Spa & Sauna
11 Korean Temple Food Center
12 Museum Kimchikan
13 Tteok Museum

SLEEPING
14 Tongtong Hotel

EATING
15 A Flower Blossom on Rice
16 Artist Bakery
17 Balwoo Gongyang
18 Bogle House
19 Galmaegisal Alley
20 Ikseon Banju
21 Ikseon Dimibang
22 Imun Seolleongtang
23 Jayeondo Sogeumbang
24 Koong
25 Oncheonjip
26 Osegyehyang

EATING
27 Soha Salt Pond
28 Soma
29 Vegan Insa
30 Yellow Dragon Curry
31 Zio Cucina

DRINKING & NIGHTLIFE
32 7.8 Makgeolli 2
33 Aledang
34 Art Monster
35 Beautiful Tea Museum
36 Brew 3.14
37 Cheongsudang
38 Craft Roo
39 Dawon
40 Ooze Whale
41 Orb of Light
42 Seoul Gypsy
43 Shortbus
44 Sikmul

ENTERTAINMENT
45 Ikseon Shooting Club
46 Saeseoul Com Com Play

SHOPPING
47 Dolsilnai
48 Guiroe
49 Jongno Jewelry District
50 KCDF Gallery
51 Kukje Embroidery
52 Leesle
53 Nakwon Musical Instruments Arcade
54 Ssamziegil
55 Teterot Salon

Three giant Buddha statues, Daeungjeon

TOP EXPERIENCE

Jogye-sa

Festooned with colourful paper lanterns in spring, Jogye-sa is the headquarters of the Jogye Order, the largest order of Korean Buddhism. A hive of activity, the attractive religious centre provides insights into Buddhist practice, particularly if you join one of its highly recommended Templestay programs.

DON'T MISS

- Daeungjeon
- Geuknakjeon
- Beomjongnu
- Museum
- Yeon Deung Hoe
- Templestay Program

Worship Hall

Daeungjeon, Jogye-sa's grand wooden hall, is Seoul's largest Buddhist worship hall. Completed in 1938, the Joseon-dynasty-style building is decorated with scenes from the Buddha's life and carved floral latticework. Inside are three giant Buddha statues: on the left is Amitabha, Buddha of the Western Paradise; in the centre is the historical Buddha; on the right is the Bhaisaiya or Medicine Buddha, holding a medicine bowl.

PRACTICALITIES

- *jogyesa.kr*
- free
- temple grounds 24hr

The small 15th-century Buddha in the glass case was the main Buddha statue before it was replaced by the much larger ones in 2006. On the right-hand side is a guardian altar with lots of fierce-looking guardians in the painting behind, and on the left side is the altar used for memorial services. Believers who enter the temple bow three times, touching their forehead to the ground – once for Buddha, once for the Dharma and once for the Sangha.

Other Buildings on the Grounds

Behind Daeungjeon is the modern **Geuknakjeon** (Paradise Hall), dedicated to Amitabha Buddha. Funeral services, dharma talks and other prayer services are held here.

Also look out for the octagonal 10-storey **stupa**, in which is enshrined a relic of the Buddha brought to Korea in 1913 by a Sri Lankan monk. Look also for **Beomjongnu**, a bell pavilion housing a drum to summon earthbound animals, a wooden fish-shaped gong to summon aquatic beings, a metal cloud-shaped gong to summon birds and a large bronze bell to summon underground creatures. The bell is rung 28 times at 4am and 33 times at 6pm.

Also in the grounds is a **museum** displaying antique woodblocks, symbol-filled paintings and other Buddhist artefacts. There are also cafeterias and restaurants on site.

Templestay Program

Near the main entrance, the Jogye-sa Information Center for Foreigners is staffed by English-speaking guides. Drop by here to make a booking for a Templestay program (from ₩10,000). There are a variety of offerings, ranging from a one-day tea ceremony to two-day-one-night experiences that include a temple tour, meditation practice, lotus-lantern making, bowing, Buddhist ceremonies and monastic meals.

To find out more about Buddhism or book a Templestay program elsewhere in Seoul or Korea, the Templestay Information Center is just across the street from Jogye-sa. Along the street you'll find many shops selling monks' robes, prayer beads, lanterns and the like.

Buddhism in Korea

When first introduced during the Koguryo dynasty in 370 CE, Buddhism coexisted with shamanism. Many Buddhist temples have a *samseong-gak* (three-spirit hall) on their grounds, which houses shamanist deities such as the Mountain God. Buddhism was persecuted during the Joseon period, when temples were tolerated only on remote mountains.

In the first half of the 20th century, the religion also suffered during the Japanese occupation. After Korea's liberation in 1945, the Jogye Order came to the fore. Its symbol – a circle enclosing three dots – represents faith in the Buddha, Dharma (moral law) and Sangha (monastic order). With around 16 million adherents, Buddhism is Korea's second most popular religion after Christianity.

SEASONAL FESTIVALS

Jogye-sa is especially worth visiting during a special event.

The most spectacular is Yeon Deung Hoe, in honour of Buddha's birthday in late April or early May, for which thousands of lotus lanterns are displayed to magical effect and a nighttime parade of illuminated floats culminates at Jogye-sa.

Another is the autumn chrysanthemum festival, when the grounds are awash in golden hues, along with Dano (p209), Chuseok and New Year's Eve.

TOP TIPS

- Being mindful of temple etiquette will ensure the best experience: remember to dress modestly (cover shoulders and knees), silence your phone, remove your hat and shoes before entering the worship hall, and don't photograph worshippers.
- Avoid the crowds by visiting in the early morning or evening. Jogye-sa after dark is a particularly beautiful sight.
- Notice the ancient trees on the temple grounds. One is a 10m-tall white pine, a natural monument in Korea, and the other is the gargantuan, 26m-tall Chinese Scholar Tree, from which the springtime lotus lanterns are spectacularly strung.

SAYAN URANAN/SHUTTERSTOCK

Changdeokgung in autumn

TOP EXPERIENCE

Changdeokgung

If you only have time to see one of Seoul's palaces, make it Changdeokgung – it's the best preserved and most beautiful. It's also World Heritage–listed because of its serene Secret Garden, which is the epitome of Joseon-dynasty landscaping. Koreans say the garden should be visited throughout the seasons to get a different perspective of its beauty, so don't hesitate to go even if it's winter.

DON'T MISS

- Donhwamun
- Injeongjeon
- Nakseonjae
- Buyongji Pond
- Juhamnu
- Buyongjeong
- Yeongyeongdang
- Ongnyucheon

Palace History

Changdeokgung was originally built in 1405 but, like Seoul's other palaces, it was destroyed during the Japanese invasion of the late 16th century. Rebuilt in 1610, it was the main palace until 1867 and remained in use by royal descendants until 1989.

PRACTICALITIES

- *royal.khs.go.kr*
- adult/youth/child ₩3000/1500/free
- 9am-6pm Tue-Sun (to 6.30pm Jun-Aug, to 5.30pm Nov-Jan)

Palace Layout

Enter through the imposing **Donhwamun** gate, turn right and cross over the stone bridge (built in 1414) – note the guardian animals carved on its sides. On the left, across a paved courtyard, is the beautiful throne hall, **Injeongjeon**. It sits in harmony with the paved courtyard, the open corridors and the trees behind it.

Next door are the government office buildings, including one with a blue-tiled roof. Further on are the private living quarters of the royal family. Peering inside the polychromatic and sparsely furnished rooms, you can get an inkling of Changdeokgung in its heyday.

Around the back is a terraced garden with decorative *ondol* chimneys. Over on the right is something completely different – **Nakseonjae**, built by King Heonjong (r 1834–49) in an austere Confucian style using unpainted wood. Royal descendants lived here until 1989.

Guided tours in English are available at 10.15am and 1.15pm and depart from the main information board.

Secret Garden

Covering almost 60% of the palace grounds, **Huwon** ('Rear Garden', aka Secret Garden) is a naturalistic wood where sinuous paths lead into glades punctuated by ornamental ponds and pavilions. This is where Joseon royalty relaxed, studied and wrote poems, and where military exercises and banquets were held.

The garden's most famous vista is that of **Buyongji Pond**, which is square to represent the earth; it is crowned by an island, which is round to represent the sky. The lotus-dotted pond is overlooked by three pavilions: **Juhamnu**, a two-storey library built in 1776 by King Jeongjo; **Buyongjeong**, said to be his favourite; and **Yeonghwadang**. Further on are a couple more ponds and **Yeongyeongdang**, built in 1828 as a place for the crown prince to study.

Ongnyucheon is a brook at the back of the garden where there's a huge rock, **Soyoam**, with three Chinese characters inscribed on it by King Injo in 1636 – *ong-nyu-cheon*, which means 'jade flowing stream' – and a poem composed in Chinese characters by King Sukjong in 1690.

Visiting the Secret Garden is only possible on a 70-minute guided tour and requires a separate ticket *(ticket.uforus.co.kr; adult/youth ₩5000/2500)*, of which there are only 100 available for each viewing session. Fifty are designated for online reservations, released six days in advance of the tour date, and 50 are held for on-site same-day bookings, sold on a first-come, first-served basis. The English tour times are 10.30am, 11.30am, 2.30pm and, from February to November, also 3.30pm.

MOONLIGHT TOUR

In spring and autumn, Changdeokgung hosts special guided moonlight tours that allow visitors to see the palace buildings lit by the glow of *cheongsachorong* (traditional lanterns). The experience includes traditional dance and music performances, as well as traditional tea and desserts.

These limited tickets are sold through a lottery system via Ticketlink, or – only for foreigners – on a first-come, first-served basis on Creatrip.com.

TOP TIPS

- Dress up in *hanbok* and get in for free.
- If you forgot to book your Secret Garden ticket in advance, don't fret. Turn up to the ticket office right at 9am and there's a good chance you'll be able to snag one.
- Save money with a combination pass (₩6000), which gives you entry to Changdeokgung and three other palaces (Gyeongbokgung, Changgyeonggung and Deoksugung) as well as Jongmyo. You don't have to visit all the sights in one day; just redeem within six months.

JOSEON SIGHTS IN JONGNO-GU

Jongchinbu: Behind the MMCA's main gallery stands the office of royal genealogy, restored to its original site after a spell by Jeongdok Library.

Sajikdan: This stone altar surrounded by low stone walls and ornate wooden gates dates to 1395 and King Taejo, founder of the Joseon dynasty.

Dongsipjagak: Once part of Gyeongbokgung's eastern wall, damaged during the Japanese occupation, this watchtower was separated from the rest to make room for a road.

Stone Pagoda of Wongak-sa: Tapgol Park was the site of Wongak-sa temple, destroyed in 1504. This 10-tier marble monument remained.

Gongpyeong Historic Sites Museum: A branch of the Seoul Museum of History, showcasing Joseon-era relics excavated during city maintenance projects.

See the Palace of Shining Celebration

MAP P53

A royal, revitalised space

Of the five major palaces in Seoul, **Gyeonghuigung** *(museum.seoul.go.kr; free)* is by far the least visited, but that only makes it all the more peaceful. In 2025, the Palace of Shining Celebration underwent the first phase of a 10-year city project to gradually transform the site and its surrounding area into a huge history and culture park that's slated to cover 136,000 sq metres. Gyeonghuigung's entrance was revitalised with a traditional stone pathway installed between **Heunghwamun** and **Sungjeongmun** gates, as well as a garden planted with native trees.

Originally called Gyeongdeokgung, the palace, closed Mondays, was completed in 1620, renamed in 1760 and largely destroyed during the Japanese occupation. Since then, three of its buildings – the main hall Sungjeongjeon, Jajeongjeon and Taeryeongjeon – have been restored.

The history park project, which is expected to be completed by 2035, will also rebuild Donuimun, the only one of Seoul's four major gates yet to be restored.

Escape to a Lesser-Known Palace

MAP P56

Visit King Gojong's childhood home

In Insa-dong, the modest-scale palace of **Unhyeongung** *(unhyeongung.or.kr; free)* has a natural-wood design reflecting the austere tastes of Heungseon Daewongun (1820–98), King Gojong's stern and conservative father. Heungseon's policies included massacring Korean Catholics, expelling foreigners from Korea and closing Confucian schools. Gojong was born and raised here until 1863, when he ascended the throne at the age of 12, with his father acting as regent. The palace, closed Mondays, is generally crowd-free and only busy when cultural events and special experiential programmes are held here, which makes it great for picture taking.

Admire Art at Two Premier Museums

MAP P63

View the MMCA and Arario collections

Dive into Korea's dynamic contemporary-art scene at **MMCA Seoul** *(mmca.go.kr; price varies by exhibition)*. The city's premier contemporary-art museum occupies a large complex that combines spacious modern galleries with the repurposed red-brick buildings of the former Defense Security

EATING IN JONGNO-GU: ASIAN FARE

MAPS P53 & P56

Yellow Dragon Curry: Many kinds of Japanese-style curry heaped over rice, with deep-fried add-ons like crispy pork cutlet and croquette. *11.30am-9pm* WW

Horapa: Bib Gourmand Thai food in Seochon: curries, soups and a divine roti dessert drizzled with condensed milk. *11.30am-3pm & 6-10pm Tue-Sat* WWW

Soma: Delicious takes on Chinese dishes such as *cheung fun* (rice noodle rolls), steamed egg with clams, and *kang pao* chicken. *5-10pm Tue-Sun* WWW

Ogawa: Top-grade sushi and sashimi at this restaurant in the basement of the Royal Building. Book, as space is limited. *noon-2pm & 6-10pm Mon-Fri* WWW

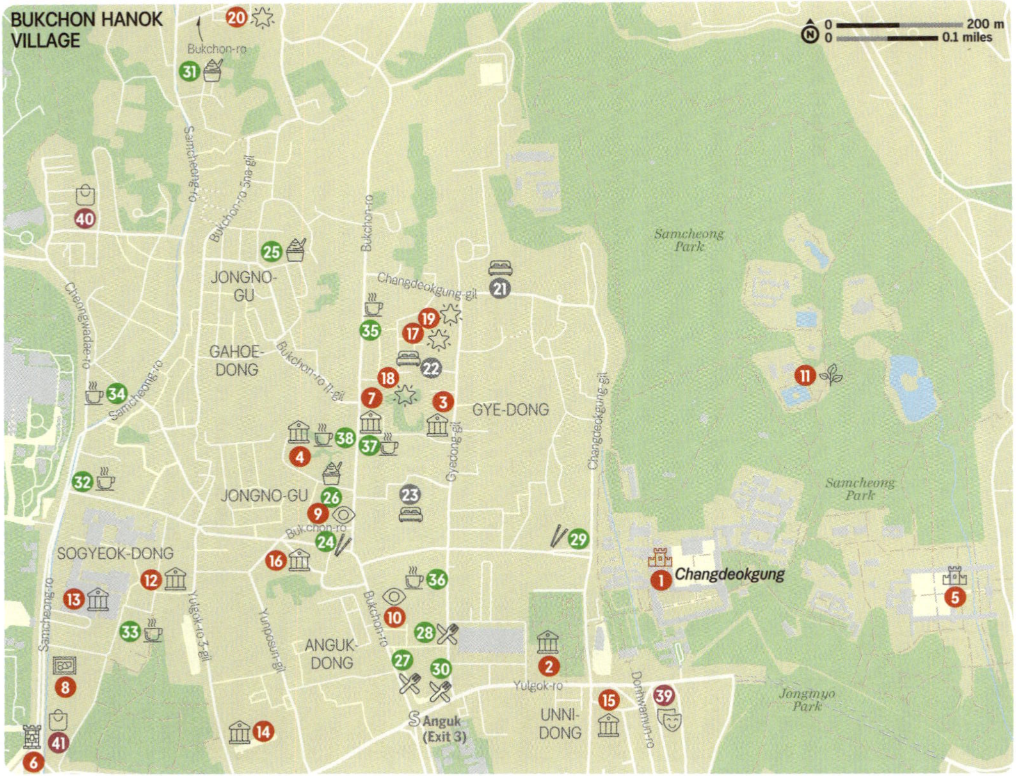

HIGHLIGHTS
1 Changdeokgung

SIGHTS
2 Arario Museum in SPACE
3 Bae Ryeom House
4 Baek In-je House
5 Changgyeonggung
6 Dongsipjagak
7 Gahoe Minhwa Museum
8 Gallery Hyundai
9 Hanji House
10 Hansik Space E:eum
11 Huwon
12 Jongchinbu
13 MMCA Seoul
14 Seoul Museum of Craft Art
15 Seoul Museum of Korean Folk Music
16 Yun Po-sun House

ACTIVITIES, COURSES & TOURS
17 Bukchon Traditional Crafts Center
18 Dong-Lim Knot Workshop
19 Kumbakyeon
20 O'ngo

SLEEPING
21 Bukchon Maru
22 Butler.Lee
23 Rak-Ko-Jae

EATING
24 Anam
25 Arari
26 Boobing
27 Cafe Layered Bukchon
28 Dotori Garden
29 Mishmash
30 Onion
31 Seoulseo Duljjaero Jalhaneunjip

DRINKING & NIGHTLIFE
32 Baekmidang
33 Cafe Cordialement
34 Cafe Husbands
35 Green Mile Coffee
36 Hollow
37 Low Roof
38 Osulloc
see 16 Tea Therapy

ENTERTAINMENT
39 Seoul Donhwamun Traditional Theater

SHOPPING
see 31 MGFS100
40 PKM Gallery
41 Seoul Selection
see 10 Sool Gallery

WHERE TO SHOP IN JONGNO-GU

Jongno Jewelry District: Hundreds of jewellery shops selling discounted gold, silver and more.

Ssamziegil: In Insa-dong, an arty four-storey complex designed by Choi Moon-gyu and Gabriel Kroiz, good for fashion and souvenirs.

Kyobo Bookshop: This Gwanghwamun Sq shop stocks a wide range of English-language books and magazines, as well as electronics.

Nakwon Musical Instruments Arcade: With over 300 shops, it's the world's largest musical-instrument complex.

Guiroe: Seonock Park's contemporary *hanbok* have been on show at London's V&A Museum. Located on Donhwamun-ro, once a road of royal processions.

Seoul Selection: Local publisher with many books in English on Korean culture.

Command. Ambitious, cutting-edge works are displayed in a variety of temporary exhibitions – to see everything would take at least half a day. The well-stocked bookshop and gift store alone make it worth a visit. The galleries are free during the museum's late opening hours, which are 6pm to 9pm on Wednesdays and Saturdays, and also on Culture Day, the last Wednesday of the month.

One of Seoul's best private art galleries, **Arario Museum in SPACE** *(arariomuseum.org; adult/youth/child ₩15,000/-9000/6000)* showcases pieces from the collection of business magnate Kim Chang-il, the first Korean on *Art Review's* list of the world's top 100 collectors. Kim's enviable trove includes works by Nam June Paik, Koo Kang, Kōhei Nawa, Tracey Emin, Damien Hirst and Cindy Sherman. The ivy-clad SPACE brick building, closed Mondays, is considered a seminal piece of early-1970s architecture. Its compact, low-ceilinged rooms and labyrinthine layout fit the artworks like a glove – you never know what wonder lies around the next corner.

On the premises, there's also a *hanok* and a five-storey glass annexe (added in 1997) housing cafes and restaurants, as well as the free **Arario Gallery** *(arariogallery.com)*, closed Sundays and Mondays.

Sweat it Out in Insa-dong

MAP P56

Spa, sip and stroll

Local bathhouses and saunas, known as *jjimjilbang* (heated rooms), can be found across Seoul. They are places where locals come to unwind, hang out and partake in a host of health and beauty rituals.

A good *jjimjilbang* with English-speaking staff is **Insadong Spa & Sauna**. In the same-sex bathing sections, get naked and enjoy soaking in different baths and the steam sauna. Pay extra for a full-body scrub from one of the attendants – as dead skin is sloughed off, you'll feel reborn. Pyjamas are provided for the mixed-sex dry sauna and relaxation area.

After your scrub, melt into a soothing cup of tea at an Insa-dong teahouse such as **Beautiful Tea Museum**, then go for

Continues on p68

DRINKING IN JONGNO-GU: OUR PICKS

MAPS P53 & P56

Bar Cham: Inspired by Korea's different provinces, with drinks that showcase Korean traditional spirits and ingredients. *6pm-1am Mon & Wed-Sun*

Bar Pomme: Skilled bartenders concoct innovative seasonal cocktails like the Crimson Foliage with rum, peanut and Aperol. *6pm-1am Mon & Wed-Sun*

Cobbler: Sophisticated *hanok* bar on an alleyway near Sajik Park, serving a complimentary piece of pie with your drink. *7pm-3am Mon-Sat*

Mutual Sound Club: Artfully presented cocktails in a cosy Seochon vinyl bar. If you like lemon and gin, get the Bee's Knees. *6-11pm Sun-Thu, to 11.30pm Fri & Sat*

Ooze Whale: By Tapgol Park, a cosy basement bar serving pasta and other mains. Food is optional, but wine is mandatory. *6pm-1am, to 2am Fri & Sat*

Orb of Light: Wine and cocktails in an intimate space on the edge of Ikseon-dong. Try the signature Florist. *6pm-2am Tue-Sun*

7.8 Makgeolli 2: Superb selection of *makgeolli*, including its own Not Applicable brand garnished with a squeeze of lemon. *5pm-midnight*

Seoul Gypsy: Near Jongmyo, an atmospheric *hanok* bar with 10 ales on tap, including a porter pilsner, Belgian white and lager. *4-11pm Tue-Sun*

EXPERIENCE HISTORY & HANOK IN SEOCHON

Hanok-studded Seochon is not overtouristed like Bukchon, making this neighbourhood west of Gyeongbokgung a pleasant place for casual wanderings.

START	END	LENGTH
Cheongwadae Sarangchae	Hong Geonik's House	1.6km; 1½ hr

Start at the museum 1 **Cheongwadae Sarangchae** to learn about Korea's presidential history. With the Blue House closed again after being reinstated as the presidential villa by President Lee Jae-myung, Cheongwadae Sarangchae is the closest you can get, for now, to Cheongwadae. Head over to 2 **Tongin Market**, pausing for lunch at the 3 **Lunchbox Cafe**, where you can buy tokens (₩5000 for 10 tokens) to spend on helpings of dishes from the various food stalls. Once you've had your fill, keep going west until you hit Ogin-gil, an attractive street lined with cafes, bakeries and boutiques.

Making your way up the road, stop at 4 **Ogin Oraksil** to try your hand at some old-school video arcade games, 5 **Visitor** for a caffeine break and 6 **Park No-soo Museum**, the one-time home of the celebrated painter Park (1927–2013). It's still decorated with his art today.

Head south to find 7 **Dae-oh Bookstore**. Opened as a bookshop in 1951, this bygone-days space, overflowing with books and memorabilia, has been preserved as a charming cafe. Further south, you'll come to 8 **Seochon Lounge**, a beautifully designed modern *hanok* hosting exhibitions of contemporary Korean craft and design. Further south still is 9 **Hong Geonik's House**, the last *hanok* in Seoul with an *ilgakmun* (two-post gate), *binggo* (ice storage) and a well.

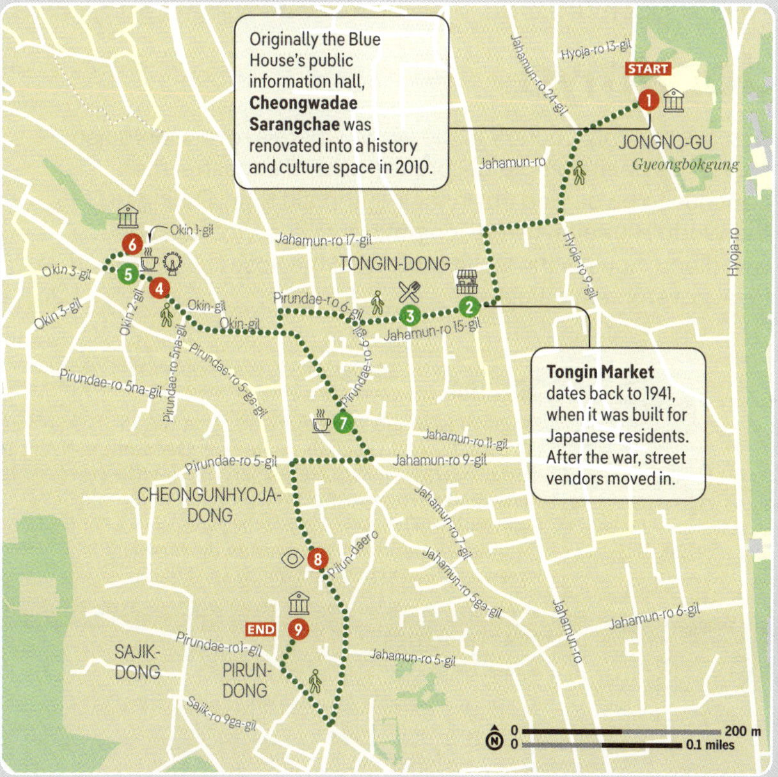

RUDY BALASKO/SHUTTERSTOCK

Jongmyo

TOP EXPERIENCE

Jongmyo

Korea is the only country in the world where a royal Confucian shrine has been completely preserved and ancestral rites continue to be carried out in their authentic form. Dating to 1395, the World Heritage–listed Jongmyo shrine, surrounded by woodland, houses the 'spirit tablets' of the Joseon royalty and loyal government officials.

DON'T MISS

- Oedaemun
- Jeongjeon
- Gongsindang
- Chilsadang
- Yeongnyeongjeon
- Jongmyo Daeje

Shrines

Jongmyo is simply decorated, befitting the shrine's solemn purpose. Enter through the main gate, **Oedaemun**. Near the entrance are two ponds, both square (representing earth) with round islands (representing the heavens). In the middle of the main path you'll notice triple stone paths – one is for the king, the other for the crown prince, with the raised middle section for the spirits. Do not walk on the spirit path.

PRACTICALITIES

- *royal.khs.go.kr*
- adult/youth/child ₩1000/500/free
- 9am-6pm Mon & Wed-Sun

Fronted by a large stone-flagged courtyard, the main shrine, **Jeongjeon**, first built in 1395, houses the spirit tablets of 49 kings and queens locked in 19 windowless rooms. Jeongjeon reopened to the public in 2025 with a Hwananje ceremony to return the tablets to their original place after five years of restoration work. In the shrine's first major renovation since 1870, the project replaced all 70,000 roof tiles with traditionally handmade ones.

To the right of the main entrance is **Gongsindang**, home to the spirit tablets of 83 meritorious subjects who served their kings well. On the left side is **Chilsadang**, enshrining the spirit tablets of the seven gods who aid the royal family.

The smaller shrine, **Yeongnyeongjeon** (Hall of Eternal Peace), built in 1421, contains the 34 spirit tablets of lesser kings and queens in 16 chambers. These include four generations of ancestors to King Taejo (the founder of the Joseon dynasty) who were made kings posthumously, and also Yi Un, the last crown prince, who died in 1970.

Behind these shrines, paths lead through a wooded park to the **North Gate**, which connects to **Changgyeonggung** (p182). Historically linked, Jongmyo and Changgyeonggung were separated by the Japanese in 1932 when they built a through road; in 2022, they were rejoined. Only on weekends, public holidays and Culture Day, when the shrine can be roamed on your own, can you currently walk between the two locations. To visit Jongmyo on weekdays, it's obligatory to join an English guided tour, which run at 10am, noon, 2pm and 4pm.

Jongmyo Daeje

Also known as Jongmyo Jerye, Jongmyo Daeje was the elaborate ancestral rite conducted by the king to honour the royal family. After he was escorted from Gwanghwamun to the shrine in a palanquin, the ancestors' tablets were placed on the altar, where their spirits were welcomed with deep bows, lavish offerings of food and liquor, and ritual music, singing and dancing. The ceremony was held five times a year.

Today Jongmyo Daeje is held on the first Sunday of May and the first Saturday of November and is conducted by the Yi clan, the descendants of the Joseon kings. After five years of restoration work on Jongmyo, 2025 marked the first time since 2019 that spectators could witness the ceremony. Considered the oldest complete Confucian ceremony in the world, Jongmyo Daeje is a UNESCO-listed intangible heritage.

SPIRIT TABLETS

While royal bodies were buried in tombs, such as those in Gangnam (p142) and northern Seoul, their spirits resided in 'tablets', or *sinju* – wooden boxes with six small holes bored in the top, bottom and four sides. The box was inscribed with the person's accomplishments.

The king's tablet is covered with a white cloth, while the queen's tablet is covered with a blue one.

TOP TIPS

- As with Seoul's major palaces, admission to Jongmyo is free on Culture Day, the last Wednesday of the month in Korea.
- On weekdays, you're required to join a guided tour group to enter Jongmyo, so if you prefer exploring on your own, opt to visit on a weekend or on Culture Day.
- Get your wide-angle camera lens ready: you'll want to capture Jeongjeon, the longest wooden building in Korea.
- Save a bit of money by purchasing a combination pass, which includes entry to Jongmyo along with four palaces. Use within six months.

MORE ART HALLS IN JONGNO-GU

GROUNDSEESAW Seochon: Contemporary gallery and cultural complex hosting exhibitions in an architecturally stunning space.

Daelim Museum: Exhibitions on photography, design and fashion. The building, once a family house, was remodelled by French architect Vincent Cornu.

Gallery Hyundai: Trailblazer of Korea's contemporary commercial-gallery scene since 1970. Represents giants like Lee Jung-seop and Nam June Paik.

PKM Gallery: Check out works by talents such as Bek Hyunjin and Sang Nam Lee.

MGFS100: Showcasing the humorous, big-footed statues of Kim Gyoung Min – you'll see many of her colourful characters around Seoul.

Kyungin Museum of Fine Art: Open since 1983, this Insa-dong gallery puts on indoor and outdoor exhibits in halls around a lovely courtyard.

Continued from p64
a stroll around nearby **Tapgol Park**, a long-time neighbourhood favourite. Opened in 1897 as Seoul's first modern-style park, it is where, on 1 March 1919, the Declaration of Independence from Japanese rule was read aloud, igniting a nationwide movement. Besides the Joseon-era pagoda (p62), you'll see a memorial to the *samil* (1 March) movement, with a copy of the declaration written in English, and a pavilion.

What's in a Name?

Insa-dong gets its name from two old neighbourhoods, combining the 'in' of Gwanin-bang with the 'sa' of Daesa-dong, and as the site of the former Royal Bureau of Painting, it's Seoul's traditional centre of arts. In the years since, antique shops, crafts vendors and commercial-art galleries (like **Sun Gallery**, one of Seoul's longest running) have all made their homes here. Visit for folk souvenirs galore – everything from *tal* (wooden masks) and *buchae* (handheld fans) to calligraphy inks and brushes, *hanji* (Korean paper) and lacquerware. Shop for locally made wares at the Korean Craft and Design Foundation's **KCDF Gallery**, *hanbok* at designers like **Dolsilnai** and **Leesle** and *bojagi* (wrapping cloths) and other fabric crafts at **Kukje Embroidery**.

Discover Korean Crafts

MAP P63

Learn about ceramics, embroidery and more

Opened in 2021, the **Seoul Museum of Craft Art** *(craft museum.seoul.go.kr; free)* showcases a spectacular collection of 23,000 craft items, ranging from Joseon-dynasty ceramics and metalwork to folding screens of embroidered birds and flowers, and beautifully decorated examples of *bojagi* (traditional wrapping cloths). The museum also champions the works of contemporary Korean artists such as the internationally renowned ceramicist Lee Hun-chung. Start by looking at the permanent exhibition, 'Artisans – Making the Better World', in buildings 1 and 2, which showcases the history of craft. Building 1 also features a special exhibition hall. In building 3 (the old high school) are fabric-based works donated by the late Huh Dong-hwa, founder of the Korea Embroidery Museum, and his wife, Park Young-sook. Register for docent tours on site, or submit your ID card to borrow a 'Craft Eye' smart guide that uses beacon technology to deliver information about exhibits and alert you when you're near a work you've 'liked'.

TEAHOUSES IN JONGNO-GU: OUR PICKS

MAPS P56 & P63

Dawon: In Insa-dong, sip your tea inside or in the garden. Try the *omija hwachae* (five-flavour berry punch). *10am-10pm*

Seoulseo Duljjaero Jalhaneunjip: (서울서둘째로잘하는집) Little has changed at 'Second Best in Seoul', a tiny medicinal tea cafe, since it opened in 1976. *11am-8.30pm*

Tea Therapy: Teas and herbal infusions for whatever ails you, and a chart to aid your selection. Footbaths outside the front door. *10am-9pm*

Osulloc: Enjoy a matcha latte, tea-based cocktail or green-tea sponge roll in this sleek Bukchon branch of the premium tea shop. *11am-8pm*

LIMLIM/SHUTTERSTOCK

Tapgol Park

At the separate **Children's Museum**, a craft village offering hands-on experiences, kids can sign up to learn how to weave fabric, make a wooden toy, or hammer their own engraved metal plate to take home with them. It has a rooftop observatory providing views over the adjacent **Yeollin Songhyeon**, a nicely designed city park that opened in 2022.

Go Gourmet with Korean Gastronomy MAP P63

All about *hansik*

Hansik Space E:eum *(hansik.or.kr; free)*, closed Mondays, is a one-stop shop for experiencing *hansik* (Korean cuisine). In addition to exhibitions about the national food culture, there is a cafe serving tea and desserts, a store, library and a learning centre where you can take classes *(₩11,000)* on how to make seasonal dishes, desserts and more. Book ahead online. A separate programme is run in the Korea Food Grand Master Center here, with courses taught by grand masters that focus on traditional ingredients such as *ganjang* (soy sauce), *gochujang* (red chilli paste) and, of course, kimchi.

WHERE TO TAKE A CRAFT CLASS

Bukchon Traditional Crafts Center: Join the programme of the day, which ranges from needle and patchwork, to painting and dying, to ceramics and beyond.

Kumbakyeon (금박연): Visit this gold-leaf gilding workshop to create decorative pouches and other items inspired by royalty.

Dong-Lim Knot Workshop: Learn how to make knotted bracelets, necklaces and other ornaments using various threads.

Gahoe Minhwa Museum: View the special exhibition and try your hand at a one-day *minhwa* (folk painting) class.

Hanji House: Browse this *hanji* showroom run by the Korean Craft and Design Foundation and make your own *hanji* bookmark.

DESSERT CAFES IN JONGNO-GU: OUR PICKS MAPS P56 & P63

Boobing: (부빙) Delicious red bean, strawberry, black sesame and other *bingsu* (shaved ice), along with coffee and tea. *1-6pm Tue-Sun* ₩

Arari: Treat yourself to ice cream with toppings such as persimmon or yuzu at this cafe by the Michelin-star restaurant Gaon. *10am-5pm* ₩

Baekmidang: Making creamy, soft ice cream, including soy-milk varieties, since 1964. *11.30am-8pm* ₩

Cafe Layered Bukchon: British-style cakes, scones and other desserts are piled high on this charming cafe's central table. *10am-10pm* ₩

LOCAL FESTIVALS

K-Royal Culture Festival: Ritual reenactments and other events across Seoul's five major palaces and Jongmyo in spring and autumn.

Lotus Lantern Festival (Yeon Deung Hoe): For Buddha's birthday, a weekend fete with dharma ceremony, cultural performances and a magical lantern parade down Jong-no to Jogye-sa.

Jongno Hanbok Festival: At Gwanghwamun Sq in October, *hanbok* fashion shows and other festivities.

Seoul Performing Arts Festival: In autumn, a month of theatre, dance and music at the Sejong Center, National Theater of Korea and beyond.

Seoul Lantern Festival: Fantastic lantern displays in Gwanghwamun Sq and Cheonggyecheon in December and January.

Insa-dong Traditional Culture Festival: Held in September, to celebrate local heritage.

Also at Hansik Space is the **Sool Gallery** *(thesool.com)*, which promotes Korean alcoholic drinks, from the milky rice wine *makgeolli*, to the clear rice wine *cheongju*, as well as various fruit wines, medicinal liquors and distilled spirits such as soju. Sign up in advance for free tasting sessions of five different liquors and buy bottles from boutique producers across Korea.

Step Back in Time in Bukchon

MAP P63

See the neighbourhood's representative *hanok*

Though it's Seoul's most famous *hanok* neighbourhood, Bukchon's structures are not the most traditional, with many of them actually built in the more modern style of the Japanese occupation period, but they are arguably the most picturesque. Trace your way through the neighbourhood to see Bukchon's most notable *hanok* – some of them, as private properties, only from the outside – which are registered as cultural heritage sites.

In Gahoe-dong is the circa-1913 **Baek In-je House** *(museum.seoul.go.kr; free)*, now a public museum, crafted out of black pine and one of the first of its kind to be constructed in two storeys. It features Japanese-style hallways that connect the *anchae* (women's quarters) and *sarangchae* (men's quarters), which traditionally were separated. The property, closed Mondays, also includes detached quarters with a lovely view overlooking Bukchon. Wander the grounds freely on your own, or join an English tour on Fridays at 2pm. Baek In-je, a prominent surgeon and hospital founder, was the third owner of this house, which previously had been built by a bank executive and transferred to a wealthy publisher.

Also in Gahoe-dong are the Han Family house, Kim Hyeongtae House and Yi Jun-gu House, all closed to the public.

A bit east in Gye-dong, stop at the **Bae Ryeom House**, an art museum that was, from 1959 to 1968, the residence of painter Bae Ryeom, and previously of archivist Song Seokha, who used it as an office of the Korean Folklore Society. Nearby is the private Kim Seong-su House.

Over in Anguk-dong, be sure to glimpse the gorgeous **Yun Po-sun House**, residence of the second president of South Korea. The house dates back to 1870, and Yun's family moved in around 1910. The house was where democracy-movement activists met from the 1950s to the 1970s, making it the birthplace of the country's first Democratic Party.

EATING IN JONGNO-GU: VEGETARIAN & VEGAN

MAPS P53 & P56

Vegan Insa: On Ikseon-dong's north side, a friendly little spot with delicious vegan Korean fried chicken, bibimbap and more. *11.30am-3pm & 5-8pm* **WW**

Osegyehyang: (오세계향) Run by members of a Taiwanese religious group, this longtime Insa-dong restaurant serves vegan versions of Korean staples. *11.30am-3pm & 5-9pm* **W**

Balwoo Gongyang: Savour formerly Michelin-starred temple cuisine, including delicate salads, dumplings and a variety of kimchi. *11.30am-3pm & 6-7.30pm* **WWW**

Rogpa Tea Stall: Freshly made, delicious vegetarian dishes at this rustic fair-trade cafe that raises awareness about Tibet. *11.30am-8pm Tue-Sun* **W**

SEE ARTS & CULTURE IN BUKCHON

Stroll through Seoul's largest concentration of *hanok* – but be mindful of the visiting-hour restrictions, as this is a real residential neighbourhood.

START	END	LENGTH
Bukchon Traditional Culture Center	Kiwa Taproom	2.3km; 2 hours

Begin at the 1 **Bukchon Traditional Culture Center**, which has a small exhibition about the area's history and its renowned architecture. Pick up a map and try your hand at a traditional game such as *gongginori*. Down the way, luxe skincare brand 2 **Sulwhasoo** occupies an award-winning renovation of a 1930s *hanok* that's been integrated with a multilevel concrete building from the 1960s. In the same complex is the premium teashop Osulloc.

It's easy to see why 3 **Gahoe-dong Hill** is Bukchon's go-to selfie spot. From the top of the steep street, the clay-tiled roofs of *hanok* contrast with the modern towers of downtown Seoul. Walk up to 4 **Jeongdok Public Library** – the small, quiet park in front of the building is a prime spot for viewing cherry blossoms in spring and the yellowing leaves of ginkgo trees in autumn. From there, check out a few of the renowned contemporary-art galleries in the area, of which there are many, such as the longstanding 5 **Kukje**, 6 **Hakgojae** (easily spotted by the robot sculpture on the roof) and 7 **Art Sonje Center**, with a cafe and arthouse cinema on site.

Tucked away in an alley behind MMCA Seoul is 8 **Kiwa Taproom**, a *hanok* bar pouring ales from one of Seoul's best microbreweries, Euljiro Brewing, and serving tasty bites. *Kiwa* is the Korean word for traditional roof tiles.

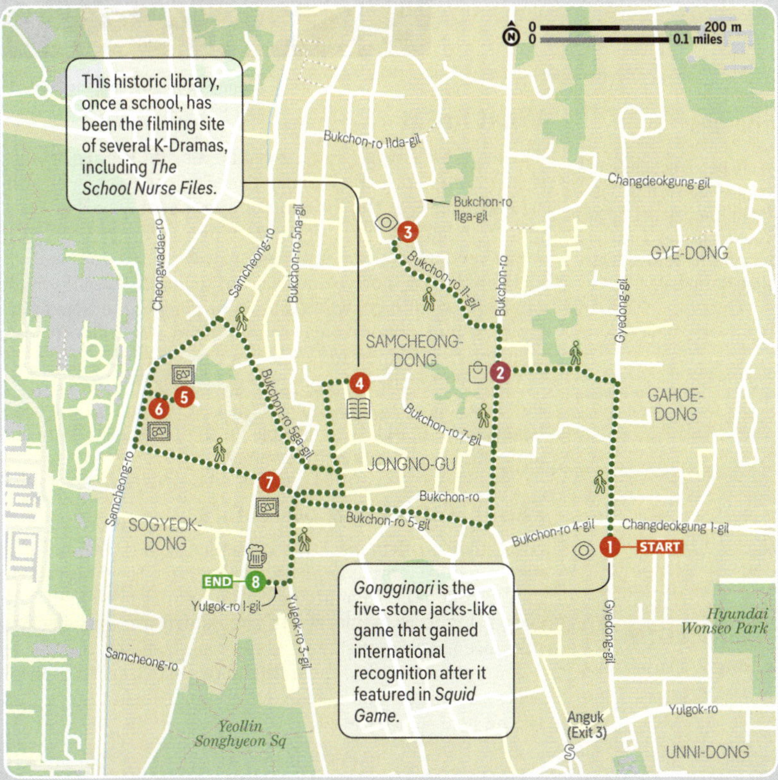

TOP EXPERIENCE

Gwangjang Market

The covered Gwangjang Market is home to Seoul's premier *meokjagolmok* (food alley), where 200-or-so street-food, kimchi and other food vendors are clustered alongside fabric, *hanbok* (traditional clothing) and bedding stalls. Head to the upper floors for vintage and secondhand clothing bargains.

DRHAO/SHUTTERSTOCK

Food vendor, Gwangjang Market

What to Eat

The food that Gwangjang is most famous for is crispy golden *nokdu bindaetteok* (mung-bean pancake) – the cluster of stalls frying them is at the junction of alleys at the market's east end. You can takeaway or squeeze onto benches beside the many vendors' stalls along the alleyways.

There's a lot more to munch on, including freshly made *mandu* (dumplings), *kalguksu* noodles, *jokbal* (braised pig's trotters) and *gimbap* (seaweed-wrapped rice rolls). There's also an alley devoted to *yukhoe*, or raw beef, stalls.

Look out for the ultra-popular *kkwabaegi* (twisted doughnuts) stall, near North Gate 2, which serves some of the city's best twisted doughnuts, notable for their extra chewy inside and cinnamon-sugar coating outside.

Fabric, Clothing & Souvenirs

Gwangjang's other speciality is textiles, sold by the metre or made up into clothing as *hanbok* or bedding. Head upstairs to hunt through the secondhand clothing stalls, piled high with everything from flannel shirts, sweatshirts and army jackets to choice pieces of vintage and designer fashion.

For cute souvenirs, including arty postcards, local craft beers and spirits and decal-covered purses, hunt down **365 Iljang** near South Gate 1.

TOP TIPS

- To get directions and a printed market map, look for the 'Red Angel' Seoul Tourism guides who stand near the first cross alley from North Gate 1.

PRACTICALITIES

- *kwangjangmarket.co.kr*
- 9am-10.30pm

Bukchon and overtourism

Called 'North Village' because of its position north of Cheonggyecheon, Bukchon was historically the home of palace retainers and other *yangban* (the noble class). In the 1890s, the Japanese placed their colonial agencies south of the stream, funnelling resources to Namchon ('South Village'), and Bukchon deteriorated. Most of Bukchon's *hanok* were built between the 1920s and 1960s, and efforts to preserve them began in 2000. Community organisations fought off redevelopment, keeping Bukchon as a beautiful traditional neighbourhood. Bukchon's beauty has attracted so many admiring travellers, it now suffers from overtourism. Residents struggle to live free of noise, litter and invasions of privacy. Learn about fair tourism at the Bukchon Traditional Culture Center (p71) and respect the rules (or risk being fined): don't visit between 5pm and 10am.

Listen to Traditional Music

MAP P63

The sounds of Korean life

Work, play and ceremonial songs are among the music showcased at the **Seoul Museum of Korean Folk Music** *(museum.seoul.go.kr/sekm; free)*. Based in a modern *hanok*-style building, the museum, closed Mondays, is a pleasant place to while away an hour listening to recordings and learning about how music has figured in the Korean national identity. At audio kiosks, hear songs about grinding grain, catching pollack in the East Sea, lamenting the harsh life of a daughter-in-law and carrying a funeral bier, among other things. The archives preserve an oral tradition that has slowly been disappearing from modern life.

Across the road is the **Seoul Donhwamun Traditional Theater** *(sgtt.kr)*, where live (sometimes free) performances are staged in a 140-seat auditorium and a grassy courtyard. It's a central spot at which to catch classical Korean music shows, including *pansori*, a UNESCO-inscribed genre of musical storytelling performed by a vocalist and a drummer.

WHERE TO TAKE A COOKING CLASS

Museum Kimchikan: Make kimchi, from radish to cabbage, and taste savoury kimchi pancakes. *(kimchikan.com)*

Seoul Kimchi Academy: Hands-on courses near Gyeonghuigung to make and take away your own pouch of kimchi. *(kimchischool.net)*

O'ngo: Operator offering cooking classes and food tours. *(ongofood.com)*

Korean Temple Food Center: On Saturdays at 10am there's a class in English on cooking vegan dishes as traditionally served at temples. *(koreatemplefood.com)*

Food & Culture Korea: Prepare and try various dishes, and leave with a certificate of attendance. *(koreanrecipe.co.kr)*

Tteok Museum: Learn how to make rice cakes – then taste them. *(tkmuseum.or.kr)*

CAFES IN BUKCHON: OUR PICKS

MAP P63

Low Roof: Multilevel coffee shop with a peaceful, pretty *hanok* patio, serving coffee and sweets. *10am-8pm Tue-Sun*

Hollow: In a neighbourhood of chaotic queues, this quiet cafe with serene rooftop seating is a welcome reprieve. *8am-9pm*

Cafe Husbands: Small, rustic spot with high-quality coffee and a killer grilled-cheese sandwich on the menu. *8am-7pm Mon & Wed-Sun*

Artist Bakery: Ultra-popular cafe with delectable pastries like the squid ink croissant and truffle baguette. Opt for the shorter takeaway queue. *7.30am-8pm*

Green Mile Coffee: With a rooftop overlooking the surrounding *hanok* and a sleek warm-wood interior, this cafe is a stunner. *9am-5.45pm Mon-Fri, 10am-7pm Sat & Sun*

Dotori Garden: Whimsical Totoro-esque cartoon cafe serving acorn-shaped madeleines and creamy yoghurt bowls. *8am-11pm*

Cafe Cordialement: Modern *hanok* cafe with a chic Euro twist. Enjoy a mocha coffee with an authentic *jambon beurre* sandwich. *10am-9pm*

Onion: Housed in a large converted *hanok*, this bakery-cafe's signature milk tea is a must-try. 7am-10pm Mon-Fri, from 9am Sat & Sun

Researched by Charles Usher

MYEONG-DONG & JUNG-GU

SHOPPING, NIGHTLIFE AND URBAN OASES

It all comes together in Jung-gu, Seoul's central district, which combines a bit of everything that makes the city special.

You could spend a lifetime exploring Seoul, but if you don't have that kind of time, a day in Myeong-dong and Jung-gu will do. This area at Seoul's heart offers up the city in microcosm. The Joseon dynasty's most interesting palace, Deoksugung, is here, but so is Euljiro's eclectic bar scene, existing side by side with machine shops. 'Myeong' means 'light' – apt for an area where Seoul's commercial razzle-dazzle reaches its apogee – while just down the road, Namdaemun Market does business much the same way it has for centuries. It's a lot to take in, but if you need a breather, you'll also find two of the city's favourite escapes here: majestic Namsan and the restored Cheonggye-cheon.

TIP

Deoksugung stays open until 9pm. Visiting after dark, when the buildings are illuminated and backdropped by the city centre's glowing skyscrapers, makes for some fabulous photo ops.

Sungnyemun (p91)

See page 215 for places to stay in Myeong-dong & Jung-gu

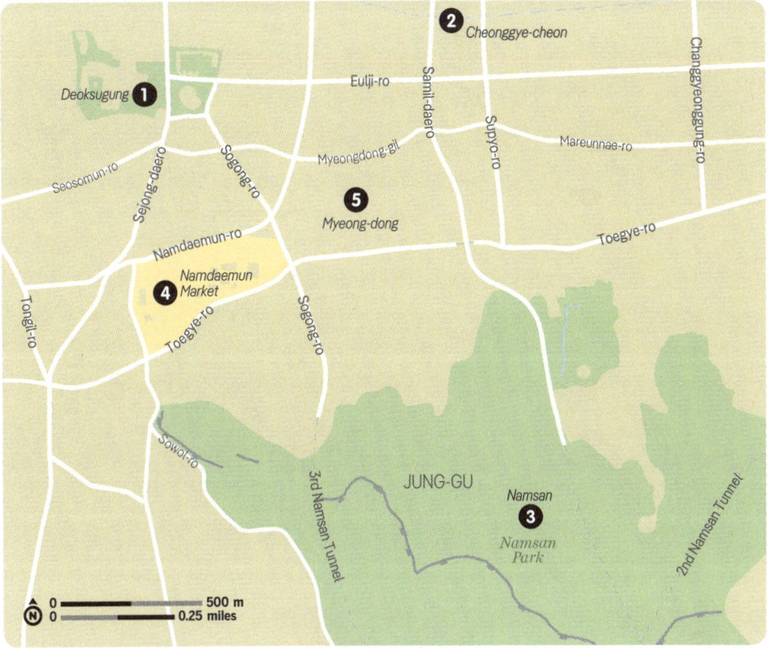

Highlights

1 Deoksugung
See eras change and outlooks shift in the eclectic architecture of this Joseon palace. **p82**

2 Cheonggye-cheon
Follow the flow of this restored stream for wildlife, public art, light shows and people-watching. **p94**

3 Namsan
Hike the mountain to find ancient city walls and cherry blossoms, then gaze over the city from N Seoul Tower. **p78**

4 Namdaemun Market
Score some souvenirs and sniff out tasty snacks in Korea's biggest traditional market. **p90**

▲ 5 Myeong-dong
Put your wallet to work in this shopping district packed with bright lights and bargain hunters. **p93**

Getting Around

Walking
Jung-gu is quite compact and – Namsan excepted – flat, and interesting sites seem to pop up around every corner, making it easy and rewarding to explore on foot.

Subway
Lines 1 to 5 all run through the area, linking local neighbourhoods and providing connections to the rest of the city. City Hall, Chungmuro and Euljiro 3-ga are major transfer stations.

Bus
Being in the city centre, the area is well serviced by public buses. Buses 01A and 01B will take you to the top of Namsan.

HIGHLIGHTS
1 Cheonggye-cheon
2 Namsan

SIGHTS
3 Beauty Play
4 Berlin Square
5 Cheonggye Plaza
6 Cheonggye-cheon Digital Canvas
see 13 Citizens' Hall
see 13 Gungisi Relics Exhibition Hall
7 Gwangtonggyo Bridge
8 Hwangudan
9 Myeong-dong
10 Myeongdong Cathedral
11 N Seoul Tower
12 Namsan Beacon Station
13 Seoul City Hall
14 Seoul Plaza
15 Studio Meditation with a Pencil
16 Waryongmyo

ACTIVITIES, COURSES & TOURS
17 Seoul Metropolitan Library

SLEEPING
18 Hotel28
19 Metro Hotel
20 Namsan Hostel Guest House
21 Small House Big Door
22 Zaza Backpackers

EATING
23 Furoa
24 Hadongkwan
25 Hansikwangbijip
26 Mari Meokja
27 Menten
28 Mokmyeok-sanbang
see 11 n.Grill
29 Odarijip
30 Street Food Stalls

DRINKING & NIGHTLIFE
31 Ace Four Club
32 Coffee Hanyakbang
33 Leesar
34 Myeongdong Sookhee

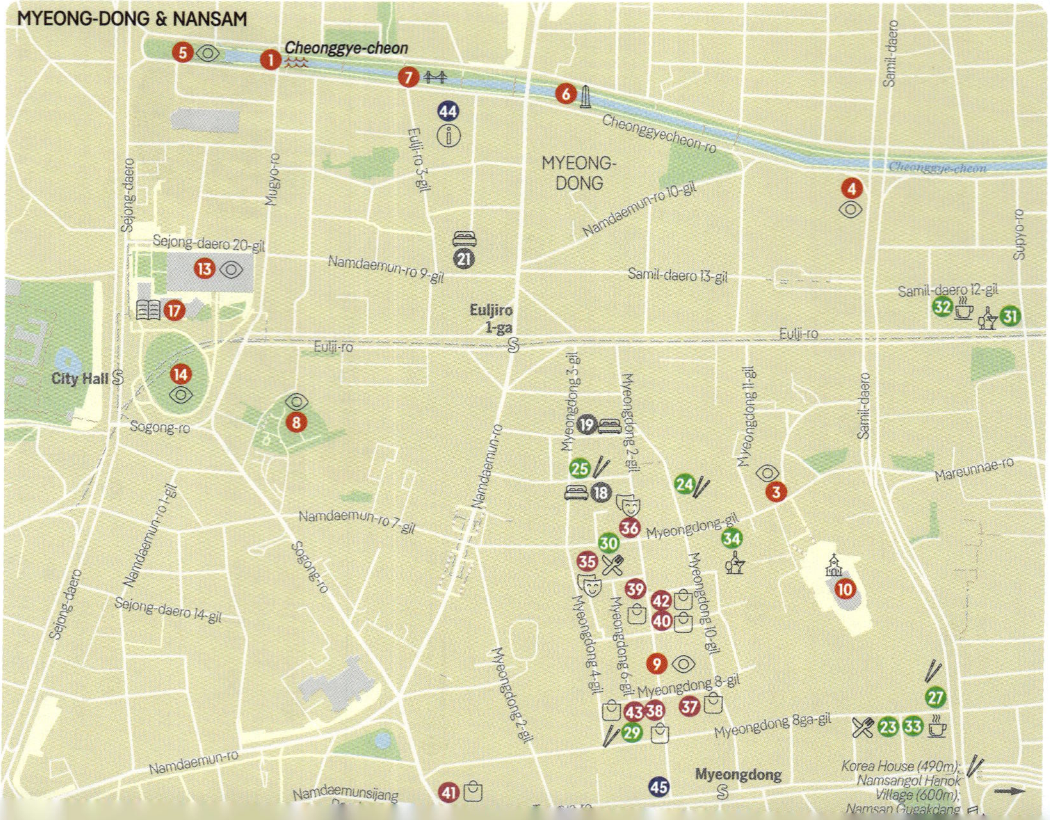

ENTERTAINMENT
35 Myeongdong Nanta Theater
36 Myeongdong Theater

SHOPPING
37 3CE Stylenanda Pink Space Hotel
38 ÅLAND
39 Covernat
40 EMIS
41 Hoehyeon Underground Shopping Center
42 Matin Kim
43 Nick Nicole

INFORMATION
44 HiKR Ground

TRANSPORT
45 Myeongdong Station
46 Namsan Cable Car
47 Namsan Oreumi

YMGERMAN/SHUTTERSTOCK

Namsan Cable Car

TOP EXPERIENCE

Namsan

When the Joseon dynasty established its royal capital, Namsan marked the city's southern boundary. Today it's smack dab in the middle of Seoul, a perfectly placed escape where locals come to exercise and get some air. Join them on the mountain's many trails to discover historic sites and flower blossoms, and ascend N Seoul Tower for the best views in the city.

DON'T MISS

- N Seoul Tower
- Namsan Cable Car
- Seoul City Wall
- Waryongmyo
- Namsan Outdoor Botanical Garden

N Seoul Tower

Visible for miles around, the 236m-high **N Seoul Tower** pokes into the sky from Namsan's summit. The views from its observation deck are unmatched – well worth the cost of admission. If you can, visit at dusk to watch the metropolis slowly light up as night descends. There are several souvenir shops and restaurants in the tower. On the plaza out front, you'll find **Namsan Beacon Station**, a 1993 re-creation of a Joseon-era signal beacon used to relay messages by fire and smoke. Lighting ceremonies are held 11am to 12.10pm Tuesday

PRACTICALITIES

- *nseoultower.co.kr*
- free; N Seoul Tower observatory adult/child ₩26,000/20,000
- 24hr (facility hours vary)

to Sunday. East of the beacon is an overlook with views of northern Seoul, while just east of that you can find a marker in the pavement indicating Seoul's geographical centre. The most enjoyable way to reach the tower is to soar over the city aboard the **Namsan Cable Car** *(cablecar.co.kr; adult/child one way ₩12,000/9000)*. A free shuttle bus to its lower boarding platform departs roughly every half-hour from Myeongdong station, exit 1. Alternatively, you can get there by riding the fun **Namsan Oreumi** *(free)* inclined elevator, which trundles up to the platform from Sogong-ro.

Historic Sites

Namsan's prominent location means it's dotted with historic sites. Foremost among these is the Seoul City Wall, which snakes across the mountain. The wall is largely a restoration here, having suffered major damage during the colonial era, but you can see an excavated original section on Namsan's west side. Look for the old post holes and inscribed stone, and note how construction methods changed over the years. Learn more about the wall at the adjacent **Hanyangdoseong Historic Site Museum**. Next to the wall are the remains of a Japanese Shinto shrine built in 1925.

Across a plaza is the **Ahn Junggeun Memorial Museum** *(ahnjunggeun.or.kr)*, dedicated to an independence fighter who was executed for assassinating Ito Hirobumi, the Japanese resident-general of Korea, in Harbin, China, in 1909. On Namsan's northern slope is **Waryongmyo**, a shrine to the Chinese statesman and military strategist Zhuge Liang that traces its origins to 1605.

Near the National Theater of Korea is **Seokhojeong**, where an archery range was established in the 1630s. You can try your hand at traditional Korean archery by reserving a spot online at yeyak.seoul.go.kr.

Walking Namsan

Only 270m high, with gentle slopes, Namsan is an inviting place to hike, whether you're looking to reach the peak or just enjoy a casual stroll. Paths crisscross the mountain, but there are three main routes to use as starting points. All three meet at the National Theater.

The North Ringway is a mostly flat 3.5km path that traces the mountain's northern edge to the Namsan Cable Car station, following the Silgae Stream much of the way. It's a great place for viewing cherry blossoms in spring.

The South Ringway loops south before heading up to N Seoul Tower and has some of the mountain's best autumn foliage. Take a short detour south to explore the **Namsan Outdoor Botanical Garden**, which has a moss garden and a garden dedicated to the Rose of Sharon, Korea's national flower.

The Seoul City Wall Perimeter Path follows the old city walls up and over the peak.

NAMSAN BUSES

Easier than walking and cheaper than the cable car, public buses 01A and 01B make the journey up Namsan, dropping passengers off just below N Seoul Tower (though you're still left with a short uphill slog to reach it). A convenient place to board either bus is exit 2 of Chungmuro station.

The **Seoul City Tour Bus** *(seoulcitybus.com)* also travels to N Seoul Tower.

TOP TIPS

- Pick up a brochure with maps of Namsan's walking trails from the info centre opposite the N Seoul Tower bus stop.
- You can use N Seoul Tower to get an idea of the city's air-pollution levels. If it's illuminated in blue at night, it means that skies are clear. Green signifies low air pollution, yellow means conditions are poor and red indicates that pollution levels are hazardous.
- Want to bring a bit of Seoul back to school or the office? Download the city's Namsan, Hangang and Alrim fonts at english.seoul.go.kr/seoul-views/seoul-symbols/5-fonts.

BEST THEATRE FOR NON-KOREAN SPEAKERS

Myeongdong Theater: Home to the National Theater Company of Korea, staging everything from Shakespeare to boundary-pushing Korean dramas. Some shows have English subtitles. *(ntck.or.kr)*

NH Arthall: Come for *The Painters*, in which talented performers with K-Pop boy-band looks mix dance with drawing and painting. *(thepainters.co.kr)*

Myeongdong Nanta Theater: The long-running *Nanta* mixes drumming, cooking, *samulnori* folk music, comedy and audience participation. *(nanta.co.kr)*

National Jeongdong Theater of Korea: A well-regarded theatre specialising in contemporary stagings of traditional stories. With English subtitles. *(jeongdong.or.kr)*

Myeongbo Art Hall: This theatre in Euljiro is the venue for the popular non-verbal show *Jump*, a mashup of physical comedy and high-flying martial arts. *(mbah.co.kr)*

BINIMIN/SHUTTERSTOCK

Namsangol Hanok Village

How Joseon's Other Half Lived

MAP P76

Tour Namsangol Hanok Village's homes

A great place to learn about traditional Korean culture, **Namsangol Hanok Village** *(hanokmaeul.co.kr)* is a collection of five Joseon-era *yangban* (upper-class) houses that were relocated here from different parts of Seoul. Explore them by yourself or join a free 90-minute guided tour; see the website for tour schedules. On Fridays, Saturdays and Sundays from April to June and September to October, the complex hosts cultural programmes where you can make straw crafts, archery bows or medicinal foods, among other things. Reserve a spot on the website.

The grounds also contain a lovely traditional garden, a teahouse and the Seoul Millennium Time Capsule. It's scheduled to be opened in 2394, the city's 1000-year anniversary. Closed Mondays.

EATING IN JUNG-GU: CLASSIC KOREAN RESTAURANTS

MAPS P84 & P92

Yurimmyeon: Puts more than 50 years of expertise into its *memil guksu*, buckwheat noodles you dip in broth. *11am-8.30pm, to 7.30pm Sat & Sun* W

Jinju Hoegwan: First dished up its famous *kongguksu* (noodles in a chilled soybean broth) and stews in 1962. *11am-9pm Mon-Fri, to 8pm Sat* W

Woo Lae Oak: Renowned for the bulgogi and Pyeongyang *naengmyeong* (noodles in chilled broth) it's been serving since 1946. *11.30am-9pm Tue-Sun* WW

Hadongkwan: Open since 1939, this Myeong-dong eatery makes perfect *gomtang* (beef and rice soup) seasoned with spring onions and black pepper. *7am-4pm Mon-Sat* WW

The Arts of Old

MAP P76

Experience a traditional meal or show

Three performance venues specialising in traditional art forms cluster on Namsan's northern slope. Within Namsangol Hanok Village is the **Namsan Gugakdang** *(sgtt.kr)*, a 306-seat theatre that hosts traditional music and dance performances, from *pansori*, a form of musical storytelling, to *seungmu*, the monk dance. Next to Namsangol is **Korea House** *(kh.or.kr)*, where you can indulge in an extravagant *hanjeongsik* (Korean table d'hôte) meal, based on royal court cuisine, or a tea service with traditional sweets.

Head to the **National Theater of Korea** *(ntok.go.kr)* to watch the national dance company, national orchestra or national *changgeuk* (Korean opera) company perform.

You can book tickets for events at all three venues through their respective websites.

Three Cool Cultural Spaces

MAP P84

Go gallery and cafe hopping

The streets west of Namsan are dotted with several cultural spaces that make for a fun few hours of exploration. Close to Hoehyeon station is the ambitious **Piknic** *(piknic.kr)*, which combines exhibition halls, a roof garden, a cafe hung with assorted chandeliers, a top-class design shop and the Michelin-starred Mediterranean restaurant **Gigas**, which gets its organic produce from the chef's dad's farm, just outside the city. From Piknic, follow Sowol-ro south to the **Whitestone Gallery** *(whitestone-gallery.com)*. The Seoul outpost of this Asian gallery occupies a building designed by the renowned Japanese architect Kengo Kuma and specialises in contemporary and emerging Asian artists. Exhibitions rotate, but the permanent collection includes pieces by Yayoi Kusama, Lee Ufan and Joan Miró. Make sure to visit the rooftop terrace, where two colourful bird sculptures by Florentijn Hofman perch above the city.

Tucked in the backstreets south of Whitestone is **Comfort** (*comfortseoul.com*), a hip multistorey space that includes a trendy streetwear and fragrance boutique, a small gallery and a cafe. Grab one of its signature lattes, which come with a salted rim and shard of honeycomb toffee, and head up to the rooftop for superlative sunset views.

DEOKSUGUNG-GIL

Deoksugung-gil, the street that runs along Deoksugung's south and west sides and leads to SeMA, makes for one of the prettiest walks in Seoul, especially in autumn, when its ginkgo trees turn golden above the old palace walls. It's also frequently the site of flea markets and street festivals.

Just be careful about whom you walk the street with, as an old superstition says that any couple who walks it together is doomed to break up. The idea likely sprang from the fact that the city's family court, where married couples went to get divorced, was once located here.

DRINKING IN JUNG-GU: OUR PICKS

MAPS P76 & P84

Myeongdong Sookhee: Slip through the secret door of this deliberately hard-to-find bar to be greeted with a Joseon-era ambience and superb cocktails. *6pm-1am*

Bar Jaerae: This classy spot has a curated whisky selection and a wide array of Korean spirits to sample. *8pm-midnight Wed & Thu, to 2am Fri, from 6pm Sat*

Cafe Gabaedo: The Namdaemun Market branch occupies an early-20th-century commercial building with Sungnyemun views. *9am-9pm, from 11am Sat & Sun*

Leesar: An Italian-style espresso bar that would get an approving nod from your *nonno*. Has several locations around the city. *7am-8pm, from 8am Sat & Sun*

MIRKO KUZMANOVIC/GETTY IMAGES

Seokjojeon

TOP EXPERIENCE

Deoksugung

You can practically see the Korean world changing at Deoksugung, Seoul's most unusual and most interesting Joseon palace. The complex embodies the country's tumultuous early 20th century with its mix of traditional wooden halls and Western-style buildings and its occasionally charming, often tragic history. It also possesses an excellent art museum and one of the city's best nighttime scenes.

- Junghwajeon
- Seokjojeon
- Jeonggwanheon
- Daehan Empire History Museum
- Hamnyeongjeon
- National Museum of Modern and Contemporary Art
- Jungmyeongjeon
- Dondeokjeon

Palace History

The complex that would become Deoksugung first served as a residence for the king in 1592, but it didn't rise to prominence until 1897, when King Gojong moved into the palace and declared the founding of the Korean (or Daehan) Empire – an attempt to modernise the country and place Joseon Korea on equal footing with more powerful nations. In the ensuing years, he set about expanding the residence from a relatively small palace to a sprawling complex. Gojong's efforts to raise the country's status and preserve its independence ultimately

PRACTICALITIES

- *royal.khs.go.kr*
- adult/child ₩1000/free
- 9am-9pm Tue-Sun

failed, and Japan forced him to abdicate in 1907, at which time the palace took its present name, meaning 'virtuous longevity'. Despite his overthrow, Gojong continued to live in the palace until his death in 1919.

The Old Palace

What you see today represents only a third of the palace at its height; the rest was either lost in a 1904 fire or dismantled under the colonial regime. Still, what remains or has been rebuilt is quite spectacular. Deoksugung's centrepiece is **Junghwajeon**, the stately throne hall where Gojong held court. While the staircases of other palace throne halls are engraved with phoenixes, Junghwajeon's is engraved with dragons, befitting Gojong's new status as emperor.

To the east is **Hamnyeongjeon**, Gojong's private chambers. At its rear is what you might consider Korea's first cafe. Gojong developed a taste for coffee during the year he spent holed up in the Russian legation following Empress Myeongseong's assassination, and he had the Russian architect Aleksey Seredin-Sabatin build **Jeonggwanheon** as a pavilion where he could enjoy a cup and entertain guests. The building blends Romanesque designs and Korean motifs, such as metal railings decorated with deer and bats, both considered auspicious. Be sure to hang around until nightfall, when these traditional halls are illuminated and form a striking contrast to the surrounding cityscape.

Western Influences

West of Junghwajeon you can see the Korean Empire breaking with Joseon's insular past and attempting to remake itself into a modern nation. Facing a very European-looking fountain and connected by a loggia are the two wings of **Seokjojeon**. The neoclassical north wing, completed in 1910, was designed by the British architect GR Harding to serve as Gojong's living quarters. It now houses the **Daehan Empire History Museum** and has been decorated to look as it would have in Gojong's time. You can visit on a guided tour that takes you through reception rooms, the dining room and Gojong's bedroom, though he never actually slept in it, preferring the traditional comforts of Hamnyeongjeon. Seokjojeon's west wing, built in 1938, hosts a branch of the **National Museum of Modern and Contemporary Art**. Exhibitions change every few months.

Behind Seokjojeon is the striking brick **Dondeokjeon**. Used as a banquet hall and accommodation for state guests, it was demolished in the 1920s and only rebuilt in 2023. Outside the current palace walls, you'll find **Jungmyeongjeon**, another Western-style brick structure. Once a royal library, it's infamous as the place where, in 1905, Japan forced Korea to sign a treaty forfeiting its sovereignty and making it a protectorate of Imperial Japan. Exhibits inside the hall recount this dark chapter.

CHANGING OF THE GUARDS

A changing of the guards ceremony takes place outside Daehanmun, the main palace gate, at 11am and 2pm Tuesday to Sunday, and lasts about 15 minutes. It's a colourful affair with flags, musicians and the exchanging of keys and passwords.

A helpful narration describes the events in both Korean and English. If you'd like to preserve your hearing, don't stand next to the drum.

Guards stick around for photos after the ceremony.

TOP TIPS

- Free one-hour guided tours of Deoksugung are provided in English at 10.45am and 1.30pm. They begin just inside the main entrance.

- You can only view the Daehan Empire History Museum on a guided tour. English tours are held at 11.50am and 2.50pm. To join, sign up in advance inside the museum entrance. The imposing front doors might appear closed, but they're open.

- For the best views of Deoksugung, head to the City Hall Seosomun Building at 15 Deoksugung-gil. Its 13th-floor **Jeongdong Observatory** (1.30pm to 5.30pm, from 9am Sat & Sun) provides a stunning bird's-eye view of the palace.

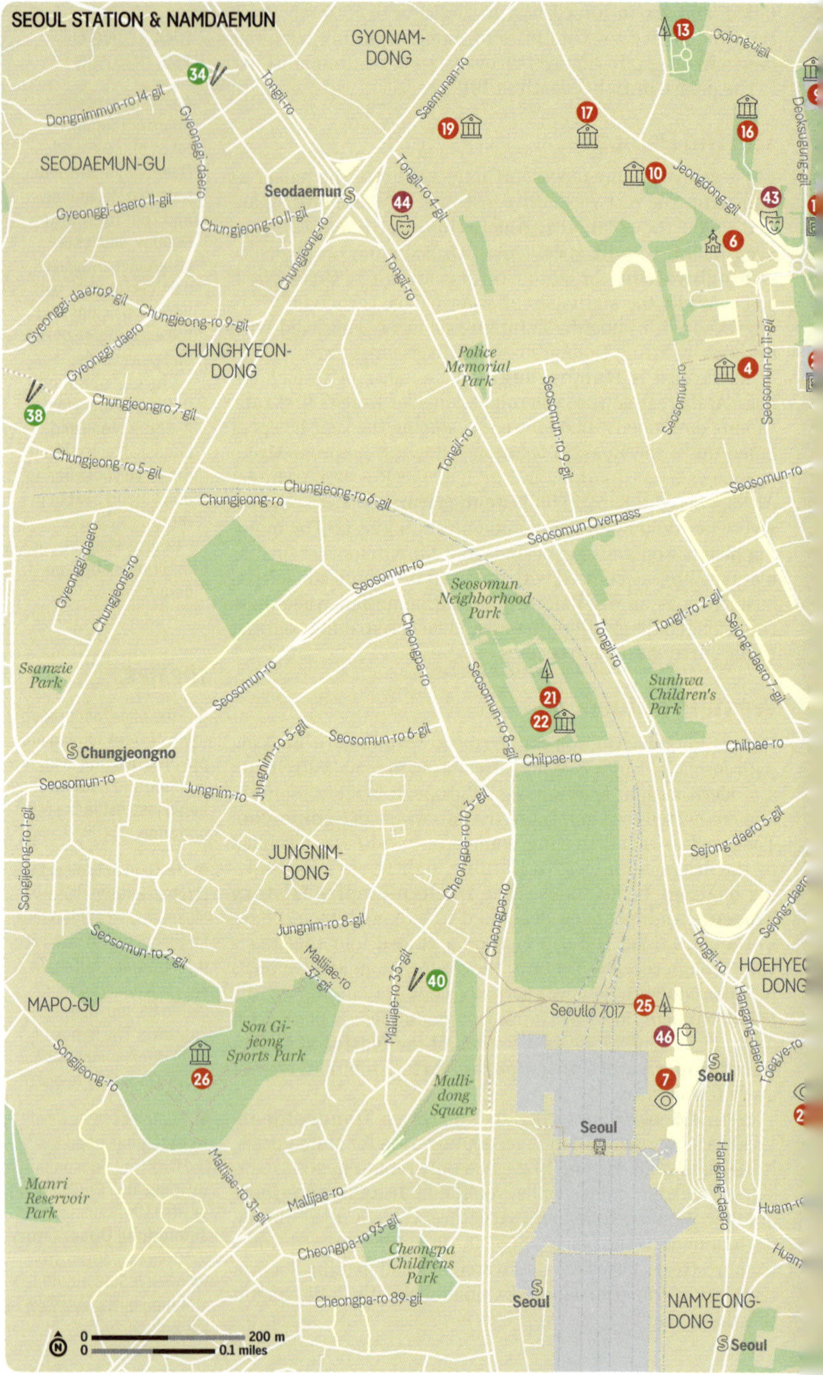
SEOUL STATION & NAMDAEMUN
GYONAM-DONG
SEODAEMUN-GU
CHUNGHYEON-DONG
JUNGNIM-DONG
MAPO-GU
HOEHYE
DONG
NAMYEONG-DONG
Seodaemun
Chungjeongno
Seoul
Dongnimmun-ro 14-gil
Gyeonggi-daero
Gyeonggi-daero 11-gil
Tongil-ro
Saemunan-ro
Tongil-ro 4-gil
Chungjeong-ro 11-gil
Chungjeong-ro
Gyeonggi-daero 9-gil
Chungjeong-ro 9-gil
Chungjeongro 7-gil
Chungjeong-ro 5-gil
Chungjeong-ro 6-gil
Jeongdong-gil
Gajang-ugil
Deoksugung-gil
Seosomun-ro
Seosomun-ro 11-gil
Seosomun-ro 9-gil
Seosomun Overpass
Police Memorial Park
Seosomun Neighborhood Park
Cheongpa-ro
Seosomun-ro 8-gil
Seosomun-ro 6-gil
Tongil-ro 2-gil
Sejong-daero 7-gil
Sunhwa Children's Park
Chilpae-ro
Ssamzie Park
Jungnim-ro
Jungnim-ro 5-gil
Songjijeong-ro 1-gil
Cheongpa-ro 103-gil
Sejong-daero 5-gil
Sejong-daero
Jungnim-ro 8-gil
Seosomun-ro 2-gil
Mallijae-ro 37-gil
Mallijae-ro 35-gil
Seoullo 7017
Hangang-daero
Toegye-ro
Songjeong-ro
Son Gi-jeong Sports Park
Malli-dong Square
Manri Reservoir Park
Mallijae-ro 31-gil
Mallijae-ro
Cheongpa-ro 93-gil
Cheongpa Childrens Park
Cheongpa-ro 89-gil
Huam-ro
200 m
0.1 miles
34
38
44
19
17
10
13
16
43
6
4
21
22
25
46
7
40
26

HIGHLIGHTS
1 Deoksugung
2 Namdaemun Market

SIGHTS
3 Ahn Junggeun Memorial Museum
4 Appenzeller/ Noble Memorial Museum
5 Bank of Korea Money Museum
6 Chungdong First Methodist Church
7 Culture Station Seoul 284
8 Daehan Empire History Museum
9 Dondeokjeon
10 Ewha Museum
11 Hamnyeongjeon
12 Hanyangdoseong Historic Site Museum
13 Jeong-dong Park
14 Jeonggwanheon
15 Junghwajeon
16 Jungmyeong-jeon
17 Korea Territorial Development Museum
18 MMCA, Deoksugung
19 Museum of Agriculture
20 Piknic Seokjoejeon
21 Seosomun Historical Park
22 Seosomun Shrine History Museum
23 Seoul Museum of Art
24 Seoul Square Building
25 Seoullo 7017
26 Son Kee Chung Memorial Hall
27 Sungnyemun
28 Whitestone Gallery

ACTIVITIES, COURSES & TOURS
29 Jeongdong Observatory

SLEEPING
30 L'Escape
31 The Plaza Seoul
32 The Westin Josun Seoul

EATING
see 20 Gigas
33 Hairtail Alley
34 Hanokjib Kimchi-jjim
35 Hotteok stand
36 Jinju Hoegwan
37 Kalguksu Alley
38 Muldwinda
39 Yurimmyeon
40 Yuzu Fine Ramen

DRINKING & NIGHTLIFE
41 Bar Jaerae
42 Cafe Gabaedo

ENTERTAINMENT
43 National Jeongdong Theater of Korea
44 NH Arthall

SHOPPING
45 Sogong Underground Shopping Center
46 Yeonnam Bangagan

INFORMATION
47 Namdaemun Market Tourist Information Booth

SHOPPING UNDERGROUND

In addition to Myeong-dong's and Namdaemun's many overground retailers, there are hundreds more to be discovered in underground arcades. The longest, stretching 2.8km from City Hall to Dongdaemun, is the **Euljiro Underground Shopping Center**. Many of its stalls stock throwback fashions, but you'll also find things such as typewriter shops and portrait studios.

Vendors selling handicrafts and antiques populate **Sogong Underground Shopping Center**, which links City Hall with Myeong-dong via Lotte Department Store.

In the 1980s, **Hoehyeon Underground Shopping Center**, between Myeongdong and Hoehyeon stations, was a destination for music fans, who flocked to its many record shops. Several secondhand vinyl dealers are still here, stocking LPs and CDs from jazz and rock to old K-Pop and J-Pop.

Art for the People

MAP P84

See SeMA's crowd-pleasing exhibitions

Operated by the city government as a public service, the **Seoul Museum of Art** (SeMA; *sema.seoul.go.kr)* holds superbly curated exhibitions, most of which are free. Many focus on the work of Korean creatives, but they run a thrilling gamut from David Hockney retrospectives to group exhibitions that tackle the issue of aging and international examinations of the occult. A permanent exhibition is devoted to the major 20th-century painter Chun Kyung-ja, who worked in the *chaesaekhwa* (colour painting) tradition. Also notable is the building itself, a 1928 structure that once housed the Korean Supreme Court. Closed Mondays.

SEMA BRANCHES

SeMA branches are scattered across the city. Check out the **Nam-Seoul Museum of Art** (p152) in Gangnam, the brand-new **Photography Seoul Museum of Art** (p192) in northern Seoul and the **Paik Ground SeMA** (p180), Nam June Paik's former home.

Jung-gu Hidden Gems

MAP P76

Surprising sights in Central Seoul

Keep an eye out for these unusual encounters in the capital. Firstly, the not-to-be-missed **Berlin Square**. This plaza exhibits three sections of the Berlin Wall, a bear statue and a Berlin streetlamp the German government donated in 2005. Shop for local produce at **Yeonnam Bangagan**, where you will find handmade pottery, small-batch sesame oil and other goodies from small Korean producers at this charming cafe/shop.

Tucked behind a luxury hotel are the remains of 1899 **Hwangudan** ritual altar, where King Gojong offered sacrifices to heaven. The aptly named **Studio Meditation with a Pencil** animation studio displays sketches of its comics and films and provides coloured pencils for you to draw your own. Last but not least is the **Appenzeller/Noble Memorial Museum**. Pai Chai Hak Dang was Korea's first modern school, founded in 1885, and its only remaining building is now a museum.

EATING IN CENTRAL SEOUL: INTERNATIONAL PICKS

MAP P76 & P84

Yuzu Fine Ramen: A cozy Japanese ramen spot that adds tangy yuzu citrus to its broth. *11am-3pm & 5-9pm, no break Sat & Sun* ₩₩

n.Grill: This French fine-dining restaurant serves multicourse meals at the top of N Seoul Tower. Lunch is slightly cheaper. *noon-10pm* ₩₩₩

Furoa: A laid-back brunch place by day (the pudding French toast is sinfully good) and a stylish lounge with DJs by night. *9am-midnight* ₩₩

Oldies Taco: Bright neon lights draw Euljiro revellers to this takeaway taco stand like moths to a flame. *11.30am-9pm* ₩

Appenzeller/Noble Memorial Museum

Seoul's Dramatic Centre of Civic Life

MAP P76

City Hall, old and new

It's impossible to miss the symbolism of Seoul's new **City Hall**, a giant glass edifice shaped like a tsunami wave about to break over its Japanese-built predecessor. Step inside and you'll be met by a lush vertical garden that rises seven storeys through the atrium and includes some 65,000 plants. At the time of its creation, it was the largest vertical garden in the world. Matching the greenery's rise is a 24m stack of blue and white 'balloons': Jheon Soo-cheon's striking art installation *Metaseosa Seobeol*. Make your own ascent and take lift No 11 up to the 8th-floor Sky Plaza Gallery, which holds rotating, typically Seoul-themed art exhibitions. Down in the building's basement is the recently renovated **Citizens' Hall**, the site of exhibitions, performances and the **Gungisi Relics Exhibition Hall**, where items discovered during City Hall's construction – primarily artefacts from a Joseon arsenal that once occupied the site – are on display.

The handsome old City Hall, built in 1926, now serves as the **Seoul Metropolitan Library** (closed Mondays). On the 3rd floor, the Old Mayor's Room reconstructs the former *sijang*'s office and planning and situation room while adding an exhibit on postwar urban planning. A small display on the 5th floor focuses on the building's architecture. Tours of both buildings are given in English at 2pm on Tuesday, Thursday, Saturday and Sunday.

In front of City Hall, **Seoul Plaza** is often used for events – everything from political protests and Seoul Pride to public World Cup viewings. In winter, it turns into a skating rink (skate rentals available), while on summer weekends in recent years it has been a venue for the Seoul Outdoor Library, filled with beanbag chairs and bookshelves.

THE FIGHT FOR THE KOREAN LANGUAGE

When Sohn Kee-chung ran in the 1936 Olympics, he competed not under his given Korean name, but under a Japanese one: Son Kitei.

Towards the end of the colonial era, Japanese authorities ramped up a campaign to repress the Korean language, pressuring schools to switch to instruction in Japanese and, in 1940, passing a law requiring Koreans to take Japanese names.

When the authorities discovered Korean scholars' clandestine attempt to produce a comprehensive Korean dictionary in 1942, they threw many of the scholars in jail.

The manuscript, more than 26,000 pages, was thought lost. But on 8 September 1945, it was rediscovered, buried in a storehouse at Seoul station. The surviving scholars resumed their work, and the first volume was published in 1947.

NIGHT LIGHTS

A walk along Seoullo 7017 is especially good at night, when you're surrounded by the city lights and have the perfect vantage point for the **Seoul Square Building**'s nightly show. The rather brick-like building, opposite Seoul station, is covered in a 7722-sq-metre media canvas containing 126,000 LED lights that display digital artworks, beginning at 8pm each night.

Stick around and you might catch Moon Kyung-won's *Sungnyemun*, depicting the nearby City Wall gate, or Kim Min-sun's *Mioon*, a shifting grid of silhouettes in colourful rooms. There's also *People Walking* by the British artist Julian Opie, who's well known for creating the album cover for Blur's greatest-hits album, *Blur: The Best Of*.

Seoullo 7017

Transport Transformations

MAP P84

A reimagined highway and train station

Just north of Seoul station are two old pieces of transport infrastructure that have been given new life as vibrant public spaces. Built in 1925, the original Seoul station is a stately Renaissance-style building with a green central dome and a grand semicircular window over its entrance. Replaced by a new, larger station in 2004, it was reopened in 2011 as **Culture Station Seoul 284** *(seoul284.org)*, a space for art exhibitions and events. Shows here are reliably excellent, but what really sets the venue apart is the ability to explore the restored station as you peruse the art. The Ladies' Waiting Room, Stationmaster's Office, The Grill (Korea's first Western-style restaurant) and other rooms are presented as they appeared in the station's heyday. Be sure to visit the 2nd-floor bathroom and barbershop, which have been left unrestored so you can see the original building materials and construction methods.

Soaring above Culture Station Seoul 284 is **Seoullo 7017**, a 17m-high vehicle overpass from the 1970s that's been turned into an elevated park stretching nearly 1km from Seoul station's west side to Hoehyeon station. Head up to the walkway – elevators and stairs provide access at several points – to watch trains pulling in and out and to stroll among potted wisteria, Chinese redbuds, hydrangeas, dogwoods and dozens of other plant species.

Korea's First Olympic Medalist

MAP P84

Hear Sohn Kee-chung's inspiring story

Sohn Kee-chung was the first Korean to win an Olympic medal, claiming gold in the marathon at the 1936 Berlin Summer Games. Except the medal wasn't credited to Korea. The country was under Japanese colonial rule at the time, and Sohn was forced to run under the Japanese flag. To this day, the International Olympic Committee attributes the victory to Japan. You can learn about Sohn's bittersweet triumph and inspiring story – he was Korea's flagbearer at the 1948 games, the country's first as an independent nation – at the **Son Kee Chung Memorial Hall** *(sonkeechung.com)* in Sohn Kee-chung Sports Park, just west of Seoul station. There's little English signage, but you can pick up a free English audio guide at the front desk. Items on display include split-toed cloth shoes of the sort Sohn wore, photos of his high-school running days and a replica of his gold medal.

On the grounds outside is the now fully grown oak tree that was presented to Sohn as a sapling upon his victory. The museum is closed Mondays.

A Martyrs' Memorial, a Grand Cathedral

MAP P84

Pilgrimage to Korean Catholic sites

In the Joseon era, Seosomun, one of the city wall's minor gates, was the site of a bustling market. The guaranteed crowds also made it a preferred venue for public executions – more witnesses to get the message. During the government's 19th-century persecution of Catholics – viewed as a threat to the social order – at least 98 believers were martyred here.

Today the site hosts the **Seosomun Historical Park** and, underground, the **Seosomun Shrine History Museum** *(seosomun.org)*, closed Mondays, dedicated to honouring their memory. Wander the park to view memorials and find the Executioner's Well, where the executioner washed his sword, then take the ramp down to the museum to learn about Catholicism's development in Korea and its conflict with Joseon's ruling Confucian ideology. Within the museum you'll also find religious artworks, the austere St Chong Hasang Chapel and the open-air Sky Square, where 44 statues made from railroad ties represent the 44 Seosomun martyrs who were canonised in 1984.

You can mark Catholicism's eventual acceptance at the grand, Gothic **Myeongdong Cathedral** *(mdsd.or.kr)*. Completed

THE HISTORY OF JEONG-DONG

When Korea opened to the outside world in the late 1800s, Seoul's new Western expat community congregated in Jeong-dong. The neighbourhood between Deoksugung and Saemunan-ro is full of reminders of that transformative era, including the country's oldest extant Protestant church, **Chungdong First Methodist Church** (1897), and its first girls' school, Ewha Hakdang (now Ewha Girls' High School and **Ewha Museum**), founded in 1886.

Many Western governments established legations in Jeong-dong. The most important of these was the Russian legation, where King Gojong took refuge after the assassination of his wife, Empress Myeongseong. It's believed he fled there via the narrow road now known as Gojongui-gil. Most of the legation burned down in the Korean War, but you can still visit its central tower in **Jeong-dong Park**.

EATING IN CENTRAL SEOUL: OUR PICKS

MAPS P76 & P84

Hanokjib Kimchi-jjim: No frills, all flavour. Specialises in *kimchi-jjim* (braised pork and aged kimchi) and *kimchi-jjigae* (stew). *10.30am-9.30pm* W

Mokmyeoksanbang: The Namsan branch of this bibimbap restaurant has great food in a lovely courtyard seating amid the mountain's greenery. *10.30am-7.30pm* W

Muldwinda: Pair *makgeolli* (unrefined rice wine) with beef tartare or boiled pork and oysters at this sophisticated tavern. *11am-2.30pm & 5-10pm Mon-Fri* WW

Odarijip: Aspiring K-Pop singers perform live while you tuck into raw crab marinated in soy sauce or grilled beef. *8.10am-midnight* WWW

TOP EXPERIENCE

Namdaemun Market

Namdaemun Market is nearly as old as Seoul itself, with roots going back to 1414. It's also Korea's largest traditional market. More than 10,000 shops spread across several city blocks, selling everything from kitchen supplies and camera equipment to souvenirs and novelty socks. Meanwhile, shoppers find sustenance at street stalls and decades-old restaurants, where hungry customers pack in shoulder to shoulder.

TRABANTOS/SHUTTERSTOCK

Namdaemun Market

- Pick up a market map from the **tourist information booth** on the central alley near Gate 5 to get oriented.
- Some light bargaining when shopping is fine, but don't expect huge discounts.
- Most restaurants in Kalguksu Alley and Hairtail Alley close at 9pm.

Shopping in the Market

Namdaemun's size can feel overwhelming. If you're just here to explore, that's part of the appeal – just dive in and see what you find. If you're shopping with purpose, however, get oriented around the main alley, which runs north-south from Gate 2 to Gate 5. You'll find lots of souvenirs, eyewear and clothes here, as well as the Central Mall Building (clothes, Korean wedding gifts, kitchenware) and Daedo Arcade Building (crafts, kitchen supplies). They're flanked by alleys selling bedding and surplus military clothes.

Buildings just west of the central alley sell lots of food products, while camera shops cluster around Gate 1. To the east are streets dedicated to women's and children's clothing.

Eating in the Market

Just inside Gate 5 is **Kalguksu Alley**. Diners down bowls of the noodle soup at counters lining either side. Squeeze between them to find a stall that looks good and pull up a stool. Not far from Gate 1 is **Hairtail Alley**, where tiny restaurants serve up clay pots of braised *galchi* (hairtail) and grilled mackerel. Next to Gate 2 you'll find a wildly popular **hotteok stand**. Along with the typical sugar-and-nut-filled version of these fried pancakes, it also does versions with vegetables and sweet red beans.

PRACTICALITIES

- *namdaemunmarket.co.kr*
- free
- shop hours vary

in 1898, it features soaring arches and lovely stained-glass windows. It also provided an important refuge for pro-democracy protesters in the 1980s. English Mass is held on Sundays at 9am.

A Legacy of Soil & Steel

MAP P84

Learn about Korea's development

If you have a deep-rooted interest in how Korea developed, you may enjoy spending a couple of hours at a pair of rather niche museums in the Jeong-dong area. The **Museum of Agriculture** *(agrimuseum.or.kr)* provides an interesting overview of the country's agricultural roots, exploring ancient farming implements, the way agricultural cycles shaped society and what may have been the world's first forcing house.

Around the corner, the **Korea Territorial Development Museum** *(molit.go.kr)* leaps forward in time to cover the country's post–Korean War growth and its 21st-century engineering accomplishments. It's all quite wonkish and rather cheerleadery, but the advancements are genuinely impressive. Both museums are closed on Mondays.

Seoul's Great South Gate

MAP P84

See the reborn Sungnyemun

Built in 1398, **Sungnyemun** is the oldest and largest of the historic City Wall gates. Its two-storey pavilion is also the city's oldest wooden building. If it doesn't quite look it, that's because the gate underwent major reconstruction following a 2008 fire, when a 69-year-old man upset with the government over a property dispute set it ablaze. Repairs were completed in 2013.

In the Joseon era, Sungnyemun was where envoys from the Chinese emperor were received and where kings presided over rituals in times of drought. Its formal name means Gate of Honouring Propriety, but it's usually just called Namdaemun, or Great South Gate. Aim to visit at either 10am or 3.30pm, when costumed guards conduct gate opening and closing ceremonies; they stay stationed at the gate during the hours between. Plaques to Sungnyemun's south display photos showing how the gate appeared before its adjoining walls were dismantled in the early 1900s. The plaza around the gate is closed on Mondays.

BEST LOCAL CLOTHING STORES IN MYEONG-DONG

EMIS: Cute sweats, T-shirts, bags and accessories. Its caps are seemingly everywhere in Seoul. Has clothes for pets, too.

Matin Kim: Men's and women's clothing basic enough to wear every day but with a bit of edge to stand out.

Covernat: A popular brand that plays it chill, with subdued workwear-inspired looks that won't go out of style.

ÅLAND: A lifestyle store that carries a wide array of trendy Korean and international labels. A good place to go exploring.

Nick Nicole: This womenswear line has a bit of the catwalk in its DNA and takes a more grown-up approach to its designs.

EATING IN MYEONG-DONG & EULJIRO: INTERNATIONAL FARE

MAPS P76 & P92

Menten: Serves just two delicious ramen varieties: *shoyu* (soy-sauce broth) and *tantanmen* (spicy broth with minced pork). *11.40am-2.30pm & 6-7.30pm Mon-Sat* ₩₩

Mari Meokja: Malaysian favourites such as *nasi lemak* and chicken curry, plus halal versions of Korean food. *8am-4.30pm & 5.30-10pm* ₩

Euljiro Las Vegas: A lively Japanese izakaya with a menu including udon, dumplings and highballs. *4pm-midnight Mon-Thu, to 1am Fri & Sat* ₩

Jangmanok: Chinese small plates served up beneath red lanterns and a mirror ball in Euljiro's nightlife district. *4pm-midnight, from noon Sat & Sun* ₩₩

SIGHTS
1 Euljiro neon signs alley
2 Seoul Film Center
3 Sewoon Electronics Museum
4 Sewoon Sangga
5 Sewoon Sangga Relics Exhibition Hall

EATING
6 Euljiro Las Vegas
7 Eunseong Nongwon
8 Jangmanok
9 Joseonok
10 Oldies Taco
11 Woo Lae Oak
12 Yongsam Sikdang

DRINKING & NIGHTLIFE
13 Art x Shift
14 Champ Coffee
15 Ciao
16 Euljiro Brewing
17 George Seoul
18 Ggeek Beer Company
19 Gong Gan Gab
20 Horangii
21 Magpie Euljiro
22 Nogari Alley
23 Ranch Brewing Company
24 Seendosi
see 23 Sunset Record Bar
25 Tabacchi

ENTERTAINMENT
26 Myeongbo Art Hall

SHOPPING
27 Euljiro Underground Shopping Center
see 20 JJMG

W.R.E.A.M. (Won Rules Everything Around Me)

MAP P84

Visit the Bank of Korea Money Museum

The **Bank of Korea Money Museum** *(bok.or.kr)* occupies the Korean central bank's former head office, a grand edifice completed in 1912. Unless you have an abiding interest in monetary policy, many exhibits are, admittedly, skippable. Others are unexpectedly captivating. You can view North Korean currency, see how unusable bills get turned into construction material and learn about Korea's shortest-lived banknote, first issued on 16 May 1962 and retired 20 days later. There are lots of good hands-on displays for kids, who can try lifting sacks of coins and get their picture put on a digital bill. Ironically, museum entry is free. It's closed Mondays.

Makeovers, Makeup & Munchies

MAP P76

Shop and eat through Myeong-dong

Myeong-dong is the bright neon bull's-eye for travellers coming to Seoul to shop. It might not have Apgujeong's (p143) high-end offerings or Dongdaemun's (p166) domestic design scene, but it makes up for that in its stores-per-block ratio and its unapologetically capitalist energy. Step into its streets at night and get swept up in the lights, the music and the international wave of bargain hunters.

Most of the clothing you'll find in Myeong-dong is the same international brands you'd see in any major city, but there are a number of trendy Korean labels, too. K-Beauty is also big in Myeong-dong. Major cosmetics retailers Olive Young and Nature Republic have multiple outlets here, while the **3CE Stylenanda Pink Space Hotel** concept store is a tower of pastel playfulness. If you want to take a deep dive into Korean cosmetics, don't miss **Beauty Play** *(beautyplay.kr)*, an experience centre where you can try out cosmetics by dozens of smaller brands, get a consultation or sign up for a beauty class (in Korean).

When you're not shopping, nosh your way through Myeong-dong's many street-food stalls, which dish up everything from grilled meat skewers and mochi-wrapped fruits to roast lobster tails coated in cheese.

MEET YOUR MONEY

Who's who on Korean bills:

₩1000 note: Yi Hwang (1501–70). The Joseon dynasty's most renowned Confucian scholar. His penname, Toegye, was given to the road linking Seoul station with Dongdaemun.

₩5000 note: Yi I (1536–84). Another famed Joseon Confucian scholar and politician. A road bearing his penname, Yulgok, passes between Jongmyo and Changdeokgung.

₩10,000 note: King Sejong the Great (1397–1450). The fourth king of the Joseon dynasty. Korea's most revered figure, he oversaw the creation of *hangeul* (the Korean phonetic alphabet) and numerous scientific advances.

₩50,000 note: Shin Saimdang (1504–51). The mother of Yi I and a celebrated poet, calligrapher and artist. Her drawings of grapes, insects and plants illustrate the bill's front.

EATING IN JUNG-GU: KOREAN BARBECUE RESTAURANTS

MAPS P76 & P92

Joseonok: A humble place that's been specialising in succulent *galbi* (beef short ribs) since 1937. *11.30am-2.30pm & 4.30-9.30pm Mon-Sat* ₩₩₩

Eunseong Nongwon: Serves everything from *samgyeopsal* (pork belly) to high-grade *hanu* (Korean beef) and stays open late. *4pm-1am* ₩₩₩

Hansikwangbijip: This basement eatery grills up quality Korean beef sirloin, tenderloin and short ribs. Enter at the corner of Myeongdong 3-gil and 7ga-gil. *11am-11pm* ₩₩₩

Yongsam Sikdang: A fun, cheap-ish place for pork belly and beer. Fills up fast with Euljiro partiers. *11am-2pm & 4-10pm, no break Sat & Sun* ₩₩₩

TOP EXPERIENCE

Cheonggye-cheon

The story of the Cheonggye Stream is shorthand for the story of modern Seoul. In the impoverished postwar years, shantytowns grew along its banks. During the 1970s developmental rush, it was replaced with an elevated highway. As the city focused on quality of life in the early 2000s, the stream was restored. Today it's an urban oasis beloved by Seoulites and visitors alike.

FLORIAN AUGUSTIN/SHUTTERSTOCK

Cheonggye-cheon

- Scan a QR code in Cheonggye Plaza to access a stream guide available in 10 languages.
- The Seoul Lantern Festival *(stolantern.com)* illuminates the Cheonggye-cheon from mid-December to mid-January. On summer weekends, the stream becomes a branch of the Seoul Outdoor Library and is lined with seats for reading.

People-Watching, Wildlife-Spotting

The Cheonggye-cheon flows through central Seoul for nearly 11km, providing a sunken pedestrian corridor with landscaped walkways and places to rest and enjoy the scenery. It's a favourite with, well, everybody: couples on dates, families out for walks, office workers on lunch breaks... The stream is quite engineered where it begins at **Cheonggye Plaza**, but the further east you go, the more 'natural' it gets, as concrete gives way to trees and vegetation. Even upstream, though, you'll likely spot herons, egrets and a few fish.

Public Art

Public art lines the stream. At Cheonggye Plaza are Coosje van Bruggen and Claes Oldenburg's shell-like *Spring* and Yeesookyung's golden rock, *You Were There_Cheonggyecheon 2025*. Near Gwanggyo Bridge is Laurent François' ***Cheonggye-cheon Digital Canvas***; a few times a night from March to November, mist jets create a watery screen for a spectral laser show. Just east of Gwanggyo Bridge, you won't miss the long mural reproducing a painting of an eight-day procession King Jeongjo made to his father's tomb in Hwaseong (p206). Next to it is a smaller mural of Suseon Jeondo, the Joseon dynasty's most famous city map, produced in 1825. At its centre? The Cheonggye-cheon.

PRACTICALITIES

- *sisul.or.kr*
- free
- 24hr

A Spotlight on Korean Cinema

MAP P92

Stop by the Seoul Film Center

The Chungmuro area used to be the heart of Korea's film industry, and the new **Seoul Film Center** *(seoulfilm center.com)*, opened in late 2025, aims to bring a bit of the silver screen's glimmer back to the neighbourhood. It hosts film-related exhibitions and screens movies – with a focus on independent and art films – in four theatres, including one on the rooftop.

K-Pop Culture Centre

MAP P76

Surf the Korean Wave at HiKR Ground

HiKR Ground *(hikr.visitkorea.or.kr)* is part tourist information centre and part *hallyu* (Korean Wave) playground. You'll find a Korea Tourism Organization info desk and a terrace with Cheonggye-cheon views on the top floor, but the fun comes on the floors below. Hold a video shoot on one of five themed stages – ranging from a laundromat to a spaceship – with controls that let you pick your soundtrack and adjust the lighting. Sing karaoke, spray digital graffiti and livestream K-Content in the HiKR Street section. On the 4th floor are rotating pop-up exhibitions related to Korea travel.

HiKR Ground's experience zones are closed on Mondays, but the info desk stays open.

A Building Where Decades Converge

MAP P92

Time travel in Sewoon Sangga

If you want to see several decades of Seoul existing simultaneously, head to **Sewoon Sangga**. The 1.2km-long development spans several blocks, but its most interesting sections are the ones immediately north and south of the Cheonggye-cheon. The concrete massif is emblematic of the 1960s development boom, while its interior is a warren of electronics shops (stereos, space heaters, karaoke machines...basically anything you can plug in) that's barely changed since the '80s.

Along the exterior 3rd-floor walkways, especially south of the stream, young entrepreneurs have set up modern shops, cafes and restaurants in formerly empty spaces. Highlights include **Champ Coffee**, **Ggeek Beer Company**, **JJMG** for handmade silver jewellery and **Horangii** for fruit sandos. There's also a tech book lounge and the **Sewoon Electronics**

THE EVOLUTION OF SEWOON SANGGA

Sewoon Sangga is more than just a brutalist behemoth. For starters, it was designed by Korea's leading 20th-century architect, Kim Swoo-geun, who also designed Seoul Olympic Stadium.

While it's now showing its age, in its day Sewoon Sangga was at the forefront of tech culture, a place where you could even find everything, as a joke went, you'd need to build a missile.

More recently, its Makercity Sewoon initiative has aimed to support aspiring creators, and the complex has become a minor drinking and dining destination.

If you're keen to see Sewoon Sangga, you might want to do it soon, though. A current proposal would raze the structure and build a skyscraper in its place.

DRINKING IN EULJIRO: TOP CAFES

MAP P76 & P92

Coffee Hanyakbang: Mother-of-pearl and old pharmacy fixtures create a time-warp aesthetic in what might be Seoul's narrowest alley. *10am-10pm, from 11am Sat & Sun, to 8pm Sun*

Art x Shift: This artist-founded cafe/gallery changes its decor to create an immersive environment that matches its current exhibition. *noon-10pm Mon-Sat, 1-7pm Sun*

George Seoul: Sodas in shades of radioactive gemstones, and cakes fit for a doll's wedding. Semi-hidden up a nondescript staircase. *noon-9.40pm Wed-Mon*

Gong Gan Gab: Mixes Euljiro's industrial feel with trendy coffee and desserts. Try the signature crème brûlée latte and pudding *bingsu* (shaved ice). *11.45am-9.50pm*

JUNG-GU AFTER DARK

When the sun goes down, Jung-gu lights up. Experience its after-hours energy on a walk through Myeong-dong, the Cheonggye-cheon and Euljiro.

START	END	LENGTH
Myeongdong station, exit 6	Euljiro neon signs alley	4km; 2hr

Come out of exit 6 of 1 **Myeongdong station** and plunge straight into 2 **Myeong-dong**'s nighttime shopping scene. Squeeze through the crowds to Myeongdong-gil. Once there, take a quick detour east to leave behind earthly pleasures for a bit of spiritual sustenance and admire the majestic 3 **Myeongdong Cathedral** (p89) illuminated against the dark. Double back and chow your way through 4 **street food stalls** cooking up lamb skewers, candied fruit and much more.

Cross 5 **Seoul Plaza** (p87), where the glass City Hall looms over its predecessor, and make sure you get to 6 **Deoksugung** (p82) by 8pm so you can see its historic palace buildings lit up, forming a captivating contrast with the surrounding skyscrapers.

Head up Sejong-daero to 7 **Cheonggye Plaza** (p94) and start a stroll down the Cheonggye-cheon, watching Seoulites at play and seeing the city lights reflected in the water.

If you get to 8 **HiKR Ground** (p95) before 7.30pm, pop inside to snap some selfies on its K-Pop stages. Watch one of the laser shows at the 9 ***Cheonggye-cheon Digital Canvas*** (p94) between 7pm and 9pm before heading to 10 **Nogari Alley** for street beers.

Finish up by heading down Eulji-ro 12-gil, the centre of Euljiro nightlife. The night is always young here, so after you bask in the glow of an 11 **alley of neon signs**, stick around to explore Euljiro's bars and restaurants.

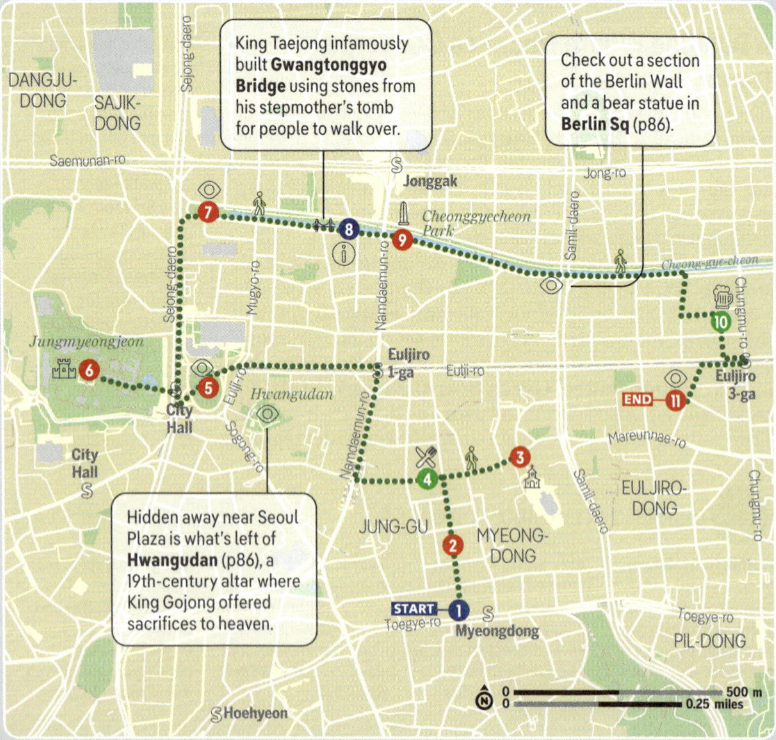

Museum, which displays both old-tech and modern electronics. Be sure to check out the **Relics Exhibition Hall**, an archaeological site at Sewoon Sangga's north end where remains of buildings from as far back as the 1400s are displayed.

Work Hard, Play Hard

MAP P92

Encounter Euljiro's split personality

Euljiro, surrounding the street of the same name, is one of Seoul's most fascinating neighbourhoods. By day, it's a hive of printers, machinists and lighting and bathroom-fixture shops – a working-class enclave that has somehow hung on in the middle of downtown. Where businesses have closed, young artists and entrepreneurs have moved in and, by night, Euljiro's alleys are packed with people spilling out of its many bars and restaurants.

Head here in the late afternoon to explore Euljiro's blue-collar side and then stick around after dark for the nightlife that's earned the area the decidedly un-hip nickname 'Hip-jiro'. The action is centred on Eulji-ro 12-gil and, if you walk down it, you're bound to see a nameless alley where a collection of **neon signs** creates an irresistible photo op.

Be sure to also visit **Nogari Alley**, where drinkers down cheap beer and bar snacks at folding tables that several old-school bars set up in the street – a perfect marriage of Euljiro eras.

KNOW YOUR KOREAN BAR SNACKS

Korean drinking is almost always done with *anju*, or bar snacks. Here are some of the most common.

Nogari: Dried pollack, usually dipped in a mix of soy sauce, mayonnaise and hot peppers.

Macaroni gwaja: Ring-shaped fried dough puffs, somehow both tasteless and addictive. Always provided free.

Golbaengi-muchim: A salad of sea snails, noodles, scallion, carrot and cucumber in a spicy sauce.

Jwipo: Filefish jerky, sometimes served roasted or grilled.

Jeon: Savoury fried pancakes. Common varieties include *kimchi-jeon* and *pa-jeon* (with green onions).

Dakbal: Grilled or stir-fried chicken feet, often served with a searingly hot sauce.

DRINKING IN EULJIRO: INTERESTING BARS

MAPS P76 & P92

Seendosi: Neon, art, a rooftop terrace, a dance space and live music, all in a random old building? Peak Euljiro. *7.30pm-1am, to 2am Fri & Sat*

Tabacchi: Styled like an Italian bar. Does wine and gelato sets – something, frankly, every bar should do. *5.30pm-1am, to 2am Fri & Sat*

Ace Four Club: One of Euljiro's best and most stylish cocktail bars. If it's full, try its sister bar, Westwing, next door. *5pm-1am, to 2am Fri & Sat*

Magpie Euljiro: This Korean craft-beer stalwart has a long list of beers on tap, including seasonal selections. *5pm-1am, closed first Wed of month*

Euljiro Brewing: Don't be put off by the ironic logo of a guy throwing up. Its beers are excellent. *3.30pm-2am*

Sunset Record Bar: You'll find retro-inspired decor and walls of vinyl at this LP bar spread across two floors. *4pm-midnight Sun-Thu, 5pm-1am Fri & Sat*

Ciao: Nurse a negroni while you listen to a DJ spin and watch the Euljiro parade from an outside table. *6pm-1am, to 2am Fri & Sat*

Ranch Brewing Company: Craft beer and Detroit-style pizza. *4-11pm Wed & Thu, 2pm-midnight Fri, noon-midnight Sat, 2-10pm Sun*

Researched by Charles Usher

WESTERN SEOUL

YOUTH CULTURE, PARK LIFE, HIP NEIGHBOURHOODS

A young population gives Western Seoul an irrepressible energy and some of the city's coolest enclaves, while former industrial sites have received green makeovers.

Seoul's west side is home to several of Korea's most prestigious universities, and the many young people mean the area has Seoul's best nightlife. The artsy Hongdae neighbourhood is a hub for all-night bars and live music, and buskers and dance crews turn streets into stages. Nearby, Yeonnam and Mangwon are hip quarters packed with cafes and boutiques, while across the river, indie artists have found a home among the machinists in Mullae Arts Village. There are also green spaces aplenty, from Seoul Botanic Park to the riverside World Cup Park and Yeouido Hangang Park, near which you'll also find the watery wonders of Noryangjin, Seoul's biggest seafood market.

INCLUDES

Yeouido Hangang Park (p112)

FROM LEFT: MIRKO KUZMANOVIC/SHUTTERSTOCK, HYOLIM/SHUTTERSTOCK

See page 216 for places to stay in Western Seoul

Highlights

❶ Hongdae
Eat, drink, dance and sing until dawn in Seoul's epicentre of after-hours fun. **p100**

❷ Noryangjin Fisheries Wholesale Market
Inspect the day's catch and get your pick sliced up at an on-site restaurant. **p116**

❸ Mullae Arts Village
Find your favourite street art amid the area's mix of studios, cafes and machine shops. **p115**

▲❹ Seoul Botanic Park
Go green in this indoor/outdoor temple to all that grows. **p118**

❺ World Cup Park
Watch a football game, stroll through the silver grass or just enjoy the river views. **p108**

Getting Around

Subway
Line 2 loops through popular areas, including Hongdae and Mullae. Lines 5, 6 and 9 connect Yeouido, Gongdeok and World Cup Park. The AREX provides easy access to the airports.

Mapo Tour Train Bus
This new hop-on, hop-off bus circulates through Mapo District tourist spots such as Hongdae, Gyeongui Line Forest Park and World Cup Park. Tickets are valid for a full day.

Bicycle
Paths along the Han River and several streams make this one of the best parts of town for cycling. Seoul Bike docking stations are ubiquitous.

Northwestern Seoul

A cluster of universities keeps the area north of the Han feeling vibrant, with a surfeit of bars, clubs, restaurants, cafes and independent cinemas to experience. All that action is balanced out by several pretty parks.

HONGDAE'S BEST LIVE-MUSIC VENUES

Jebi Dabang: A hole in the floor offers a bird's-eye view of indie and acoustic shows in the basement.

Club FF: This Hongdae staple likes it loud. Mostly sticks to a tried-and-true guitar-bass-drums formula.

Rolling Hall: Hosts a wide array of genres and pulls in some big names in the Korean indie scene.

Strange Fruit: A tiny underground space with cheap drinks – in other words, your classic university club.

Club Evans: This 2nd-floor venue has been nurturing up-and-coming jazz musicians since 2001.

Senggi Studio: A recording studio and performing space with an experimental streak.

Seoul's Fountain of Youth

MAP P102

Revel in Hongdae's nightlife

Hongik University possesses a prestigious arts school and, for decades, Hongdae, as the surrounding neighbourhood is known, has been at the forefront of Seoul's alternative culture. Its popularity has seen it gentrify in recent years, but it remains a haven for punks, club kids, hip-hop heads, LGBTIQ+ youth and anyone who does things differently.

To experience Korea's most infectious after-hours scene, show up on a weekend night and join the throngs swelling Hongdae's streets and bars. The mostly pedestrianised Eoulmadang-ro, often just called **Hongdae St** (it's also been rebranded as Red Road), cuts through the heart of the area. North of Hongik-ro, its plazas play host to festivals, b-boys and buskers; south, it's lined with fashion boutiques and fortune tellers, while crowds form around impromptu street performances. Peek up at the divas singing karaoke in **Luxury Su Noraebang** *(sunoraebang.com)*, the rooms of which overlook the street, or go dancing in the clubs that cluster around the intersection of Jandari-ro and Wausan-ro, including **NB2** (hip-hop), **MODECi** (house) and **Club Ocean** (EDM).

At some point during the night, be sure to swing by the **Hongdae Playground**, the plaza near the university's front gate that's the neighbourhood's unofficial meeting point and hosts everything from craft markets to b-boy battles.

Walk the Line

MAP P102

Park people and cool neighbourhoods

Built atop railroad tracks that once ran all the way to the Chinese border, the 6.3km **Gyeongui Line Forest Park** extends from Hyochang Park station to Gajwa station. Its most popular stretch is right outside Hongdae University station, where it's a proper urban planner's dream. Maples and ginkgos flank patches of grass, locals walk dogs, photographers set up fashion shoots and visitors crisscross the

LEEBORN/SHUTTERSTOCK

Street performance, Hongdae

park on their way to the surrounding restaurants, photo booths and board-game cafes.

Snack on a *hotteok*, a pancake filled with caramelised brown sugar, from **Seoul Hotteok** while you mosey through the park or people-watch, then dive into the streets to the northeast to explore Yeonnam, a trendy neighbourhood bursting with small cafes and indie shops of the sort that used to fill Hongdae before its rents shot up.

You'll likely get lost in the twisting, dead-end streets, but serendipitous discovery is the name of the game here. Keep angling northeast, across Seongsan-ro, to check out the Yeonhui area, which has similar, if slightly more upscale, vibes, with jewellery ateliers, gelato shops and the like.

BEST YEONNAM & YEONHUI SHOPS

YOUR-MIND: An art bookstore that also stocks zines and stationery. Sometimes hosts artist pop-ups.

Bowlow: This men's fashion brand sells *au courant* styles in muted tones, from jackets to bags.

Acorn Caricature: Get a cute K-Cartoon drawn of yourself. Has four-frame and one-minute options.

Youssoful: A local cosmetics brand that makes perfume, hand cream and diffusers.

Juuneedu: Sells charming women's pyjamas.

Banul Story: Shelves full of colourful yarn and other knitting supplies, plus knit hats, scarves and sweaters.

Gravel: This vintage shop specialises in things such as French work jackets and skateboard backpacks.

DRINKING IN HONGDAE: BARS & CAFES

MAPS P102 & P105

Bar Da: Largely unchanged over 20 years, this 2nd-floor hideout is a favourite of locals and expats alike. *7pm-2am Sun-Thu, 6pm-3am Fri & Sat*

UniQorn Craft Beer & Wine: Laid-back and LGBTIQ-friendly, with vegan food options. Down a quiet side street. *5pm-2am Wed-Sun, 6pm-midnight Mon & Tue*

Gopchang Jeongol: Classic '60s to '90s pop occasionally inspires singalongs at this enthusiastically retro bar. *7.30pm-1am Tue-Thu, to 2am Fri & Sat*

Shinleedoga: A bit of Bukchon in Hongdae, this lovely *hanok* cafe has a courtyard with a small pond that becomes a firepit in winter. *11am-11.30pm*

d.still: Hongdae for adults. A low-key spot serving elevated cocktails in a speakeasy setting. *7pm-2am, closed 1st Sun of the month*

Sanullim 1992: Try some of 250 traditional alcohols, like *makgeolli* or soju, at this joint styled like a country *jumak* (tavern). *5pm-1am Tue-Sun*

Seoul Brewery: It makes six year-round brews, seasonal offerings and beers fermented with wild yeast. *5pm-midnight, from 1pm Sat & Sun*

Yri Cafe: A neighbourhood staple, this boho cafe has packed bookshelves and sometimes hosts concerts or author talks. *11am-midnight*

SIGHTS
1 Ansan
2 Eunpyeong Hanok Village
3 Eunpyeong Historical Hanok Museum
4 Gyeongui Line Forest Park
5 Hongdae Playground
6 Hongdae Street
7 Hongje-cheon Artificial Waterfall
8 Jingwan-sa
9 KT&G Sangsang-madang
10 Myeongin Museum
11 Solhyangjae
12 Yeonhui Forest Rest Area

ACTIVITIES, COURSES & TOURS
13 Yonsei University

SLEEPING
14 Hongyugain
15 L7 Hongdae
16 Roi Guesthouse
17 RYSE
18 Time Travelers Relax

EATING
19 Chuncheonjip Dakgalbi & Makguksu
20 Everything Bagel
21 Fell + Cole
22 Gyeongju Sikdang
23 Hongdae Jopok Tteokbokki
24 Hongik Sutbul Galbi
25 Hongojip
26 Joseon Sidae
27 Kotetsu
28 Kyo-ramen
29 Seoul Hotteok
30 Sinchon Hwangso Gopchang
31 Tuk Tuk Noodle Thai

DRINKING & NIGHTLIFE
32 Bar Da
33 Cafe Pokpo
34 Channel 1969
35 Club Ocean
36 Coffee Libre
37 d.still
38 Gopchang Jeongol
39 Irin Iljan
see 20 Manufact Coffee
40 MODECi
41 Morning Calm Coffee Lab
42 NB2
43 Sanullim 1992
44 Shinleedoga
45 Yri Cafe

ENTERTAINMENT
46 Club Evans
47 Club FF
48 Jebi Dabang
49 Laika Cinema
50 Luxury Su Noraebang
51 Rolling Hall
52 Senggi Studio
53 Strange Fruit

SHOPPING
54 Acorn Caricature
55 Banul Story
56 Bowlow
57 Gravel
58 Juuneedu
59 YOUR-MIND
60 Youssoful

MANGWON FAVOURITES

Illustrator and publishing studio co-owner **Kelly Belter** *(@bybelter)*, who has lived in Mangwon since 2018, shares her top spots.

Always Au8ust: My go-to cafe for its delicious vegan desserts (the seasonal roulade is my favourite) and coffee. I love its warm atmosphere and friendly staff.

Hongje Stream: My favourite place for a morning stroll, and it connects to popular neighbourhoods like Yeonnam and Yeonhui.

Athoce: A vintage shop with a curated selection of men's and women's fashion.

Rowing Coffee: Plenty of outlets and table space for those days I want to work outside the office. Has cute desserts, like Japanese fruit sandos.

Dalgona: Its soups and noodles have that handmade touch that makes waiting for its opening days (Friday-Sunday) worth it.

A Place of Pilgrimage

MAP P105

Learn about Korea's Catholic history

When Catholicism arrived in Korea, the religion was seen as a dangerous foreign threat and its practitioners were persecuted for undermining Confucian hierarchies. During the Byeongin Persecution of 1866, many hundreds were martyred, often beheaded on the riverside promontory that the **Jeoldusan Martyrs' Shrine** *(jeoldusan.or.kr)* now occupies. You can learn about this little-known history at the on-site Korean Catholic Martyrs' Museum (closed Mondays), which displays items such as an 18th-century rosary and tells the story of 103 martyrs who were canonised in 1984. Outside, Jeoldusan's (the name means Beheading Hill) solemn grounds display numerous memorials.

Old & New Meet in Mangwon

MAP P105

See the city's changing face

For a glimpse of how Seoul evolves in microcosm, spend a few hours hanging out in Mangwon. On the banks of the Han River, this appealing middle-class area mixes older touches such as a traditional market and small brick apartment buildings with a lively energy that young entrepreneurs have brought with them.

To get a feel for these two sides of Seoul, walk the aisles of **Mangwon Market** *(mangwonmarket.com)* to see the rice cakes and many varieties of kimchi for sale and to sit down to a bowl of noodles at one of its eateries. Then mosey over to Poeun-ro, a street colloquially known as **Mangnidan-gil**, where a slew of restaurants, cafes and shops that have opened in recent years pull in young Seoulites from across the city.

Remembering Victims of Sexual Violence

MAP P105

Hear Korean comfort women's stories

The thoughtfully laid-out **War & Women's Human Rights Museum** *(womenandwarmuseum.net; adult/child ₩5000/3000)*, closed on Mondays, shares the stories of Korean 'comfort women' – victims of sexual trafficking and slavery by the Japanese military from 1932 to 1945. While signage and videos are largely in Korean, the English audio guide included with admission narrates the route through the exhibits,

DRINKING IN YEONNAM & YEONHUI: OUR PICKS

MAP P102

Coffee Libre: Look for the lucha libre mask to find this cafe, which helped kick-start Korea's craft-coffee revolution. *11.30am-8pm*

Morning Calm Coffee Lab: This very Zen place has a rock garden out back and a temple-like basement with a reflecting pool. *10am-10pm*

Channel 1969: Attracting a more mature crowd, this bar has DJs spinning anything from J-Pop to psychedelic, plus concerts. *7pm-midnight Wed, Thu & Sun, to 2am Fri & Sat*

Manufact Coffee: A sleek upstairs space with an industrial vibe and a bar and seating area that blend into each other. *8.30am-6.30pm*

HIGHLIGHTS
1 World Cup Park

SIGHTS
2 Football Fæntasium
3 Haneul Park
4 Hongje Stream
5 Jeoldusan Martyrs' Shrine
see 31 Korean Film Museum
6 Mangnidan-gil
7 Nanji Hangang Park
8 Nanji-cheon Park
9 Noeul Park
10 Oil Tank Culture Park
11 Pyeonghwa Park
12 Seoul Battleship Park
13 Seoul World Cup Stadium
14 War & Women's Human Rights Museum

ACTIVITIES, COURSES & TOURS
15 World Cup Spa Land 24

EATING
16 Dalgona
17 Dangdo
18 MistaGyoza
19 Okdongsik
20 Oreno Ramen
21 Spacca Napoli
22 Tsubu Curry

DRINKING & NIGHTLIFE
23 Always Au8ust
24 Anthracite Seogyo
25 Brown Front Door
26 Han River Espresso
27 Hard Material
28 Rowing Coffee
29 Seoul Brewery
30 UniQorn Craft Beer & Wine

ENTERTAINMENT
31 Cinematheque KOFA

SHOPPING
32 Athoce
33 Mangwon Market

EATING IN MANGWON: TASTY CHOICES

Okdongsik: Just 10 seats at the bar, but the wait for its *dwaeji gomtang* (pork and rice soup) is worth it. *11am-3pm & 5-10pm Mon-Fri, 11am-9pm Sat & Sun* WW

Tsubu Curry: Good Japanese curries with pork cutlets and veggies, plus big windows that look onto the Mangnidan-gil parade. *11am-4pm & 5-9pm Mon-Sat* WW

MistaGyoza: A lively izakaya serving up highballs, fried dumplings and a few good vegetarian options. Great for groups before or after a night out. *5pm-2am* WW

Dangdo: There's often a line out the door at this small gelato shop on Mangnidan-gil, which changes its menu daily. *noon-9pm* W

THE SEATED GIRLS

Every Wednesday since 8 January 1992, former 'comfort women' and their supporters have held protests outside the Japanese Embassy in Seoul to demand an official apology and sufficient compensation from the Japanese government.

To commemorate the 1000th protest in December 2011, they were joined by a new demonstrator: a statue of a young girl seated on a chair, her fists clenched, her stoic gaze directed straight ahead. Created by Kim Seo-kyung and Kim Eun-sung, the figure depicted in the *Statue of Peace* represents a young 'comfort woman'.

In the years since, similar Girl Statues, as they're commonly known, have been erected throughout Korea and across the globe as gestures of support and remembrance.

KOREA BY BIKE/SHUTTERSTOCK

Seoul Battleship Park

taking you outside to a gravel alley lined with victims' artwork, downstairs to a video display and upstairs to a history and memorial hall. View the testimonials, belongings and photos of survivors while learning about their ongoing fight for justice. The museum concludes with an exhibit about sexual violence against women in war and conflict worldwide, including the Vietnamese survivors of sexual violence by Korea's own soldiers during the Vietnam War.

Ships Ahoy!

MAP P105

Tour three retired naval vessels

On (and in) the Han River is **Seoul Battleship Park** *(seoul battleshippark.com; adult/student/child ₩3000/2000/1000)*, where a trio of retired naval ships is on display. A small museum looks at the history of the Han and of Korea's navy, but the real attraction is getting to scramble through the three vessels: a 25m-long Dolgorae-class submarine, a high-speed craft and a 102m-long battleship that's anchored in the river. On the battleship, you can squeeze through narrow

DRINKING IN MANGWON: BEST SPOTS

MAP P105

Anthracite Seogyo: Sip a hand-drip coffee in this quiet wood-and-brick space while gazing at the courtyard's persimmon trees. *9am-10pm*

Hard Material: The staff at this intimate bar mix up creative cocktails and spin some excellent vinyl. *6pm-2am*

Han River Espresso: Grab a coffee from this little neighbourhood spot and stroll down to nearby Mangwon Hangang Park. *8am-10pm Wed-Mon*

Brown Front Door: A cafe and select shop by day, this place transforms into a lounge bar with a DJ after dark. *noon-midnight Tue-Sun*

passageways to check out barracks, the bridge, the radio room and more. Be sure to peer through the submarine's periscope to spy on the **National Assembly Building** (p112) in Yeouido. If you're visiting with any young admirals who want to look the part, there are adorable little sailor uniforms for rental.

Seoul's World Cup Showpiece

MAP P105

Watch football, visit a spa

Seoul World Cup Stadium was built for the 2002 FIFA World Cup, which Korea cohosted with Japan. Its roof resembles a traditional kite. Today the stadium hosts national team matches and is the home ground of FC Seoul. Within the stadium you'll find **World Cup Spa Land 24**, a 24-hour *jjimjilbang* (sauna) with hot baths and saunas, and **Football Fæntasium** *(faentasium.com; ₩15,000)*, a small museum with displays on the history of the sport and Korea's storied 2002 squad that was the only Asian men's team to reach a World Cup semifinal. Content is aimed at kids and is almost exclusively in Korean, so the high entry fee might only be worth it if you've got a young football fanatic in tow. There's also a department store and movie theatre in the stadium.

Out with Oil, In with Art

MAP P105

Explore a reimagined industrial space

Oil Tank Culture Park *(parks.seoul.go.kr/culturetank)* opened in 2017 as a symbol of Seoul's urban renewal. Four giant tanks that once stored diesel fuel and kerosene have been reimagined as an exhibition pavilion, amphitheatre, culture complex and media hall, while a fifth has been preserved in its original form. A sixth structure, a community space with a cafe and library, was constructed out of the dismantled pieces of two other tanks.

Wander the grounds (open 24 hours) – once a designated national security facility – stopping at the tanks (closed on Mondays) to appreciate the architecture and artwork and to snap some post-industrial pics.

GOING TO A FOOTBALL MATCH

Korea's domestic soccer season runs from February to November, and if you happen to be in town on an FC Seoul match day, going to a game at World Cup Stadium makes for a fun experience.

Tickets can be purchased at the stadium's ticket office, located at the top of the stairs at the stadium's north end, which is also the end the team's core supporters occupy. You'll find the team store, merch stalls and food trucks in the plaza outside exit 2 of World Cup Stadium station.

There are no issues with hooliganism in Korea, and matches are exceedingly family-friendly.

EATING IN HONGDAE: POPULAR PICKS

MAP P102

Hongik Sutbul Galbi: This Hongdae institution is popular for late-night pork barbecue that's grilled over charcoal for a richer flavour. *3.30pm-4am* ₩₩

Oreno Ramen: Original branch of a Michelin-listed chain. Savour chicken ramen with fresh noodles and stock made in-house daily. Try the *tori paitan. 11am-10pm* ₩₩

Spacca Napoli: Owner Lee Young-woo trained in Naples and his cosy spot was recently named Korea's best pizzeria. *11.30am-3pm & 5-9.30pm Wed-Sun* ₩₩

Hongdae Jopok Tteokbokki: Rumoured to have been started by an ex-gangster, this *tteokbokki* place has been around for 40 years. *11.30am-1.30am* ₩

Gyeongju Sikdang: Grilled meat and Korean comfort food served in a house that feels like the chef's home. *11.30am-3.30pm & 5.30-11pm* ₩₩

Joseon Sidae: A Joseon-dynasty-themed bar/restaurant done up to look like a traditional tavern. *4.30pm-2.30am Sun-Thu, to 4am Fri & Sat* ₩₩

Fell + Cole: Forget plain vanilla; this gastronomic ice-cream parlour serves flavours like cognac, perilla leaf and white-chocolate ginger. *noon-9pm Mon-Sat* ₩

Kotetsu: A little joint that fries up mighty okonomiyaki (Japanese pancakes). Best paired with a whisky highball. *5pm-midnight, from 2pm Sat & Sun* ₩₩

CLASSIC KOREAN FILMS ONLINE

You don't need to visit the Korean Film Archive (KOFA) to dive into the country's cinematic history. You don't even need to leave your couch. KOFA's YouTube channel, Korean Classic Film, has 110 films available to stream for free, stretching all the way back to the oldest existing Korean movie, *The Turning Point of the Youngsters*. Made in 1934, it was only rediscovered in 2007.

Other seminal films on the channel include *Aimless Bullet* (1961), which depicts a family's post-Korean War struggles, and *The March of Fools*, a 1975 comedy about students coming of age in a modernising country.

Fans of animation will love KOFA's Korean Animation YouTube channel, which has nearly 500 classic animations from the 1960s to the 2010s.

Trash to Treasured Green Spaces

MAP P105

Chill in the World Cup parks

You'd never know it, but parts of **World Cup Park**, created for the 2002 FIFA World Cup, were built atop a giant landfill. The enormous green space is divided into five smaller parks. Across the bridge from World Cup Stadium, **Pyeonghwa (Peace) Park** features a pond and is a popular picnic spot. Westwards, **Haneul (Sky) Park** offers excellent views across the city, art installations and photo ops amid fields of silver grass. The adjacent **Noeul (Sunset) Park** is known for its hilltop campsites. To the north is **Nanji-cheon (Nanji Stream) Park**, where wooden boardwalks cross the water and kids fly kites on a large lawn.

To the south, along the river, **Nanji Hangang Park** has more campsites and boardwalks snaking through a marsh that's home to otters and waterfowl. Playgrounds, sports facilities and convenience stores dot the parks.

EATING IN WESTERN SEOUL: MEATY MORSELS

MAPS P102 & P105

Sinchon Hwangso Gopchang: If you're keen to try *gopchang* (offal) barbecue, this decades-old joint in the lively Shinchon area is a good pick. *2pm-1.30am* ₩₩

Chuncheonjip Dakgalbi & Makguksu: *Dakgalbi* (spicy stir-fried chicken) with add-ins like cheese and noodles. *11am-3pm & 4-10.30pm Tue-Sun* ₩₩

Old Shanghai: Stop here for a pot of beef or lamb *malajeongol* (spicy stew with numbing pepper). It also serves great dumplings. *4pm-1am* ₩₩

Gongdeok Traditional Market: A cluster of market restaurants specialises in *jokbal* (pork trotters) or *jeon* (savoury fried pancakes). *hours vary* ₩₩

SANGA PARK/SHUTTERSTOCK

World Cup Park

Seoul on the Silver Screen

MAP P105

Learn about Korean film history

If international hits such as *Parasite* and *Train to Busan* have piqued your interest in Korean cinema, spend a couple of hours at the Korean Film Archive's **Korean Film Museum** *(koreafilm.or.kr)*, closed Sundays and Mondays. Exhibitions begin with the arrival of film in Korea in 1901 and culminate in the current golden age. There's archival footage of old movies and fascinating explorations of how factors such as post-WWII film shortages and 1970s government censorship shaped the country's film industry. The archive also houses **Cinematheque KOFA**, which hosts film festivals and indie movies.

Western Seoul has several other small cinemas that cater to anyone whose taste in films is more arthouse than blockbuster.

In Yeonhui, the 40-seat **Laika Cinema** *(laikacinema.com)* offers intimate screenings. **Arthouse Momo** *(arthouse momo.com)*, on the Ewha Womans University campus, shows auteur-driven movies and has the added benefit of letting you

FESTIVALS IN WESTERN SEOUL

Yeongdeungpo Yeouido Spring Flower Festival (April): Crowds flock to Yeouido to view the many cherry trees and other flowers in full bloom.

Hangang River Festival (July & August): Events in the riverside parks include outdoor movie screenings, concerts and circus acts.

Seoul International Fireworks Festival (late September/ early October): Spectacular displays of aerial artistry in the skies over Yeouido.

Red Road Festival (October): Buskers, art exhibitions, flea markets and more along Red Road in central Hongdae.

Seoul Silver Grass Festival (October): Cultural and music festival against the illuminated backdrop of Haneul Park's silver grass.

EATING IN YEONNAM & YEONHUI: TOP TASTES

MAP P102

Tuk Tuk Noodle Thai: Thai chefs whip up authentic dishes that earn this spot regular Michelin Bib Gourmand recognition. *11am-3.30pm & 5-9pm Thu-Tue* ₩₩

Hongojip: Most barbecue places only serve parties of two or more, but Hongojip does single servings, perfect for solo travellers. *11.30am-10pm* ₩

Everything Bagel: A loving shrine to New York, with bagels that do the city justice. Terrific breakfast sandwiches. *8am-5pm Tue-Sat* ₩

Kyo-ramen: There's typically a line out the door at mealtimes for the Japanese ramen served here. *11.30am-2.50pm & 5-7.30pm Tue-Sun* ₩

KOREAN LANGUAGE PROGRAMMES

Anyone thinking of moving to Korea to study the language will find ample opportunity in Seoul. With its concentration of universities, Western Seoul is home to some of the country's most popular language programmes, including those at **Sogang University** *(klec.sogang.ac.kr)*, **Yonsei University** *(yskli.com)* and **Ewha Womans University** *(elc.ewha.ac.kr)*. Elsewhere in the city, the courses at **Korea University** *(klcc.korea.ac.kr)* and **Seoul National University** *(lei.snu.ac.kr)* are also well regarded.

Expats already living in Seoul can take free language classes at the **Seoul Global Center** *(global.seoul.go.kr)* and other government-run foreign-resident centres across the city.

check out architect Dominique Perrault's frankly cinematic Campus Center. In Hongdae, the **KT&G Sangsangmadang** *(sangsangmadang.com)* cultural space has a small theatre as well as art galleries and a fun shop selling quirky goods by Korean designers.

Sign Up for Some Makgeolli 101

MAP P105

Join a class or tasting

Makgeolli, an unrefined rice wine, is Korea's most unique alcoholic drink. Long dismissed as a farmer's brew, it's now treated with the same seriousness as beer or whisky, and craft *makgeolli* breweries have sprung up all over the country.

If you've developed a taste for the sweet, sour, slightly fizzy stuff, you can learn how to make your own at **Baekusaeng Makgeolli** *(baekusaeng.com)* in Ahyeon Market. The brewery offers one-day classes, three-day intensive courses and a class on making *nuruk*, a traditional fermentation starter. It also runs *makgeolli* and soju tasting sessions. If you don't have time for a full class, craft *makgeolli* brewer **Chowol** *(chowolhada.com)* offers short tasting sessions in its basement space near Mapo station.

A Waterfall in the City

MAP P102

Hike Ansan's mountain trails

A relatively easy climb, 296m **Ansan** is topped with a *bongsudae*, a beacon tower used to relay smoke signals during the Joseon dynasty. The mountain's numerous trails include the accessible Ansan Jarak-gil. On the northwest flank is

Eunpyeong Hanok Village

the **Yeonhui Forest Rest Area**, filled with flower beds, a herb garden and a babbling stream. From here, you might be able to hear the soothing sounds of the **Honjge-cheon Artificial Waterfall**, which pours off the mountain's base and into the Hongje Stream. Despite being artificial, it's quite lovely, with multiple cascades. Admire the scene from a small beach, a beanbag chair or the large **Cafe Pokpo** across the stream.

Hanok for the 21st Century

MAP P102

Stroll serene Eunpyeong Hanok Village

Way up in Seoul's northwest corner is **Eunpyeong Hanok Village**. Developed in the early 2010s, it's the city's largest neighbourhood of neo-*hanok*, two-storey structures that combine traditional materials and craftsmanship with modern technologies. The views of Bukhansan and the homes' tile roofs from **Irin Iljan**, a multistorey cafe at the village's entrance, are breathtaking – as close to a Joseon landscape as you'll get in Seoul.

To learn about *hanok* construction and local history, visit the adjacent **Eunpyeong Historical Hanok Museum** *(museum.ep.go.kr; adult/child ₩1000/500)*, closed Mondays, which touches on the area's past as a Joseon burial site as well as what was basically Joseon's version of the Pony Express. As you wander the village's charming streets, two more good places to drop in are the **Myeongin Museum**, which displays a collection of masks from around Asia and Africa, and **Solhyangjae**, a cultural space where you can partake in a tea tasting.

JINGWAN-SA

Near Eunpyeong Hanok Village is **Jingwan-sa** *(jinkwansa.org)*, one of Seoul's most prestigious Buddhist temples. It dates to at least the first years of the 11th century. During the Joseon dynasty, scholars studied the newly created *hangeul* alphabet here.

In 2009, temple repairs uncovered 19 copies of pro-independence newspapers wrapped in an old Korean flag, suggesting that Jingwan-sa served as a base for activists during the colonial period. Most of the complex was destroyed in a fire during the Korean War, but it's been beautifully rebuilt and enjoys a lovely setting in the Bukhansan foothills.

You can savour the atmosphere at a pleasant thatch-roofed teahouse, or take part in a three-hour Templestay program.

Southwestern Seoul

Southwestern Seoul is largely residential, though Yeouido is a major political and financial centre and there are several marquee attractions scattered among the apartments, including Seoul Botanic Park and the city's largest seafood market.

KOREAN PROTEST CULTURE

South Koreans are enthusiastic protesters, and odds are you'll come across a demonstration while you're in Seoul, whether it's a lone grievance-holder with a sign or a massive candlelight rally. The most common protest locations are Gwanghwamun Plaza, City Hall and the National Assembly Building.

Despite the yelling and the large police presence, today's protests are generally peaceful. Protests often feature musical performances and singalongs and, as seen during the mass demonstrations against President Yoon Suk-yeol's 2024 declaration of martial law, clever signs and K-Pop light sticks have become essential protest accessories. After the demonstration, it's common for protestors to clean up and pack out their rubbish.

An Island Embraced by Parks

Enjoy Yeouido's greenery

Yeouido, a large island in the Han River, is a curious mix of power and parkland. At its northwestern tip is the **National Assembly Building** *(assembly.go.kr)*, where the legislature determines Korea's course. Meanwhile, the interior is home to major financial institutions, the world's most-attended church and the headquarters of KBS, the national public broadcaster.

Despite all that muscle, it's parks that are Yeouido's main attraction. When the weather is nice, give yourself a few leisurely hours to explore them. **Yeouido Hangang Park** runs along the river for the full length of the island. There are public swimming pools, sports facilities and convenience stores for picnic supplies. Don't miss **Mulbit (Water Light) Sq**, where fountains and a shallow pool fill a vast plaza, and the droplet-shaped Waterlight Stage floats just offshore. The opposite side of the island is skirted by **Yeouido Saetgang Ecological Park**. Stroll the boardwalks and dirt paths that wend between trees and beds of cattails, spot herons and magpies and see how quickly you forget you're in the city.

Connecting these two parks down the island's middle is **Yeouido Park**. In 1916 the Imperial Japanese Army built Korea's first airport here, but today it's a pleasant collection of trees, ponds and open spaces. There are plans for a major performing arts centre to be built here in the coming years.

Get Out on the Water

Cruise the Han River

If you're keen to find out what Seoul looks like from the water, **E-Land Cruise** *(elandcruise.com)* operates an array of Han River pleasure cruises. Boats depart from a wharf just north of Wonhyo Bridge in Yeouido Hangang Park. Daytime, sunset and starlight cruises sail west to Seogang Bridge, passing Bamseom, an undeveloped island that's a bird sanctuary and Ramsar wetland. Longer moonlight cruises sail east to Banpo

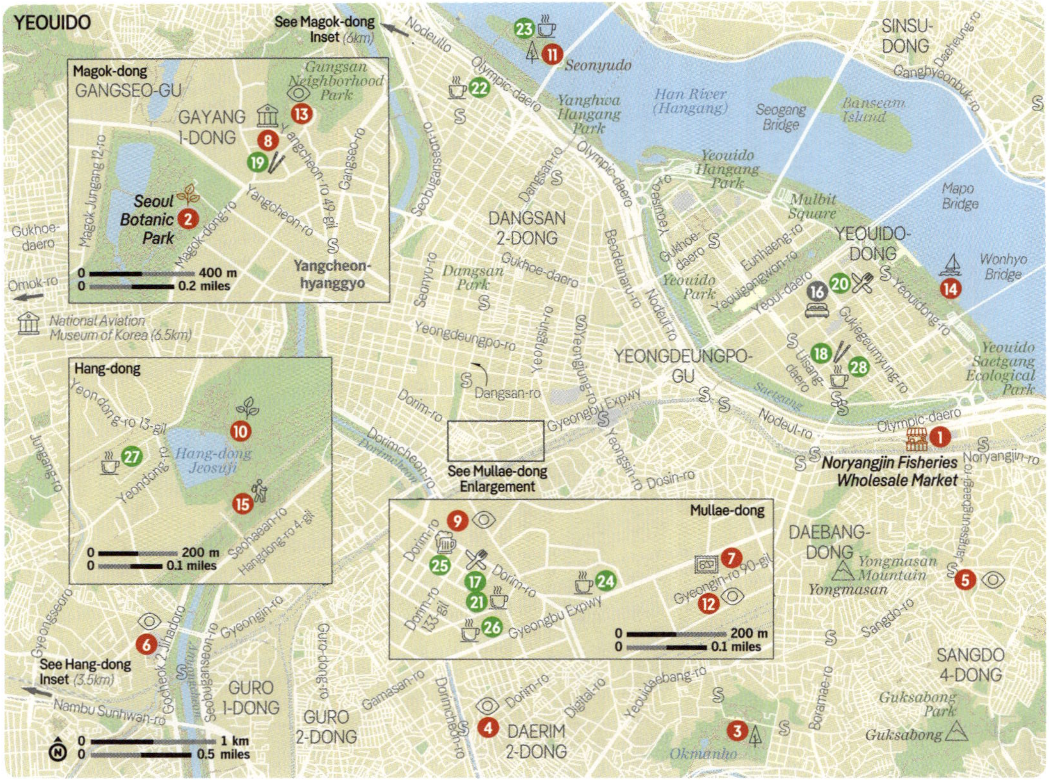

HIGHLIGHTS

1 Noryangjin Fisheries Wholesale Market

2 Seoul Botanic Park

SIGHTS

3 Boramae Park

4 Daerim-dong Chinatown

5 Dongjak District Office

6 Gocheok SkyDome

7 Gong Gan Tou

8 Gyeomjae Jeong Seon Art Museum

9 Mullae Arts Village

10 Pureun Arboretum

11 Seonyudo Park

12 Seoul Art Space Mullae

13 Yangcheon Hyanggyo

ACTIVITIES, COURSES & TOURS

14 E-Land Cruise

15 Hangdong Railroad Trail

SLEEPING

16 Conrad Seoul

EATING

see 1 Busan Ilbeonji

17 Gallery Mullae

18 Jinju House

19 Sogon Myeonok

20 The Hyundai Seoul

DRINKING & NIGHTLIFE

21 Baekya

22 Bright Size

23 Cafe Naru

24 Mullae Banggu

25 Old Mullae

26 Saintrust

27 Shelter

28 TFT Coffee Roasters

TAKE A SPIN AROUND YEOUIDO

Flat terrain and pretty parks make Yeouido perfect for cycling. Hop on two wheels to explore the island's architecture and green spaces.

START	END	LENGTH
National Assembly station, exit 3	KDB Bank Building	8 km; 1½ hrs

Grab a public Seoul Bike from the docking station outside National Assembly station, exit 3, and pedal in the direction of the domed 1 **National Assembly Building** (p112). Completed in 1975, it's open to foreign visitors who apply by email in advance. Soon after, you'll pass 2 **Yoido Full Gospel Church**, which boasts the largest congregation of any church in the world.

Briefly pop into Yeouido Park to take a pedestrian tunnel to 3 **Mulbit Sq** (p112), where kids splash in the fountains and shallow pool. Take your time pedalling through 4 **Yeouido Hangang Park** (p112), stopping to take in the river views or slurp up some convenience-store ramen when the mood strikes.

The golden, 249m-high 5 **63 Square** used to be Korea's tallest building. It now hosts a branch of France's Centre Pompidou. Around the island's corner is a traditional Turkish vineyard house in 6 **Jamae Park**, which celebrates Seoul's sister-city relationship with Ankara.

Cross the street and head into the beautiful 7 **Yeouido Saetgang Ecological Park** (p112), where you'll find reed beds, ponds and waterfowl. After heading back up to street level, cycle to 8 **Yeouido Park** (p112). Its trees, ponds and pavilions are a stark departure from the surrounding skyscrapers. When you're done, return your ride to the Seoul Bike docking station in front of the KDB Bank Building.

Bridge's Moonlight Rainbow Fountain (p152). Some cruises include dinner or live music and there are special seasonal cruises as well. You can book tickets in advance at the website, or simply purchase them at the wharf's ticket office.

A New Kind of Industrial Park

Witness Seonyudo's transformation

Seonyudo, an island in the Han River, has lived several lives. Once, Joseon poets admired the views from its 40m-high hill. In the early 1900s, that hill became a quarry. In the '70s, a water treatment plant was built here. Then, in the early 2000s, the island was turned into **Seonyudo Park**. Instead of being dismantled, however, the plant's infrastructure was incorporated into the park's award-winning design.

Set aside a couple of hours to explore the island, where a former chemical settling basin has been turned into a multilevel aquatic garden and other parts of the plant have been reborn as amphitheatres and play areas. The whole thing feels like what you might get if the postapocalypse was landscaped. To reach the island, walk across the footbridge north of Seonyudo station, disembark at the island's Seonyudo Park bus stop, or cycle across Yanghwa Bridge from one of the neighbouring stretches of Hangang Park.

Mullae's Creative Spark

See art and industry coexist

The area south of Mullae station seems an unlikely tourist destination at first blush. Machine shops line the streets, filling the air with clanking and the acrid smell of hot metal. But dive into the alleys and you'll find yourself in **Mullae Arts Village**, where, beginning in 2003, young creatives have transformed empty factories into visual-art studios. South of Dorim-ro, in particular, you'll come across numerous small galleries, ateliers, watering holes and restaurants serving everything from traditional Korean to upmarket Italian.

It's a photogenic neighbourhood where street art abounds, so take your time poking around. Come on a weekday when the machinists are at work to get the full industrial-artistic experience, or show up at night, or on a weekend, to see the artworks on closed shop doors on display.

TOP SECRET SPOTS

This Southwestern part of town sees relatively few tourists, but it has some great niche attractions.

Yangcheon Hyanggyo: Dating to 1411, this quiet complex is Seoul's only remaining *hyanggyo*, a Joseon-era Confucian academy.

Daerim-dong Chinatown: The neighbourhood around Daerim station is home to a large Chinese population, with some of Seoul's best Chinese food.

Dongjak District Office: In 2025, the office unveiled a twisting three-storey slide called the D-Lide. Who says bureaucrats don't know how to have fun?

Boramae Park: On the former site of the Korean Air Force Academy, displaying decommissioned fighter jets, supply planes and a helicopter.

Gocheok SkyDome: If the game at Jamsil Baseball Stadium is rained out, you can still watch the Kiwoom Heroes play at their domed park.

CAFES IN SOUTHWESTERN SEOUL: OUR PICKS

TFT Coffee Roasters: Order an Iceberg, the cafe's signature take on an Einspänner, available in plain or chocolate. *7am-9pm Mon-Fri, 10am-7pm Sat & Sun*

Cafe Naru: This Seonyudo cafe has great views over the Han River. Also serves food such as pizza and fries. *10am-7.30pm Mon-Fri, to 9pm Sat & Sun*

Bright Size: On the way from Seonyudo station to the island, this tidy cafe does hand drips and refreshing fruit ades. *7am-7pm Mon-Fri, from 9am Sat*

Shelter: A good place to pick up a coffee before exploring Pureun Arboretum or the Hangdong Railroad Trail. *8am-3pm Tue, Wed & Sun, to 8pm Thu-Sat*

TOP EXPERIENCE

Noryangjin Fisheries Wholesale Market

Seoul's largest seafood market, Noryangjin Fisheries Wholesale Market, opened in 1927 and has occupied its current building since 2016. Some 300 tonnes of marine products pass through here every day, amounting to half of all the capital's seafood. Explore around 700 stalls to encounter unusual sea creatures, tuck into the freshest fish in the city and stick around for the spectacle of late-night auctions.

MARIUSZ_PRUSACZYK/GETTY IMAGES

Noryangjin Fisheries Wholesale Market

TOP TIPS

- As a wet market, Noryangjin is, well, wet. Wear close-toed shoes and clothes that can withstand the errant splash or two.
- You'll find more upscale restaurants on Noryangjin's 5th floor.
- Cross the 3rd-floor car park to find a deck with killer views of the golden 63 Square (p114) building.

PRACTICALITIES

- *susansijang.co.kr*
- free
- 24hr

Market Stalls

Noryangjin's stalls are spread across the building's 1st and 2nd floors. Wander the aisles to see crabs stacked like Frisbees, ribbony silver cutlass fish and rubber-booted fishmongers displaying some serious knife skills. It's fine to gawk and take pictures – vendors are used to it – but stay aware of your surroundings. The place is a hive of activity, with workers scooping fish out of tanks and rolling dollies through the aisles. For the liveliest action, come between midnight and 3am Monday to Saturday, when the fish auctions are held.

Eating at Noryangjin

For the full market experience, pick out a fish and eat it at one of the 2nd-floor restaurants. Haggling is expected at stalls, so have a calculator app at the ready. Many vendors partner with specific restaurants, in which case someone will lead you to the appropriate establishment. The most typical preparations include *hoe* (sashimi) and *maeuntang* (spicy fish soup). If you don't know where to start in the market, some restaurants, such as **Busan Ilbeonji**, can help with interpretation, or you can just order off a restaurant's menu. You can also buy presliced sashimi platters at many stalls. Feeling adventurous? Try *gaebul* (penis fish, a type of spoon worm), *san-nakji* (sliced live octopus) or *hongeo* (fermented skate). Just be warned: there are no refunds.

Be sure to drop by the small **Gong Gan Tou** *(gongcraft.net)* and **Seoul Art Space Mullae** *(sfac.or.kr)* to see what's showing in their galleries.

A Locals-Only Green Space

An arboretum and railroad trail

In Seoul's far southwestern corner, **Pureun Arboretum** makes for a pleasant place to decompress. The city's first municipal arboretum has a cafe, walking paths, several themed gardens, a pond and flower beds. It also provides a habitat for frogs, kingfishers and little grebes. Join the local dog walkers and retired couples enjoying the scene; you'll probably be the only non-local there. Running past the arboretum's south side is the **Hangdong Railroad Trail**, a walking path along an old railroad bed. It runs for 4.5km and connects to Cheonwang station.

A True View of Joseon Art

See Jeong Seon's influential paintings

Korea's most important painter was arguably 'Gyeomjae' Jeong Seon, who was born into an aristocratic Seoul family in 1676. He pioneered Jingyeong, or 'true-view' landscape painting, a style that influenced generations of Korean artists. Located where Jeong Seon once served as a government magistrate, the **Gyeomjae Jeong Seon Art Museum** *(adult/child ₩1000/500)* is dedicated to his legacy and his bewitching depictions of the country's natural scenery, often produced in a stark, nearly colourless palette.

The museum displays some original paintings, but the majority are reprints of works in the collections of major institutions such as the **National Museum of Korea** (p124) and the **Leeum Museum of Art** (p136). Most likely, you've also got a reprint in your pocket – before you hand over your ₩1000 note for your entry ticket, flip it over. That's Jeong Seon's painting *Secluded Life over a Creek* on the back.

Up, Up & Away

Discover Korea's aviation history

Located next to Gimpo Airport, the **National Aviation Museum of Korea** *(aviation.or.kr)* glides through Korea's history of flight, from the establishment of the country's first flight school to its current cutting-edge experiments with air taxis

WHY I LOVE WESTERN SEOUL

Charles Usher, Lonely Planet writer

Every weekend during the first year I lived in Korea, I'd make the 90-minute trip from the small village in which I lived to Hongdae to careen from barbecue joint to bar to music venue until the morning, when buses started running again.

I'm too old for that now, but whenever I'm back in Seoul, I find myself drawn to this side of the city, pulled in by Hongdae's inexhaustible energy, by Mullae's blend of the blue collar and the artistic and by my need to see what's new in indie-inflected neighbourhoods such as Yeonnam and Mangwon. These places always make me feel young, and they'll likely have the same effect on you – maybe even enough to keep you out until the sun comes up.

DRINKING IN MULLAE ARTS VILLAGE: TOP PICKS

Saintrust: On the eighth day, God created dessert. Probably. Prayers for good coffee and sweets are answered at this cafe with church-inspired design. *noon-10pm*

Mullae Banggu: Near Seoul Art Space Mullae, this little cafe also sells fun stationery and home goods by local designers. *11.30am-6pm Mon-Fri, noon-8pm Sat & Sun*

Baekya: Enjoy coffee and cake or a glass of chardonnay on the rooftop terrace. Sometimes has DJs spinning vinyl. *2-11pm Mon-Fri, 1-9.30pm Sat & Sun*

Old Mullae: Brewpub with beer from several of Korea's most popular craft breweries on tap, including Magpie, Artmonster and Galmegi. *noon-midnight, to 1am Fri & Sat*

TOP EXPERIENCE

Seoul Botanic Park

Despite its address, Seoul Botanic Park feels worlds away from the capital's congestion. Opened in 2019, it includes a massive greenhouse, a botanic garden, a wetland and plenty of green space, all spread across more than 48 hectares. Go on a round-the-world horticultural journey, picnic on the shores of its artificial lake, or just stop and smell the roses, more than 20 varieties of which grow here.

AHEWER/SHUTTERSTOCK

Seoul Botanic Park

TOP TIPS

- The greenhouse and botanic garden require paid admission, but the Forest Field, Lake Garden and Wetland sections are free and always open.
- The greenhouse is quite warm, so if you're visiting in winter, use one of the on-site lockers to store your coat.

Greenhouse & Botanic Center

Claiming to be the world's only such facility with a concave roof, the park's greenhouse is divided into tropical and Mediterranean zones. In the former, you'll see plants from Southeast Asia and South America as you stroll along a skywalk that takes you into the canopy. The latter includes specimens from destinations as diverse as Italy, Uzbekistan and Australia. Listen to the audio guide and Bao Bao, the greenhouse's resident alien, will chaperone you through the exhibits. Connected to the greenhouse is the Botanic Center, which has a rooftop garden and a large library of gardening and horticulture books.

Botanic Gardens

Outside, wander through eight themed gardens. Among these are a traditional Korean garden, a garden composed of reeds and silver grass, a space devoted to garden designers and a garden displaying plants used as folk remedies. Trails connect to a park with picnic-ready grass lawns, a research greenhouse, an artificial lake with wooden walkways and iris beds, and a wetland by the Han River. On your way to the wetland, you'll pass **Magok Cultural Hall**, a drainage pump station that was built in 1928 and now hosts art exhibitions.

PRACTICALITIES

- *botanicpark.seoul.go.kr*
- adult/student/child ₩5000/3000/2000
- 9.30am-6pm Mar-Oct, to 5pm Nov-Feb

SANGA PARK/SHUTTERSTOCK

Pureun Arboretum (p117)

and hydrogen-powered aircraft. There are lots of planes on display and some fun exhibits that take you behind the scenes of how an airport operates.

You can also take part in simulation experiences – from flight-crew training to piloting a plane – which you can reserve online. (The Black Eagles aerobatic VR experience can only be booked in person.) There's also an airport experience programme just for kids. The museum is closed on Mondays.

KOREAN PAINTERS TO KNOW

If Jeong Seon's works have piqued your interest in Korean painting, check out these other artists.

Kim Hong-do & Sin Yun-bok: These Joseon-era painters were masters of the everyday, depicting farmers, wrestlers and tavern patrons, often in a humorous light.

Lee Jung-seob: A major 20th-century artist, Lee was known for his paintings of cattle and kinetic human figures.

Kim Whanki & Lee Ufan: Separated by two decades, both pioneered abstract art and Korea's monochromatic Dansaekhwa movement.

Chun Kyung-ja: Working in the colourful tradition of *chaesaekhwa* painting, Chun is best known for her arresting portraits of women.

Hejum Bä & Hun Kyu Kim: Bä's vivid, abstract works and Kim's intricate canvases make them up-and-coming artists to know.

EATING IN WESTERN SEOUL: TERRIFIC TASTES

Sogon Myeonok: Presses its own sesame oil and mills the buckwheat for its delicious *naengmyeon* (cold noodles) on site. *11am-3pm & 4.30-9.30pm* ₩₩

Gallery Mullae: Tucked down a small alley, this Italian restaurant doubles as a live-music venue for local indie acts. *11am-midnight* ₩₩

Jinju House: Basement place famous for its *kongguksu* (noodles in chilled soybean broth). Packed with office workers at lunch. *10am-8pm Mon-Fri, to 7pm Sat* ₩₩

The Hyundai Seoul: This posh department store has a terrific food court, with Korean, Chinese, Japanese and Western offerings. *10.30am-8pm* ₩₩

Researched by Ann Babe

ITAEWON & YONGSAN-GU

TOP MUSEUMS, MULTICULTURAL VIBE, VIBRANT NIGHTLIFE

A multicultural restaurant scene, with a dynamism that extends to nightlife, arts, entertainment and beyond, makes Itaewon and Yongsan-gu the city's ultimate area of diversity.

Home to the city's most vibrant LGBTIQ+ scene and largest Muslim community, Itaewon has long been an international centre of Seoul. The broader Yongsan district is dominated by the huge Yongsan Park, nestled around the country's No 1 museum, the National Museum of Korea, and the former US Army Garrison, which is in the process of opening up to the public as part of a project to revitalise the green space. Itaewon's neighbourhood of Gyeongnidan and adjacent Haebangchon (HBC for short) are diverse enclaves of laid-back restaurants, bars and cafes, while eastward, ultra-bougie Hannam-dong is the preferred neighbourhood of many a celebrity Seoulite. Over by Yongsan station is another hip pocket, Hangangno-dong.

TIP

For Yongsan-gu's best riverside sunset-watching, walk halfway across Hangang Bridge to Nodeul Island – its west end looks out onto the skyscrapers of Yeouido.

Gyeongnidan (p133)

See page 216 for places to stay in Itaewon & Yongsan-gu

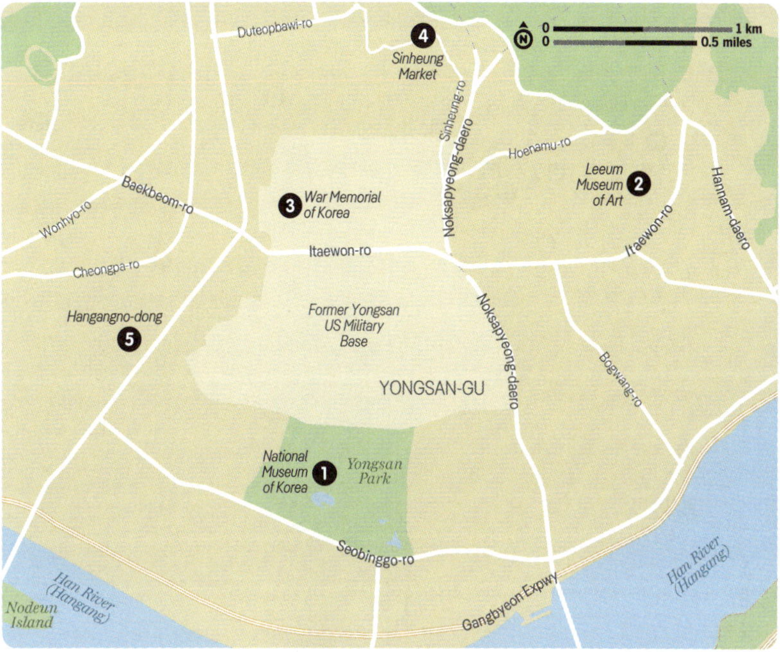

Highlights

❶ National Museum of Korea

Survey centuries of Korean culture, history and art at the country's most visited museum. **p124**

▶❷ Leeum Museum of Art

Admire contemporary showstoppers and Korean classics in an architecturally stunning space. **p136**

❸ War Memorial of Korea

Learn about the military history of Korea, including an unresolved conflict. **p128**

❹ Sinheung Market

Eat, drink and be merry in a one-time textiles centre turned buzzy back-alley dining district. **p131**

❺ Hangangno-dong

Feel the newtro vibes in a historic railway centre brimming with restaurants, bars and shops. **p137**

Getting Around

Subway

Use line 6 to access Haebangchon, Itaewon and Hannamdong. For the War Memorial of Korea and Yongnidan-gil, get off at Samgakji; also transfer here to line 4 for the National Museum of Korea.

Walking

Be prepared to hoof it to explore all the hilly alleys of Haebangchon and Gyeongnidan.

Bus

The green mini village buses can be handy for visiting the main streets of Haebangchon and Gyeongnidan-gil, to expedite the walk to and from Noksapyeong station.

SIGHTS
1 Itaewon Antique Furniture Street
2 Itaewon Bugundang History Park
3 P21
4 Whistle

SLEEPING
5 G Guesthouse Itaewon
6 H Hostel Itaewon
7 Seoul Cube Itaewon

EATING
8 ALT.a
9 Braai Republic
10 Burger Snack
11 byTOFU
12 Casablanca Sandwicherie
13 Comme Moa
14 Crispy Pork Town
15 Egg & Flour
16 EID
17 Ginn-Laoo
18 Gino's NY Pizza
19 Hemian Brunch Bar
20 Honfleur
21 Lazzat
22 Linus' BBQ
23 LOCOS BBQ
24 Morococo Cafe
25 Normal Brunch
26 Pad Kapaw
27 Petra Palace
28 Plant Cafe & Kitchen
29 Rocka Doodle
30 Spoonery
31 Sunday Arvo
32 The Baker's Table
33 The States
34 Troika
35 Vegetus
36 XOLO Pub Mexicano
37 Ya Shanghai

DRINKING & NIGHTLIFE
38 Blacklist
39 Booth
40 Burn
41 Cafe TRVR
see 38 Cakeshop
42 CrownB Bar
43 Dank Yard
44 DRESSER
45 Faust / Tanz Bar
46 Fountain
47 Gil Bar Dak
see 38 hype
48 Jazz Garage
49 Karma
50 Kenya Kiambu Coffee
51 Kockiri
see 12 Le Cafe
see 38 Lit Lounge
see 32 Magpie Brewshop
52 Mr Ahn's Craft Makgeolli
53 Namsan Sool Club
54 Pet Sounds
55 Queen
56 Rabbithole Arcade Pub
57 Social Haven
58 Southside Parlor
59 Sunset Beach
see 34 The Craic House
60 Tiger Espresso
61 Trance
62 Ugly Society
63 Vin Vin
64 Why Not
65 Woori Super
66 Y.Pot Coffee

ENTERTAINMENT
see 54 Boogie Woogie

SHOPPING
67 Cat Allergy
68 Graphic
69 Woori Bookstore

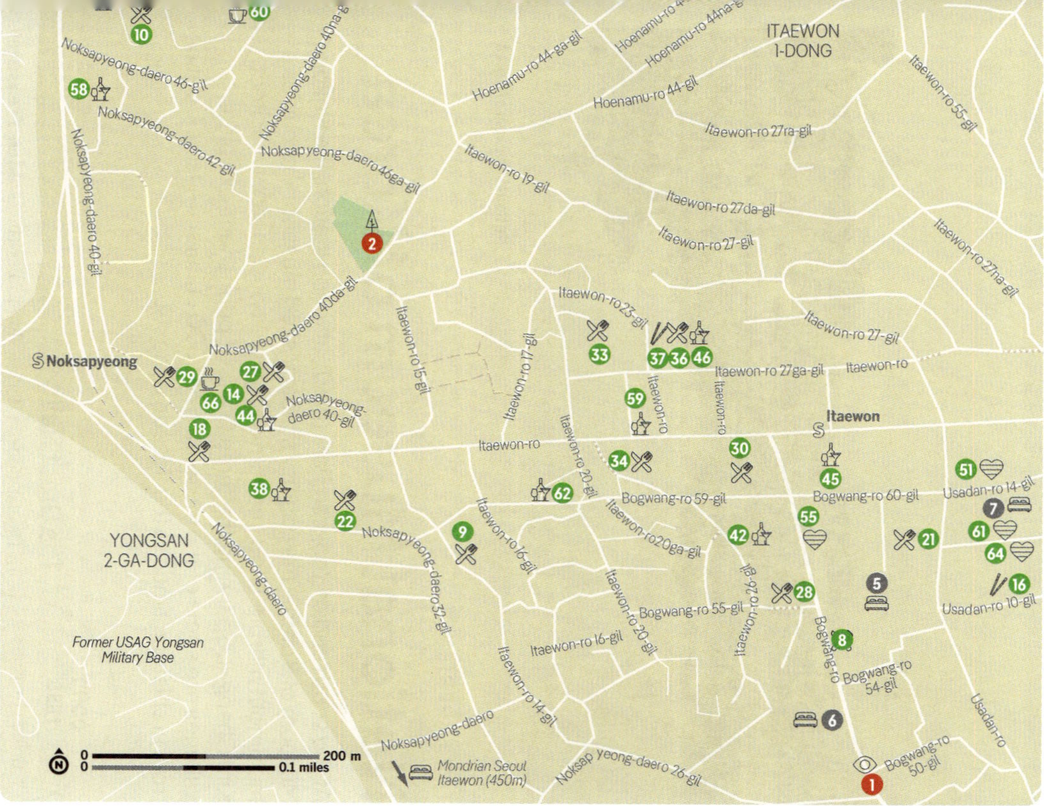

© KOREA TOURISM ORGANIZATION - CHOI RIN

National Museum of Korea

TOP EXPERIENCE

National Museum of Korea

At the south end of Yongsan Park (p130), at Ichon station, the National Museum of Korea – the country's most visited museum – occupies a mammoth marble-lined, modernist complex designed by architect Kim Chang-il. Spanning the three floors of permanent-exhibition galleries are some of the museum's 270,000 cultural treasures, dating from prehistoric times to the Joseon dynasty.

DON'T MISS

- Golden Treasures from the Great Tomb of Hwangnam
- Baekje Incense Burner
- Ten Storey Pagoda
- Pensive Bodhisattva
- Mirror Pond
- Bosingak Bell
- Dragon Falls

The Great Hall

In the 1st-floor galleries, don't miss the **Golden Treasures from the Great Tomb of Hwangnam**, a delicate 5th-century Silla Kingdom gold crown and belt dripping with jade gems; the **Baekje Incense Burner**, a decorative metal piece that's an extraordinary example of the artistry of the 6th- to 7th-century Baekje Kingdom; and the Goryeo-dynasty **Ten Storey Pagoda**, carved out of marble, from the one-time Gyeongcheon Temple in Gyeonggi Province.

PRACTICALITIES

- *museum.go.kr*
- free
- 10am-6pm, to 9pm Wed & Sat

On the 2nd floor, the Room of Quiet Contemplation contains the 7th-century **Pensive Bodhisattva**. In the 3rd-floor sculpture and crafts gallery, view the lopsided beauty of the 18th-century **Moon Jar**, a white porcelain vessel from the Joseon dynasty. There are also several immersive digital galleries where you can see projections of paintings and 3D renderings of cultural artefacts. Virtual-reality experiences in Digital Gallery 2 require advance registration.

Hour-long English-language tours leave from the lobby at 10.30am and 1pm daily. The museum's app serves as an excellent audio guide.

Food and drink options can be found on all three levels, with a food court, restaurant and cafe on the 1st floor, a cafe on the 2nd floor and a tearoom on the 3rd floor. There are three gift shops selling a nice selection of Korean souvenirs.

Special Exhibition Hall & Children's Museum

At the **Special Exhibition Hall** *(price varies by exhibition)*, two galleries host blockbuster shows on anything from Impressionist painting and Viennese art to East Asian lacquerware and Buddhist art. There's also a theatre for special performances, including musicals, plays and *pansori* (a type of musical storytelling).

At the free but reservation-only **Children's Museum**, there are plenty of hands-on features and play areas that let kids interact with artefacts. Register online for one of five daily sessions.

Museum Grounds

Outside, the surrounding grounds are best appreciated in clear conditions, when the Great Hall is perfectly reflected in the large **Mirror Pond** to the south and the short-lived Presidential Office is visible from the museum deck looking north. On the grounds is an outdoor exhibition area showcasing pagodas, stupas, steles and other ancient stoneworks, such as a twin lion stone lantern from the Goryeo dynasty. The highlight of the outdoor exhibitions is the original **Bosingak Bell**, located near the picturesque **Dragon Falls**. There's also a pavilion and gardens.

On the southeast corner of the grounds is the temporarily closed **National Hangeul Museum** *(hangeul.go.kr)*, scheduled to reopen in October 2028 after it undergoes repairs from fire damage. The museum, which celebrates Hunminjeongeum (the book explaining the principles of *hangeul*), was already undergoing a planned expansion in 2025 when the fire sparked and spread across the entire 3rd-floor ceiling. Fire-extinguishment efforts partially flooded a storage facility, leading to the transfer of more than 25,000 items to the National Museum, as well as the National Folk Museum of Korea and the National Museum of World Writing Systems in Incheon. The National Hangeul Museum continues to hold exhibitions and educational programmes at other venues across the city. Check its website for event details.

BOSINGAK BELL

Cast in 1468 at Wongak-sa, the temple formerly at **Tapgol Park** (p68), this 3.18m-tall, 2.28m-wide bronze bell weighing 17.8 tonnes was first moved to Myeong-dong and then to Jongno-gu. Housed in the Bosingak Pavilion, it was used to tell time, announce curfew and sound the alarm for fires.

It rang in the New Year until 1985, when it was replaced by a replica and relocated to the National Museum for preservation.

TOP TIPS

- The National Museum of Korea is one of the best in the country for accessibility. It has barrier-free smart galleries featuring height-adjustable AI kiosks with 3D avatars that can interact with visitors through voice, sign language and braille. Wheelchairs are offered free of charge.
- Special exhibits are half-price on Culture Day, the last Wednesday of the month.
- Free coat check, strollers and storage lockers are available.
- For picnic snacks in the park, there's a convenience store and cafe near the main entrance.

FOREIGNERS IN KOREA

Korea is a mono-cultural society. The number of foreigners, or *waegukin*, living in the country has reached an all-time high, with government data putting it at 2.73 million as of 2025; that amounts to just over 5% of the country's population.

These foreigners are here as international students, workers and marriage visa holders, and most are from China, Vietnam, the USA, Thailand and Uzbekistan. This includes ethnic Koreans with foreign citizenship like Joseonjok (Korean Chinese) and adopted Koreans. More than half live in the Greater Seoul Area, which includes Incheon and Gyeonggi Province.

While Seoul has the highest number of foreigners in a city, Ansan, in Gyeonggi-do, has the highest concentration.

Eat Your Way Through Itaewon

MAP P122

A round-the-world culinary adventure

Seoul's most internationally diverse district delivers with its copious bounty of cuisines from all over the world. Latin, Southeast Asian, European, Middle Eastern and North African – all these and more can be found here, with more than a few only-in-Korea fusion surprises among them. So loosen your belt and get excited! One block north of the main street, Itaewon-ro, you'll spot everything from Irish, British and American-style pubs to Indian eateries, Mexican restaurants and Turkish kebab stalls.

Stop at **XOLO Pub Mexicano** for tacos and *birria ramyeon*, **Ya Shanghai** for *mapo tofu* and dim sum, or **The States**, an Americana-themed diner-bar serving 'calorie buckets', 'protein monsters' and cocktails named after states in an interior so gaudy it's good. The south side of Itaewon-ro is where you'll find **Linus' BBQ** for delicious pulled-pork and brisket platters, Russian restaurant **Troika** right above Irish pub **The Craic House**, **Braai Republic** for South African meat pies, an amazing array of Muslim restaurants clustered around **Seoul Central Mosque** (p129) and a plethora of Vietnamese eateries around Quy Nhon St.

Revel in Itaewon's Nightlife

MAP P122

Party 'til the sun comes up

Itaewon is a top location for late-night drinking and clubbing. The lights are kept low at **Lit Lounge**, a hookah lounge known for its inclusive atmosphere and approachable staff. It's also great for dancing.

Cakeshop, a small club with a huge reputation, has been a mainstay of Itaewon's club scene for a decade. Listen to new and niche genres, as well as visiting international acts.

Entertainment complex **Fountain** offers a dance floor on the 1st level that plays top-40 music, bar games on the 2nd and a VIP lounge on the 3rd. It gets packed at peak hours.

For full-on techno, head to **Faust / Tanz Bar**, where the mood is welcoming and the party goes very, very late.

EATING IN YONGSAN-GU: INTERNATIONAL CUISINES

MAP P122

Comme Moa: In Haebangchon, with Michelin-recommended French fare like duck-leg confit and stuffed quail. *6-10pm Mon-Fri, noon-3pm & 6-11pm Sat & Sun* ₩₩₩

Crispy Pork Town: Tacos and quesadillas served in a colourful, casual setting. *noon-3pm & 5-10pm Tue-Sun* ₩₩

Morococo Cafe: Spice-scented spot serving a small menu of dishes like chicken with preserved lemon and the must-try 'Morocco Over Rice'. *noon-10pm Tue-Sun* ₩₩

Youhan: Chef Kim Yu-han, who trained in Thailand, brings Thai flavours to Hannam-dong. Try the house-made sausage. *6pm-midnight Tue-Fri, 2-9pm Sat & Sun* ₩₩₩

Petra Palace: Stop at this blink-and-you-miss-it joint for fresh, vibrant Middle Eastern dishes like tabouli, kebab and falafel. *11am-8pm Thu-Tue* ₩₩

Chakra: Authentic Indian food in Hannam-dong, with a welcoming atmosphere and delicious curries, biryani and more. *11.30am-4pm & 5-10pm* ₩₩

Egg & Flour: Bib Gourmand Italian with a prime Namsan view. The freshly made pasta is on point. *noon-3pm & 5-10pm* ₩₩₩

Casablanca Sandwicherie: By the same crew as Morococo, half loaves of bread filled with chicken, lamb, chilli and other fillings. *noon-10pm Tue-Sun* ₩

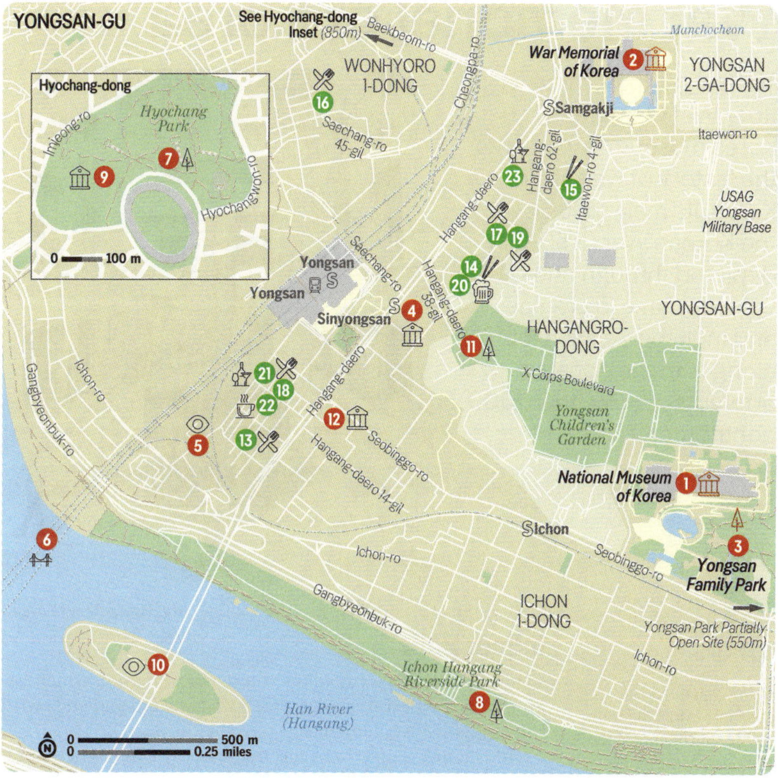

HIGHLIGHTS

1 National Museum of Korea
2 War Memorial of Korea
3 Yongsan Family Park

SIGHTS

4 Amorepacific Museum of Art
5 Baekbin Railroad Crossing
6 Hangang Railway Bridge
7 Hyochang Park
8 Ichon Hangang Park
9 Kim Koo Museum
10 Nodeul Island
11 Yongsan Children's Garden
12 Yongsan History Museum

EATING

13 Ferments
see 13 Hi Thai
14 Neungdong Minari
15 Oilje
16 Plantude
17 Sam Sam Sam
18 Shawnino
19 Teddy Beurre House

DRINKING & NIGHTLIFE

20 Hand and Malt Brewlab
21 Hay Coffee and Bar
22 Pont Coffee
see 17 Tangled Cassette
23 VIBD BLVD

TOP EXPERIENCE

War Memorial of Korea

The gargantuan, three-floor War Memorial of Korea museum documents the history of warfare in Korea. Its main focus is the Korean War (1950–53), depicted through photos, video footage, dioramas and multimedia exhibits, along with the donated artefacts of more than 1000 contributors.

War Memorial of Korea

TOP TIPS

- You will need your passport to join the free daily English tours of the 2nd floor. Tours of the Korean War Room 1 depart at 10am and 2pm, and those of the Korean War Room 2 at 10.30am and 2.30pm.
- Free lockers are available.

Indoor Halls

The main entranceway takes you to the 2nd floor, which begins with North Korea's surprise 4am invasion and ends with the Armistice Agreement.

On the 3rd floor, there are exhibits on UN participation and a reproduction of the UN Memorial Cemetery in Busan. Other displays cover Korea's involvement in the Vietnam War, North Korean attacks on the South since 1953 and Korea's UN peacekeeping roles.

On the 1st floor, war history rooms depict ancient battles fought against invading Mongol, Japanese and Chinese armies. There is also a replica of one of Admiral Yi Sun-sin's famous iron-clad turtle warships (called *geobukseon*), which he used to defeat the Japanese navy in the 1590s.

Outdoor Exhibits

The outdoor exhibition area includes more than 150 tanks, helicopters, missiles and planes, including a huge B-52 bomber. Several stirring monuments symbolising Koreans' hopes for reunification include the 11m-high **Statue of Brothers**, which portrays the true tale of two brothers who fought on opposite sides of the war and met in battle.

There's also a **Children's Museum**, presenting the history of war in Korea with an introduction to national war heroes of old.

PRACTICALITIES

- *warmemo.or.kr*
- free
- 9.30am-6pm Tue-Sun

See Seoul's Little Arabia

MAP P132

Learn about the city's Islamic community

With its twin minarets rising high above 'Halal Hill', Seoul's only mosque anchors the city's Islamic community, standing at the centre of its many Arabic restaurants, food marts and other businesses below. Open to worshippers and visitors, the **Seoul Central Mosque**, established in 1976, houses the Korean Muslim Association office on the 1st floor, the men's prayer hall on the 2nd floor and the women's prayer hall on the 3rd floor. In addition to being a place of worship, the mosque aims to educate Korea's broader public, less than 1% of whom are Muslim, mostly immigrants.

Stop at the mosque (remember to wear modest clothes), then enjoy a hearty halal lunch nearby. Two recommended options: **EID** for Korean classics made halal, and **Lazzat** for halal Uzbek and Central Asian fare.

Treasure Hunt on Antique Street

MAP P122

Shop for heirlooms and other delights

A 1km stretch along Bogwang-ro and Noksapyeong-daero has been a go-to destination in Seoul for antique furniture, vintage dishes, paintings, light fixtures, curios and other home decor since the 1990s. Among the dozens of stores around **Itaewon Antique Furniture Street**, some standouts include Shim's Antique, Queens Antique, Vintage More, Daedong Antiques and Notting Hill.

Books & Beats

MAP P132

A literary, musical smorgasbord

Take a peek at **Book Park**, a beautiful multilevel reading lounge inside the cultural space **Blue Square** *(bluesquare.kr)*. For the price of entry (₩9900), you can browse and read a curated selection of books and enjoy a drink from their cafe. Also part of Blue Square are a theatre and concert hall, which host big-time musicals and shows like *Wicked*. Check the schedule ahead.

BEST LGBTIQ+ SPOTS

Lesvos: Since 1996, this lesbian bar has been a safe space for sexual minorities and women in Korea.

Rabbithole Arcade Pub: Located in Haebangchon, this basement venue offers weekly drag shows and a welcoming vibe.

Kockiri: A hip gay bar that plays disco and caters to a diverse clientele. A plus is its beautiful terrace.

Why Not: The perfect place to begin the night before hitting the clubs next door. Known for being foreigner-friendly.

Trance: Famed for its late-night drag shows, this small basement club has been a scene staple for almost three decades.

Queen: In a new location and popular among foreigners for its fun atmosphere that doesn't really get going until 2am.

DRINKING IN ITAEWON: COCKTAIL BARS

MAP P122

Southside Parlor: A pioneer of Seoul's cocktail scene. Check out its new sister bar downstairs. *6pm-midnight Sun & Tue-Thu, to 2am Fri & Sat*	**Blacklist:** Head to the 3rd floor and try an old fashioned, martini or other top-shelf cocktail, and food from the late-night charcuterie menu. *6pm-2am*	**DRESSER:** An upscale cocktail bar with an interior that recalls Victorian England. *6pm-2am Wed-Mon*	**Ugly Society:** Weird and delightful; a rooftop joint serving up strong drinks and a nice view of the surrounding area. *5pm-1am*
CrownB Bar: Lit by a mix of chandeliers and neon, this eclectic watering hole features an open-air bar. *7pm-2am Sun & Tue-Thu, to 4am Fri & Sat*	**Social Haven:** A mainstay of the HBC expat community, this bar specialising in Aperol spritz gets crowded after aperitif time. *6pm-2am Mon-Fri, 4pm-3am Sat, to 2am Sun*	**Sunset Beach:** There's no sunset and there's no beach, but this tiny alleyway bar offers an island of respite in Itaewon's heart. *7pm-2am Sun-Thu, to 4am Fri & Sat*	**hype:** A rooftop hookah bar with a wide variety of flavours on offer, set in a chill R&B hip-hop ambience. *7pm-1am Tue-Thu, 6pm-3am Fri, 7pm-3am Sat, 6pm-1am Sun*

TOP EXPERIENCE

Yongsan Park

The Yongsan Park area has long been mostly under the control of foreign hands, first by the Japanese and then by the Americans, with the former army garrison occupying a sizeable chunk. In a drawn-out affair, Yongsan, or 'Dragon Hill', is slowly being transferred back to Korea, as the city expands and revitalises the park to open up formerly closed-off spaces to the public.

OLIVIA JUNG/SHUTTERSTOCK

Yongsan Family Park

Lay of the Land

This huge green space is only partly accessible, with many areas still barricaded. Across from the War Memorial of Korea stands the old Defence Ministry compound that, from 2022 to 2025, served as the Presidential Office.

To the south, surrounding the National Museum of Korea, is a swathe of public parkland. **Yongsan Family Park** is the site of sculptures, picnic pavilions, a barefoot walking path (store your shoes in the rack) and the Taegeukgi (Korean Flag) Memorial, while **Yongsan Children's Garden** features sports fields, play centres and cafes.

Former Officers' Quarters

Around Yongsan Children's Garden and at the **Partially Open Site**, in the southeast corner of the park, you can see the former 5th residential complex of the US military. The area resembles a little America and offers a fascinating glimpse into a long-secretive space. Take a look inside the officers' quarters, which display exhibitions and art, and have a coffee at the cafe.

In 2018, Yongsan Garrison was relocated to Camp Humphreys in Pyeongtaek, setting the stage for the garrison's partial reopening – the first time in 120 years the site was accessible to the Korean public. So far, less than half of the garrison's approximate 2.43 million sq metres have been returned.

TOP TIPS

- Different parts are best accessed by different subway stations – Seobinggo for the Partially Open Site, Ichon for Yongsan Family Park and Sinyongsan for Yongsan Children's Garden.
- The Children's Garden requires registration 11 days in advance for foreigners *(yongsanparkstory.kr)*.

PRACTICALITIES

- *parkyongsan.kr*
- free
- Partially Open Site 9am-6pm Tue-Sun, Children's Garden 9am-6pm Tue-Sun (to 9pm Sat)

Down the street, the Hyundai Card Music Library and its adjacent warehouse-sized music store, **Vinyl & Plastic**, offer a relaxing ambience for sitting back and listening to your pick of LPs. Their enormous collections – more than 10,000 records spanning many genres – range from Korean hip-hop and pop classics to rarer gems.

Honour Korea's Liberation Activists

MAP P127

A visit to Hyochang Park

Learn about Korea's liberation movement and one of its most well-known activists, Kim Koo, the one-time president of the Korean Provisional Government in Shanghai. Set in **Hyochang Park**, the two-storey **Kim Koo Museum** *(kimkoomuseum.org; free)* includes exhibitions about his humble origins, rise to prominence and assassination, and showcases his personal artefacts with a view onto his burial site outside. Also on the park premises are the burial sites of Koo's compatriots Lee Bong-chang, Yun Bong-gil and Baek Jeong-gi, known as the **Graves of the Three Martyrs**, plus there's an empty grave for Ahn Jung-geun, whose remains have yet to be found.

Walking the trails of the park, designated as a cultural heritage site, makes for a scenic stroll past Korea's first international soccer stadium, various sports facilities and verdant gardens. Originally a cemetery for the Korean royal family, Hyochang Park was turned into a golf course by the Japanese – who first left the tombs in the line of play, then later moved them to Gyeonggi Province – before it was made into a memorial for Korean independence activists in 1946 after liberation.

Explore the Alleys of Sinheung Market

MAP P122

Dinner and drinks in a revived cultural space

In the back streets of hilly Haebangchon hides an old marketplace that's gained new appeal. The 1960s-era **Sinheung Market**, which once sold textiles, has been revived as a buzzy cultural space full of fine-dining restaurants, rooftop lounges and wine and cocktail bars with an intimate speakeasy vibe.

Ginn-Laoo and **Pad Kapaw**, a duo of Thai restaurants run by Sriprateep Paw, serve authentic and immaculate northeastern Thai fare, while **Vin Vin** is a sleek wine bar featuring a protein-forward menu of seafood, beef tartare and other beautifully presented plates. Follow up dinner with a cocktail at **Karma**, which boasts an impressive menu that includes nonalcoholic options, or **Gil Bar Dak**.

LOCAL FESTIVALS

Itaewon World Music Spirit Festival: Annual festival honouring the memories of victims of the Itaewon Halloween crowd-crush tragedy, which killed 159 people in October 2022.
Olive Young Festa: By the hit cosmetic commerce company, a spring 'beauty-tainment' festival featuring brand booths, performances and lots of samples.
Itaewon Global Village Festival: October weekend celebration of the district's cultural diversity, with global street foods, performances, exhibitions and other events.
Itaewon Film Festival: Launched by five local filmmakers, this selection of international film screenings takes place in autumn. Its inaugural edition was in 2025.
HBC Music Festival: Haebangchon's long-standing autumn block party showcases a packed lineup of live music at bars and clubs across the neighbourhood.

DRINKING IN ITAEWON: CRAFT BEER

MAP P122

Woori Super: Browse the coolers, pick your poison and take a seat at a plastic table at this corner bottle shop with an amazing selection and a fun vibe. *2pm-2am*

Magpie Brewshop: Korea craft-beer pioneer pouring some of the country's finest brews. Pull up a stool at the tiny bar or duck into the pizza-pub basement. *3-11pm*

Dank Yard: A friendly HBC joint serving an excellent craft-beer selection and delicious *anju* (food eaten while drinking). *6pm-midnight Tue-Thu, to 1am Fri & Sat, 4-11pm Sun*

Booth: The original Booth brewpub looks the part with its pop-art murals and warehouse-chic interior, pouring craft suds and serving pizza since 2013. *11am-9pm*

HIGHLIGHTS
1 Leeum Museum of Art

SIGHTS
2 FOUNDRY SEOUL
3 Gallery Joeun
4 Lehmann Maupin
5 Pace Gallery
6 Pipe Gallery
7 Seoul Central Mosque

SLEEPING
8 Grand Hyatt Seoul
9 Imperial Palace Boutique Hotel

EATING
10 Chakra
11 Passion5
12 Summer Lane
13 Youhan

DRINKING & NIGHTLIFE
14 Cafe Le Sens
15 Lesvos
16 Milestone Coffee
17 Not Bad Coffee

ENTERTAINMENT
18 All that Jazz
19 Blue Square

SHOPPING
20 BOMARKET
21 Kinki Robot
22 MIMI Got the MUSEUM
23 Vinyl & Plastic

See Sunset at Bugundang Park

MAP P122

A view of N Seoul Tower

The doors to Bugundang Shrine are almost always closed, but locals know that the tiny **Itaewon Bugundang History Park** at the top of a hill is worth a visit anyway, as it makes for one of the best spots to watch the sun set over N Seoul Tower – and a rather fitting one at that, since the circa-1619 altar that resides here was relocated in 1917 from Namsan itself. Also on the premises is a monument in honour of the female Christian freedom fighter Ryu Gwan-sun, who died while imprisoned by the Japanese at just 17 years of age.

Go Up & Down Gyeongnidan

MAP P122

Explore Seoul's original international street

Because of its history as a residential area for foreigners connected to the US military, Gyeongnidan St (Hoenamu-ro) gained a reputation as being an exotic place that today remains an epicentre for expats, with many international restaurants, bars and embassies lining its steep ascent towards Namsan. Starting from the bottom and making your way to the **Grand Hyatt** (p216) at the top, poke around the cute off-alley spaces, such as the reading lounge **Graphic** (₩20,000 for the day), the **Whistle** and **P21** art galleries, and the luxe housewares stores Nouhaus and Oaos.

Going up and down hilly Gyeongnidan-gil can feel like a real hike, so treat yourself to Korea's customary hiking companion, a cup of *makgeolli* (milky rice wine), at the bottom at the Michelin-recommended **Mr Ahn's Craft Makgeolli**, or **Namsan Sool Club**.

Check out Yongnidan

MAP P127

Cafes, contemporary art and cosmetics

Between Sinyongsan and Samgakji stations, a couple of blocks east of the main road, is the popular Yongnidan St. Starting at the north end, near Samgakji exit 3, work your way southwest. Along the route is the **Teddy Beurre House** bakery-cafe packed with plush stuffed bears, the ever-popular **Sam Sam**

QUIRKY SHOPS IN YONGSAN-GU

Kinki Robot: In Hannam-dong, with wonderfully weird toys, art and lifestyle collectibles, with a second location in Apgujeong.
MIMI Got the MUSEUM: Selling gorgeous Art Deco, modernist and other jewellery, this vintage shop also puts on the occasional exhibition.
Cat Allergy: A cat-themed collectibles store brimming with all the weird and wacky trinkets you never knew you needed; it's sure to make you chuckle.
Woori Bookstore: (우리책방) If dogs are more your thing, a bookstore dedicated to our beloved canine companions. Pet-friendly, of course.
BOMARKET: Inside Nine One Hannam, this kitsch kitchen and homewares shop sells vivid, modern designs that are good for adding a pop of colour to your life.

DRINKING IN ITAEWON & HANNAM-DONG: CUTE CAFES

MAP P122 & P132

Le Cafe: On the Haebangchon main drag, a cosy little shop with a friendly owner-barista and excellent brews for taking a break from a busy day. *9am-10pm*	**Tiger Espresso:** Perfect espressos, pour-overs and lattes, plus homemade scones with a homey ambience. *7am-6pm Mon & Wed-Sun*	**Kenya Kiambu Coffee:** Next to the Kenyan Embassy, serving Kenyan coffee and a prime view of Namsan. *9.30am-9pm*	**Y.Pot Coffee:** One of the least pretentious cafes in the area, run by a mild-mannered coffee nerd who roasts his own beans. *noon-10pm Tue-Sun*
Cafe Le Sens: A lovely bakery-cafe inside the chic Hannam Sounds shopping complex. Grab a seat on the terrace if it's nice out. *10am-10pm*	**Not Bad Coffee:** Near the Leeum Museum of Art, a multilevel cafe with hipster decor and tasty pastries. A second location in Gangnam. *9am-8pm*	**Cafe TRVR:** Stylish and serene cafe on a back alley in Gyeongnidan, with a beautiful rooftop. *7.45am-6.30pm*	**Milestone Coffee:** The popular Sinsa-dong cafe's atmospheric Hannam-dong branch, known for its Viennese coffee. *10am-8.30pm*

STROLLING HAUTE HANNAM-DONG

Tread one of Seoul's hottest, most-high-end neighbourhoods and see what all the hype is about.

START	END	LENGTH
Leeum Museum of Art	Hannam-dong Cafe Street	3km; 2hr

Start at the immaculate 1 **Leeum Museum of Art** (p136), where the spiral staircase and Gravity Stairs will wow you. Admire more art at some of the numerous nearby galleries: 2 **Amado Art** and 3 **Hippie Hannam** are two options that feature up-and-coming artists.

Turn right onto Hannam-daero and stop for lunch at 4 **Gourmet 494 Hannam**, an upmarket food court inside the luxury Nine One Hannam condo complex. K-Pop idols G-Dragon and Jimin are said to live here. Also in Nine One are some galleries, including a branch of GROUNDSEESAW, fine-dining restaurants, high-end boutiques and lifestyle shop BOMARKET.

Further on is 5 **Tartine**, a San Francisco bakery known for its pecan pie, cream tarts and other scrumptious sweets. It's expanded around Seoul, but Hannam is its first and flagship location.

Nearby, peer from a distance at 6 **UN Village**, another ultra-affluent apartment favoured by a number of Korean celebs. The glamorous village has even had a song by EXO's BaekHyun named after it. Heading back west, stop at 7 **Sounds Hannam**, an upscale, brick-enclosed shopping centre with clothing boutiques, eateries and a jazz lounge. Down the road and to your right, stroll along 8 **Hannam-dong Cafe Street**, an attractive stretch of coffee shops, restaurants, boutiques and bars.

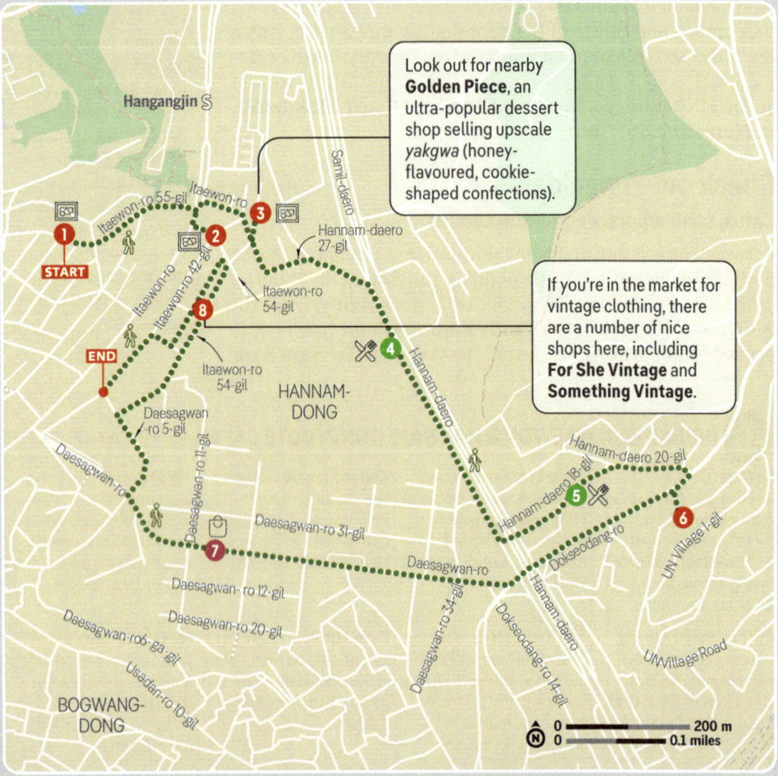

Sam Western restaurant and the retro-chic **Tangled Cassette** bar. If you're in the mood for Korean food, search out the nearby, Michelin-recommended **Oilje**, where the perilla *miyeok-guk* (seaweed soup) is a must, or **Neungdong Minari**, another Michelin Guide eatery, serving *gomtang* (beef bone soup) dressed with water dropwort.

Past the end of Yongnidan is the **Amorepacific Museum of Art** *(apma.amorepacific.com; price varies by exhibition)*, housing contemporary works on the bottom level of a corporate office headquarters. Here you can also shop for Amorepacific brands such as Sulwhasoo, Innisfree and Etude.

What's in a Name?

It's become the trend in Korea, when a certain street has reached peak it-factor status, to nickname it by portmanteau-ing the name of its neighbourhood with the suffix '-nidan'. From Yongsan's Yongnidan to Songpa's Songnidan to Mangwon's Mangnidan (p104), these postfixed '-nidan' streets stand out across Seoul as the next fashionable places to hang out for shopping, dining, drinking and more. But before them all was Gyeongnidan. Named after the Army Financial Management Corp at the base of the road ('Gyeongnidan' being the last three syllables of the group's title), it's the original '-nidan' street in Korea.

Revitalised River

MAP P127

An artsy park plus an island

Enjoy the newly revived **Ichon Hangang Park**, undergoing restoration as part of the city's overall river conservation efforts to regain the shoreline's natural environment and increase its biodiversity. The redesigned park has more wetland and observations decks and is a lovely place to have a picnic, rent a bicycle (₩3300 for one hour) and walk among sculptures. Among the most impressive is the 8m-tall *Scroll-Flowing Stories*, a larger-than-life coil crafted out of steel and fibreglass.

Nearby, floating in the Han, **Nodeul Island** *(nodeul.org)* hosts musical and cultural performances, and is the site of

ART GALLERIES IN HANNAM-DONG

Pipe Gallery: Showcasing emerging talents, this contemporary-art gallery seeks to be an open cultural space connecting art with the public.

Gallery Joeun: Since 2016, this contemporary-art gallery highlights rising and established artists who work across different media.

Pace Gallery: The Hannam-dong outpost of the international gallery founded by Arne Glimcher in 1960.

FOUNDRY SEOUL: Launched in 2021 by TK Corp, a Busan-based pipe fittings manufacturing company, curating exhibitions and experimental shows.

Lehmann Maupin: Seoul branch of the global gallery with locations in New York, London and Hong Kong. Appointment only.

EATING IN ITAEWON: AMERICAN & VEGAN SPOTS

MAP P122

ALT.a: Bib Gourmand plant-based Asian cuisine in Itaewon. Get the hot and sour vEEF and stir-fried spicy eggplant. *11.30am-3pm & 5-10pm* ₩₩₩

byTOFU: Cute little restaurant in Haebangchon where tofu is the star of wraps, bowls and sandwiches. *9am-4pm Mon & Thu-Sun* ₩₩

Plant Cafe & Kitchen: One of Seoul's original vegan eateries (now with a second location in Yeonnam), making a stellar sesame peanut soba bowl. *11am-10pm Tue-Sun* ₩₩

Vegetus: A vegan favourite in Haebangchon with friendly staff serving veggie burgers, pastas and more. *noon-2.45pm & 5-9.30pm Mon & Wed-Sun* ₩₩

Burger Snack: Drip-down-your-arm juicy burgers and cheeseburgers served from a takeaway window. *11am-1pm & 6-8.30pm* ₩

Rocka Doodle: Authentic Nashville hot chicken. Select your sandwich (go for the 'Grandpa') and your spice level (cayenne to Carolina reaper). *11.30am-9pm Mon-Sat* ₩

LOCOS BBQ: Tender, fall-off-the-bone meats served with baked beans, coleslaw and other sides. Get the sampler platter. *11.30am-10pm* ₩₩

Gino's NY Pizza: Baking a range of New York-style pizzas; now with another location in Apgujeong. *11.30am-3pm & 5-10pm Mon-Fri, 11.30am-10pm Sat & Sun* ₩₩

TOP EXPERIENCE

Leeum Museum of Art

Tucked amid a luxury residential neighbourhood on the south side of Namsan is the Leeum Museum of Art, one of Korea's premier art galleries. Stunningly designed and arranged, it balances Korean traditional art with modern and contemporary art across its three museums joined by a central lobby.

STEVE JANGS/SHUTTERSTOCK

Joseon dynasty ceramics, M1

Korean Traditional Art

Museum 1, or **M1**, is a fortress of terracotta bricks by Swiss architect Mario Botta that takes you on a journey through four floors of Korean painting, calligraphy, ceramics, Buddhist art and metal and wood craft covering the Goryeo and Joseon dynasties. Begin with a lift ride to the top floor and circle your way down around a sun-drenched spiral staircase to reach the Olafur Eliasson light installation *Gravity Stairs* at the end.

Modern & Contemporary Art

M2, a rusted stainless-steel structure designed by French architect Jean Nouvel, showcases early and mid-20th-century paintings, sculptures and installations by acclaimed Korean and international artists, including Nam June Paik, Kim Whanki, Salvador Dalí, Jean-Michel Basquiat, Cecily Brown, Damien Hirst and Jeff Koons. The museum's third area, designed by Dutch architect Rem Koolhaas, is a cultural centre hosting mostly paid special exhibitions. There is also a sculpture garden out front containing Anish Kapoor's tower of mirrored orbs *Tall Tree and the Eye* and satellite-like dish *Sky Mirror*.

Audio Guide & Amenities

The free digital docent audio guide is highly recommended. (Be prepared to surrender an ID to borrow.) There's also an enticing gift shop and a cafe on site.

TOP TIPS

- You can buy tickets on site, but during peak visiting hours it's recommended to book online in advance.
- On Culture Day, the last Wednesday of the month, tickets are half-price.
- If all you want to see is traditional art, M1 is free.

PRACTICALITIES

- *leeumhoam.org*
- adult/youth/child ₩12,000/6000/free
- 10am-6pm Tue-Sun

an art gallery, bookstore, lounge and several restaurants. Formerly known as Jungji-do, the artificial island, originally built by the Japanese in 1917, was once a popular recreation spot that eventually fell into disuse, but underwent revitalisation beginning in 2012. As of the end of 2025, Nodeul is undergoing another redevelopment project to add elevated gardens, and will remain partly open during construction (slated for completion in 2028).

Learn about Yongsan's Railway History MAP P127

Where the past and future meet

The neighbourhood around Yongsan station, Hangangno-dong, is an interesting pocket of central Seoul, where old-town newtro vibes and futuristic smart city collide.

At the **Baekbin Railroad Crossing**, Korean nostalgia rings out every time a train comes through, lending the intersecting street its *'ttaeng ttaeng!'* nickname. Popularised by the K-Drama 'My Mister', it's one of the few remaining active railroad crossings in the capital. For the sensation of stepping into an earlier Seoul, come and see the train, then wander the narrow surrounding streets, dotted with cute restaurants, bars, cafes and shops.

Stop also at the **Yongsan History Museum** *(museum.yongsan.go.kr; free)*, housed in a former railway station turned railroad hospital, for an overview of the area's past (bring your ID to borrow an English audio guide). The museum also has a lovely rooftop terrace.

To the south, spanning the Han River, you can see Korea's first railway bridge, the **Hangang Railway Bridge**, completed in 1900 by the Japanese and since rebuilt.

Yongsan has a lengthy history with Japan. In the 1880s, Yongsan was the hub for Korea's commercial trade with France, China and Japan. After the Sino-Japanese War (1894–95), Japan began eyeing the area as key to realising its colonial ambitions, and solidified plans to annex Korea. They took steps to turn Yongsan into a railway hub, building Yongsan station, which was completed in 1906. Later, to manage all

KOREA'S 3.1 MOVEMENT

In 1919, inspired by the Paris Peace Conference's principle of self-determination and the recent death of King Gojong, 33 Korean religious leaders drafted a Declaration of Independence proclaiming freedom from Japanese colonial rule, signing it on 1 March.

From then, *sam-il* (1 March) movement demonstrations spread quickly across the nation, as students, religious leaders and ordinary citizens rose up in nonviolent protest. They were ruthlessly suppressed by Japanese authorities, who arrested, injured and killed thousands.

Despite this, the movement energised Korean nationalism and led to the establishment of the Provisional Government of the Republic of Korea in Shanghai.

EATING IN ITAEWON & HANNAM-DONG: BREAKFAST/ BRUNCH —MAP P122 & P132

Normal Brunch: A normal name with an elevated menu; the food is scrumptious. *11am-8.30pm Mon, Tue, Thu & Fri, from 10am Sat & Sun* ₩₩

Hemian Brunch Bar: French toast, pastas and more at this tiny spot near the pedestrian bridge over Noksapyeong St. *10.45am-3pm & 5-9pm Mon-Thu, 10.45am-9pm Fri-Sun* ₩₩

Honfleur: Near the Grand Hyatt, a charming little restaurant with tasty pastas, smoothies and a brioche French toast that's out of this world. *9am-6pm Tue-Sun* ₩₩

Summer Lane: Popular Australian brunch cafe in Hannam-dong. Try the salmon eggs Benedict, or assemble your own creation from the a la carte menu. *7.30am-6pm* ₩₩

Sunday Arvo: Fresh takes on old favourites like French toast and pancakes. Sandwiches, soups and salads, too. *10am-6pm Mon & Wed-Fri, 9am-7pm Sat & Sun* ₩₩

The Baker's Table: Serves breakfast, sandwiches, schnitzel and bratwurst. Also bakes sweet and savoury pastries, and is generous with free samples. *8am-9pm* ₩₩

Passion5: A pastry paradise, with more glistening, glazed treats than you can imagine, along with salads and sandwiches. *7.30am-10pm* ₩

Spoonery: By Itaewon station, with hearty breakfast platters, sandwiches and rice bowls. *8am-6pm* ₩₩

WANDERING THE HILLS OF HAEBANGCHON

Meaning 'Independence Village', Haebangchon is a former refugee shantytown, full of winding alleyways with plenty to reveal.

START	END	LENGTH
Undebt	Coley	2.2km; 1½ hours

Kick off with a sugar high in Huam-dong at **1 Undebt**, a unique cave-themed cafe converted from a Japanese colonial house. Setting the mood with stone walls and a warm-wood interior, it serves up a decadent menu of desserts.

Next, come to the **2 staircase of 108 Steps**, another vestige of the occupation, which was built by the Japanese as a pathway to their Shinto shrine honouring Japanese war casualties. After liberation, the shrine was demolished but the stairs remain. Not far beyond is **3 Storage Book & Film**, an indie shop with an alluring ambient playlist and some real treasures tucked within its tightly packed cases.

Heading southeast to a web of alleyways, you'll stumble into **4 Sinheung Market** (p131), which began by cooking North Korean food for war refugees and later became a centre of textiles. Today it's a hip dining and drinking sector. Just outside the market is a branch of **5 Nuldam Space**, a small cafe chain selling letter-writing sets along with its lattes.

Follow Sinheung-ro, the main Haebangchon street, which goes past a strip of international eateries and a stretch of kimchi pots stacked outside **6 Hansin Pottery**, in operation since 1967. On the way to Noksaypyeong station, stop across the street at **7 Coley**, a cosy corner bar with convivial vibes.

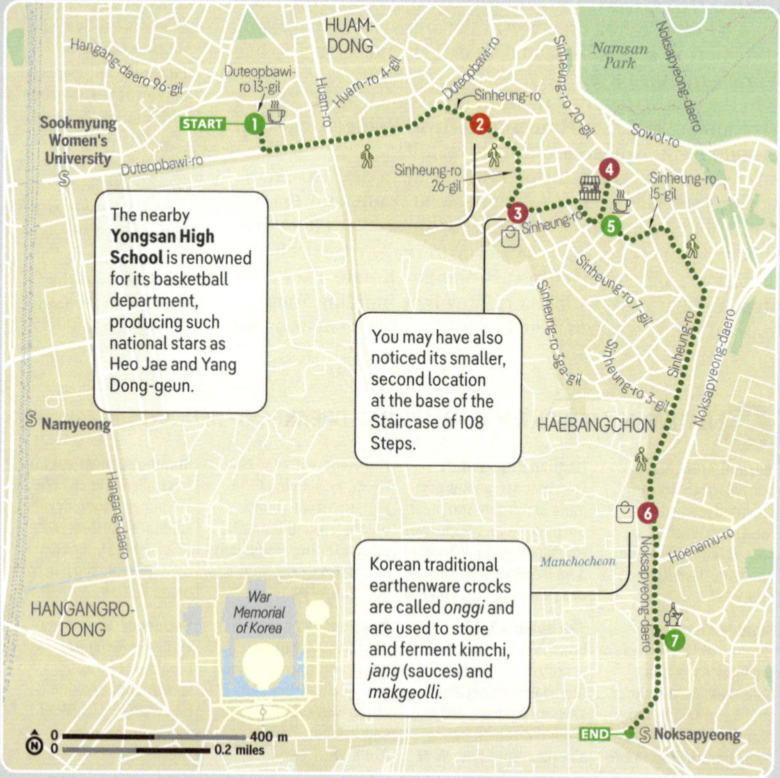

TRAVERS LEWIS/SHUTTERSTOCK

Baekbin Railroad Crossing (p137)

the injured railroad workers, they established the Yongsan Railway Hospital – today a museum (p137). Then, to cement their power, they began building Yongsan Garrison in 1906, forcibly evicting residents to make way for it, and established their Imperial Army headquarters there in 1910.

Hangangno-dong, though, is undergoing a transformation, with the construction of the Yongsan International Business District, a long-delayed project that is finally underway. At the end of 2025, ground broke on what was considered to be the last major undeveloped plot of land in central Seoul. By 2030, the Korail-owned former rail-yard site is expected to be remade into a high-density vertical city with skyscrapers (some with more than 100 storeys), sky trails, green space and housing. While the neighbourhood will stay intact, the scenery around it will change.

LIVE MUSIC IN ITAEWON

All That Jazz: A fixture on the Seoul jazz scene since 1976. There are usually two sessions of live music a night, with the first starting around 7pm.
Jazz Garage: Live jazz, along with whisky, wine and barbecue, at this intimate Gyeongnidan lounge with an open-air patio.
Boogie Woogie: A neon-clad live-music den featuring local jazz acts and a smattering of blues, funk and hip hop.
Pet Sounds: Named after Korean owner Jay's love affair with the Beach Boys' Pet Sounds album, this friendly upstairs rock bar features live local acts and DJs.
Burn: Blaze up a top-class Cuban, swirl your aged single malt and kick back in a leather club chair at this throwback cigar bar. Live jazz nightly (cover ₩7000).

EATING & DRINKING IN HANGANGNO-DONG: OUR PICKS

MAP P127

Ferments: Vegan menu with kombucha-dough pizzas, fermented hummus and fermented curry. *11.30am-11pm Sun-Thu, to midnight Fri & Sat* ₩₩	**Hi Thai:** This terrific Thai restaurant from Daegu has opened a Yongsan branch, cooking scrumptious noodles, curries and soups. *11am-3.30pm & 5-9pm* ₩₩	**Shawnino:** Pastas and seafood shine at this vibrant Italian restaurant styled after the Amalfi Coast. *10am-4pm & 6-10pm Mon-Sat, 9am-8pm Sun* ₩₩₩	**Plantude:** On the 7th floor of iPark Mall, delicious plant-based stews and pastas are served in a plant-filled ambience. There's another branch in CoEx. 11am-9pm ₩₩
Hay Coffee and Bar: Premium coffee and cocktails set in a rustic, dark-wood *hanok*. Pull up a seat at the bar and order a tiramisu. *noon-1am Tue-Sun*	**VIBD BLVD:** Hidden near Samgakji station, the vibes are impeccable at this 2nd-storey vinyl bar with the ideal ambient lighting. *8.30pm-1am Tue-Sun*	**Pont Coffee:** Named after the French word for bridge, this cafe sees its baristas as bridges between coffee and people. *10am-9pm*	**Hand and Malt Brewlab:** At Yongnidan's south end, a convivial microbrewery with a great happy hour. *5-11pm Mon-Thu, to midnight Fri, 2pm-midnight Sat, 2-11pm Sun*

Researched by Charles Usher

GANGNAM & SOUTHERN SEOUL

LUXE LIFESTYLES REFLECT SEOUL'S METEORIC RISE

Nowhere revels in Korea's rags-to-riches trajectory quite like Gangnam, where corporate headquarters share boulevards with designer shops, stylish cocktail bars and sleek art galleries.

The name 'Gangnam' can indicate everything south of the Han (it translates to 'south of the river'), but most often it refers to Seoul's posh southeastern districts. An oft-lampooned realm of new money and conspicuous consumption, this upper-class area is also an undeniable testament to Korea's economic achievements. Skyscrapers puncture the horizon around Gangnam station and Starfield COEX Mall, while closer to the river, high-end boutiques and restaurants fill the Apgujeong and Sinsa neighbourhoods. It's wild to think that, until Korea's 1970s development boom, most of this was just farmland. Look past the flash and cash, though, and you can still find pockets of blissful tranquillity, including Joseon-era royal tombs, one of Seoul's oldest temples and the sprawling green space of Olympic Park.

INCLUDES

Gangnam (p150)

FROM LEFT: SAYAN URANAN/GETTY IMAGES, CHUNG SUNG-JUN/GETTY IMAGES

See page 217 for places to stay in Gangnam & Southern Seoul

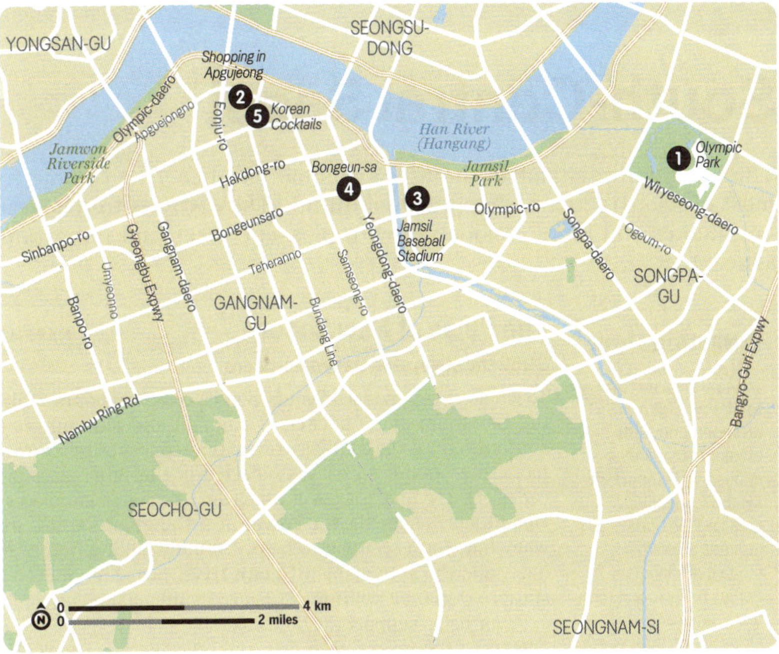

Highlights

❶ Olympic Park
Combine art, athletics and ancient history in one of Seoul's largest green spaces. **p158**

❷ Shopping in Apgujeong
Browse edgy venues such as Haus Nowhere Dosan in this super-stylish neighbourhood. **p143**

▼❸ Jamsil Baseball Stadium
Join the raucous crowd at a game and cheer on the home team. **p161**

❹ Bongeun-sa
Break from Gangnam's bustle and breathe deep at this tranquil temple. **p148**

❺ Korean Cocktails
Sip modern drinks made with traditional ingredients at renowned bars such as Zest and Pine&Co. **p149**

Getting Around

Subway
Line 2 connects several major stations, including Gangnam, Samseong and Jamsil. Line 3 and the Suin-Bundang Line are major north–south routes, while Lines 5 and 8 go to Olympic Park.

Bus
Buses reach places without immediate subway access, including the Seoul Arts Center (bus 406 to Seoul Arts Center) and Seorae Village (bus Seocho 13 to Seorae Village Entrance).

Walking
Gangnam is more car-centric than other parts of Seoul, but remains walkable within individual districts. Apgujeong, Garosu-gil and Seorae Village are good to explore on foot.

South-Central Seoul

The Gangnam district is the area's commercial heart and home to most of its attractions, shopping and dining. The districts to the west are quieter and more residential, with pleasant parks and important art centres.

SYMBOLS IN STONE

Joseon-dynasty royal tombs are elaborate arrangements with elements that are imbued with important symbolic meaning. Flanking the burial mounds are *seokho*, stone guardian tiger deities that protect the tomb, and *seogyang*, stone sheep that repel evil spirits and ensure the deceased's peaceful repose. In front of these are *mangjuseok*, towers meant to guide the soul home. Further forward are several *muninseok*, stone scholars and military officers who serve and guard the dead monarch.

The Pulse of New Seoul

MAP P144

Stroll the always-on Gangnam-daero

To get a grip on modern Seoul, spend a couple of hours walking Gangnam-daero between Gangnam and Sinnonhyeon stations. This is the contemporary city in concentrate. Korea's modern economic success is reflected in the shiny glass facades of skyscrapers, some of which are true statement pieces. Headliners include the **GT Tower** near Gangnam station, its wavy blue form seeming to be perpetually baking in a heat haze, and the aptly named **Urban Hive**, near Sinnonhyeon station. Designed by Kim In-Cheurl, its unusual honeycomb exterior helps support the building.

Beneath the towers, shoppers and office workers pack the footpaths. Join the crowds filling their bags with makeup from **Chicor** *(chicor.com)* and clothing from **Musinsa** *(musinsa.com)*, or just soak up the K-Culture vibes – pop music pouring out of cosmetics stores, idols shilling contact lenses from giant video billboards, and visitors still crossing their wrists and striking a pose at the **Gangnam Style 'Horse Dance' Stage** a decade after Psy's satirical hit put the district on everyone's playlist.

EATING IN SOUTH-CENTRAL SEOUL: OUR PICKS

MAPS P144 & P146

Samwon Garden: Samwon has been serving top-class *galbi* (beef ribs) amid a traditional garden for over 40 years. *11.30am-9.30pm* ₩₩₩

One Degree North: Singaporean favourites such as chicken rice and *char siu* transport you (almost) to the equator. *11.30am-10pm Mon-Sat* ₩₩

Solsot: Among the many rice-pot options at this chain restaurant are steak, salmon, freshwater eel and cheese *dakgalbi* (spicy chicken). *11am-9pm* ₩₩

Monks Butcher: The menu at this stylish vegan restaurant ranges from pastas and risotto to meatless burgers and cottage pie. *noon-10.30pm* ₩₩

Jinmi Pyeongyang Naengmyeon: Soothing Pyeongyang-style *naengmyeong* (noodles in a cold broth), plus dumplings, bulgogi and pork. *11am-9.30pm* ₩₩

Orabang: This cosy joint brings the flavours of Jeju to Seoul. Try the *gosari yukgaejang*, a spicy beef soup with bracken. *11.30am-10pm Mon-Fri, from 1pm Sat & Sun* ₩₩

Yukgak Gogi: This barbecue restaurant has a unique location: on the roof of the old Express Bus Terminal. Great views. *11am-10pm* ₩₩

Jeongdon: Serves crispy, juicy Japanese-style pork cutlets. Fried chicken and fish cutlets are also on offer. *11.30am-9.30pm* ₩₩

Final Royal Resting Places

MAP P144

Contemplate the Seonjeongneung tombs

Amid the Gangnam skyscrapers, the earthen mounds of the **Seolleung and Jeongneung Royal Tombs** *(royal.khs.go.kr; adult/child ₩1000/free)*, often referred to as Seonjeongneung, cut a relatively modest figure. On the west side is Seolleung, the twin tombs of King Seongjong and Queen Jeonghyeon. Jeongneung, the tomb of their son, King Junjong, lies to the east. At each tomb, you can pass through the red *hongsalmun* gate and follow the route later kings used when paying their respects. Keep off the upper path, the *sindo*, which is reserved for spirits. Also on site is a small history centre, while serene trails threading the forested premises take you past a tomb-keeper's house and royal kitchen. Seonjeongneung is closed on Mondays.

A Mall That Has It All

MAP P144

Entertain yourself at Starfield COEX

The gargantuan **Starfield COEX Mall** *(starfield.co.kr/coexmall)* packs in enough to keep you occupied for an entire day or more. Beyond its 250-plus shops and restaurants, you can catch a movie at **Megabox COEX** cinema, test your fortune at **Seven Luck Casino** and see sharks, rays and penguins at **SEA LIFE COEX, Seoul Aquarium** *(visitsealife.com/coex-seoul; adult/child ₩35,000/31,000)*. Young ones will delight in the daily otter feedings and mermaid performances. At the mall's centre is the eye-candy **Starfield Library** and its two-storey bookshelves. A must for K-Pop fans is the **Ktown4u** complex, which includes a shop, cafe and photo zone. Aspiring idols can even take dance or voice classes at the **Ktown4u Academy** *(ktown4uacademy.com)*. Enquire through the website's contact form.

Get a New High-Style Look

MAP P146

Shop Apgujeong's trendy fashion scene

To head home with a wardrobe that will have folks asking, 'Where'd you get that?', spend a few hours in the streets around Apgujeong Rodeo station. Just outside the exit is the **Galleria** *(dept.galleria.co.kr)* department store, stocked with international luxury brands such as Dior and Fendi. For more street swagger, check out **10 Corso Como** *(ssfshop.com)*,

Continues on p149

THE GROWTH OF GANGNAM

The neighbourhoods south of the Han River are among Seoul's most sought-after, but this wasn't always the case. For much of the city's modern history, this land was an afterthought, a swampy expanse of farmland and mulberry fields.

That changed when a post-Korean War population boom created an acute housing shortage. In response, the government turned its gaze across the river. In the mid-1960s, it launched a plan to spur relocation to Gangnam, promoting apartment construction, building subway lines, moving government offices, designating Gangnam a financial hub and relocating the country's most prestigious university.

Today southern Seoul is home to corporate headquarters, Korea's most exclusive schools and some of Seoul's most expensive real estate.

DRINKING IN GANGNAM: BEST FOR PINTS

MAP P144

Dublin: Irish pub with frothy pints of Guinness and large windows that open onto the street, making for great people-watching. *3pm-1am Sun-Thu, to 2am Fri & Sat*

Bulldog Pub: Toss darts and throw back ales at this upstairs pub. Serves casual bar food and has a never-ending drinks menu. *7pm-1am Mon-Thu, to 2am Fri & Sat*

Goose Island Brewhouse: The Chicago brewery's American-style brewpub serves Korea-exclusive pours among its long list of lagers and more. *11.30am-midnight*

Thursday Party: Pushing the weekend to its limits, Thursday Party has all you need for a good time: bar games, cheap drinks, late hours. *7pm-2am Sun & Tue-Thu, to 5am Fri & Sat*

★ **HIGHLIGHTS**
1 Bongeun-sa

★ **SIGHTS**
2 Gangnam Style 'Horse Dance' Stage
3 GT Tower
4 Gugak Museum
5 Jamwon Hangang Park
6 Ktown4u
7 Montmartre Park
8 Moonlight Rainbow Fountain
9 Seolleung and Jeongneung Royal Tombs
10 Seorae Island
11 Seorae Village
12 Seoripul Park
13 Seoul Arts Center
14 Some Sevit
15 Urban Hive
16 Yangjae-cheon

ACTIVITIES, COURSES & TOURS
17 SEA LIFE COEX, Seoul Aquarium
18 Starfield Library

SLEEPING
19 H Avenue Hotel Yeoksam
20 Josun Palace
21 Owall Hotel
22 Park Hyatt Seoul

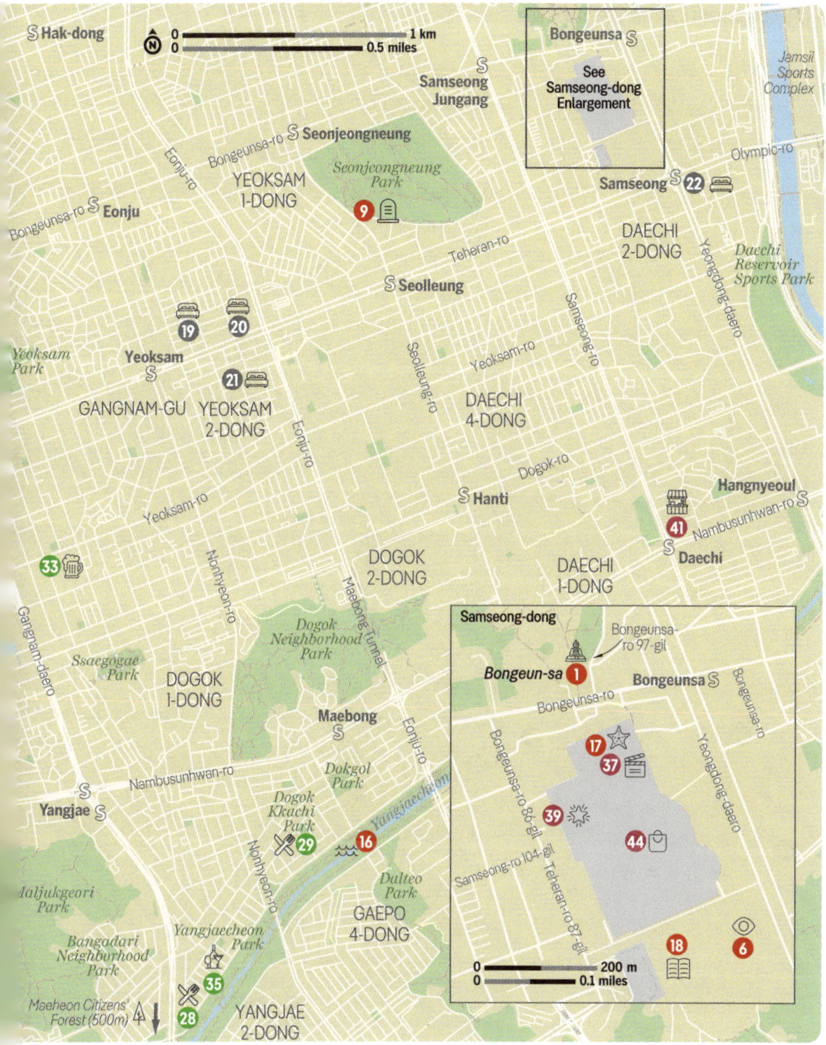

EATING
23 Gangnam Gyoja
24 Jeongdon
25 Mom Korean Bistro
26 Muwol Table
27 Neurin Maeul Brewery
28 Pâtisserie Crémiel
29 Sun's Donut
30 Yukgak Gogi

DRINKING & NIGHTLIFE
31 Bulldog Pub
32 Dublin
33 Goose Island Brewhouse
34 Maillet
35 Terrace
36 Thursday Party

ENTERTAINMENT
37 Megabox COEX
38 National Gugak Center
39 Seven Luck Casino

SHOPPING
40 Chicor
41 Eunma Shopping Mall
42 Fromagerie Le Meunier
43 Musinsa
44 Starfield COEX Mall
45 Toudou

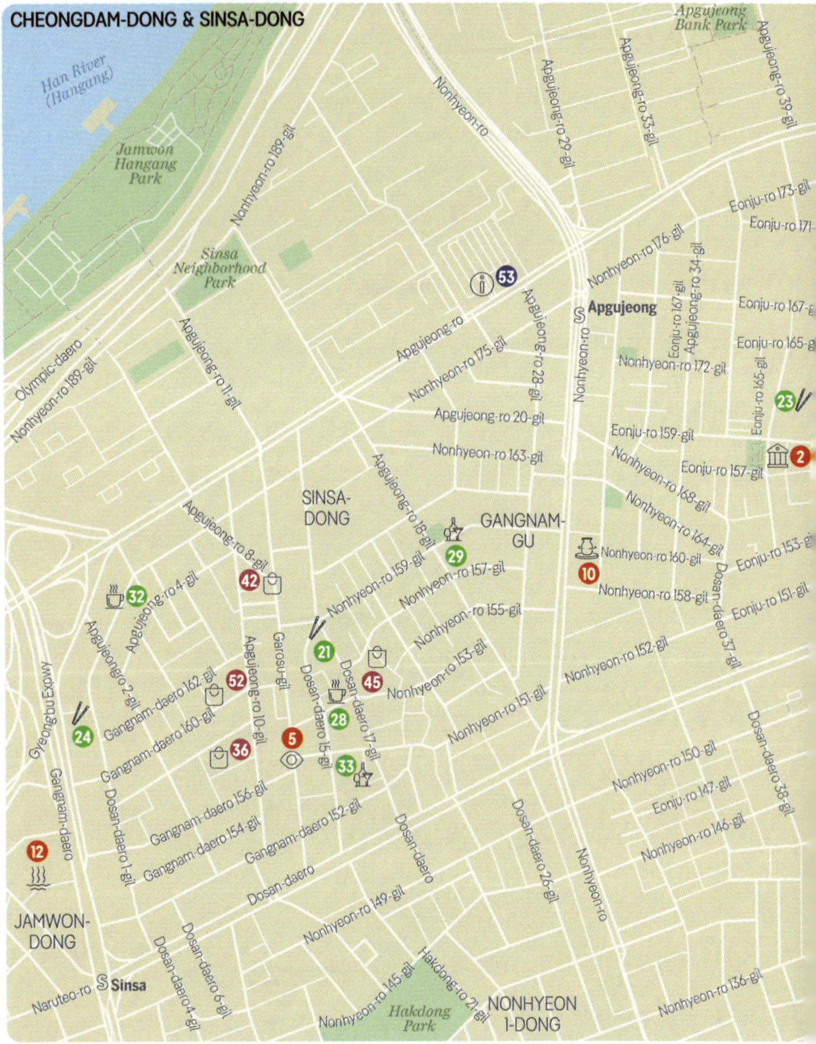

SIGHTS

1 Apgujeong Rodeo Street
2 Coreana Cosmetics Museum
3 'Dosan' Ahn Chang-ho Memorial Hall
4 Dosan Park
5 Garosu-gil
6 Horim Museum
7 K-Star Road
8 SONGEUN
9 White Cube Seoul

ACTIVITIES, COURSES & TOURS

10 Fold and Tie
11 Jenny House
12 Spa Lei

EATING

13 Butter Finger Pancakes
14 Jinmi Pyeongyang Naengmyeon
15 Jungsik
16 Mingles
17 Monks Butcher
18 New York Lots O Bagels
19 Oasis
20 One Degree North
21 Orabang
22 Ryunique
23 Samwon Garden
24 Soigné
25 Solsot

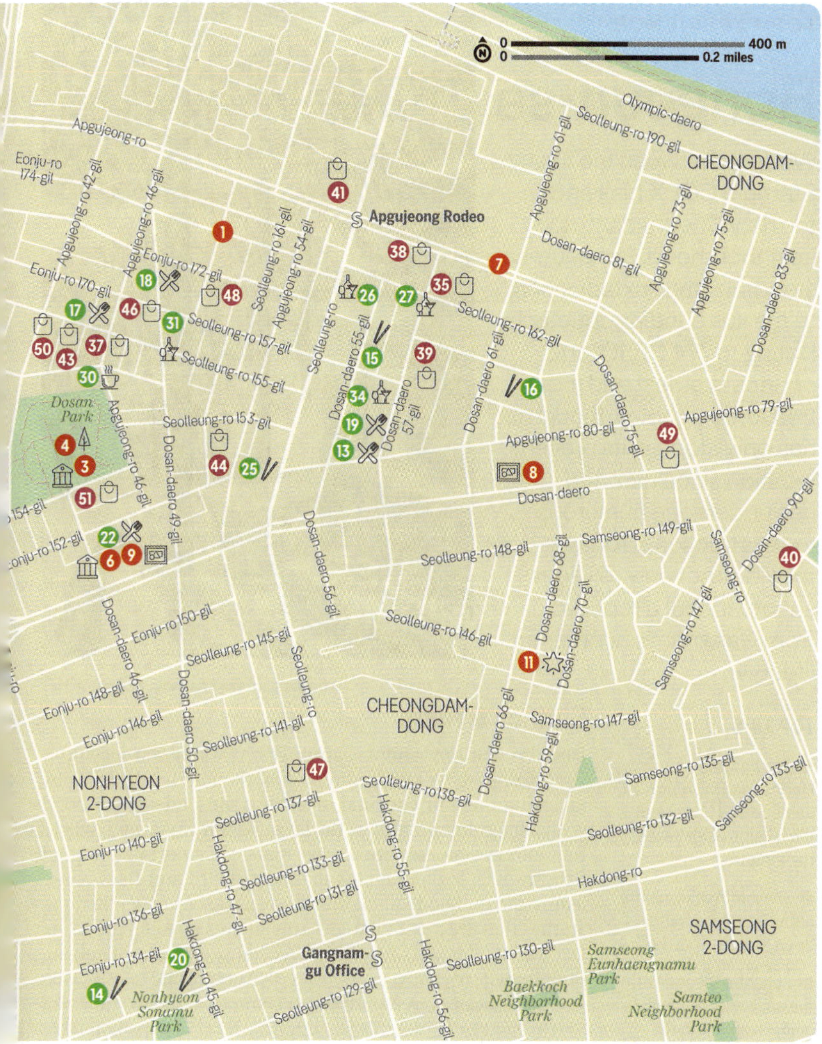

DRINKING & NIGHTLIFE

26 Alice Cheongdam
27 Bar Tea Scent
28 Conflict Store
29 Kompakt Record Bar
30 Nudake
31 Pine&Co
32 Steamers Coffee Factory
33 Villa Records
34 Zest

SHOPPING

35 10 Corso Como
36 ADERERROR
37 ATiiSSU
38 Beaker
39 BOONTHESHOP
40 Brown Hat
41 Galleria
42 Gentle Monster Sinsa Flagship Store
43 Glowny
see 30 Haus Nowhere Dosan
44 Instant Funk
45 Klairs
46 MSCHF
47 Notdam
48 Opener
49 Seoul House of Dior
50 Sinoon
51 Sulhwasoo
52 Tamburins

INFORMATION

53 Gangnam Medical Tour Center

TOP EXPERIENCE

Bongeun-sa

Wedged between the flashy Starfield COEX Mall and the ritzy Cheongdam-dong neighbourhood, Bongeun-sa stands in stark juxtaposition to the surrounding spectacle. Dating to 794 CE, it's one of Seoul's oldest and most treasured temples, though it has only stood in its present location since 1562 and has undergone numerous reconstructions. Today, it provides not only religious sanctuary but a reprieve from Gangnam's high-tempo lifestyle.

MAREMAGNUM/GETTY IMAGES

Lotus Lantern Festival, Bongeun-sa

TOP TIPS

- The peaceful Meditation Trail runs past bamboo and flowers on the hillside at the rear of the temple.
- The information centre at the temple entrance is open 10am to 4pm daily.
- Scan the QR code at the entrance for a mobile guide available in 10 languages.

Shrines & Halls

Pass through Jinyeomun (Gate of Truth), where you encounter the four heavenly kings who protect the Buddha-Dharma by guarding the four cardinal directions. Beyond a small pond with a laughing Buddha is the large Beopwangru hall, where religious ceremonies are held at 10am each morning. Behind Beopwangru is the temple's main courtyard and Daewoongjeon, its main Buddha hall. Inside are a trio of wooden Buddha statues that are a designated National Treasure. Surrounding Daewoongjeon are several smaller halls, including Panjeon. Built in 1855, it's Bongeun-sa's oldest structure and houses 3503 wooden blocks carved with the 81 volumes of the Avatamsaka Sutra. Next to Panjeon is the temple's most conspicuous feature, the 23m Great Statue of Maitreya Buddha, who, it's believed, will one day return to relieve people of their suffering.

Templelife & Templestay

If you're able, visit Bongeun-sa on a Thursday to take part in one of its Templelife programs – either a temple tour followed by a tea ceremony or an experience that combines Buddhist crafts, sound meditation and sutra copying using golden ink. Overnight Templestay programs are held on the first Saturday of the month. These include *Seon* (Zen) meditation, monastic meals and a conversation with a monk. Both programs should be booked ahead online (*templestay.com; Templelife/Templestay ₩30,000/120,000*).

PRACTICALITIES

- *bongeunsa.org*
- free
- 5am-10pm

Continued from p143

Beaker *(ssfshop.com)* and **BOONTHESHOP** *(boontheshop.com)*, where you can track down popular Korean labels such as thisisneverthat, San San Gear and OPEN YY. All three are clustered around Apgujeong-ro 60-gil. Several of Korea's trendiest and edgiest shops are near Dosan Park. **MSCHF** *(mischief.co.kr)* and **Instant Funk** *(instantfunk.kr)* are popular for women's wear, while **ATiiSSU**'s *(atiissu.com)* hats feel appropriate for a post-apocalyptic anime. Don't miss **Haus Nowhere Dosan**, a multistorey complex housing global eyewear fave Gentle Monster *(gentlemonster.com)*, its sister cosmetics brand Tamburins *(tamburins.com)* and **Nudake** *(nudake.com)*, a bakery-cafe with artistic aspirations. Even if you're not shopping, the building's trippy art installations alone are worth the visit.

Find Something Beautiful

MAP P146

Go gallery hopping in Apgujeong

Apgujeong's good looks extend to art, and there are a number of galleries to peruse here. The best of the bunch is **SONGEUN** *(songeun.or.kr)*, housed in a silver shard designed by the Swiss studio Herzog & de Meuron. Its rotating contemporary exhibitions can range from sound installations to explorations of links between Asian and African cultures. You're asked to reserve your visit in advance, but it's possible to just show up and register on site. A few blocks down Dosan-daero, **White Cube Seoul** *(whitecube.com)* has frequently changing shows, while the adjacent **Horim Museum**'s *(horimmuseum.org; adult/child ₩5000/3000)* collection consists of incense burners, Buddhist paintings and other centuries-old artefacts. Anyone who's a fan of Korean cosmetics should pop by the **Coreana Cosmetics Museum** *(spacec.co.kr; adult/student ₩6000/4000)* to get a primer on Korean beauty practices stretching back 2000 years and to see historic oil bottles and hairpins.

Treatment for Tourists

MAP P146

Get a medical-service consultation

Korea has become a major destination for medical tourism, and not just for plastic surgery, which grabs most of the headlines, but for dental care, dermatology and plenty more. If you're considering treatment, the **Gangnam Medical Tour Center** *(medicaltour.gangnam.go.kr)* provides information, arranges

GANGNAM FASHION

Kim Minji (@minjiena), stylist and owner of the minjiena fashion brand, shares where she goes to get the look in Gangnam.

Brown Hat: Discover truly unique hats you won't find anywhere else. Its high prices are reasonable considering the unbelievable quality.
Sinoon: The flagship branch of this designer brand in Apgujeong is a must-visit if you love cute and charming things.
Glowny: The label has several locations, but I recommend its newest branch, by Dosan Park. It makes high-quality basic items with a Korean touch.
Opener: A select shop that imports distinctive international brands. It's a great place to explore and discover new styles. It's also a favourite with celebrities.

DRINKING IN APGUJEONG: TOP COCKTAILS

MAP P146

Zest: Named one of the world's best bars, Zest focuses on upcycling ingredients such as corn silk that would normally go to waste. *6.30pm-2am, from 3pm Sat & Sun*

Pine&Co: Creative concoctions riff on traditional Korean ingredients like shiitake mushrooms, *omija* (five-flavour) berries and fermentation starter *nuruk*. *7pm-2am*

Alice Cheongdam: This *Alice in Wonderland*–inspired bar has more than a few surprises. Drinks might feature a flower pot or bubble tower. *6pm-2am, to 3am Fri & Sat*

Bar Tea Scent: Tea-based spirits and tea-infused cocktails like the 'Sencha Sonic' (with green-tea gin) and 'Iron Daiquiri' (oolong-tea rum), presented with a flourish. *7pm-3am*

STROLL GANGNAM IN STYLE

Put on your best look and strut through Sinsa and Apgujeong, neighbourhoods synonymous with luxury brands and K-Pop swagger.

START	END	LENGTH
Sinsa station	SONGEUN	4km; 2hr

1 **Garosu-gil** used to be one of Seoul's 'it' shopping streets, but now most of the action is on the blocks to the west. Here you'll find photo booths, skincare shops and the flagship store of local streetwear favourite 2 **ADERERROR**. Near the road's north end are the ritzy Hyundai Department Store and 3 **Gangnam Medical Tour Center** (p149), where you can learn about the latest medical procedures.

Follow Eonju-ro south to leafy 4 **Dosan Park**, named after the independence activist 'Dosan' Ahn Chang-ho, who served as prime minister in the Korean Provisional Government and is buried here. Exit the park and pop into 5 **Haus Nowhere Dosan** (p149) for mind-bending art installations and the avant eyewear brand Gentle Monster. Break for coffee and sculptural baked goods at the basement-level Nudake cafe.

Window-shop through the boutique-packed roads collectively known as 6 **Apgujeong Rodeo Street**. Emerge in front of the 7 **Galleria** (p143) department store, which is covered in shimmering, scalelike glass discs that turn a psychedelic pink at night. Heading east, Apgujeong-ro is lined with architecturally audacious luxury-brand stores. These blocks also make up 8 **K-Star Road**, where cutesy bear sculptures pay homage to OG K-Pop icons such as SHINEee and Kara. Around the corner is the excellent 9 **SONGEUN** (p149) gallery, where contemporary art offers a reprieve from the neighbourhood's commercial pressures.

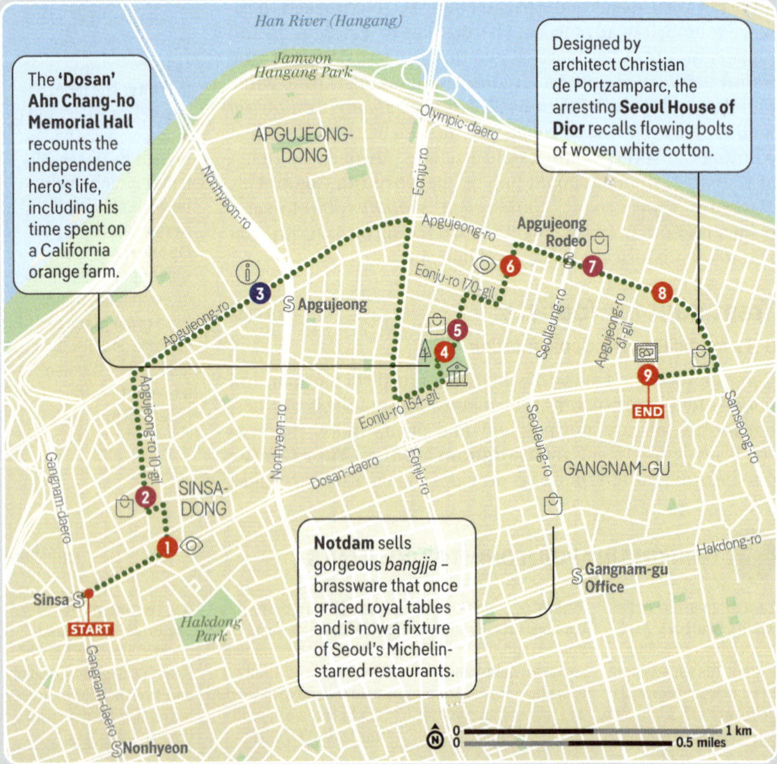

consultations and offers interpretation support. If you're not, you can still join one of the centre's K-Culture programmes to do a bit of yoga or discover your personal colour. Reserve a spot through the website. Alternatively, indulge in some self-care and relax with a cup of robot-prepared coffee in the plush lounge.

Commerce Meets Art

MAP P146

Scope Garosu-gil's high-concept shops

Things change fast in Seoul. Not long ago, Garosu-gil was one of the city's best shopping streets, but now it's full of largely international brands and empty storefronts. The surrounding streets still have some marquee shops, though. A block west, the uber-popular brands **Gentle Monster** *(gentlemonster.com)*, **Tamburins** *(tamburins.com)* and **ADERERROR** *(adererror.com)*, for eyewear, cosmetics and streetwear respectively, have high-concept flagship stores with art installations that turn browsing into a whole experience. Elsewhere in the neighbourhood, you can find good vintage offerings and plenty of stylish cafes.

Seoul's French Connection

MAP P144

Be a Seorae Village flaneur

The charming **Seorae Village** neighbourhood took shape in 1981, when the Lycée Français de Séoul moved here and the city's French expats followed. You won't confuse it with the 8th arrondissement, but the enclave does have a distinct feel, more relaxed than the rest of the city, with little Gallic touches such as street signs in both Korean and French. Spend an afternoon casually exploring its bistros and wine bars, making sure to pick up some chocolates at **Toudou** and savor **Maillet**'s superb pastries – *mille-feuilles*, éclairs, lime tarts – in the cafe's leafy back garden. If the weather is nice, grab some brie, Adarré or *la marotte* from **Fromagerie Le Meunier** and picnic in **Montmartre Park**, Seorae's pleasant hilltop green space, where you'll find a rose garden, plaques with French poems and kids playing soccer on a grassy lawn.

South Side Arts & Culture

MAP P144

Major museums and performance venues

The southern edge of Seoul is home to a trio of important arts institutions along Nambusunhwan-ro. Together they give culture vultures just about everything they could ask for: painting,

BEST SPOTS FOR SELF-CARE

Gangnam's all about looking and feeling fabulous. These are its top self-care spots:

Sulhwasoo: The flagship store of this esteemed cosmetics brand has an Oriental medicine spa and a rooftop lounge.

Jenny House: Splurge on a K-Idol makeover at this top-tier salon, which has styled some of Korea's biggest celebrities.

Klairs: For Klairs, doing good equals looking good. All cosmetics at its Garosu-gil store are vegan and ethically sourced.

Spa Lei: A relaxing women-only spa with an open-air bath, sitz baths and saunas. Provides massages and facials, too.

Fold and Tie: Take a class *(fold-tie.com)* to learn the Korean art of cloth gift wrapping so you can pay all that good feeling forward.

DRINKING AROUND GAROSU-GIL: BARS & CAFES

MAP P146

Villa Records: Cocktails in this mid-century-modern space can be made straight up or 'molecular,' like a negroni with warm citrus and cacao foam. *7pm-2am*

Conflict Store: This minimalist cafe takes its coffee seriously, offering *omakase* tasting courses, though you can also just relax with a (very good) latte. *10am-10pm*

Kompakt Record Bar: Owned and operated by bartenders who also DJ. The unique atmosphere sometimes attracts figures from Korea's hip-hop industry. *7pm-2am*

Steamers Coffee Factory: Third-wave coffee shop doing Ethiopian and Colombian single-origin brews in a sleek setting. *8.30am-6pm, from 9am Sat & Sun*

TRADITIONAL MUSIC FORMS

Before there was K-Pop, there was *gugak*, Korea's traditional music. *Gugak* comes in a vast array of forms. These are some of the major genres you may hear at a National Gugak Center concert.

Jeongak: Formal music reserved for banquets and events such as Confucian ceremonies. It's performed by soloists or small ensembles.

Pansori: Epic dramas sung and acted out by a solo singer. Traditionally, a performance could last several hours.

Nongak: Lively, percussive songs performed in rural communities to accompany agricultural labour or scare off evil spirits.

Sanjo: Solo instrumental music, often played on a *gayageum* or *geomungo*, which are both types of zithers. Occasionally accompanied by a drummer.

sculpture, music, calligraphy, opera and more. At the **Seoul Arts Center** *(SCA; sac.or.kr)*, lovers of the performing arts can catch the national opera, ballet or orchestra in an opera house that resembles a traditional hat, listen to a piano recital in the music hall, or watch a play in a theatre dedicated to experimental works. Purchase tickets in person or at interparkglobal.com. Prefer the visual arts? The Hangaram Art Museum has seven galleries, the changing exhibitions of which might display anything from furniture to French Impressionist works. Galleries 1 to 6 are free; Gallery 7, which displays the headline exhibitions, is ticketed. The Hangaram Design Museum was Korea's first such venue dedicated to design when it opened in 1999. A separate building hosts the Seoul Calligraphy Art Museum, which may just change your idea of what the art form can be.

Next to the SAC is the **National Gugak Center** *(gugak.go.kr)*. Head to its **Gugak Museum** to view and hear traditional instruments and to try interactive features that take you on a listening journey through Korean music history. Free guided English tours are held on Saturdays at 2pm. At 3pm, the centre holds its weekly Saturday Gugak Concert, a medley of several different musical styles. Book tickets through the centre's website.

A short bus ride west, the **Nam-Seoul Museum of Art** *(sema.seoul.go.kr)* occupies a stately red-brick and granite structure that once housed the Belgian consulate. An outpost of the **Seoul Museum of Art** (p86), its permanent exhibition displays work by the 20th-century sculptor Kwon Jin-kyu, while rotating exhibitions change every three months. All three venues are closed on Mondays.

Somewhere Under the Rainbow

MAP P144

See an aqueous spectacle

In the evening, make your way to Banpo Hangang Park to see the wonderful water- and light-show put on by the **Moonlight Rainbow Fountain**. Running for 570m along both sides of the double-decker Banpo Bridge, it's the longest bridge fountain in the world. Some 380 jets rain water down from the upper level, moving up and down in dancing arcs and combining with 10,000 coloured lights and K-Pop recordings to create a playful display.

Occasionally, the city hosts festivals where the bridge's partially pedestrianised lower level is closed to traffic and turned

EATING IN GANGNAM: FINE DINING

MAP P146

Mingles: Chef Kang Mingoo is known for his innovative cookery with clean flavours and artful presentation. Reserve far in advance. *noon-3pm & 6-10pm Tue-Sat* **WWW**

Ryunique: French and Japanese influences combine in platings incorporating wood and moss, to reflect reverence for the natural world. *noon-3pm & 6-10.30pm Tue-Sun* **WWW**

Jungsik: Chef-owner Yim Jungsik serves neo-Korean food at its finest. Bookings open on the first of even-numbered months for two-month periods. *noon-3pm & 5.30-10pm* **WWW**

Soigné: Contemporary Seoul cuisine tells a story of Korean culture in a chic minimalist dining room. Book well in advance. *noon-3pm & 6-10pm Tue-Sun* **WWW**

Moonlight Rainbow Fountain

over to food trucks, artist stalls and beanbag chairs.

If the bridge fountain isn't playing, you can still enjoy coloured lights reflecting on the water at the adjacent **Some Sevit** *(somesevit.co.kr)*. The trio of floating artificial islands houses restaurants, a cafe, event spaces and a beer garden, its views of the Moonlight Rainbow Fountain almost justifying its inflated prices. For fun on the water, charter a yacht, book a boat tour or rent a kayak from Some Sevit's Golden Blue Marina, or take a spin on a round Tubester boat.

Distinguished Final Resting Places

Seoul National Cemetery's serene scenes

Set on 144 hectares above the Han River, **Seoul National Cemetery** is where many of modern Korea's most important figures are buried, including presidents Park Chung-hee and Kim Dae-jung, Ju Si-gyeong, who helped standardise *hangeul* in the early 20th century, and the Canadian missionary Frank Schofield, an advocate for Korean independence. Others, such as the martyred independence activist Yu Gwan-sun, are

WHY I LOVE GANGNAM

Charles Usher, Lonely Planet writer

When I lived in Seoul, it was always on the river's north side, and it took me a while to come around on Gangnam. Better late than never, as they say. The area can get a bad rap, often portrayed as image-obsessed and money-hungry. Those things aren't untrue, exactly, but they don't tell the whole story.

There's an appealing sophistication here, one that connects art galleries, fine-dining restaurants and craft-cocktail bars. And despite being the centre of Korea's demanding work culture, Gangnam actually has some of the city's most relaxing neighbourhoods.

There's something practically therapeutic about ambling along the Yangjae Stream – time always seems to slow down here, an almost impossible thing for it to do in Seoul.

EATING IN GANGNAM: KOREAN COMFORT FOOD

MAP P144

Muwol Table: An inviting eatery serving elegantly presented home-cooking classics like bulgogi and *bossam* (boiled pork belly) with cool barley tea. *11am-10pm* ₩₩

Gangnam Gyoja: Specialises in big bowls of *kalguksu* (handmade knife-cut noodles) and steamed pork dumplings. Has English menus with pictures. *10.30am-9pm* ₩

Neurin Maeul Brewery: The 'Slow Village' brewpub serves savoury pancakes and other filling faves alongside its own *makgeolli*. *5pm-midnight Mon-Sat, 4-11pm Sun* ₩₩

Mom Korean Bistro: In Seorae Village, Mom gives home cooking the French-bistro treatment. The bibimbap lunch specials are terrific value. *11.30am-3pm & 5-9pm Tue-Sun* ₩

HONORARY KOREANS

Three foreigners have received the honour of burial in Seoul National Cemetery. Two of them, Jiang Hui Lin and Wei Xu-fang, were Chinese nationals who joined the South Korean army during the Korean War. Jiang was killed in action on a reconnaissance mission in February 1951. Wei, a doctor of Oriental medicine, survived the war and spent the ensuing decades providing free medical treatment to the poor.

Dr Frank W Schofield, a Canadian, arrived in Korea in 1916 to do missionary work and lecture at Seoul's Severance Union Medical College. He would go on to play a major role in bringing the Koreans' plight under colonial rule to international attention, photographing the 1 March 1919 independence protest at Tapgol Park and writing for overseas publications.

enshrined in memorial tablets.

Unless you have an abiding interest in Korean history, the burial plots and memorials may be of limited interest, but this is an unexpectedly great place to view cherry blossoms in spring, when weeping cherry trees droop pink and white boughs over a small stream.

MAP P144

An Underground Portal to Early Gangnam

Snack through Eunma Shopping Mall

Gangnam is known today as the epitome of aspirational luxury, but it had humble beginnings, with its earliest apartment complexes built mainly to relieve overcrowding on the city's north side. One of these was the Eunma Town Apartments, constructed in 1979 for low-income residents. If you ever tire of Gangnam's shiny surfaces, come to this complex by Daechi station and wander through **Eunma Shopping Mall**, its underground warren of food stalls and shops. A few concessions to the modern world have been made, such as a pizza place, but for the most part, things feel delightfully stuck in the past.

Do as generations of Korean students have done and stop by one of its snack bars, such as Oneul Twigim at stall A-65, for *tteokbokki* (rice cakes in a spicy sauce) and Korean tempura, but do it soon. Plans are afoot to replace Eunma with a 35-storey tower.

Go Slow with the Flow

MAP P144

Savour a Yangjae Stream stroll

When Seoul's fast pace gets to be a bit much, melt your stress away by the **Yangjae-cheon**. This peaceful stream runs across the southern part of the Gangnam district and is lined with walking paths that pass drooping willows, reed beds and rows of metasequoia trees. Egrets swoop over artificial cascades, and fat carp congregate beneath bridges.

The west end of Yangjaecheon-ro, a 15-minute walk south of Yangjae station, is fronted by cute wine bars and cafes. Grab a bottle from **Terrace** to enjoy at a table along the path, or pick up a coffee and pastry from **Pâtisserie Crémiel**, run by a French-Korean couple, and join the local dog walkers and stroller pushers for a calming ramble along the water.

EATING IN GANGNAM: BRUNCH SPOTS

MAPS P144 & P146

Oasis: Draws a stylish Cheongdam crowd for salads, eggs Benedict, fresh orange juice and indulgent pancakes in homemade toffee sauce. *9am-6pm* **WW**

Butter Finger Pancakes: Fluffy pancakes done five ways, plus all the breakfast standards and diner classics like burgers and meatloaf. *8am-7pm, from 7am Sat & Sun* **WW**

New York Lots O Bagels: Homemade bagels, cream cheese, lox and egg sandwiches. Has a patio surrounded by bamboo. *8.30am-8pm, from 8am Sat & Sun* **W**

Sun's Donut: This oddly otter-obsessed joint's adventurous homemade doughnuts include Earl Grey hibiscus and mugwort chocolat blanc. *11am-8pm* **W**

FANGIZ_BASHKORT/SHUTTERSTOCK

Gwanak-san

GANGNAM'S BEST GREEN SPACES

Here are great spots to escape southern Seoul's concrete sprawl.

Seorae Island: In spring, take the footbridge to this tiny Han River island to wander amid fields of yellow rapeseed flowers.

Gwanak-san: This mountain on Seoul's southern edge serves up amazing city views. A hermitage near the summit sits atop a sheer cliff.

Maeheon Citizens' Forest: This 26-hectare park has lots of shady walking paths, a playground and a memorial to independence fighter Yun Bong-gil.

Jamwon Hangang Park: An outdoor pool, pink muhly grass and a Starbucks floating on the Han River (with views of Moonlight Rainbow Fountain!).

Seoripul Park: Pedestrian bridges link Seoripul's two halves with Montmartre Park, creating a long green corridor amid the apartment buildings.

Southeastern Seoul

This corner of the city is where Seoul was born and where it announced itself on the world stage 6000 years later. Encounter ancient sites, major sports venues and lots of family fun.

THE BAEKJE KINGDOM

Most of Seoul's major historic sites date to the Joseon era, but it was the Baekje kingdom that first established the area as an important settlement.

Baekje was one of several kingdoms to emerge from the collapse of the northern Gojoseon kingdom, and in 18 BCE it founded its capital in what's now the Songpa district. Baekje flourished thanks to its economically and militarily strategic Han River location and its close ties to Tang China.

It grew into a maritime power, came to control much of the peninsula's western half and developed an advanced culture, even introducing Buddhism to Japan. Its demise finally came in the mid-7th century, when it was conquered by the southeastern Silla kingdom.

The First Seoulites

See Korea's largest Neolithic site

The land south of the Han River is the newest part of Seoul. It's also the oldest. Ten minutes' walk from Amsa History Park station is the **Amsa-dong Prehistoric Site Museum** *(sunsa.gangdong.go.kr; adult/child ₩500/300)*, located on the site of a village that dates to at least the 4th millennium BCE. Discovered after a 1925 flood, it's the largest Neolithic site in the country. See how these early Seoulites lived through museum exhibits, reconstructed pit houses and a shelter that displays excavated items such as stone arrowheads and pottery. Closed Mondays.

Where the City Began

Explore ancient Baekje ruins

This part of the city was also where the Seoul region's first major settlement arose. In 18 BCE, the emerging Baekje kingdom established its capital, Wiryeseong, on the banks of the Han. You can discover Seoul's urban origins at a series of ancient sites scattered throughout the Songpa district.

Wiryeseong is thought to have centred on the **Pungnap-toseong** and **Mongchon-toseong** (p159) fortresses. The former, near Cheonho and Gangdong-gu Office stations, likely held the royal palace. Any traces of the buildings are long gone, but you can still walk more than 2km of earthen ramparts, which reach 15m high in spots.

Tucked into residential neighbourhoods to the south are two Baekje burial sites. At the **Ancient Tombs in Bangi-dong**, paths wind between the grassy mounds of eight stone-chamber tombs. A metal grate lets you peer into the gloomy interior of Tomb No 1. More impressive still are the **Ancient Tombs in Seokchon-dong**. This collection of stone mound tombs and terraced stone tombs in the shadow of the Lotte World Tower was a Baekje royal cemetery. The three-tiered Tomb No 3, measuring 51m by 48m, is thought to have belonged to King Geunchogo.

HIGHLIGHTS
1 Lotte World
2 Olympic Park

SIGHTS
3 Ancient Tombs in Bangi-dong
4 Ancient Tombs in Seokchon-dong
5 Lotte Museum of Art
See 1 Lotte World Folk Museum
see 5 Lotte World Tower
6 Mongchon-toseong
7 Pungnap-toseong
8 Seoul Baekje Children's Museum
9 Seoul Baekje Museum
10 Seoul Olympic Museum
11 Seoul Olympic Museum of Art
12 Songpa Book Museum
13 World Peace Gate

ACTIVITIES, COURSES & TOURS
14 Lotte World Aquarium
see 1 Lotte World Ice Rink

SLEEPING
15 Lotte Hotel World
16 Seoul Olympic Parktel
see 5 Signiel Seoul

EATING
17 Bangi Shabu Shabu Kalguksu
18 Bogil
19 Byeolmi Gopchang
20 Cafe Pepper

ENTERTAINMENT
see 1 Lotte World Adventure

SANGA PARK/SHUTTERSTOCK

Olympic Park

TOP EXPERIENCE

Olympic Park

The mammoth Olympic Park served as one of the primary sites for the 1988 Summer Olympic Games, but it's not merely an athletics afterthought. The park has avoided the fate of so many rusting Olympic facilities and remains a vibrant place, combining still-active arenas, historic sites, museums and art venues. Seoulites cherish its green spaces, flocking here to play and picnic.

DON'T MISS

- World Peace Gate
- Mongchon-toseong
- Seoul Olympic Museum of Art
- Seoul Baekje Museum
- Seoul Olympic Museum
- 88 Lawn Field

Olympic Facilities

The 1988 Summer Olympics were the moment South Korea announced itself on the world stage after decades of colonialism, war, poverty and dictatorship. You get a sense of the country's aspirations for the Games when you pass beneath the soaring red-and-blue wings of Kim Choong-up's **World Peace Gate** at the park's entrance. Look up to see four mythological animals painted on the wings' undersides. The gate opens onto the 28,000-sq-metre Peace Plaza. Look down to see pavement

PRACTICALITIES

- *ksponco.or.kr/olympicpark*
- free (SOMA adult/student/child ₩5000/4000/3000)
- 5am-10pm, facility hours vary

decorated with a motif inspired by a Goguryeo-era tomb mural. If you're an Olympics buff, visit the **Seoul Olympic Museum**, just north of the plaza. Recently reopened following renovations, it explores the '88 Games and Korea's Olympic history. Sporting venues cluster on the park's east side. Some continue to hold competitions, while others host concerts, including major K-Pop spectacles.

Baekje History

Snaking for 2.3km through Olympic Park are the rammed-earth walls of **Mongchon-toseong**, a 4th-century fortress that formed part of Wiryeseong, capital of the Baekje kingdom (18 BCE–660 CE). Walking paths along the top of the walls provide great views across the park. Learn all about the fortress and the Baekje people at the **Seoul Baekje Museum** *(baekjemuseum.seoul.go.kr)*, on the park's south side. The museum, closed Mondays, displays a full-scale model of workers constructing **Pungnap-toseong** (p156) fortress and an exhibit on the rivalry between Baekje, Goguryeo and Silla as they fought for control of the Han River basin during the Three Kingdoms era. Don't miss the remarkable Chiljido, a seven-branched ritual sword. Most exhibits are in Korean, so use the QR codes to read descriptions and watch videos in English.

If you're travelling with kids, the **Seoul Baekje Children's Museum** on the opposite side of the park has great hands-on activities that bring the era to life. The Seoul Baekje Museum operates an active excavation site nearby where the oldest wooden plough in East Asia was unearthed.

Seoul Olympic Museum of Art

Between the Peace Plaza and Seoul Baekje Museum is the **Seoul Olympic Museum of Art** *(SOMA; soma.kspo.or.kr; adult/student/child ₩5000/4000/3000)*, a bright space full of modern and contemporary pieces (closed Mondays). Its collection contains several video artworks by Paik Nam-june, including *Golden Crown*, a piece inspired by Baekje culture, and *Coubertin*, a tribute to the father of the modern Olympics. SOMA is best known for its sculpture collection, which debuted five days before the '88 Olympics' opening ceremony. Nearly 200 pieces by artists from across the world are installed inside the museum and across the Olympic Park grounds. Some are larger than a house.

Green Spaces

Plenty of folks come to Olympic Park not to do any of the above, but to simply enjoy a break from the surrounding city. Follow their lead and settle in for a picnic among the kite-flyers on the vast **88 Lawn Field** at the park's centre, or stop and smell the roses in the park's southeast corner, site of the **Rose Plaza** and **Wildflower Garden**. Alternatively, rent a bike from the stall near the World Peace Gate or stroll along Mongchon Lake, 88 Lake or the Seongnae Stream, which formed a natural moat for Mongchon-toseong in Baekje times.

PICNICKING IN THE PARK

If you didn't prepare a picnic in advance, don't sweat it. Just outside Olympic Park station on the park's east side are several places where you can throw a meal together. (If you see the *Thumb* sculpture, you're in the right spot.)

Besides two cafes and a bakery, the CU convenience store stocks drinks, *gimbap* (rice and fillings wrapped in seaweed), instant ramen, chips, fruit and anything else you might need.

TOP TIPS

- Want to attend a show at one of the Olympic Park concert venues? You'll find performance schedules and links to booking sites on the Olympic Park website.
- SOMA's handy Olympic Sculpture Park guide includes a map displaying the location of every piece and a QR code that links to an audio tour.
- Olympic Park's most picturesque photo op is One Tree Hill. The lone tree backdropped by Mongchon-toseong's earthen ramparts is a popular setting for films and commercials.
- Head to the Wildflower Garden in spring to find it carpeted in red poppies and in autumn for a vivid display of yellow cosmos.

TOP EXPERIENCE

Lotte World

Welcome to Planet Lotte. The chaebol's massive complex is home to Lotte World Tower (Korea's tallest building), Lotte World Adventure amusement park, Lotte World Mall, Lotte World Aquarium and a slew of other entertainment options with 'Lotte' in their names. Is it all rather corporate? Exceedingly. Is it a tonne of fun anyway? Absolutely.

Lotte World Tower

TOP TIPS

- It's not cheap, but Lotte World Adventure's Magic Pass provides limited access to faster queues.
- If you plan to see several of Seoul's top sites, purchasing a Discover Seoul Pass *(discoverseoulpass.com)* might be worth it. Most pass options include entry to Lotte World Adventure and discounts on other Lotte World attractions.

Family Fun

Thrills await at **Lotte World**. Buy a silly headband and spend a day at **Lotte World Adventure** *(adult/youth/child ₩61,000/54,000/47,000)*, Seoul's premier amusement park. Attractions in the large indoor section are tamer – a carousel, 'flying' hot-air balloons – while the outdoor Magic Island has a gyro drop and roller coasters. Kids will also enjoy the **Lotte World Folk Museum**'s *(adult/youth/child ₩5000/3000/2000)* detailed historic models. On the building's lower level is the **Lotte World Ice Rink** *(weekends adult/child ₩18,000/15,000, weekdays ₩15,000/13,000)*. Rent some skates and channel your inner Kim Yuna. Inside the Lotte World Mall is the **Lotte World Aquarium** *(adult/child ₩35,000/31,000)*, with a rainforest tunnel and play nooks for kids.

Elevated Experiences

The 555m **Lotte World Tower**'s sleek design was inspired by Korean ceramics and calligraphy. A ticket to **Seoul Sky** *(adult/child ₩31,000/27,000)* whisks you up to an observatory that spans the 117th to 120th storeys and features a glass floor, outdoor terraces and epic views. Adventurous types can join a **Sky Bridge Tour** *(₩130,000)* to walk across an 8m-long bridge outside the 124th floor. Within the tower, exhibitions at the **Lotte Museum of Art** *(lottemuseum.com; adult/child ₩20,000/13,000)* range from French street artist JR to up-and-coming Korean artists.

PRACTICALITIES

- *lotteworld.com*
- prices vary by facility
- hours vary by facility

Take Yourself Out to a Ballgame

Catch some Korean baseball

Baseball is Korea's most popular sport, so even if you're not a fan, attending a game is a fun way to live like a local. The antics in the stands are just as good as the action on the field, with dancing cheerleaders, fans belting out personalised cheers for each player, and stadium snacks such as fried chicken and squid jerky.

The 25,000-seat **Jamsil Baseball Stadium** is shared by two of Korea's pro teams: the Doosan Bears *(doosanbears.com)* and LG Twins *(lgtwins.com)*. If you can't purchase tickets through the teams' websites, you can usually buy them at the stadium up to 90 minutes before games. The Korea Baseball Organization season runs from March to October.

Paper & Ink, Through the Ages

Browse the Songpa Book Museum

At the **Songpa Book Museum** *(bookmuseum.go.kr)*, closed Mondays, you can learn about the progression of Korean reading culture, beginning with Joseon-era literati and ending with modern-day bookmakers. In between are fascinating exhibits that span a century of Korean media consumption as experienced by three generations of readers, explaining the rise of popular book culture and displaying some of the nation's quintessential reads. QR codes link to English explanations and an audio guide. A central staircase, flanked by bookshelves and cosy reading nooks, leads up to the exhibitions.

Don't miss the printing-press station, where you can stamp your own bookmark. On the 1st floor is a children's studio and cafe.

KOREAN AUTHORS TO KNOW

Thanks to growing interest in Korean culture, more of the country's literature is available in English translation than ever.

Anyone curious about K-Lit should start with the 2024 Nobel Prize winner Han Kang. Her novel *Human Acts* is a moving look at the 1980 pro-democracy Gwangju Uprising and its aftermath.

Other modern Korean writers to know include Park Wan-suh, whose *Who Ate Up All the Shinga*? offers an intimate account of the colonial and Korean War years, and Kim Young-ha, author of *Your Republic Is Calling You*, a spy story that makes the peninsula's postwar division personal.

A new generation of Korean authors includes Cho Nam-joo, whose *Kim Ji-young, Born 1982* became a feminist touchstone, and Park Sang-young, whose *Love in the Big City* was a breakthrough for queer Korean literature.

EATING IN SOUTHEASTERN SEOUL

Bangi Shabu Shabu Kalguksu: A neighbourhood favourite serving *kalguksu* with mushrooms and sliced beef to cook in the broth. *11am-9.30pm Mon-Sat* ₩

Bogil: Abalone, eel and other superb seafood sourced from the south-coast island of Bogil-do, where the chef grew up. *11am-4pm & 5-10pm Tue-Sun* ₩₩

Cafe Pepper: This adorable cafe makes gluten-free desserts like strawberries and cream cake, pistachio cherry tarts and banana poundcake. *noon-9pm* ₩

Byeolmi Gopchang: Dishes up grilled beef intestines so popular it had to open a second location a block away. *11am-3am, to 5am Thu-Sat* ₩₩

Researched by Simon Richmond

DONGDAEMUN & EASTERN SEOUL

AMAZING ARCHITECTURE, MARVELLOUS MARKETS, VERDANT PARKS

Past and present Korean retail collide in areas around and east of Dongdaemun. Negotiate massive markets, hunt down the latest pop-ups and chill out in leafy parks.

Dongdaemun is synonymous with retail. Here labyrinthine markets and malls, mostly selling fashion and fabric, orbit the spaceship-like Dongdaemun Design Plaza (DDP), an architectural icon of contemporary Seoul. In Sindang, cool cafes, hidden cocktail bars and offbeat boutiques are colonising the area's old rice warehouses near Jungang Market. Inevitably, it's been dubbed 'hip-dang'. Further east is Seoul Yangnyeongsi Herb Medicine Market, Korea's largest herbal-medicine market and Dapsimni, one of the best places in Seoul for antiques. The old shoemaking and light industrial district of Seongsu-dong is now awash with trendy boutiques and cafes. It's also close by Seoul Forest, one of the city's best parks.

INCLUDES

Dongdaemun Market (p164)

FROM LEFT: DECNUI/GETTY IMAGES, ANTHONY WALLACE/AFP VIA GETTY IMAGES

See page 217 for places to stay in Dongdaemun & Eastern Seoul

Highlights

❶ Dongdaemun Design Plaza (DDP)

Get up close to a 21st-century architectural wonder. **p166**

❷ Seoul Forest

See the deer, butterflies and insects that live in one of the city's loveliest parks. **p173**

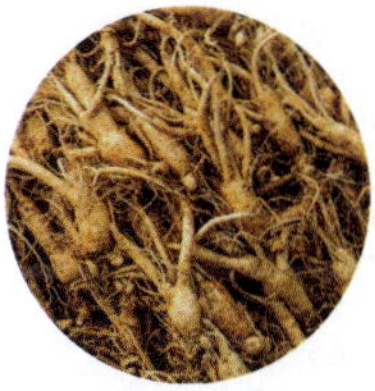

❸ Seongsu

Hunt for the latest fashions and other goods in the superb boutiques and pop-ups. **p174**

❹ Sindang

Hang out in cool cafes and cocktail bars, and try local cuisine, including the rice-cake dish *tteobokki*. **p164**

▲❺ Seoul K-Medi Center

Learn about traditional Korean medicine, get massaged by a machine and shop for herbs. **p167**

Getting Around

Subway

Dongdaemun or Dongdaemun History & Culture Park stations are best for the Dongdaemun area. Jegi-dong is the hop-off point for Yangnyeongsi Herb Medicine Market and Gyeongdong food market.

Walking

Paths alongside the Cheonggye-cheon provide pleasant strolling between Dongdaemun and Seoul Yangnyeongsi. The market areas themselves and Seongsu are best explored on foot.

Bus

Handy for quick hops around these spread-out areas.

Dongdaemun, Sindang, Jegi-dong & Dapsimni

Markets for fashion, food, medicinal herbs and antiques are at the heart of this neighbourhood quartet. Dongdaemun itself is part of Jung-gu, as is the upmarket district of Jangchung-dong around Dongguk University subway station.

BEST SHOPPING IN DONGDAEMUN

Cécile Cédric: Gardening-themed store in Sindang with gifts for plant lovers, including scented candles, T-shirts and vintage housewares.

Hyundai City Outlets: One of the fanciest malls in Dongdaemun, with many international fashion brands and a branch of Kyobo bookstore.

DDP Design Store: Creative Korean designers showcase their wares in this store stocking lots of cool items.

DunDun: For fashion, including a branch of Uniqlo and a big 7-Eleven stocking cosmetics and instant *ramyeon*.

Dongdaemun Market: For ready-to-wear (and made-to-measure) *hanbok* (traditional clothing) outfits, bedding and fabric accessories.

Historic City Wall Gate

Admire majestic Heunginjimun

Meaning 'Gate of Rising Benevolence', **Heunginjimun**, which is also known as Dongdaemun (Great East Gate), is one of the eight entrances through Seoul City Wall. First built in 1396, and rebuilt several times since (the last full reconstruction was in 1869), this grand gate is the only one of the eight to feature an *ongseong*, a half-circle-shaped wall that's an added defence feature. Forming a traffic island, the gate is closed to pedestrians, but there are good photo ops of it from Dongdaemun Seonggwak Park to the north.

Hang Out in Sindang

Sample street food in Jungang Market

In recent years Sindang, a market area specialising in dried goods, furniture and restaurant fittings, has morphed into a hot spot for cool hangouts such as **Mailroom**, a cafe styled like an antique post office, and **Showflix** *(@showflix_seoul)*, a dining bar with live musical performances.

More traditional is the covered arcade of **Jungang Market**, lined with stalls selling tasty snacks, including *haemul pajeon* (seafood pancake) and *hoe* (raw fish). The **stall** of an old woman constantly making mammoth *hotteok* (glutinous rice-dough pancakes) is very popular. Just off the main arcade, sample craft beers at **Kokkiri Brewery**.

Look for steps going beneath the central arcade to find **Seoul Art Space Sindang**, with units occupied by artists specialising in contemporary craft and design.

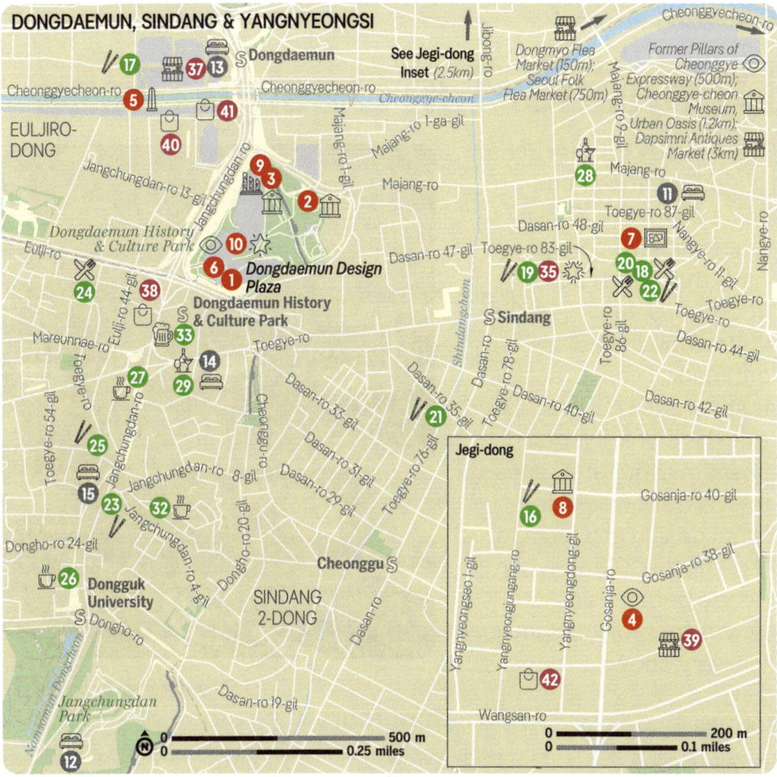

HIGHLIGHTS

1 Dongdaemun Design Plaza

SIGHTS

2 Dongdaemun History Museum
3 Dongdaemun Stadium Memorial
4 Goldstar Electronics Refresh Center
5 Jeon Tae-il statue
6 Oullim Square
7 Seoul Art Space Sindang
8 Seoul K-Medi Center
9 Yigansumun

ACTIVITIES, COURSES & TOURS

10 Diki Diki

SLEEPING

11 ABP Sindang
12 Hotel Shilla
13 JW Marriott Dongdaemun Square
14 Mangrove Dongdaemun
15 PIPE Hostel Dongdaemun

EATING

16 Chamdajeong
17 Dongdaemun Grilled Fish Alley
18 Gosari Express
19 Hani Kalguksu
20 Hotteok stall
21 I Love Sindangdong
22 Sindang Gyeryugwan
23 Soop Mama Kitchen
24 Star Samarkand
25 Woori Yeah Sool

DRINKING & NIGHTLIFE

26 Cafe Fritz
27 Conhas
28 Gu Seoul
29 Jean Frigo
30 Kokkiri Brewery
31 Mailroom
see 11 Manmool
see 4 Starbucks Gyeongdong 1960
32 Starbucks Jangchung Lounge R
33 Woori Yeah Sool Brewery
34 Zoo Sindang

ENTERTAINMENT

35 Showflix

SHOPPING

36 Cécile Cédric
see 6 DDP Design Store
37 Dongdaemun Market
38 DunDun
39 Gyeongdong Market
40 Hyundai City Outlets
41 Pyeonghwa Market
42 Seoul Yangnyeongsi Herb Medicine Market

TOP EXPERIENCE

Dongdaemun Design Plaza

Designed by the late Zaha Hadid, Dongdaemun Design Plaza (DDP) is a spaceship-like complex that's the largest 3D amorphous building in the world. An architectural landmark, it serves as a multipurpose cultural space for exhibitions, events, museums and retail, and acts as a showcase for Seoul design and fashion. At night, the 222m silvery facade becomes a giant canvas for projected image-and-light shows.

PANTA CREATION, VIA SEOUL DESIGN FOUNDATION

Dongdaemun Design Plaza

TOP TIPS

- **Oullim Sq** hosts an excellent farmers' and craft market *(@marchefriends)* between April and November on Sundays.
- Shop for local design products at the DDP Design Store (p164).
- **Diki Diki**, a fun play space for kids, is on the 4th floor of DDP Museum (closed Mondays).

PRACTICALITIES

- *ddp.or.kr*
- exhibitions free-₩24,000
- exhibitions 10am-7pm

Architecture Tours

Covered in 45,133 aluminium panels, no two alike, DDP has graceful curved walls both inside and out. Spread across five levels, it can be a confusing building to navigate – to fully appreciate its architectural ingenuity, join the free English tour at 1.30pm Tuesday to Sunday, starting from the complex's M3 entrance off the Miraero Bridge.

Check the DDP website to see if rooftop tours (₩38,000) are running – they're well worth joining for an elevated perspective on the building and surrounds.

Dongdaemun History & Culture Park

In 2008, during the dismantling of the Dongdaemun Stadium to make way for DDP, major archaeological remains were uncovered, including Seoul City Wall foundations going as far back as the late 14th century, as well other Joseon-dynasty buildings. The remains have been incorporated into the Dongdaemun History & Culture Park and include the two-arched floodgate **Yigansumun**.

The **Dongdaemun History Museum** provides the historical background to the ancient foundations preserved outside, while the **Dongdaemun Stadium Memorial** presents the history of the sporting complex that occupied the site from 1925 to 2007. Two of the stadium's floodlight towers have been preserved.

Rummage for Flea Market Finds

Browse Dongmyo and Seoul Folk Flea markets

One of Seoul's coolest (not to mention sustainable) shopping locations is **Dongmyo Flea Market**. In the streets surrounding Dongmyo Shrine, this market is all about hand-me-down fashion. If sifting through piles of clothes, shoes and bags spread on the ground is not your scene, the more curated selection at scores of little boutiques will appeal.

A short walk east is the covered, two-storey **Seoul Folk Flea Market** *(@seoulfolkfleamarket)*. You could kit out half the world's hipster cafes from the teetering stacks of items here, which include traditional Korean bric-a-brac such as wooden masks and ink drawings. On the 2nd floor there's a section styled as Seoul of the 1960s and '70s. The market is closed Tuesday.

Explore Yangnyeongsi Herb Medicine Market

Visit Seoul K-Medi Center

To get a handle on the weird and wonderful products sold at the surrounding **Seoul Yangnyeongsi Herb Medicine Market**, swing by the museum at the **Seoul K-Medi Center** *(kmedi.ddm.go.kr; adult/child ₩1000/500)*. The exhibition is a great primer on the vast array of natural ingredients that are used in Korean medicine and the philosophies underpinning its practice.

Housed in an impressive building partly styled to resemble the Bojewon, a hospital from the early Joseon era, the centre also offers massages of hands, feet and back (30 minutes ₩5000), all done by machines. Between March and November, you can also treat your feet to a herbal bath of mugwort and mint while sipping herbal tea (20 minutes ₩6000).

Across the central courtyard is **Chamdajeong**, open 9am to 7pm, a cafe serving herbal teas and traditional food such as pumpkin porridge or a lotus-leaf rice set meal.

KOREAN MEDICINE MARKET

Plants form a large portion of the pharmaceutical ingredients of Korean medicine, and parts of plants that have medicinal uses are called *boncho.*

Jegi-dong, location of Seoul Yangnyeongsi Herb Medicine Market, has been associated with traditional medicine since the 17th century – that's when the Bojewon, providing lodging for travellers and free medical treatment for the sick and poor, was established here. It was outside the city walls to prevent the spread of infection.

Today the market has more than 1000 specialised traders and businesses. Shopfronts are piled with roots, seeds, barks, dried flowers, fruits and vegetables, from *youngji* mushrooms and cinnamon sticks to deer antlers and Korean red ginseng.

EATING & DRINKING IN DONGDAEMUN & JANGCHUNG: OUR PICKS

Dongdaemun Grilled Fish Alley: Small, no-frills restaurants specialising in charcoal-grilled *samchi* (Spanish mackerel) and other fish. *8.30am-8.30pm* ₩₩

Star Samarkand: Try *plov* (a rice-and-meat dish), *lagman* noodles, *manti* dumplings and freshly baked breads at this friendly Uzbeki restaurant. *10am-11pm Wed-Mon* ₩₩

Woori Yeah Sool: (우리예술) Wash down plump deep-fried prawns and delicious spicy pork ribs with its house-made *makgeolli. 5-11pm Tue-Sun* ₩₩

Soop Mama Kitchen: Homemade Korean meals, including various bibimbap, as well as an all-day breakfast platter and craft beer from Jeju. *11am-8pm* ₩

Starbucks Jangchung Lounge R: A stylish 1960s house and garden is the base for this upmarket Starbucks. Also serves cocktails. *9am-9pm Sun-Thu, to 10pm Fri & Sat*

Cafe Fritz: Split across three *hanok*-style buildings, this bakery-cafe is a chilled hangout serving good drinks and food. *8am-10pm*

Conhas: There are fantastic views of DDP from the upper floors of this industrial-style cafe serving quality brews. *10am-11pm*

Woori Yeah Sool Brewery: Sample a range of *makgeolli*, including one fermented with basil and apple, at this cosy taphouse. *3-11pm Tue-Sun*

DONGDAEMUN SINDANG LOOP

Encounter some of Seoul's eclectic architecture and a traditional food market on this circuit of sights around Dongdaemun.

START	END	LENGTH
Dongdaemun Design Plaza	Heunginjimun	4.5km, 2hr

Admire the sweeping metallic surface of ❶ **Dongdaemun Design Plaza** (p166). Head south down Jangchungdan-ro to ❷ **Kyungdong Presbyterian Church**, a red-brick church designed by Kim Swoo Geun in 1981, its unusual shape inspired by hands clasped in prayer. Further along is ❸ **Shinsegae Namsan**, a handsome beige-brick building that's the department store's training centre – step inside to admire its grand entrance.

Either side of the intersection of Jangchungdan-ro and Dongho-ro are the family-run bakery-cafe ❹ **Taegeukdang** and the ❺ **Jangchung Arena**. Opened in 1955 as an army gymnasium, the arena's domed roof was added in 1963. Running along the eastern edge of the Shilla Hotel's grounds is a section of ❻ **Seoul City Wall**. Fuel up on coffee and brunch dishes at ❼ **Sunday Arvo Yaksu**, then check out what art is on show at ❽ **Frieze House Seoul**.

From Yaksu station, either walk north along Dasan-ro or hop on the subway for two stops to Sindang. Navigate to ❾ **Jungang Market** (p164), where you can sample traditional street food. Keep on north until you reach the ❿ **Cheonggye-cheon**. Follow the stream-side path back west, enjoying the respite from the urban hubbub on the way to the historic ⓫ **Heunginjimun** (p164) east gate.

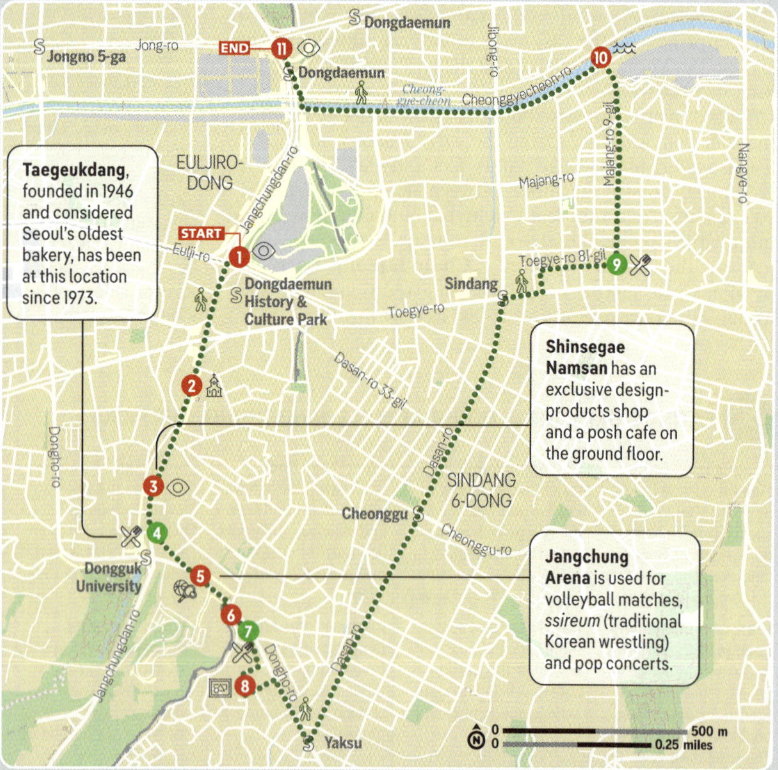

Go Shopping at Gyeongdong Market

Find a theatrical branch of Starbucks

Gyeongdong Market is one of Seoul's biggest wholesale fresh-produce markets. It's a really popular place, but as a way of attracting even more customers, the traders association teamed up with Starbucks to take part in its Community Store charitable programme. **Starbucks Gyeongdong 1960** is an impressive revamp of an old theatre within the market, featuring tiered seating, a giant artwork hung over the serving counter and a small stage for musical performances. In the lobby is the **Goldstar Electronics Refresh Center**, a creative project by electronics giant LG with a focus on sustainability.

MORE DESTINATION CAFES

Large-scale cafes such as Starbucks Gyeongdong 1960 that are destinations in themselves are massively popular across Korea. In the greater Seoul region, also check out **COSMO 40** (p197) in Incheon and **Joyang Bangjik** (p201) on Ganghwado.

Visit the Cheonggye-cheon Museum

A stream through Seoul

The mammoth and costly effort to resurrect Seoul's long-buried east–west stream is detailed at the excellent **Cheonggye-cheon Museum** *(museum.seoul.go.kr; free)*. Learn how the stream evolved from a Joseon beauty spot to a sewer dubbed 'Seoul's cancer' to a beacon of urban regeneration.

Opposite the museum, the **Urban Oasis** museum is housed inside a re-creation of some of the wooden shanties that lined the stream after the Korean War. The space is dedicated to changing exhibitions on themes of sustainability.

The museum, which is closed Mondays, is a fine starting point for a walk along the banks of the waterway. Heading west, you'll soon encounter the remains of three concrete **pillars** from the elevated highway that was dismantled before the stream's resurrection. They stand in the midst of the stream near the Muhakgyo bridge and the confluence with Seongbuk-cheon.

JEON TAE-IL'S STATUE

After the Korean War, the banks of the Cheonggye-cheon through Dongdaemun became a shanty town for North Korean refugees. To make a living, they sold clothes refashioned from US army uniforms. So began the area's association with fashion.

In 1962 a market building was created to house the small clothing factories and stalls selling the fabric and accessories. It was named **Pyeonghwa**, meaning 'peace'.

Working conditions in Pyeonghwa's sweatshops were appalling and, in 1970, Jeon Tae-il, a 22-year-old tailor at the market, died after setting himself alight in protest. His death spurred the formation of labour unions to advocate for workers' rights. A **statue of Jeon** stands on the bridge over the Cheonggye-cheon beside the market.

EATING IN SINDANG: OUR PICKS

Hani Kalguksu: Simple joint serving tasty hand-cut noodles in a spicy broth topped with pollock milt, roe and water parsley. *10.30am-2.30pm & 5-9pm* ₩

I Love Sindangdong: Cook the comfort food *tteokbokki* (a spicy rice-cake stew) at your table at this mainstay of Sindang-dong Tteokbokki Town. *24hr* ₩₩

Sindang Gyeryugwan: Sink your teeth into super-succulent and crispy whole chicken stuffed with garlic rice and vegetables. *4-10pm* ₩₩

Gosari Express: Inventive plant-based takes on Korean cuisine, including noodles at this Michelin-tipped restaurant. *11.30am-9pm Tue–Sat* ₩₩

DAPSIMNI SHOPPING LIST

Summer Song from Hyangmidang *(@hyangmidang)* recommends popular, portable items to pick up from Dapsimni Antiques Market:

Bojagi: Wrapping cloths handmade from stitched-together pieces of cloth – usually ramie (a type of linen) but silk at times.

Baneulggoji: Pin-cushions, beautifully decorated with hand-stitched embroidery.

Nohtsutgarak: Brass spoons – the smaller ones are decorated with delicate engravings.

Jaegi: Wooden plates used for displaying food in ancestral rites.

Soban: Small wooden tables, used for individual dining or serving tea – they reflect Korea's refined craftsmanship and modest beauty.

Mokgirogi: Wooden carvings of wild geese or ducks, traditionally given as a present to newlyweds as they symbolise eternal love.

SIMON RICHMOND

***Baneul Saam*, Dapsimni**

Treasure Trove of Korean Crafts

Browse Dapsimni Antiques Market

Antiques dealers have clustered in two buildings in **Dapsimni** since the 1980s. Here you can find a wealth of Korean arts and crafts – mostly old, sometimes new – ranging from silk tassel decorations for *hanbok* to fish-shaped wooden locks and a stone carved Bodhisattva astride an elephant. It's a fascinating place to rummage for unique pieces, and the selection of goods is larger and prices tend to be cheaper than at dealers in Insa-dong (p68). Often you'll have to sift through shelves and piles of dusty old items. In the larger of the two buildings, however, are dealers with a more curated and contemporary-styled presentation, such as **Gobokii** *(@gobokii_kr)*, **Hyangmidang** *(@hyangmidang)*, **Of** *(@ofjec_t)* and **Hobak Folk Art Gallery** *(@hobakfolkartgallery)*. If you have cash, you can haggle for discounts of between 5% and 10%. The market is closed on Sundays.

DRINKING IN DONGDAEMUN & SINDANG: BARS

Jean Frigo: Push against a fridge door to find this chic cocktail bar hidden behind a daytime greengrocers. *6pm-1.30am Tue-Sat, 5pm-midnight Sun*

Gu Seoul: Chris Jang is the friendly, English-speaking mixologist running this spacious bar decorated with his own furniture designs. *6pm-1am Thu-Tue*

Zoo Sindang: Sip Chinese-zodiac-themed cocktails at this fun speakeasy hung with a jungle of fake plants. *6pm-2am*

Manmool: Enjoy the retro vibes of this vintage-furnished cafe-bar serving coffee, wine, cocktails and desserts. *3pm-1am Tue-Sun*

Seongsu & Seoul Forest Park

In rapidly developing Seongsu, it's all about eye-catching design and fashion. For a respite from the crowds thronging its main streets, head to one of the area's trio of verdant parks.

Surreal Retail Playground

Behold Haus Nowhere

In recent years, Seongsu has become a testing ground for retail experimentation. Imaginatively designed pop-ups are integral, offering interior design that blurs the line between retail, art and entertainment. Leading the way is **Haus Nowhere**, a showcase for a suite of IICOMBINED brands: Gentle Monster (eyewear), Tamburins (cosmetics), Nudake (tea and desserts), Attissu (hats) and Nuflaat (tableware).

The wow factor begins before you step across the threshold, with the 14-storey building, designed by The_System Lab, led by architect Kim Chanjoong, looming ominously above the Seongsu roofline. This sci-fi vision in concrete is also the HQ of IICOMBINED. Outside, the *More Is More* installation by conceptual artist Max Siedentopf features a life-sized elderly white man holding up a single gold bin bag amid a sea of black ones.

The installations inside are just as weird, wonderful and outsized, eclipsing the products they're promoting and making Haus Nowhere a selfie-snapping glimpse into the future of offline retail. Book ahead for the 5th-floor's **Nudake Teahouse**, serving flavoured teas and designer desserts in a sage and purple boudoir straight out of a Stanley Kubrick movie.

Also jaw-dropping is **Blue Elephant Space Seongsu**, an eyewear boutique offering up a giant sphere onto which media art is projected.

Kayak the Han River

Hang out in Ttukseom Hangang Park

Among the series of parks fringing the Han River, **Ttukseom Hangang Park** *(hangang.seoul.go.kr)* has carved a niche for itself as a base for kayak and stand-up paddleboard (SUP) operations that cluster at the eastern end of the waterside reserve. **Koa Travel** *(@koa.travel_kr)*, run by English-speaking Koa, offers two-hour rental of kayaks and SUPs (₩40,000) and guided tours (₩70,000) along the river. Paddling the

Continues on p175

SEONGSU POPUPS

Choi Wonseok is the CEO of Project Rent *(project-rent.com)*.

We pioneered pop-ups in Seongsu-dong back in 2018, and now operate eight spaces dedicated to brand communication. Our clients include Lotte (Ghana chocolate, Xylitol chewing gum), Apple TV (*Pachinko*) and Hyundai Motors.

A successful pop-up is about quality over quantity. For the Ghana Chocolate House pop-up, which attracted 32,000 visitors over four weeks in 2024, we used experiential design rather than traditional advertising to convince customers of the product's premium value.

When I started in Seongsu, I dreamed of creating a street that felt like walking through a magazine – a collection of small, curated brands. Now, it feels more like an offline theme park where digital content comes to life.

HIGHLIGHTS
1 Seoul Forest

SIGHTS
2 Seoul Children's Grand Park
3 Ttukseom Hangang Park
4 Ttukseom Jjabeolle

ACTIVITIES, COURSES & TOURS
5 Koa Travel

SLEEPING
6 Hotel Poco
7 Seoul Forest Stay

EATING
8 Glow Seongsu
9 Grandmother's Recipe
10 Nanpo Seongsu
11 Neungdong Minari Seongsu

DRINKING & NIGHTLIFE
12 Amazing Brewing Co
13 Daelim Changgo
14 Magpie&Tiger Seongsu Tearoom

SHOPPING
15 Adererror
16 CU convenience store
17 Kwangya
18 Olive Young N Seongsu

INFORMATION
19 Seoul Forest Visitor Center

TOP EXPERIENCE

Seoul Forest

Bounded by the Han River and the Jungnang Stream, Seoul Forest covers nearly 481,000 sq metres. A serene location for a relaxing stroll or picnic throughout the year, it's split into five areas: the Culture & Art Park, Experiential Learning Park, Eco Forest (which includes a sika deer enclosure), Marsh Plants Gardens and the riverside Hangang Park.

SANGA PARK/GETTY IMAGES

Seoul Forest in autumn

Culture & Art Park

The land on which Seoul Forest is located was once a royal hunting ground. In 1908, Seoul's first public waterworks opened here and later there was a horse-racing track – hence the dynamic sculpture of galloping horses at the park's east entrance. Behind the sculpture is the **Splash Fountain**, where 100 water spouts cool down delighted kids in the summer, the **Sculpture Garden** and **Mirror Lake**, a shallow pond that provides a beautiful reflective foreground for scenic photography.

Nature in the City

The **Experiential Learning Park** contains the Butterfly Garden (May to October) and Insect Garden – both these enclosed spaces are closed on Mondays.

Each spring the **Cherry Tree Path** is an explosion of fluffy blossoms – follow it to the **Eco Forest**,where there's a fenced corral for Korean water deer and sika deer. Climb to the footbridge to get a good overhead view of the deer and to access the Hangang riverside section of the park across the expressway. In autumn, don't miss **Ginkgo Road** for its profusion of golden-leaved ginkgo trees.

TOP TIPS

- Park maps are available at the **visitor centre**, where you can also borrow strollers and wheelchairs for free.
- Inside the park, the only place to buy food and drink is at the **CU convenience store** beside the Butterfly Garden.

PRACTICALITIES

- *parks.seoul.go.kr/template/sub/seoulforest.do*
- free
- 24hr

SEONGSU STROLL

Spend a visually stimulating half-day cruising Seongsu's arty, surreal boutiques, cafes and pop-ups.

START	END	LENGTH
Onion	Seoul Brewery Seongsu	3.5km, 2hr

Fuel up on coffee and baked goods at 1 **Onion**. Nearby at 2 **Amore Seongsu**, the flagship of beauty company Amorepacific, there's a lovely rock garden with grasses and trees. Further east is 3 **Common Ground**, a hip shopping mall created from converted shipping containers. Standing for Le Conte Des Contes, meaning 'a story within a story', 4 **LCDC Seoul** hosts pop-up exhibitions and small stores championing Korean creatives and lifestyle brands such as Hanahzo for handmade soaps. Head south to marvel at the contemporary architecture and art at 5 **Haus Nowhere** (p171).

A cavernous converted *changgo* (warehouse) is home to both the long-running cafe 6 **Daelim Changgo** and 7 **Musinsa Store Seongsu@ Daelim Changgo**, one of several physical branches of the major Korean online fashion platform. Gawp at the giant media globe rising three floors through 8 **Blue Elephant Space Seongsu** (p171). The 9 **Dior** pop-up store has been such a hit it's likely to be around a few more years; across the way is another architectural and branding showpiece – the flagship for cosmetics brand 10 **Tamburins**.

Shop a superb range of stationery from Korea and overseas at 11 **Point of View**, then enjoy a beer and a bite to eat at 12 **Seoul Brewery Seongsu** – you've earned it!

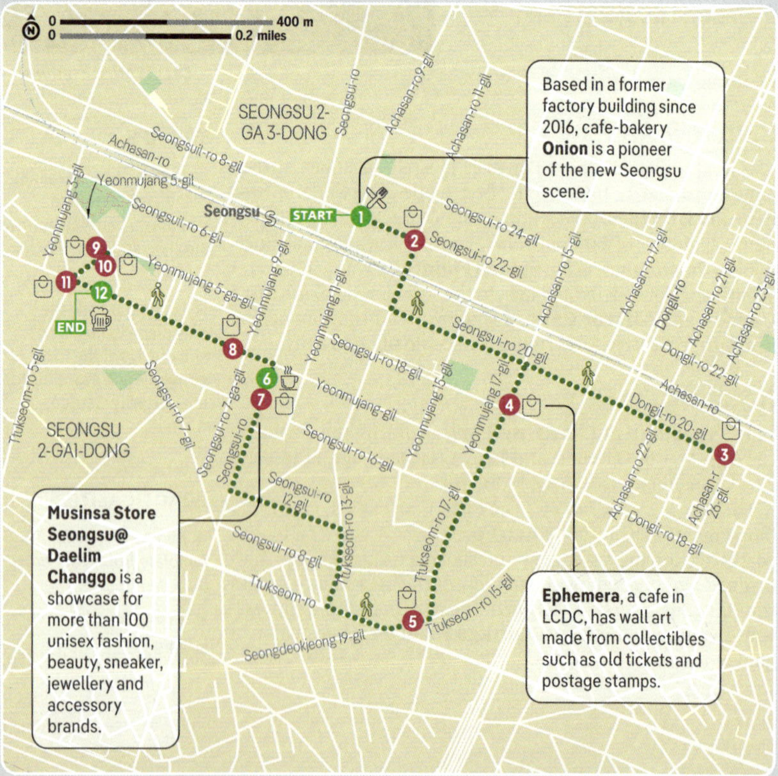

Continued from p171
Han around sunset, with the light glittering off the soaring Lotte Tower and Gangnam's skyline, is especially memorable.

Other facilities and attractions in the park include a sculpture park packed with many excellent works, a rock-climbing wall and, in summer, an outdoor swimming pool. At the time of research, the **Ttukseom Jjabeolle**, a giant doughnut-shaped and elevated structure that houses an exhibition on the Han River, was closed for renovations.

A Park Dedicated to Kids

Run wild in Children's Grand Park

Opened in 1973, **Seoul Children's Grand Park** *(sisul.or.kr/open_content/childrenpark; free)* is a place that generations of locals view fondly as a place for play and education. Within the enormous and well-designed green space are amusement rides, a free zoo, a botanical garden, a wetland ecology area, a giant musical fountain and a children's museum with plenty of hands-on edutainment. Star attractions in the zoo include elephants, tigers and lions – in 2005, six elephants broke out of their enclosure, causing havoc in the area until their recapture.

The park's main entrance is next to the Children's Grand Park subway station, with a second entrance beside Achasan station at the foot of 295m Achasan mountain.

BEST SHOPPING IN SEONGSU

Common Ground: Complex built from 200 shipping containers. Includes **Up Cycle Hug** for sustainably made items and lots of good vintage stores.

Olive Young N Seongsu: The N stands for new and next level at this mega branch of the beauty-store chain. Sign up for free consultations.

Point of View: Superbly curated store stacked with stationery from Korea and overseas.

Adererror: High-concept art alongside one of Korea's hottest fashion brands, known for its deconstructed streetwear.

Kwangya: Heaven for K-Pop fans is this basement souvenir store featuring SM Entertainment artists.

EATING & DRINKING IN SEONGSU & SEOUL FOREST: OUR PICKS

Grandmother's Recipe: Family-run restaurant serving delicious, great-value meals featuring classics such as bulgogi beef. *11.30am-3.40pm & 4.40-9pm* WW

Nanpo Seongsu: Relaxed joint attracting a young crowd for its fusion Korean dishes – try the rice balls wrapped in greens. *11am-9.30pm* WW

Neungdong Minari Seongsu: Expect to line up for delicious *yukhoe* (raw beef) bibimbap and water-parsley-topped *gomtang* (beef-bone soup). *9.30am-midnight* W

Glow Seongsu: Take your pick from stalls selling 10 types of global cuisine at this dining village set around a fairy-lit pond and garden. *11am-11pm* WW

Amazing Brewing Co: Wash down wood-fired pizza with draft beers at this Seongsu-based microbrewery. *5pm-midnight Mon-Fri, from 3pm Sat & Sun*

Seoul Brewery Seongsu: Fascinating selection of in-house ales, including a rice lager, rye IPA and chocolatey porter. Good food, too. *noon-11.30pm*

Magpie&Tiger Seongsu Tearoom: Flying the flag for tea in coffee-dominated Seongsu is this oasis of calm above a Musinsa boutique. *11am-9.30pm*

Daelim Changgo: Check out contemporary art while sipping lattes at this cafe-gallery in a red brick warehouse *(changgo)* that was once a rice mill. *11am-10pm.*

Researched by Simon Richmond

NORTHERN SEOUL

CITY WALL & NATIONAL PARK HIKING TRAILS

Get up close to the old fortress wall, visit fine museums and meditate at serene temples in Seoul's mountainous northern neighbourhoods.

It's hard to resist following the Seoul City Wall as it snakes across Naksan, Bukaksan and Inwangsan, three of the city's guardian mountains. Further north, urban development ceases at the boundaries of the majestic Bukhansan National Park, home to higher peaks, ancient temples and myriad hiking trails. Learn about key episodes in Korean history at the Changgyeonggung royal palace and the sombre Seodaemun Prison History Hall. Dive into Daehangno theatre scene and visit museums devoted, among other things, to Korean furniture, stone carving and pioneers of 20th-century Korean art. Here, too, lies an elegant late-Joseon villa and garden, the perfect escape from contemporary Seoul.

INCLUDES

FROM LEFT: STOCK PHOTOS 2000/SHUTTERSTOCK, YLLYSO/SHUTTERSTOCK

Changgyeonggung (p182)

See page 218 for places to stay in Northern Seoul

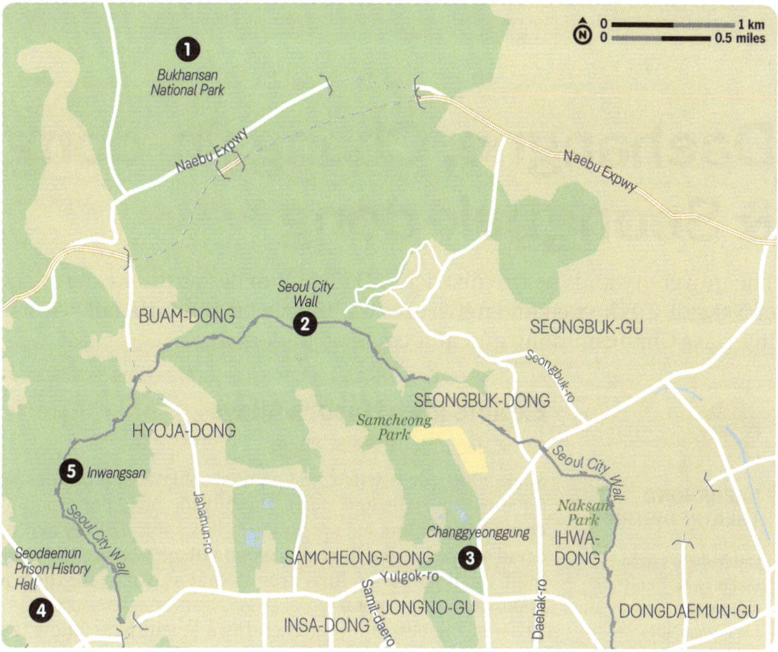

Highlights

1 Bukhansan National Park
Summit Seoul's tallest peaks in this 76,922-sq-km reserve. **p194**

2 Seoul City Wall
Hike beside the historic fortress walls as they connect Naksan, Bukaksan and Inwangsan mountains. **p181**

3 Changgyeonggung
Cross an ancient stone bridge, view a Joseon throne room and stroll around leafy gardens. **p182**

4 Seodaemun Prison History Hall
Learn about the local martyrs in the fight for independence. **p189**

▲ 5 Inwangsan
Hike up this mountain for Seoul City Wall views and to witness shamanistic ceremonies. **p190**

Getting Around

Subway
Daehangno and Seongbuk-dong are accessed by Hyehwa and Hangsung University stations. For Seodaemun, alight at Dongnimmun. For Bukhansan National Park trails, head to Dobongsan or Bukhansan Ui stations.

Walking
There are hiking routes alongside Seoul City Wall over Naksan, Bukaksan and Inwangsan, as well as other trails up these three city-centre mountains.

Bus
Buses are handiest for reaching Buam-dong and for the further-flung sites of Seongbuk-dong, such as the Korean Stone Art Museum and Korea Furniture Museum.

Daehangno, Changsin-dong & Seongbuk-dong

The university and theatre district of Daehangno lies at the western foot of Naksan. To the east and north are two hillside neighbourhoods – working-class Changsin-dong and affluent Seongbuk-dong.

DAEHANGNO THEATRE DISTRICT

Daehangno's association with youth culture and the performing arts goes back decades. The district was the original home of Seoul National University and remains the base for Arts Council Korea.

There are some 170 theatres in the area, the largest ones being **Hongik University Daehakro Art Center** *(artscenter.hongik.ac.kr)* and **Arko & Daehakro Arts Theater** *(theater.arko.or.kr)*. At Marronnier Park, **Daehangno Information Center**, open 10am to 8pm Tuesday to Sunday, has flyers for most of the shows playing. Staff here can point out shows that have subtitles in other languages, or are performed in English, such as the long-running comedy-thriller *Hangover*. Tickets are typically around ₩15,000.

Explore Ihwa Maeul's Alleys

Mural-decorated hillside village

Since 2006, when artists first painted colourful murals across its alleyway walls and stairs, the hillside neighbourhood of **Ihwa Maeul** has been a tourism hot spot. This is one of Seoul's *daldongnae* (literally 'moon village'), where the poor built small homes on high ground that at least gave them a good view of the moon.

One of the best ways to reach Ihwa Maeul is to follow the footpath beside Seoul City Wall from Dongdaemun. At the top of the village, the **Gaebbul** cafe includes the gourmet bakery **Baeogae**, where you can buy cutely designed macrons. It also has an outdoor deck that is a prime sunset viewing spot. At the foot of Ihwa Maeul is **Ihwajang** *(syngmanrhee.or.kr)*, once the family home of Syngman Rhee, the Republic of Korea's first president. Rhee led South Korea from August 1948 until April 1960. At the time of research, the property was closed for renovations.

Hang Out in Marronnier Park

Home to Arko Art Center

The heart of the university and performing-arts district of Daehangno is **Marronnier Park**, named after the horse chestnut trees planted here. The plaza-like park usually has something happening on afternoons and evenings at the outdoor stage, as well as various sculptures to admire. The ginkgo trees turning golden and contrasting against the surrounding red-brick buildings also make it a fine spot to admire autumnal foliage.

One of those red-brick buildings to the park's east side is **Arko Art Center** *(arko.or.kr/artcenter; free)*. Operated by Arts Council Korea, this centre's galleries host regularly changing, often avant-garde exhibitions by mostly Korean artists. Opened in 1979, it was designed by celebrated architect Kim Swoo Geun. The centre is closed Monday.

DAEHANGNO, CHANGSIN-DONG & SEONGBUK-DONG

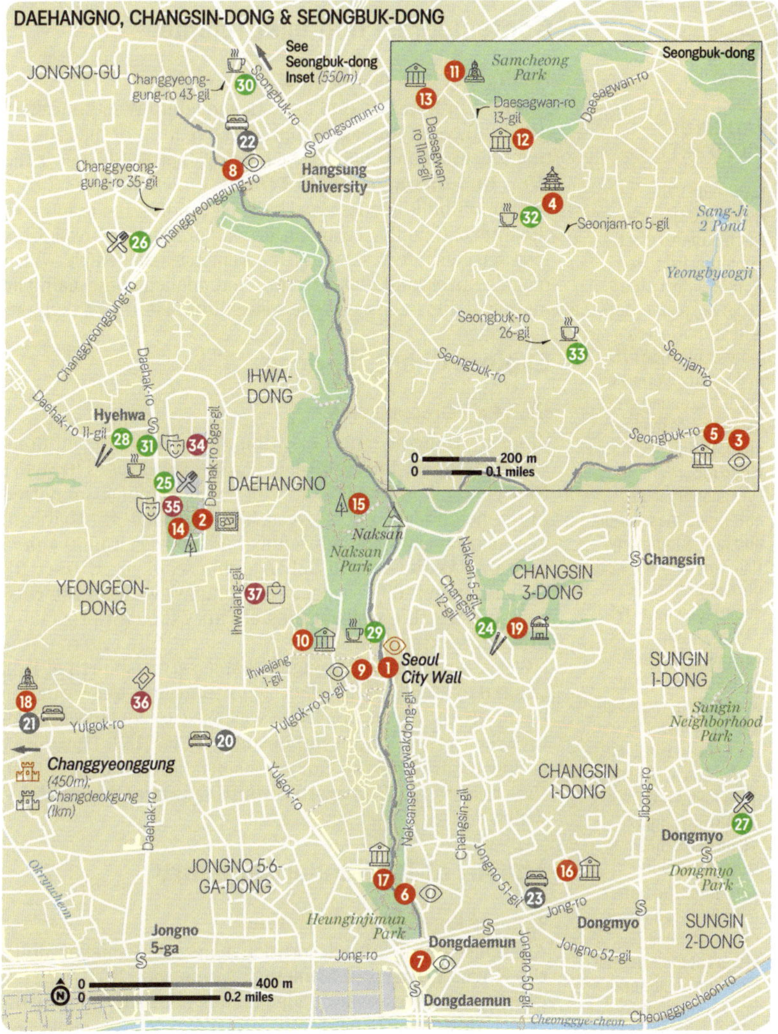

HIGHLIGHTS
1 Seoul City Wall

SIGHTS
2 Arko Art Center
3 Choi Sunu House
4 Gilsang-sa
5 Han Sang Soo Embroidery Museum
6 Hanyangdoseong
7 Heunginjimun
8 Hyehwamun
9 Ihwa Maeul
10 Ihwajang
11 Jeongbeopsa
12 Korea Furniture Museum
13 Korean Stone Art Museum
14 Marronnier Park
15 Naksan Park
16 Paik Ground SeMA
17 Seoul City Wall Museum
18 Won Buddhism Wonnam Temple

ACTIVITIES
19 Changsin Sungin Quarry Observatory

SLEEPING
20 Glue Hotel
21 Mayplace
22 Nabijam
23 Original Backpackers

EATING
24 Chang Chang
25 Dalgona Stall
26 Hyehwa Kalguksu
27 Olden Grey
28 Solnamugil Deongjang Yesool

DRINKING & NIGHTLIFE
see 24 Donut Jungsu
29 Gaebbul
30 Haero Coffee
31 Hakrim
32 Space.Supernormal.Cafe
33 Suyeonsanbang

ENTERTAINMENT
34 Arko & Daehakro Arts Theater
35 Daehangno Information Center
36 Hongik University Daehakro Art Center

SHOPPING
37 ithinkso Archive

FATHER OF VIDEO ART

Nam June Paik (1932–2006) is one of South Korea's most famous artists. He worked with a wide variety of media, but is best known as a pioneer of video art. In the early 1960s, he started creating art using one of the first commercially available video recorders.

A visionary who embraced mass media and new technology, Paik coined the phrase 'electronic superhighway' in 1974.

Paik Ground SeMA will give a taste of what Paik's art is all about. For a thorough overview, head to the more extensive collection at the Nam June Paik Art Center (p208) in Yongin.

One of his most impressive works, *The More, The Better* from 1988, is a tower of TVs screening videos at the National Museum of Modern and Contemporary Art in Gwacheon.

Contemporary Buddhist Temple

Meditate at Wonnam Temple

Founded in Korea in 1916 by Park Joongbin, Won Buddhism (Won Bulkyo in Korean) is a progressive form of the religion that is centred on equality. The religion's spiritual home is the **Won Buddhism Wonnam Temple**, which occupies a contemporary building designed by Mass Studies, the practice of the internationally acclaimed Korean architect Minsok Cho. Exposed concrete in sinuous curves encircles the temple, which includes an elegant *hanok* (traditional wooden home) hall. The main worship hall is a serene space illuminated by a skylight.

Explore Changsin-dong

Visit Paik Ground SeMA

Close by Dongdaemun's clothing markets, Changsin-dong was once home to small-scale sewing factories. The artist Nam Jun Paik, whose father was a textile manufacturer, lived in the neighbourhood between 1937 and 1950. It's that connection that saw Seoul Museum of Art convert a 1960 *hanok* here into **Paik Ground SeMA** *(sema.seoul.go.kr; free)*. It's a small exhibition space (closed Monday) with an attached cafe, but worth a visit for fans of Paik's thought-provoking, groundbreaking artworks.

Weave your way up through the steep streets north of Paik Ground to eventually overlook a former granite quarry dating to the 1920s. Stone from here was used to construct buildings such as Seoul train station and old City Hall. The quarry is now a park and you can get a splendid view over it from the cantilevered **Changsin Sungin Quarry Observatory**, which houses a cafe.

The Art of Traditional Carpentry

Tour the Korea Furniture Museum

As exclusive as its hillside location in upscale Seongbuk-dong, the **Korea Furniture Museum** *(kofum.com; ₩20,000)* is a gem. Advance reservation via email is necessary to tour the collection of handsome furniture, including chests, bookcases and dining tables made from varieties of wood, such as persimmon, maple and paulownia. Some are decorated with lacquer, mother of pearl or tortoise shell. The museum is the personal

EATING IN DAEHANGNO & CHANGSIN-DONG: OUR PICKS

Solnamugil Doenjang Yesool: (솔나무길 된장예술) Serves a veggie bibimbap with a tofu stew and many tasty side dishes. *10.30am-2.30pm & 3.30-9pm* ₩₩

Chang Chang: Retro-themed Cantonese restaurant serving warming bowls of beef-brisket noodles and stir fries. *11.30am-3pm & 5-9pm* ₩₩

Hyehwa Kalguksu: (혜화 칼국수) Old-school eatery specialising in Andong *guksi* noodles in a milky-white beef-bone broth with leeks. *11am-9.30pm* ₩

Olden Grey: Trendy brunch restaurant close by Dongmyo and sharing premises with the Olden Brown cafe. Also has a rooftop garden. *11am-10pm* ₩₩

TOP EXPERIENCE

Seoul City Wall

Completed in 1396 during the reign of King Taejo, Hanyangdoseong (Seoul City Wall) was built to defend the capital. Today, the stone fortifications, which connect Seoul's four inner 'guardian' mountains of Bukaksan, Naksan, Namsan and Inwangsan, are a top visitor attraction. Hiking trails alongside the wall bring you up close to historic architecture and provide awesome views across the city.

NGHIA KHANH/SHUTTERSTOCK

Seoul City Wall, Naksan Park

Seoul City Wall Museum

To learn all about the 600-year history of the fortifications, it's worth dropping by the **Seoul City Wall Museum** *(museum.seoul.go.kr; free)*. Feng shui principles were used in the wall's construction, which follows the city's natural topography. Joseon-dynasty builders carved their names on the stones of the original fortress – you can do likewise via an interactive display onto a video projection of the wall. The museum is closed Monday.

Hiking the Wall

Between 5m and 8m in height, the wall runs for 18.6km around central Seoul, with just under 80% of it restored. While it's possible to hike the entire route in a single (exhausting) day, it's better to split the circuit over two days, or focus on one of the four sections.

The shortest and least strenuous route is 2.1km over **Naksan Park** between the sub-gate **Hyehwamun** and **Heunginjimun** (p164), one of the four original principal gates in the wall. Here the fortress wall cuts a graceful, sinuous curve through the city and provides beautiful vistas. The most challenging section is that up and over **Bukaksan** (p186; 4.7km).

TOP TIPS

- A free map and walking guide is available at the Seoul City Wall Museum.
- A night hike beside the illuminated wall up to Naksan is recommended so as to enjoy the twinkling panorama of city lights.

PRACTICALITIES

- *seoulcitywall.seoul.go.kr*
- free
- 24hr

TOP EXPERIENCE

Changgyeonggung

The history of Changgyeonggung, one of Seoul's 'five grand palaces', goes back to the mid-15th century when King Sejong built a retirement home here for his father, Taejong. Much renovated and reconstructed in the centuries since, it contains a few original structures and is impressive for its lushly wooded grounds and Korea's first Western-style greenhouse, built in 1909.

TAKASHI IMAGES/SHUTTERSTOCK

Daeonsil

TOP TIPS

- Between March and November, the Moonlight Lotus Show, a nighttime media art show, is projected across Chundangji.
- Join free English guided tours at 11am and 3pm Tuesday to Sunday.
- Entry is free for those wearing traditional *hanbok*.

PRACTICALITIES

- *royal.khs.go.kr*
- adult/child ₩1000/free
- 9am-9pm Tue-Sun

Palace Buildings

The palace's main entrance is **Honghwamun**, an impressive double-hipped roof structure dating to 1616. Dead ahead is **Okcheongyo**, a stone bridge completed in 1483, making it the oldest surviving structure of the original palace, and the throne hall, **Myeongjeongjeon**. The oldest surviving hall in all of Seoul's palaces, it is a rare example of early-17th-century Joseon architecture and is decorated inside with a splendid *irworobongdo* folded screen painted with five mountains, the sun and the moon.

The smaller buildings beyond the main hall were where royals and concubines lived – sometimes these buildings are used for special exhibitions.

Gardens & Greenhouse

Like Seoul's other palaces, Changgyeonggung was destroyed twice by the Japanese – first in the 1590s and again during the colonial period of the first half of the 20th century, when the grounds were turned into a park containing a zoo. That is when the **Chundangji** ornamental pond was added, as well as **Daeonsil** (Great Greenhouse), a European-style glasshouse. Stocked with Korean plants, including lovely examples of *bunjae* (bonsai), it's a popular spot for couples to hang out.

project of a former Yonsei University professor, who displays the pieces from the collection in a series of elegant *hanok*. The wooden buildings include a kitchen house with a seemingly contemporary design of windows, and a villa that was once part of **Changdeokgung**. A bonus is the panoramic city views from the property, which is closed Sunday and Monday.

Hillside Garden of Old Stone Statues

Explore the Korean Stone Art Museum

An army of centuries-old stone sentinels stand guard on the hillside overlooking Seongbuk-dong at the **Korean Stone Art Museum** *(koreanstonemuseum.com; ₩5000)*. This unique collection was amassed over several decades by Chun Shin-Il, chairman of the industrial Sejoong corporation. Start by viewing the interior displays, which are mainly of *beoksu* (village guardians), before emerging on the museum's roof, which blends into landscaped, hillside gardens. Meander paths lined by enigmatic stone figures, elegant Buddhist deities and lanterns as you also take in the marvellous city views. The museum is closed Monday.

Next door is the colourfully decorated Buddhist temple, **Jeongbeopsa**, which includes a peaceful cafe. The temple is the start of a hiking trail up Bukaksan.

Templestay in Seongbuk-dong

Meditate at Gilsang-sa

Gilsang-sa *(kilsangsa.info)* was once Daewongak, a restaurant where *gisaeng* (female entertainers accomplished in traditional arts) performed. In 1995 the property was donated by its owner Kim Yeong-han to the venerable Buddhist monk Beopjeong, who turned it into a branch temple of the Jogye order. A tiny museum dedicated to Beopjeong, who passed away in 2010, is located at the top of the complex, beside the creek that flows down the mountainside.

The temple runs overnight templestay programs. It's a particular pleasure to visit in May, when the grounds are festooned with lanterns for Buddha's birthday, and November for the autumn colours.

Opposite the temple, **Space.Supernormal.Cafe** is a pleasant spot for drinks and to view good exhibitions of contemporary art by Korean and international artists.

KNOW YOUR STONE CARVINGS

A staple of Korean arts and crafts down the centuries, stone statues had various functions in relation to religious beliefs. Obvious figures of veneration are the images of Buddhas and Bodhisattvas.

There's also an assortment of guardians – *seokho* (tigers), *seogyang* (sheep), *dongjaseok* (child attendants) and *muninseok* (scholar attendants) – placed to protect the tombs of royal families and aristocrats. *Jangmyeongdeung* (lanterns) were both practical for illuminating graveyards and a spiritual beacon to pray for the deceased's immortality in the afterlife.

Commoners also carved *beoksu* – small totems placed at the entrance to villages to protect against evil spirits and illnesses. These carvings have different facial expressions that give them distinct personalities.

DRINKING IN DAEHANGNO & CHANGSIN-DONG: OUR PICKS

Hakrim: Little (save drink prices) has changed at this classic Daehangno *dabang* (cafe) since it opened in 1956. *10am-11pm*

Donut Jungsu: Catch your breath and take in the view after the trudge up steep Changsin-dong streets at this cute cafe serving gourmet doughnuts. *11.30am-9pm*

Changsin Sungin Quarry Observatory: There are occasional live music performances at this chilled cafe with superior views. *10am-8pm Mon-Fri, to 10pm Sat & Sun*

Haero Coffee: The speciality coffee comes with tasting notes at this *hanok* cafe hidden away north of Daehangno. *11am-10pm*

CLIMB NAKSAN

Follow the old fortress walls to the mural-covered alleyways of Ihwa Maeul and the summit of guardian mountain Naksan.

START	END	LENGTH
Heunginjimun	Hakrim	1.5km, 2hr

Admire ❶ **Heunginjimun** (p164), the majestic Great East Gate, before learning all about the historic fortifications at ❷ **Seoul City Wall Museum** (p181). Follow the wall uphill for the brief, steep climb to ❸ **Ihwa Maeul** (p178). Take a rest at the ❹ **Gaebbul** (p178) bakery-cafe near the top of the village.

Continue to ❺ **Naksan Park** (p181), which is bordered by more impressive sections of the wall and offers splendid urban views. Retrace your steps to Ihwa Maeul and head downhill, passing ❻ **Ihwajang** (p178), the historic home of Syngman Rhee, the first president of South Korea.

Drop into ❼ **ithinkso Archive**, a design store selling bags, stationery and house plants. Continue to ❽ **Marronnier Park** (p178), where you can see what art is being exhibited at the ❾ **Arko Art Center** (p178).

Along Daehak-ro, beside the entrances to Hyehwa subway station, are some tempting street-food stalls, including a ❿ **vendor** who prepares and sells *dalgona*, the honeycomb toffee that featured in the Netflix drama *Squid Game*. Step back in time at the classic ⓫ **Hakrim** (p183) *dabang* (cafe) and order a creamy Vienna coffee, its signature drink.

SIMON RICHMOND

Han Sang Soo Embroidery Museum

Be Charmed by Hanok Architecture

Suyeonsanbang and Choi Sunu House

Meaning 'a home in the mountains for reading and scholarly gatherings', **Suyeonsanbang** *(@sooyeonsanbang)*, open Wednesday to Sunday, was the residence of the novelist Yi Tae-jun from 1933 to 1946. Today it is one of Seoul's most charming *hanok* teahouses. Sit inside the cosy and beautifully constructed wooden building, or take a table on the verandah with a view of the garden, to enjoy drinks and sweets including matcha, honey ginger tea and pumpkin soup.

From the teahouse, it's about a 10-minute walk to another elegant *hanok*, **Choi Sunu House** *(choisunu.com; free)*. Built in the 1930s, and once the home of the former director of the National Museum of Korea, the building was purchased in 2002 by the National Trust of Korea. A box of outer walls contains the L-shaped inner and outer wings of the home and its garden.

Admire Korean Embroidery

Visit the Han Sang Soo Embroidery Museum

The small **Han Sang Soo Embroidery Museum** *(hansang soo.co.kr; ₩5000)* spotlights the art of Korean needlework through temporary exhibitions of pieces from a collection of antiques and works by master artisan Han Sang Soo (1932–2016). Han's daughter, Susana Youngran Kim, the museum's curator, also teaches classes and continues to work on some of her mother's amazingly detailed large-scale embroideries. The museum is closed Monday.

EMBROIDERY ART

Traditionally made with silk thread, embroidery was a skill handed down from mother to daughter among all classes of Korean society. Royal embroidery is known as *gungsu*, while that produced by the general public is called *minsu*.

Embroidery features on wrapping cloths, pillows and clothing. There are motifs and images that are common designs. For example, specific Chinese characters, peonies and lotuses are symbols of health, happiness and long life, while grapes and strawberries stand for fertility.

Hyungbae are the insignia embroidered on clothing to indicate the wearer's rank – birds indicated civil servants, and four-legged animals were for military officers.

Apart from the Han Sang Soo Embroidery Museum, you can see beautiful examples of this art at the Seoul Museum of Craft Art (p68).

Buam-dong & Seodaemun

The upmarket neighbourhood of Buam-dong shelters to the northwest of Bukaksan, while some of Seodaemun's key sights are at the foot of Inwang-san, another of Seoul's guardian mountains.

Summit Bukaksan

Follow the Seoul City Wall route

Although just 342.5m high, **Bukaksan's** rocky terrain and steep granite outcrops make it a challenging mountain to climb. For more than half a century, most trails up and across Bukaksan were strictly off-limits to protect the **Cheong Wa Dae** presidential compound. Now that the 'Blue House' has been decommissioned, all routes on the tallest of Seoul's four guardian peaks are open to the public.

There's a spectacular 2.5km section of the **Seoul City Wall** over Bukaksan that rises steeply from **Changuimun**, the old sub-gate in Buam-dong. The trail hops over the peak above Cheong Wa Dae to the **Malbawi Information Center** near **Sukjeongmun**, the main north gate, which can also be accessed from **Samcheong Park**. The wall is in excellent condition and there's a vivid sense of its original purpose as the city's last line of defence, especially in the sections where barbed-wire-topped fences and guard posts remain as vestiges of the mountain's prior high-security status.

Historic Villa & Garden

Swoon at Seokpajeong Seoul Museum of Art

Your ticket for **Seokpajeong Seoul Museum of Art** *(seoulmuseum.org; adult/child ₩20,000/13,000)* will grant you access to at least two major exhibitions of modern and contemporary art and photography from Korea and around the world. On permanent display are a couple of works by the Japanese artist Yayoi Kusama, including one of her famous polka-dot *Pumpkin* sculptures.

However, the best reason for visiting is hidden behind the museum buildings. Here you'll find **Seokpajeong**, an elegant late-Joseon villa that once belonged to Heungseon Daewongun, regent to King Gojong. Paths meandering through the leafy hillside gardens are poetically called the Walk of Clouds and the Walk of Water – follow them to find a resting pavilion

A MOUNTAINSIDE RETREAT

When Yi Ha-eung's 12-year-old son Yi Myeongbok became King Gojong in 1863, his father gained the title Heungseon Daewongun and effectively ruled Korea as regent for his young son.

Until this point, the Andong Kim clan had been powerful in the Korean court. To exert his new authority, Heungseon Daewongun devised a plan to acquire the villa Seokpajeong, which was built and owned by Kim Heunggeun, a member of the Andong Kims.

Kim was reluctant to sell but allowed Heungseon Daewongun to stay a night. The wily regent took along his son, a shrewd move as vassals, such as Kim, could no longer own a property where an emperor had stayed. Thus the villa became royal property and Heungseon Daewongun got his mountainside retreat.

AARONCHOI/GETTY IMAGES

Seokpajeong Seoul Museum of Art

and ancient carvings in the rocks. Themed exhibitions of sculpture and ceramics are held in the gardens and the rooms of the villa, usually between June and November. The museum is closed Monday and Tuesday.

An Accomplished Artist

Visit the Whanki Museum

For a glimpse into the creative mind of Kim Whanki (1913–74), a pioneer of Korea's avant-garde and modernism art movements, a visit to **Whanki Museum** *(whankimuseum.org; adult/child ₩18,000/9000)* is highly recommended. The museum was built in 1992 by the Whanki Foundation, established by Kim's wife Hyangan. From its collection of some 2000 works by Kim, it stages one or two different themed exhibitions each year. It also displays works by other modern and contemporary Korean artists. Trained in Japan in the 1930s, Kim was a professor of fine arts in Seoul during the 1940s and '50s before moving to Paris and later to New York. His paintings developed from colour-saturated figurative compositions to later abstract works made up of dots. The museum is closed Monday.

FOLK RELIGION

Musok is Korea's ancient, highly ritualised and somewhat taboo folk religion. Scholars believe it is not wholly correct to compare this belief system to shamanism, or call the *mudang* (often females with the skills to connect to the supernatural) shamans, but there are similarities.

The stigmatisation of *musok* goes back to the Joseon era, when the ruling class, who were followers of Confucianism, rooted out anything considered superstitious or mystical.

Today, there is government recognition of *musok* as an intangible part of Korean cultural heritage, and people still turn to *mudang* for spiritual support in their lives.

Mudang perform *gut* (rituals) to connect with the spirits. At Inwangsan Guksadang, you might witness a *gut* to bless a marriage, bring good fortune or cure illness.

EATING IN BUAM-DONG & SEODAEMUN: OUR PICKS

Gyeyeolsa Chicken: Dig into golden-fried chicken and crisp potato wedges. One basket serves two nicely. *noon-10.30pm Tue-Sun* ₩₩

Jaha Sonmandoo: Posh *mandu* (dumpling) house for heavenly dough parcels stuffed with veggies, beef and pork, served boiled or in soup. *11am-9.30pm* ₩₩

Scoff: Lemon drizzle sponge, Earl Grey scones and sausage rolls are among the many tempting bakes at this long-running cafe. *10am-8pm Mon-Fri, from 9am Sat & Sun* ₩

Neungra Bapsang: Famous North Korean restaurant serving specialities like Pyongyang cold noodles and *gamja mandu* (potato dumplings). *11am-9pm* ₩₩

HIGHLIGHTS

1 Seodaemun Prison History Hall

SIGHTS

2 Changuimun
3 Cheong Wa Dae
4 Dilkusha
5 Dongnimmun
6 Inwangsan Guksadang
7 Samcheong Park
8 Seodaemun Independence Park
9 Seokpajeong Seoul Museum of Art
10 Seonamjeong
11 Seonbawi
12 Sukjeongmun
13 Whanki Museum
14 Woram Park

ACTIVITIES, COURSES & TOURS

15 Bukaksan
16 Inwangsan

SLEEPING

17 Guesthouse The Kims

EATING

18 Gyeyeolsa Chicken
19 Jaha Sonmandoo
20 Neungra Bapsang
21 Scoff

DRINKING & NIGHTLIFE

22 Club Espresso
23 Inwangsan Mountain Chosochaekbang
24 Okba
25 Sanmotoongi

INFORMATION

26 Malbawi Information Center

TOP EXPERIENCE

Seodaemun Prison History Hall

Symbolic of the colonial oppression of Korea by Japan in the early 20th century, and of suffering during the post-independence years of dictatorship, Seodaemun Prison History Hall is a place of tragedy and sacrifice. Much of the red-brick compound has been carefully restored since the prison's closure in 1987, transforming it into a museum that honours those who were imprisoned and executed here.

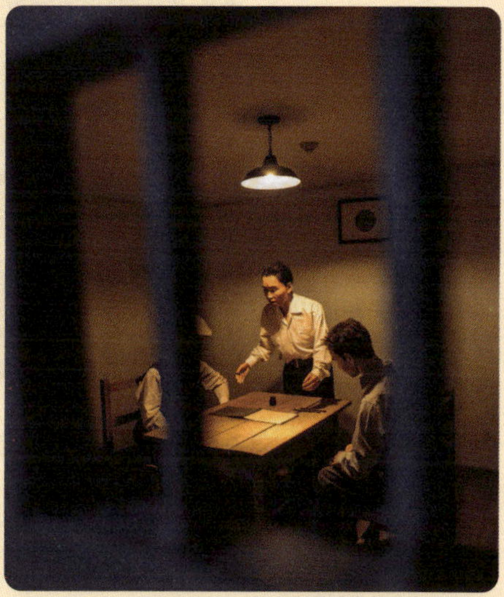

MIRKO KUZMANOVIC/SHUTTERSTOCK

Seodaemun Prison History Hall exhibit

Victim Memorials

The prison was designed to house 500 prisoners. However, during the height of the anti-Japanese protests in 1919, up to 3500 prisoners were packed inside. On a self-guided tour, you can explore the cellblocks where independence fighters and democracy campaigners were held, as well as the nightmarish interrogation and torture rooms and execution building.

A memorial lists the names of 90 Koreans known to have died here, but up to 600 nameless others are thought to have perished from torture, execution, malnutrition and disease. The most famous of the victims is Yu Gwan-sun, an 18-year-old Ewha high-school student who was tortured to death in 1920 – learn about her in the Women's Prison Building.

Seodaemun Independence Park

The prison history hall is on one side of **Seodaemun Independence Park**, dedicated to those who fought for Korean independence. At the park's southern end is **Dongnimmun**, an impressive granite archway modelled after the Arc de Triomphe. Completed in 1898, Dongnimmun stands where the 16th-century Yeongeunmun gate (a symbol of Imperial China's suzerainty over Korea) was located. A pair of stone plinths are all that remain of the older gateway.

TOP TIPS

- Seodaemun Prison History Hall is closed on Monday.
- On the 1st floor of the Exhibition Hall, a short movie in Korean introduces the history of the prison.
- Look for the bronze statue of democracy martyr Yu Gwan Sun in Independence Park.

PRACTICALITIES

- *sphh.sscmc.or.kr*
- adult/teen/child ₩3000/1500/1000
- 9.30am-6pm Mar-Oct, to 5pm Nov-Feb

MARY LINELY TAYLOR

A British stage actress, Mary Linely Taylor (1889–1982) arrived in Seoul as a newlywed in 1917. She kept accounts of her life in the city and travels around Korea – a draft feature about a journey to Mt Kumgang (now in North Korea) on display at Dilkusha demonstrates she could have been a Lonely Planet author! She was also an accomplished artist.

The Taylors were arrested soon after Japan's attack on Pearl Harbor in 1941 and eventually deported to the US. In 1948, before they could return to Seoul, Albert died of a heart attack, aged 51. Mary brought his ashes back to be buried near his father's grave in Seoul's Foreigners' Cemetery.

Her memoir, *A Chain of Amber*, was published by her son Bruce in 1992.

CHANOOB/SHUTTERSTOCK

Panoramic Views of Seoul

Climb Inwangsan

The summit of **Inwangsan** (339.9m) offers a sweeping vista of the city and the Seoul City Wall flowing over Bukaksan, Naksan and Namsan. You can clearly see how the old city nestled inside its guardian mountains. The mountain is a strenuous but relatively easy climb, with several different routes to the summit.

For the least amount of climbing, start at Changuimun (p186), the sub-gate in Buam-dong, and follow the Seoul City Wall. Alternatively, start or finish at **Woram Park**, also with a section of the Seoul City Wall. Another popular route is the Seonbawi Trail from the historic Dongnimmun (p189) arch beside Independence Park. Along this, you will pass **Seonamjeong** (선암정사), a Buddhist temple, before reaching the *musok* shrine **Inwangsan Guksadang**. The Japanese demolished the original shrine on Namsan in 1925, and it was later rebuilt here. Climb above the shrine to find **Seonbawi**, a rock formation that resembles a robed monk praying. Women wanting to become pregnant come here to ask for blessings.

DRINKING IN BUAM-DONG & SEODAEMUN: OUR PICKS

Club Espresso: Perfect for a caffeine kick before climbing Bukaksan is this long-running cafe roasting beans from around the globe. *9am-10pm*

Sanmotoongi: (산모퉁이) Mountainside cafe, famously featuring in a TV drama, offering superb views and quirky bric-a-brac decoration inside and out. *11am-7pm*

Inwangsan Mountain Chosochaekbang: Old police station remodelled into a popular bakery and book cafe on the upper slopes of Inwangsan. *8am-9.30pm*

Okba: Charming *hanok*-based cafe-bar serving coffee, traditional teas, wine and highball cocktails. *11.30am-6pm Tue-Thu & Sun, to 9pm Fri & Sat*

City views from Inwangsan

Drop by Dilkusha

Historic expat house

Meaning 'heart's delight' in Persian, **Dilkusha** *(museum.seoul.go.kr; free)* was built in 1924 by the American miner, entrepreneur and journalist Albert Wilder 'Bruce' Taylor and his British wife Mary. The story goes that the couple were walking along the old city walls when they came upon a large ginkgo tree and thought this would be an ideal location for their home. That ginkgo still stands outside the red-brick house, which was restored and reopened in 2021 as a museum.

The rooms hold displays about the Taylors' fascinating life as expats in Korea in the early 20th century, with personal items, photographs and Mary's paintings bringing the stories alive.

Albert's 1919 article about Korea's independence movement for the *New York Times* was important in bringing to world attention the situation in the colonised country. He also photographed the state funeral of Emperor Gojong.

HISTORY AND NATURE

If ancient sites, beautiful trees and nature take your fancy, visit **Jeondeung-sa** (p201), Korea's oldest temple, where there's a 700-year-old ginkgo tree.

Chang-dong & Dobongsan

Seoul is cultivating Chang-dong as a cultural industries hub, so has recently opened a couple of museums here. Further north, explore a botanical garden and a former military defence post turning into an arts space.

Seoul's New Creative Hub

Photographs, robots, AI and K-Pop

Notable for its architecture etched with lines and dynamic curves, **Photography Seoul Museum of Art** *(sema.seoul.go.kr; free)* is Seoul's first public museum dedicated to photographic images. Exhibitions change fairly regularly. Photo lovers will want to browse the library, stocked with more than 5000 titles.

Next door, in a space-ship-like building, is the **Robot and AI Museum** *(RAIM; science.seoul.go.kr; free)*. You need to make a booking to join the interactive tour of the main exhibition, which includes working examples of various robots and AI tech. The tours are in Korean, but there are English explanations in the associated displays. Both museums are closed Monday.

Scheduled to open in the first half of 2027, **Seoul Arena** will be a cultural venue dedicated to K-Pop. The main performance arena will seat 28,000 people, making it one of the largest in Seoul. There will also be a mall and multiplex cinema.

Anti-Tank Defence Facility Reimagined

Art at the Peace Culture Bunker

Immediately east of Dobongsan station is the **Seoul Iris Garden** *(parks.seoul.go.kr; free)*, planted with some 300,000 irises across 130 different species. This beautiful botanical garden also includes medicinal, wetland and wildflower gardens.

Close by is **Peace Culture Bunker** *(culturebunker.or.kr; free)*, an arts and community centre crafted ingeniously from the concrete bones of a former military facility. Its observation tower provides views of the surrounding mountainous landscape and there are wall murals and sculptures to admire.

ARCHITECTURAL ADAPTIVE REUSE

Peace Culture Bunker is one of several inspiring examples across Seoul of defunct pieces of architecture that have been imaginatively adapted for new use. The site gets its name from a 1970 public-housing complex that was used to conceal a bunker to house tanks that could be deployed in the event of an attack from North Korea.

The ageing apartments were demolished in 2004, leaving the 1st floor and bunker relatively intact. In 2017 CoRe Architects transformed the site into studios and resting spaces for resident artists and visitors. The concrete structure of the bunker was left visible and a 20m-tall Brutalist-style observation tower was added.

EATING IN UI-DONG, BUKHANSAN NATIONAL PARK: OUR PICKS

Bukhansan Lounge: Pleasant modern cafe overlooking a stream and serving snack foods to fuel up for a hike. *8.30am-8pm Mon-Fri, from 6am Sat & Sun* ₩

Highground Bakery: Spacious, forest-surrounded cafe with great bakes and occasional live-music performances. *10am-10pm* ₩

Sunwoongak: Enjoy the traditional architecture of this large *hanok* cafe dating from 1967. Serves drinks and desserts such as pecan pie. *noon-8pm Thu-Tue* ₩

Woorikong Sundubu: Popular eatery serving meals made with *sundubu* (soft tofu) as well as other traditional, hearty Korean dishes. *9.30am-7pm* ₩₩

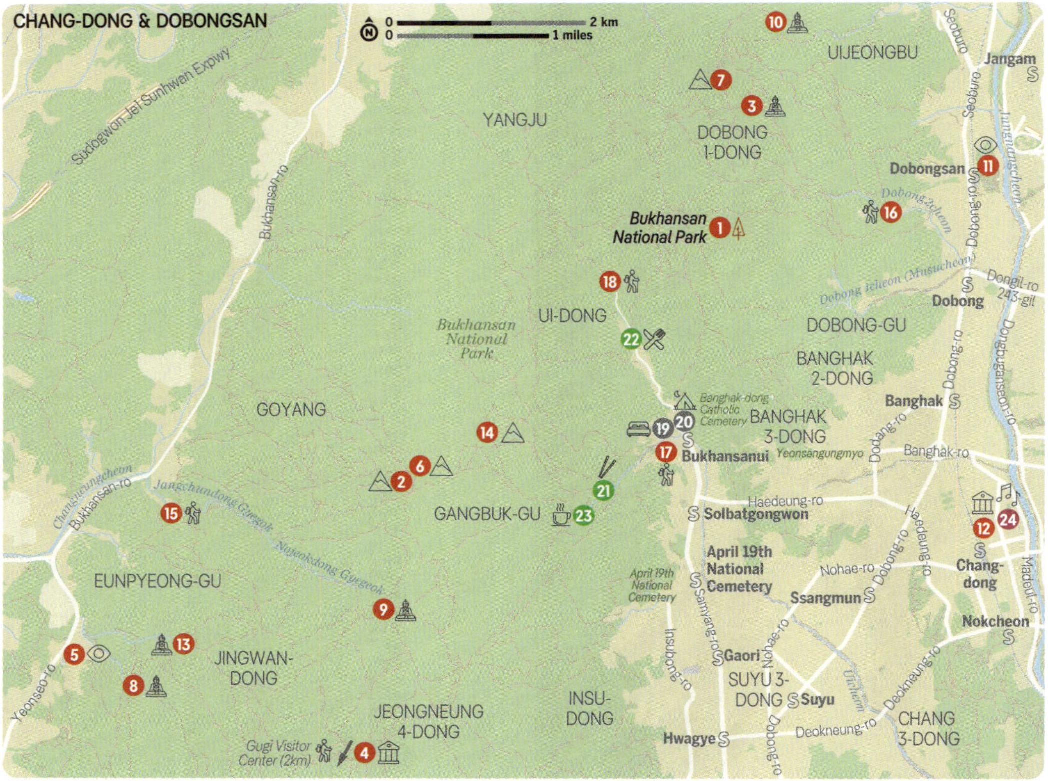

★ **HIGHLIGHTS**
1 Bukhansan National Park

★ **SIGHTS**
2 Baegundae
3 Cheonchuk-sa
4 Daenammun
5 Eunpyeong Hanok Village
6 Insubong
7 Jaunbong
8 Jingwan-sa
9 Jungheung-sa
10 Mangwol-sa
11 Peace Culture Bunker
12 Photography Seoul Museum of Art
see 12 Robot and AI Museum
13 Samcheon-sa
see 11 Seoul Iris Garden
see 7 Sinseondae
14 Yeongbong

ACTIVITIES, COURSES & TOURS
15 Bukhansan-seong Visitor Center
16 Dobong-san Visitor Information Center
17 Seoul Hiking Tourism Center
18 Uiryeong-gil

SLEEPING
19 Anto Resort
20 Ui-dong Family Camping Ground

EATING
21 Bukhansan Lounge
22 Highground Bakery
see 17 Woorikong Sundubu

DRINKING & NIGHTLIFE
23 Sunwoongak

ENTERTAINMENT
24 Seoul Arena

MONGKOL CHAI/SHUTTERSTOCK

Dobong-san in autumn

TOP EXPERIENCE

Bukhansan National Park

Less than an hour by subway from central Seoul, 78.5-sq-km Bukhansan National Park is riddled with hiking trails and rock-climbing sites. To reach the park's tallest peaks is challenging, but the rewards are sweeping vistas and a sense of achievement. On the lower slopes, the pleasures include abundant nature, rushing streams, serene temples and the remains of Joseon-dynasty fortifications.

DON'T MISS

- Baegundae
- Insubong
- Samcheon-sa
- Jingwan-sa
- Sinseondae
- Cheonchuk-sa
- Mangwol-sa
- Uiryeong-gil

About the Park

There are multiple entry points into the park, which is divided by the Uiryeong Pass into two sections: the southern Bukhansan area, accessed via Bukhansan Ui subway station, and the northern Dobong-san area, reached via Dobongsan station.

Bukhan-san Trails

Seoul's highest peak, **Baegundae** (836.5m) offers 360-degree views of the city and parts of Gyeonggi-do. The shortest

PRACTICALITIES

- *knps.or.kr*
- free
- 24hr

route up the mountain (around 8km return, taking about four hours) is the **Baegundae Ui Gugok Trail**. This starts and finishes at the **Seoul Hiking Tourism Center**, a five-minute walk from Bukhansan Ui station, the terminus of the Seoul LRT Ui Sinseol Line. Hiking shoes and gloves are necessary, as parts of this trail are steep and can be slippery. A short detour off the Baegundae Ui Gugok Trail takes you to the peak of **Yeongbong** (604m). Opposite here is the granite outcrop **Insubong** (811m), which has some of the best multipitch rock climbing in Asia and routes of all grades.

The 10.2km **Bukhansanseong-Daenammun Trail**, between the **Bukhansanseong Visitor Center** and **Gugi Visitor Center**, is a popular route. Along it you can visit **Jungheung-sa**, an old temple that has been restored, the remains of a temporary palace from the Joseon dynasty and **Daenammun**, a principal gate along the 11.6km Bukhansanseong Fortress wall built in 1711.

The **Samcheon-sa Trail** (7.33km, around 2½ hours) starts at **Samcheon-sa**, a temple founded in 661 CE, and ends at **Jingwan-sa** (p111), a beautiful temple close by **Eunpyeong Hanok Village** (p111).

Dobong-san Trails

Jaunbong (740.2m) is the tallest peak in the Dobong-san section of the park, but access to its steep rock cliffs is restricted. Instead, hikers aim for **Sinseondae** (726m), a 6.3km (2½-hour return) journey from Dobongsan subway station. Note that the final part of the ascent is very steep and the trail can get busy on weekends and public holidays.

An alternative is the 9.32km, six-hour **Dobong-san Main Ridge Trail** between Mangwolsa station and **Dobong-san Visitor Information Center**. It's physically demanding but offers panoramic views from the ridge. Along the route, take signed detours to visit the atmospheric, forest-surrounded **Cheonchuk-sa** and **Mangwol-sa** temples.

Bukhansan Dulle-gil

An alternative to scaling the park's exposed peaks is to hike the **Bukhansan Dulle-gil**. Split into 21 sections, with a total length of just over 75km, this gently undulating path circumnavigates the park through the forest on the lower slopes of Bukhan-san and Dobong-san.

Section 21 of the trail is the **Uiryeong-gil**, an unpaved path over a pass between the park's two mountains. Between 1968, when 31 North Korean commandos crossed the national park in a failed attempt to assassinate the then South Korean president Park Chung-hee, and 2009, this 6.5km route (two hours) was closed to the public for security reasons. That four-decade hiatus in human intervention helped preserve the ecosystem. Reservations (via the park's website) are required from September to the end of November and every weekend through the year. Access is from 9am, with last entry at 4pm (3pm in winter). Bring photo ID as this will be checked at the trailhead.

EASY HIKING

If time is short, or you'd prefer an easy hike in the park, Cho Juhyon, a guide at Seoul Hiking Tourism Center, recommends the Sogwicheon Trail (7km return) to Daedongmun, one of the gates in the Bukhansanseong Fortress wall.

It's also possible to reach Yeongbong peak along an easier 8.6km route that is moderately challenging and still provides fine panoramas of Seoul.

TOP TIPS

- Seoul Hiking Tourism Center (closed Monday) offers free maps, guidebooks and gifts, as well as lockers and showers.
- If you need hiking boots and other gear, you can rent them from Seoul Hiking Tourism Center.
- Although not especially high, some of the park's peaks are physically challenging ascents, so choose hiking routes with care.
- Bring plenty of water and waterproof clothing.
- It's possible to arrange a templestay at Jingwan-sa.
- Peak season is from mid-October to mid-November, when the autumn leaf colours are at their peak.

Researched by Charles Usher

Day Trips from Seoul

Peer into North Korea, explore historic fortresses and find tonnes of family fun, all in easy reach of the capital.

Places

TOP TIP

If you rent a car, download the Naver Maps app for navigation. Google Maps doesn't provide driving directions in Korea.

It can be hard to escape the gravitational pull of Planet Seoul, but achieve escape velocity and you'll discover a fascinating mix of things to do, nearly all of them easily accessible by public transport. The surrounding region is steeped in history, from Suwon's majestic Hwaseong Fortress, the apex of Joseon achievement, to Incheon's Open Port, where modern Korea began. Then there's the infamous Demilitarized Zone (DMZ); join a tour to see North Korea with your own eyes. Schedule kid-centric outings to Everland amusement park and the immersive Korean Folk Village, have inspired encounters at Bucheon Art Bunker B39, or just decompress on a rural break to Ganghwado Island. Whichever direction you go, a different world awaits.

Incheon

TIME FROM SEOUL: 1¼HR

Slurp your way through Chinatown

Step off the train at Incheon station and pass through an eye-catching red and gold pai-loo gate into Korea's biggest and oldest **Chinatown**. The year after Incheon's port opened to the outside world in 1883, this area became a Qing Dynasty concession, and merchants began arriving from across the Yellow Sea. Wander the curving streets to spot old Chinese row houses, watch incense curl toward the dragons atop the **Uiseondang Temple** and dig around in souvenir shops. Most of all, eat. The area is filled with restaurants specialising in *jajangmyeon*, a dish of noodles in savoury black bean sauce. Learn about it and see delivery containers through the ages at the fun **Jajangmyeon Museum** *(adult/child ₩1000/700)*.

A portal to the past

When Incheon's port was opened, the former fishing village suddenly became Korea's doorway to the world. Along with the Chinese settlement, Japanese and Western enclaves were established in the Incheon Open Port area. Visit the **Incheon Open Port Museum** *(adult/student/child ₩500/300/200)* and **Incheon Open Port Modern Architecture Museum** *(adult/student ₩500/300)* to learn about this transformative period and how developments in Incheon gave rise to many

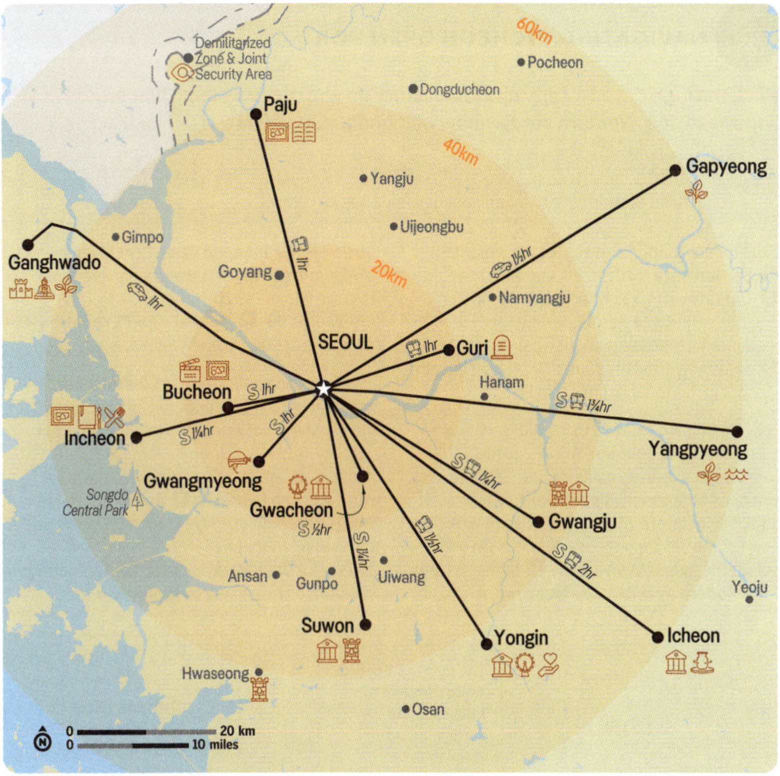

national firsts (postal service, railway, modern hospital...) and to see models of the area's historic buildings. Down the street, the **Daebul Hotel Exhibition Hall** *(adult/child ₩1000/700)* has re-creations of when the building housed Korea's first Western-style hotel, 14 years before one opened in Seoul. The connected **Jung-gu Life History Museum** shows what life was like here in the 1960s.

Artistic ex-industrial spaces

On the edge of the Incheon Open Port area is **Incheon Art Platform** *(inartplatform.kr)*, a grouping of squat red-brick warehouses from the 1930s and '40s now turned into a creative space and artist residency. Stop by to peruse its galleries, installations and performances. Most events are free. The structure housing IAP's offices is the country's oldest Western-style office building, dating to 1888.

For more industrial-artistic mashups, venture to **COSMO 40**, near Gajaeul station. The former chemical factory is now a super-cool cafe/bakery/gallery/performance space. Wander Void Hall, where giant illuminated metal columns stretch two storeys, play ping-pong on the 2nd floor and scramble around catwalks before settling in for a latte beneath dangling crane hooks.

NAVIGATING INCHEON OPEN PORT

Walk through Korea's early modern history as you traverse the Chinese, Japanese and Western settlements of Incheon Open Port.

START	END	LENGTH
Incheon Station	Seokjeongnu Pavilion, Jayu Park	1.3km; 1½hr

Exit Incheon station and aim for the vibrant ❶ **pai-loo gate** marking the entrance to ❷ **Chinatown** (p196). Snack your way through dumplings and noodles at the neighbourhood's restaurants, then learn about what you ate at the ❸ **Jajangmyeon Museum** (p196), which tells the story of Incheon's most moreish invention.

Leaving Chinatown, walk to the old warehouses that make up ❹ **Incheon Art Platform** (p197) to see what's on in its galleries and performance spaces. At the complex's eastern end, take a left and go to Sinpo-ro 23beon-gil. You're now in the heart of the old Japanese settlement. On either side of the intersection are the ❺ **Incheon Open Port Modern Architecture Museum** (p196) and the domed ❻ **Incheon Open Port Museum** (p196). Both occupy erstwhile Japanese banks from the turn of the 20th century. A few steps further on is the ❼ **Daebul Hotel Exhibition Hall** (p197), site of Korea's first Western-style hotel.

Turn right and you'll arrive at ❽ **stairs** that once marked the border between the Chinese and Japanese settlements. Note the different styles of stone lanterns on either side. Before climbing up, break for *pat-bingsu* (shaved ice with sweet red beans) at ❾ **Pot-R**, housed in a well-preserved *machiya* (Japanese wooden townhouse) from the 1880s. At the top of the stairs is ❿ **Jayu Park**. Head to ⓫ **Seokjeongnu Pavilion** for views over the Port of Incheon.

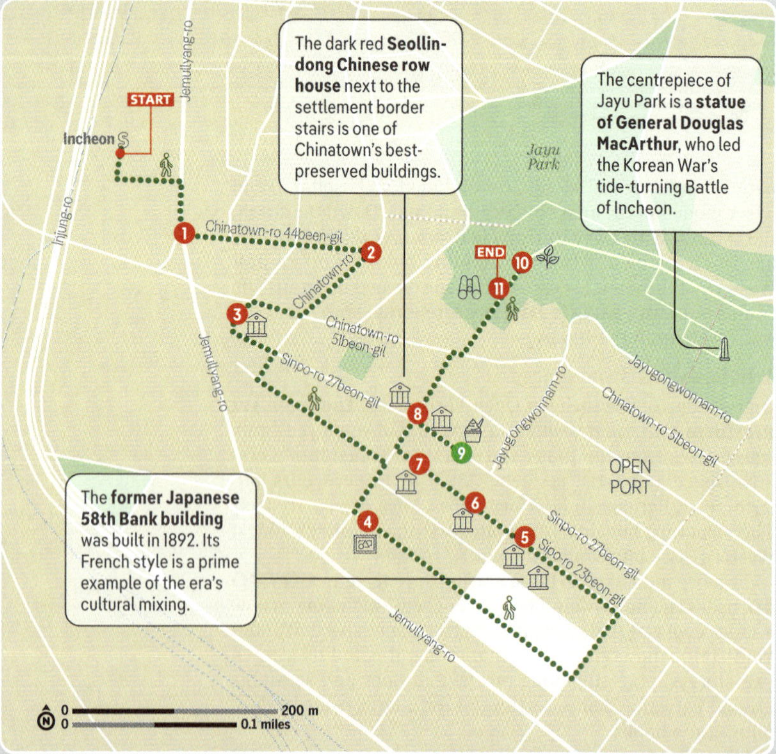

Downtown Incheon's 'island' escape

Jump on the **Wolmi Sea Train** *(wolmiseatrain.or.kr; adult/student/child ₩14,000/10,000/8000)* to **Wolmido**, a former island that was connected to the mainland after the Korean War. Leaving from near Incheon station, the monorail makes three stops around the island. You need a Korean phone number and bank card to book online. If you need assistance, try the tourist info centre at the station. Buses also make the trip. On the 'island', a waterfront boardwalk has amusement parks, arcades, cafes and restaurants. The forested **Wolmi Park** contains an observatory for views and a large traditional garden. On the park's southern edge is the fascinating **Museum of Korea Emigration History** *(incheon.go.kr)*, chronicling the Korean diaspora starting in the early 20th century, when thousands emigrated to work on Hawaiian sugar-cane plantations.

Learn about the Korean War

The strikingly designed **Memorial Hall for Incheon Landing Operation** *(landing915.com)* commemorates the daring September 1950 attack, codenamed Operation Chromite, that was a turning point in the Korean War. Displays go into granular detail about the operation's planning and execution using archival newsreels, displays of weaponry and a room-sized scale model of the battle. Outside, amphibious landing vehicles and other materiel are on display. Next door, the **Incheon Metropolitan City Museum** *(incheon.go.kr)* has some good exhibitions on Joseon-era farming tools and Open Port history, though English info is limited.

See Korea's city of the future

After decades of development, the 'smart city' of Songdo, built on 600 hectares of reclaimed land, is mostly complete. The planned neighbourhood lacks the soul of other Korean cities, but it's worth a visit to marvel at the engineering and see the future of Korean urbanism.

Songdo's highlight is **Songdo Central Park**, which is surrounded by glassy skyscrapers and has walking paths and a canal. Rent pleasure boats from the boat house at the canal's east end. There are several sights of note in and around the park. Most arresting is the **Tri-Bowl** *(tribowl.kr)*, a curving, metallic arts and culture complex that seems to only be visiting our planet temporarily. It's especially stunning lit up at night. Inside are a concert hall and exhibition space. The **Incheon Urban History Museum** *(incheon.go.kr)* gives a

KNOW YOUR NOODLES

One of Korea's favourite delivery foods, *jajangmyeon* was invented in Incheon. Sometime around 1910, chefs at Gonghwachun (which now houses the Jajangmyeon Museum) tweaked a Chinese recipe to create a dish of noodles in fermented bean sauce. Tasty, filling and cheap, it became a staple of Chinese dockworkers and bricklayers in Korea.

In the post-Korean War years, imported American wheat flour helped a taste for *jajangmyeon* spread among the public. By 2015, Koreans were slurping up some 7 million bowls of the stuff each day.

Today, *jajangmyeon* is in every Chinese restaurant, sold in instant noodle form and served many ways. Two of the most common versions are *ganjajang*, a slightly drier, made-to-order style, and *hayan* (white) *jajang*, made with a lighter Chinese bean paste.

EATING IN INCHEON'S CHINATOWN

Mandabok: Specialises in *hayan baengnyeon jajang*, a white *jajangmyeon* with pork, seafood and vegetables. *11am-9.30pm, from 10.30am Sat & Sun* ₩

Yanjing: An unmissable place cooking up *jajangmyeon*, *jjamppong* (spicy noodle soup with seafood) and Chinese classics like Peking duck. *10.30am-9.30pm* ₩

Taehwawon: This century-old restaurant makes its own bean paste for its signature Incheon *hyangto jajang*. Has an all-veg menu too. *11am-9pm, to 8.30pm Sat & Sun* ₩

Sinseung Banjeom: Run by a granddaughter of the man whose restaurant invented *jajangmyeon*. Large menu runs from dumplings to *mapo tofu*. *11am-3pm & 4.45-9pm* ₩

INCHEON HISTORY

Incheon's – and, it's fair to say, Korea's – modern history began in 1883, when its port opened to international trade. Japanese, Chinese, American, French, Russian and other foreign merchants poured in, transforming the fishing settlement, then known as Jemulpo, into a major city.

Incheon's most famous chapter came during the Korean War. Pushed back to the peninsula's southeastern corner and in danger of losing the war only months after it began, South Korea and its UN allies plotted a daring raid behind enemy lines. In September 1950, 75,000 troops and 261 naval vessels under the command of US General Douglas MacArthur landed at Incheon, overwhelming North Korean forces and retaking Seoul.

Today, Incheon is a major trade and transport hub.

good overview of the city's past 150 years, while across the canal, the **National Museum of World Writing Systems** *(mow.or.kr)* is a captivating odyssey through the history of the written word, from Egyptian hieroglyphs to whatever AI is. Don't miss the Akkadian cuneiform tablet from at least 1600 BCE. On the park's south side, the **Songdo Hanok Village** is a collection of restaurants in newly built *hanok* – pretty, but not exactly rich in history.

Be sure you visit the **G-Tower** observation deck. Take the elevator beside the info desk, and you'll be treated to a 33rd-floor view of Songdo in all its hubris and accomplishment. From this vantage point, imagining that everything you see was once ocean is genuinely mind-boggling.

Ganghwado

TIME FROM SEOUL: **1HR**

Tour Goryeo & Joseon sites

When the Mongols invaded Korea in the 13th century, the Goryeo royal court hightailed it to this large island at the Han River mouth. King Gojong built a new capital at what's now the north edge of the island's main town, Ganghwa-eup, but within four decades Goryeo had established a truce with the Mongols, moved back to Kaesong and demolished its Ganghwa capital. What's seen at the **Goryeo Palace Site** (*adult/child ₩1200/900*) are actually reconstructions of Joseon government offices destroyed by the French in 1866. Most interesting is a royal library with displays on valuable records the French looted.

Just downhill are the 19th-century **Yongheunggung Royal Residence**, where King Cheoljong lived before ascending to the throne, and the **Ganghwa Anglican Church**. Built by a royal architect in 1900, its traditional Korean exterior and Western interior create a distinctive dissonance. View photos of early-20th-century parishioners and masses in the nave. Services are held on Sunday.

Ganghwa's location made it a frequent place of conflict, and the Joseon government built 53 defensive facilities around the island. The most impressive is **Gwangseongbo Fort** (*adult/child ₩1500/1100*). Constructed in 1658, it was the site of an 1871 battle with the US navy. Walk the walls to check out observation posts, bulwarks and the wicked currents in the strait below. Overlooking the primary bridge to the mainland is **Gapgot Dondae** (*adult/child ₩1200/900*), which dates to 1679. Besides the fortress walls and cannons, there's a small war museum and a 400-year-old orange tree.

EATING ALONG INCHEON'S HIP GAEHANG-RO

Sinpo International Market: The market is famed for *dakgangjeong* (fried chicken pieces in spicy sauce). Wonjo Sinpo and Channuri are popular. *10am-9pm* ₩₩

Taxco Market: Unexpectedly respectable *birria* and *carnitas* tacos, plus a shelf of Mexican snacks. Skip the nachos. *11.30am-3pm & 5-9pm Wed-Mon* ₩

Mekong Sarong: A stylish restaurant with checkerboard floors and plants. Serves Vietnamese staples like pho and banh mi. *11.30am-3pm & 5-9pm Tue-Sun* ₩₩

Gaehangro Tongdak: Old-fashioned fried chicken in a retro setting decorated with old family photos and glass lamps. *5pm-midnight, from 4pm Sat & Sun* ₩₩

SEUNG HA KIM/SHUTTERSTOCK

Gwangseongbo Fort

Follow the thread of Ganghwa textiles

In the 1900s, Ganghwado was known for its *sochang*, a light, breathable cotton fabric. You can encounter this legacy at a trio of Ganghwa-eup sites. Learn about the industry, watch a weaving demonstration and sew a *sochang* souvenir at the **Sochang Fabric Experience Hall** (closed Mondays). You can also sample the local *sunmu* radish tea in a *hanok* built in 1938. Down the street, the **Dongkwang Textile Living Culture Center** displays old *sochang* manufacturing machines in a former factory. Also nearby is **Joyang Bangjik**. It's not exactly educational, but it's definitely something. Occupying another former textile factory, it's nominally a cafe and bakery, but mainly it's a fever dream that seems to have emptied out every antique store in a 100km radius. Amid preserved sections of the factory are carousel horses, phone booths, a camera collection, religious memorabilia and who knows what else. Order a coffee and embrace the chaos.

Korean Buddhism's beginning

Established in 381 CE, **Jeondeung-sa** *(jeondeungsa.org)* is Korea's oldest temple. Located within the walls of Samnang Fortress in the island's south, it has a beautiful forested setting on the slopes of Jeongjok-san. Views reach all the way to the mainland. Take a couple of hours to soak up the vistas

BEST INCHEON ISLANDS

Dozens of islands are accessible from Incheon by road or ferry. These are some of the best.

Yeongjongdo: This large island is home to a pair of glitzy casino resorts: **INSPIRE Entertainment Resort** and **Paradise City**.

Sindo, Sido & Modo: These bridge-linked islands are a 10-minute ferry ride from Yeongjongdo's **Sammok Port**. Aim for the sculpture park at Modo's end.

Jangbongdo: A 40-minute ferry ride from Sammok Port and known for camping, strangely shaped rocks and fine sunsets.

Muuido: A bridge links Yeongjongdo to this small island with forested hiking trails and sandy **Hanagae Beach**.

Deokjeokdo: Suntan on spectacular 2km-long **Seopo-ri Beach**, backed by a grove of 200-year-old pines. Two hours by ferry from Incheon.

EATING ON GANGHWADO

Wangjajeong Mukbap: Next to the Goryeo Palace Site, specialising in *mukbap*, an acorn-jelly-and-rice soup with diced cabbage. *10am-9pm Tue-Sun* ₩

Manisan Sanchae: Real country fare. Superb bibimbap with wild mountain vegetables, served with a rich soybean-paste soup. *9.30am-7pm, from 9am Sat & Sun* ₩

Toga: Soft tofu stew made with salted and fermented shrimp and sliced hot peppers. *9.30am-5pm Mon, Tue, Thu & Fri, 9am-7pm Sat & Sun* ₩

Wondumak Garden: Try its signature soup made with *galbi* and salted shrimp, a Ganghwado speciality. *10am-2.30pm & 5-9pm Thu-Tue, no break Sat & Sun* ₩₩

GANGHWADO PRACTICALITIES

Buses from the mainland end up in the island's largest town, Ganghwa-eup, which is a handy base from which to explore. The town has numerous hotel options, while pensions dot the island's rural interior and cluster on its southern and western coasts.

You can reach the main sites by public transport, but Ganghwado is big and buses infrequent, so if you're aiming to visit numerous sites, consider joining an organised bus tour from Seoul or Incheon, or renting a car. If you rent, do so from an agency at Incheon or Gimpo international airports. Rates there are considerably cheaper than at agencies in Seoul, and English-speaking staff are always available to help.

CSTRIKE/SHUTTERSTOCK

and the peaceful setting, seeking out the temple's 900-year-old iron bell and a 700-year-old ginkgo.

The temple's marquee attraction is Daeungjeon Hall, built in 1681. Beneath a coffered ceiling decorated with dragons, mythical birds and lotus flowers, it holds a treasured gilded Buddha triad. Outside, carved wooden figures appear to hold up each corner of the roof. According to legend, they depict a barmaid who stole from the hall's carpenter. After you've toured the grounds, pause for a drink at the temple's charming teahouse, **Jungnim Dawon**. You can also spend the night at Jeondeung-sa as part of the templestay program.

After leaving Jeondeung-sa, pop into nearby **Geumpung Brewery**, which has been making *makgeolli* (unrefined rice wine) since the 1930s. The original building has a shop and an upstairs exhibition space where you can watch a video about the brewing process and see artefacts from the brewery's history. Contact Geumpung in advance to join one of its brewing or tasting classes.

A sacred mountaintop altar

The peak of **Mani-san** is crowned by Chamseongdan Altar, said to originally have been built by Dangun, the mythical first Korean. The views from here are phenomenal. Of the three different routes to the 472m summit, the shortest (4.8km, three hours return) starts at Hamheodongcheon campsite in Hwado-myeon village. Alternatively, follow a 6.4km route to the summit from the Manisan Tourist Information Centre in the village of Sangbang-ri. After you descend, recover at the broad **Dongmak Beach**, with plenty of restaurants and convenience stores.

Jeondeung-sa (p201)

Rock of ages

Ganghwado's position as the gateway to Seoul means it's seen its fair share of history. Seven kilometres northwest of Ganghwa-eup, the imaginative **Ganghwa History Museum** *(ganghwa.go.kr; adult/child ₩3000/2000)* will help you better grasp what you encounter across the island. Displays start with the island's ancient dolmen sites, tell how the Goryeo capital relocated here and examine islanders' role in the anti-colonial struggle for independence.

Speaking of dolmens, you can view several of them in a park just outside the museum. There are about 45,000 of these Bronze Age megalithic tombs around the globe, and close to 40% are on the Korean Peninsula, including 160 on Ganghwado. None are quite as impressive as the **Bugeun-ri Dolmen**, the three giant stones of which form a slanting table, with the enormous capstone weighing 48 tonnes. When the glow of the setting sun hits it, it feels almost spiritual.

Gaze across the northern border

Rising from Ganghwado's northern tip is the **Ganghwa Peace Observatory** *(adult/student/child ₩2500/1700/1000)*. There are some information displays in Korean, but the main attraction is the views into North Korea, just across the Han River. Note the South Korean military facilities along the riverbank. Another, prettier, place to spy across the border is the **Hwagae Garden** *(ganghwa.go.kr/hwagae; adult/child ₩5000/3000)* on Gyodongdo Island, connected to Ganghwado by bridge. Divided into themed zones, the garden climbs a mountain slope; at the top is a glass-floored observatory that looks into North Korea and over a scattering of small islands. Come at sunset for the most drama. It's a 45-minute climb to the observatory, or you can ride the slow monorail up *(adult/child ₩14,000/12,000)*. Near the garden is the old-timey **Daeryong Market**, with retro cafes and places to eat.

GETTING TO THE OBSERVATORIES

The easiest way to visit the Ganghwa Peace Observatory and Hwagae Garden is by car, though with a bit of patience it's possible to get to both by bus from either central Ganghwa-eup or the Ganghwa Bus Terminal. Departures are infrequent, but buses 26, 27 and 28 all run to the Peace Observatory, taking 20 to 45 minutes.

To reach Hwagae Garden, take bus 18, which departs roughly every 80 minutes and takes close to an hour.

You'll pass through a South Korean military checkpoint en route to each site. It's nothing to worry about, but you'll need to show ID, so make sure you bring your passport.

TOP EXPERIENCE

The DMZ & Imjingak Resort

Less than 50km north of Seoul is the Demilitarized Zone (DMZ), the 4km-wide, 240km-long no-man's land separating North and South Korea. It's a sinister place where the tension is palpable, but it's also a major tourist attraction, fascinating and forbidding in equal measure. Join a tour to enter the DMZ, or travel independently to Imjingak to get as close as you can on your own.

GUILLAUME B/SHUTTERSTOCK

Dora Observatory

TOP TIPS

- At the time of writing, DMZ tours were not permitted to visit the JSA. Check with tour operators to see if this changes.
- For all tours, you'll need to bring your passport. There are other rules to be observed – check with your tour company beforehand.
- You can reach Imjingak Resort from Seoul by bus or a combination of bus and train; 2¼ hours one way.

PRACTICALITIES

- *dmz.gg.go.kr*
- tour prices vary
- Imjingak Resort 9am-6pm

DMZ Tours

The only way to access the heavily mined DMZ is on a tour. Most operators offer half- and full-day options. Both typically visit **Imjingak Resort**, the **Third Infiltration Tunnel** and **Dora Observatory**. Discovered in 1978, the tunnel is one of four that North Korea is known to have dug under the DMZ for a potential surprise attack. Creeping along 265m of this 73m-deep tunnel isn't for the claustrophobic, or the tall. At Dora Observatory, you can peer through binoculars into North Korea. On a clear day, you can make out the city of Kaesong. When geopolitical conditions permit, longer tours also visit the **Joint Security Area** (JSA), where the Military Demarcation Line separates the two countries and North and South Korean troops stand face to face.

Imjingak Resort

This park on the banks of the Imjin River makes for a surreal day. Solemn sites such as the **National Memorial for Abductees During the Korean War**, a bullet-riddled locomotive and the remains of a bridge that once connected the two countries share space with art installations, fast-food restaurants and an amusement park. Take the gondola across the river to visit an observatory and **Gallery Greaves**, a museum space in a former US-army-camp bowling alley.

Paju

TIME FROM SEOUL: 1HR

A book city...

There's something almost noble about Paju's commitment to the arts, considering it borders a hostile country. Visit this charming city northwest of Seoul, though, and it's easy to forget that North Korea is just across the river.

Paju is the centre of Korea's publishing industry. Soak up the literary vibes in **Paju Book City** *(pajubookcity.org)*, a collection of some 900 publishing houses, bookshops, bookbinders and related businesses that began to take shape in 1989. Many occupy architecturally striking buildings. Lovers of books – the physical, paper and ink kind – should visit the **Book City Letterpress Museum** *(letterpressmuseum.co.kr; ₩4000)*, which displays working presses, typewriters from around the world and a restoration of the office that published Korea's Declaration of Independence. The museum's collection of 35 million metal printing blocks, weighing a cumulative 22 tonnes, is truly...ahem...impressive. Next door, the **Asia Publication Culture & Information Center** houses the Forest of Wisdom library and Booksori Bookstore. Both offer plenty of places to curl up with a good read from the towering shelves. Hunt around and you'll find some books in English.

If you've ever wished you could just live at the library, book a room at **Jijihyang** *(jijihyang.com)*, the centre's on-site guesthouse. A short walk away is the contemporary **Mimesis Art Museum** *(mimesisartmuseum.co.kr; adult/student/child ₩10,000/8000/5000)*, a curvaceous concrete building designed by Portuguese architect Álvaro Siza.

...and an art village

Several kilometres north of Book City is **Heyri Art Valley** *(heyri.net)*, a cultural complex with dozens of museums, galleries, studios and performance spaces. They tend to offer more kitsch than culture – there are museums dedicated to Coca-Cola, dolls, dinosaurs etc – but there are also some gems, a good deal of interesting architecture and lots of charming cafes. By far the complex's best site is the free **National Folk Museum of Korea, Paju** *(nfm.go.kr/paju)*, a branch of, and storage facility for, the main **museum** (p51) in Seoul. Two-storey glass cabinets showcase a fascinating range of artefacts, from ceramics and beer glasses to an amulet for cows meant to ward off misfortune. There are also fascinating displays that take you behind the scenes of how the museum conducts its conservation work.

Bucheon

TIME FROM SEOUL: 1HR

Trash transformed into art

Midway between Seoul and Incheon, the city of Bucheon can seem like a slightly anonymous bedroom community, but it's got an enticingly strange side. To experience it, catch a bus from Bucheon City Hall station to **Bucheon Art Bunker B39** *(artbunkerb39.org)*, a decommissioned rubbish incinerator that re-opened as an exhibition space in 2018. In its past life,

GANGHWADO HISTORY

Dangun – grandson of a god, son of a bear-woman – is said to have created the Korean people in 2333 BCE. Whether you believe that or not, Ganghwado's history stretches back almost as far. Some 160 dolmens provide proof of a civilisation existing here by at least 1500 BCE.

Fast-forward to the 13th century CE, and Ganghwado had its 39 years of fame when King Gojong moved his Goryeo capital here while Mongols rampaged on the mainland.

The island also played a major role in modern history, as the scene of a bloody 1866 skirmish with the French, who were seeking revenge for the execution of French Catholic missionaries, and an 1871 conflict with a US naval mission attempting to open Korea to trade.

TOP EXPERIENCE

Hwaseong

Completed in 1796, this majestic citadel represents the apex of Joseon achievement, combining mountain and lowland fortress design with Chinese and Western construction techniques. It wasn't just a defence installation, though. It was also a grand expression of filial piety, part of King Jeongjo's project to move his father's tomb from Seoul to a more auspicious location in Suwon.

BASTIEN ALTERMATT/GETTY IMAGES

Hwaseong Haenggung

TOP TIPS

- The **Hwaseong Fortress Tourist Trolley** links some of Hwaseong's main sites from 9.40am to 5pm Tuesday to Sunday.
- See Hwaseong from 150m in **Flying Suwon**'s *(flyingsuwon.com)* tethered hot-air balloon near **Changnyongmun** gate.
- The Suwon Museum Agency app provides English info at the Suwon Hwaseong Museum.

Walk the Walls

The best way to experience **Hwaseong** is to set aside a day to walk its walls, which extend for 5.7km through central Suwon, running over the top of 143m Paldal-san and along the lowlands to the east. En route, you'll encounter four imposing gates, command posts, fire beacons and secret exits where troops could pass undetected. Hwaseong sustained considerable damage during the Japanese colonial period and Korean War, and much of what you see today is the product of reconstruction carried out in the 1970s. At the fortress' northern and southern points are **Janganmun** and **Paldalmun** gates. Janganmun, where Jeongjo would arrive, served as the main gate, while Paldalmun was a conduit for merchants from the south. There are still markets there today. In good weather, be sure to relax at **Hwahongmun**, a military facility/pleasure pavilion built directly over the Suwon-cheon stream.

Hwaseong Haenggung

Located at the centre of the fortress, **Hwaseong Haenggung** (*adult/student/child ₩2000/1500/1000*) was where Jeongjo stayed when visiting his father's tomb. With 600 rooms, it was the largest palace outside of Seoul. It's been meticulously reconstructed after all but two buildings (Nangnamheon and Noraedang) were destroyed during the colonial period. Learn more about the fortress and palace at the nearby **Suwon Hwaseong Museum** (*adult/child ₩2000/1000*).

PRACTICALITIES

- *swcf.or.kr*
- free
- 24hr

the facility burned 180 tonnes of garbage every day, and much of its infrastructure has been left intact – the control room, ash storage room, draft fan room – only now they're venues for exhibitions by Korean and international contemporary artists. There's something exhilarating about exploring the building, navigating metal pipes and puddles where rain has seeped through the concrete, and suddenly coming upon an installation tucked in the shadows. It's closed Monday.

Gwangmyeong

TIME FROM SEOUL: **1HR**

Underground wonders

Gwangmyeong Cave *(gm.go.kr/cv; adult/student/child ₩10,000/5000/3000)* has gone through a few different chapters. A mine for most of the 20th century, it later spent three decades as a storage site for fermented shrimp. Today it's a family-friendly tourist attraction. There are a few historical displays along the 2km route through the cave, but most are pretty kitschy: glowing artificial flowers, treasure stashes, robotic fish. The gigantic dragon created by New Zealand's famed Weta Workshop is admittedly pretty cool. Kids will likely have a grand old time, and parents will find a wine cellar at the end. Catch a bus from Gwangmyeong station to reach the cave, which is closed on Mondays.

Gwacheon

TIME FROM SEOUL: **30MIN**

Family fun in Seoul Grand Park

Just outside of Seoul, the suburb of Gwacheon is home to the enormous **Seoul Grand Park** *(grandpark.seoul.go.kr)*, a favourite with local families. The park contains **Seoul Zoo** *(adult/student/child ₩5000/3000/2000)*, home to elephants, flamingos and many other animals; the **Seoul Grand Park Botanical Garden**, which has a children's zoo where you can watch Border collies herd sheep; and Korea's first theme park, **SeoulLand** *(seoulland.co.kr; adult/student/child ₩52,000/46,000/43,000)*, which has rides, stage shows and seasonal events. Travellers without kids might be more drawn to the Gwacheon branch of the **Museum of Modern and Contemporary Art** *(mmca.go.kr; adult/child ₩3000/free)*, located within the park. Begin on the top floor and work your way down to trace the history of Korean modern art. Besides these facilities, Seoul Grand Park also makes a great place for a picnic, with lots of walking paths and a large artificial lake.

TIPS FOR VISITING SEOUL GRAND PARK

The most scenic way to reach the zoo and botanical garden is the Skylift *(skylift.co.kr)*, a chairlift that soars over the lake and zoo.

The Elephant Train (₩2000) loops between Seoul Grand Park station, Seoul Zoo and SeoulLand. A free bus loops around the zoo and botanical garden.

A free shuttle bus runs from Seoul Grand Park station to the MMCA, Gwacheon. To find the bus stop, make a U-turn from exit 4. The MMCA also runs a free shuttle bus between its Seoul, Deoksugung and Gwacheon branches Tuesday to Friday.

Try to time your visit to the MMCA, Gwacheon for between 2pm and 4pm, when Paik Nam-june's monumental video artwork *The More, the Better* is turned on.

EATING IN GYEONGGI PROVINCE

Samddle Tofu: Just outside Imjingak Resort, this cosy eatery serves tofu soups and platters of tofu and boiled pork belly. *11am-8pm* ₩

Golden Bell: *Naengmyeon* (cold noodles), ox-bone soup, pork cutlets and barbecue at a family-friendly place near Everland amusement park. *6am-3pm & 5-10pm* ₩

Meogeoyasanda: Hearty options like mountain vegetable bibimbap and homemade tofu perfect for pre- or post-hike meals at Namhan-sanseong. *10am-10pm* ₩

Naruteoga: Dumulmeori restaurant serving regional specialities *dakgalbi* (spicy stir-fried chicken) and *makguksu* (chilled buckwheat noodles). *10am-7pm, to 8pm Sat & Sun* ₩

THE BUCHEON INTERNATIONAL FANTASTIC FILM FESTIVAL

If your taste in film skews more *Oldboy* than *KPop Demon Hunters*, consider attending the **Bucheon International Fantastic Film Festival** *(bifan.kr)*, which has been bringing the weird and wonderful to the city for 30 years.

Held each July, BIFAN is dedicated to genre films, and over the course of 10 days it screens more than 200 movies from three dozen countries in categories that span horror, fantasy, experimental and more. The festival embraces new technologies such as AI and virtual reality, and supplements its on-screen entertainment with a night market, concerts and other events.

Most films screen at Bucheon City Hall, CGV Sopung and Bucheon Art Bunker B39. Purchase tickets through the festival website.

Suwon

TIME FROM SEOUL: 1¼HR /

Art at the heart of a fortress

If you're visiting Suwon to see Hwaseong Fortress, it's worth popping in to the **Suwon Museum of Art** *(suma.suwon.go.kr; adult/student/child ₩4000/2000/1000)*, next to Hwaseong Haenggung. The facility hosts rotating exhibitions of modern and contemporary art and has some large spaces that can be used for sound installations and the like. The museum is closed Mondays and doesn't accept foreign cards, so bring cash.

Yongin

TIME FROM SEOUL: 1½HR /

Time travel at a folk village

The **Korean Folk Village** *(koreanfolk.co.kr; adult/child ₩37,000/30,000)* has been transporting visitors back to the Joseon dynasty since 1974. Its picturesque grounds are filled with 270 thatch- and tile-roofed buildings that have been relocated here from around the country. If you're sceptical about the authenticity, consider that the village is realistic enough to have served as a filming location for some of Korea's most popular historical dramas, including *Dae Jang Geum* and *Kingdom*.

The village is much more than just a collection of buildings, though. The past comes alive through its many performances and hands-on activities. You may come across cast members dressed in traditional *hanbok* tending to vegetable plots, conducting tightrope-walking demonstrations or putting on *pungmul* music and dance performances. Stroll down Craft Workshop Street to watch artisans make things such as fans and straw shoes. If you want to get in on the 16th-century action yourself, try out old tools such as A-frame carriers and treadle mills in the Traditional Lifestyle Experience area and play folk games like *tuho* (arrow tossing) in the Swing Yard. There's also a children's amusement park.

Korea's video art star

The father of video art, Paik Nam-june was arguably Korea's most influential modern artist and his works still feel fun and fresh decades after they were created. The **Nam June Paik Art Center** *(njp.ggcf.kr)* has regularly changing exhibitions of pieces pulled from Paik's archive, as well as by avant-garde creators who share his experimental approach. Viewing works by Paik, who died in 2006, you get the sense that no one better understood the way video would come to shape our lives.

EATING IN SUWON: OUR PICKS

Bonsuwon Galbi: Suwon is famous for its beef *galbi* (ribs), and this is one of the best places in the city to get them. *11.30am-8.30pm, to 8pm Sun & Mon* ₩₩₩

Yeonpo Galbi: Grills up mouthwatering beef *galbi*. For lunch, it also serves *galbitang*, a beef-rib soup that's a good option for solo diners. *11.20am-9pm* ₩₩₩

Yongseong Tongdak: Popular *chimaek* (chicken and beer) spot for juicy, golden chicken and cold, cheap brews. *11am-11pm Wed-Mon* ₩₩

Starfield Suwon: This large mall has a good range of dining outlets, including a big 7th-floor food court. *10am-10pm* ₩

SUDONG KIM/SHUTTERSTOCK

Korean Folk Village

In the adjacent park, the **Gyeonggi Province Museum**'s *(musenet.ggcf.kr)* handsome displays trace life in the region from Paleolithic to modern times. Special attention is paid to Gyeonggi-do's historic role as the gateway to the capital. The province produced most of Joseon's porcelain, and the exhibits related to the area's pottery are a particular highlight.

Escape to (never-n)Everland

Korea's largest amusement park, **Everland** *(everland.com; from ₩46,000)* makes for a fun-filled family day out, but it's also a good time for anyone who likes thrill rides and sugary snacks. The park is split into several themed areas. Magic Land is mostly dedicated to kid-friendly rides, while American Adventure ups the adrenaline. Ride the T Express, a gargantuan wooden roller coaster, in European Adventure, and see elephants, tigers and the panda twins Rui Bao and Hui Bao in Zoo Topia. Purchase tickets online or at the ticket booth dedicated to foreign visitors.

Caribbean Bay *(adult/child ₩45,000/39,000)* is the resort's separate water park with indoor and outdoor pools, an impressive assortment of rides, a lazy river and a not-so-lazy wave pool. Both sites are best visited on a weekday, when crowds are more manageable.

Everland is owned by Samsung, and selections from its founder Lee Byung-chull's extensive collection

SAMSUNG'S SISTER MUSEUM

See more art from Lee's collection at the **Leeum Museum of Art** (p136) in Itaewon, where items range from a 1500-year-old gilt-bronze crown to works by Salvador Dalí, Louise Bourgeois and Bahc Yiso.

KOREAN FOLK VILLAGE EVENTS

The Korean Folk Village hosts special events on Korean holidays, giving you a rare opportunity to take part in traditional ceremonies that are fast disappearing in the modern world.

On Dano, the 5th day of the 5th lunar month, you can have your hair washed with iris-infused water. On Chuseok, the autumn harvest festival, sample sweet *songpyeon* rice cakes.

On the winter solstice, tuck into warming red-bean porridge.

Check the village's website for exact dates, as holidays based on the lunar calendar change dates from year to year. Even if you can't time your visit to a holiday, you'll still be treated to some of the village's many seasonal events that follow the rhythms of traditional life, such as spring rice planting.

CERAMIC FESTIVALS

Icheon has been a centre of ceramics production for at least 500 years. It's a craft that continues to thrive today, with more than 400 workshops in and around the town.

The Korea Ceramic Foundation is based in Icheon, which is part of UNESCO's Creative Cities Network thanks to its pottery heritage. The best time to visit is in April and May to catch the annual **Icheon Ceramic Festival**, when artists and enthusiasts gather to buy and sell pottery and to take part in a packed programme of craft activities.

In autumn of even-numbered years, the foundation hosts the **Gyeonggi Ceramics Biennale** at sites across Icheon and the nearby cities of Gwangju and Yeoju, important ceramics centres themselves.

AGAROSE/SHUTTERSTOCK

feature in rotating exhibitions at the superb **Hoam Art Museum** *(leeumhoam.org; adult/student ₩25,000/13,000)*. Buddhist art, paintings by the 18th-century master 'Gyeomjae' Jeong Seon and international augmented-reality works are just some of what you might come across. The museum cafe is an architecturally eye-catching, if pricey, place for a meal. Outside, the beautiful Heewon traditional garden has a lotus pond, plum trees and sculptures.

Icheon

TIME FROM SEOUL: **2HR** (bus/train)

See Korea's ceramics capital

Icheon is one of Korea's most famous centres for pottery. Learn about this history and see what today's ceramicists are up to at a pair of museums within Seolbong Park. The **Icheon Municipal Museum** *(artic.or.kr/icmus/main/view)* covers more than a millennium of ceramics culture, while up the hill, the international collection at the **Gyeonggi Museum of Contemporary Ceramic Art** *(gmocca.org; adult/child ₩3000/2000)* ranges from modern takes on traditional styles to works that will have you rethinking what's possible with the medium.

Northwest of the museums is **Ye's Park** ceramics village, where more than 200 stores and studios cluster. Shop for

DRINKING IN GYEONGGI PROVINCE

Brown Hands: In Incheon, the Gaehang-ro branch of this small cafe chain has left much of its old building fashionably untouched. *11.30am-9.30pm*

Gardenus: Sip an iced Americano and snack on photo-worthy baked goods next to a small reflecting pool at this Heyri Art Valley cafe. *10am-10pm*

Cafe Dohwa: This modern, two-storey *hanok* cafe has good desserts and a great location overlooking the Suwon Traditional Culture Center. *7am-11pm*

Kraemerlee: More than a dozen different brews are on tap at this microbrewery near the Garden of Morning Calm. Serves up American-style barbecue, too. *11am-10pm*

Traditional ceramics, Icheon

tableware, decorative figurines and more, in styles ranging from traditional to sleekly contemporary. You can also book a pottery class with Kwak Kyung Tae, a master of creating *onggi* jars; contact him via ceramicmasterclass.com.

Gwangju

TIME FROM SEOUL: 1¼HR 🚌/🚆

Hike 17th-century fortress walls

The World Heritage-listed **Namhan-sanseong** fortress once guarded Seoul's southern entrance and served as a backup capital in times of emergency. Today the fortress walls, of which 12.3km remain, are protected within a provincial park threaded with hiking trails through beautiful pine and oak forests. The most popular route is a two-hour loop past three of the fortress' four gates that serves up sweeping panoramas along the way. Budget a full day to trek the wall's entire perimeter.

Just inside Namhan-sanseong's main entrance is a fine reconstruction of the **Namhan-sanseong Emergency Palace** *(adult/child ₩2000/1000)*. Considering its beautiful setting, you have to imagine the Joseon king would have been tempted to make his residence here permanent. Outside the gate is a collection of restaurants to fuel your hike and the informative **Namhansanseong Historical Museum**, where you can learn about the fort's construction and the warrior monks who defended it.

Guri

TIME FROM SEOUL: 1HR 🚆/🚌

Pay your respects to Joseon royalty

Donggureung *(royal.khs.go.kr)* is the largest and most attractive of the World Heritage-listed Joseon royal tomb complexes scattered around Seoul and Gyeonggi-do. Spend some time in the small History Center near the entrance to learn about the elaborate burial rites and pick up a site map before

TEMPORARY PALACES

When Joseon's rulers travelled around Korea, they needed somewhere fitting to stay. In places they visited regularly, such as the tombs of ancestors or a regional fortress, a *haenggung* (temporary palace) was constructed.

The Namhan-sanseong Emergency Palace was built in 1625 and proved useful to King Injo a decade later, when he was forced to take shelter here from the invading Qing army.

Unlike other *haenggung*, Namhan-sanseong was designed to function as a temporary capital in times of crisis. Subsequent kings stayed here when visiting Yeongneung and Nyeongneung, the tombs of King Sejong and King Hyojong, respectively. Other temporary palaces are in Suwon and Ganghwado.

FAMILY FUN

There's lots for parents and kids to do together close to Seoul.
Gyeonggi Children's Museum: English displays and copious opportunities for play make learning lots of fun. *gcm.ggcf.kr*
Aquafield: This *jjimjil-bang* (sauna) at Star-field Goyang Mall has a rooftop pool, food court and kids zone. *aquafield-ssg.co.kr*
Anseong Farmland: Children can feed rabbits, meet cows, ride horses and go on amusement-park rides. *nhasfarmland.com*
Korail Tourist Trains: Themed trains depart on sightseeing trips to rural Gangwon and Chungcheong provinces. *korail.com*
Ilsan Lake Park: This 99-hectare park has a lake, artificial islands, a playground and a musical fountain. *goyang.go.kr/park*
Mr Toilet House: Kids will find this museum (also known as Haewoojae) about digestion and toilets hilarious. *haewoojae.com*

visiting the tombs of the seven kings and 10 queens buried here. Note the silver grass atop the tomb of Joseon-dynasty founder King Taejo, which comes from his hometown of Hamheung, North Korea. Plan on 1½ hours to explore Donggureung in its entirety.

Yangpyeong

TIME FROM SEOUL: 1¾HR

See where the waters meet

When the weather's good, few places make for a better outing than **Dumulmeori**, the spot where the northern and southern branches of the Han River meet before flowing through Seoul. You'll find cafes and restaurants catering to day-trippers, a regal 400-year-old zelkova and a traditional sailboat moored just offshore, a tribute to when this was an important merchant port.

If you get here early enough, you might be treated to the sight of the rivers covered in a blanket of morning fog. While here, be sure to try the corn dogs and ice cream made with lotus leaves, Dumulmeori specialities. From Dumulmeori, cross a bridge built atop anchored boats to **Semiwon** *(semiwon.or.kr; adult/child ₩7000/4000)*, a garden known for its many lotuses and water lilies. Peak bloom for the lotuses is early June, while the water lilies are at their best in July and August.

Gapyeong

TIME FROM SEOUL: 1½HR

Explore an Edenic garden

Deep in Gapyeong's verdant hills is the astonishing **Garden of Morning Calm** *(morningcalm.co.kr; adult/student/child ₩11,000/8500/7500)*. Horticulture professor Han Sang-kyeong and his wife, Lee Young-ja, began constructing the garden in 1994, and it has since grown to cover 33 hectares and include 20 different themed gardens, including a traditional Korean garden, an English cottage-style garden and a bonsai garden. You could easily spend an entire day here, admiring the countless beautiful views, filling your camera roll and lingering in the garden's cafes and restaurants.

The garden offers starkly different, though equally beautiful, experiences in different seasons. In spring, expect cherry blossoms and colourful tulips; in summer, hydrangeas burst into cheerful spheres and streams offer respite from the heat; in autumn, ginkgos light up in gold and pink muhly grass creates feathery pastel waves. Even in winter, snow and an elaborate light display make the garden worth a visit.

While it's possible to get to the garden via a combination of train and bus, it's a time-consuming process, so you might want to consider renting a car. The surrounding valley has many good pensions and places to eat.

CHIARA SAKUWA/SHUTTERSTOCK

Garden of Morning Calm

KOREAN GARDEN DESIGN

Although it incorporates a wide range of styles, the Garden of Morning Calm is part of a venerable tradition of gardens on the peninsula.

Whereas gardens in the West often seek to shape and apply order to the natural world – think of all those trimmed lawns and clipped hedges – traditional Korean gardens seek to blend in with their surroundings.

Garden locations are often chosen for their favourable *pungsu*, or feng shui, and follow the existing topography. When being laid out, Korean gardens typically factor the surrounding view (often mountains) into their design. Informality, simplicity and an unforced appearance are prized, thus strengthening the connection between people and the natural world.

Where to Stay

From budget hostels to five-star hotels, Seoul's accommodation options are wide ranging. There's the opportunity, too, to stay in uniquely local lodging – traditional *hanok* (Korean wooden houses) with *ondol* (heated floors).

Where to Stay if You Love ...

Grand palaces & historic *hanok*

Gwanghwamun & Jongno-gu (p48) For a *hanok* guesthouse experience, the neighbourhoods around Gwanghwamun offer midrange and high-end options within walking distance of palaces, museums, arts and crafts.

Hallyu, shopping & street snacks

Myeong-dong & Jung-gu (p74) You can't get more central than Jung-gu, which offers plenty of hostels and midrange hotels. It's a great area to stay for shopping, walking between sights and sampling the nightlife of hip areas such as Euljiro.

Bar-hopping, global flavours & clubbing

Western Seoul (p98) Owing to their large student populations, Hongdae and Sinchon have a glut of guesthouses, hostels and small hotels at lower and midrange prices. Yeouido has some high-end options.

Hipster 'hoods & post-industrial parks

Itaewon & Yongsan-gu (p120) Full of no-frills hostels at the doorstep of some of the city's best nightlife. The best have communal kitchens, roof terraces and a backpacker vibe, but can get noisy.

Designer fashion & fine dining

Gangnam & Southern Seoul (p140) Lodging abounds in Gangnam, from high-end hotels to midrange chains. Distances between local sights and those across the river can be long, so stay near a subway station.

Modern architecture & traditional markets

Dongdaemun & Eastern Seoul (p162) Much of the area's midrange accommodation is concentrated around the malls and markets of Dongdaemun, with a few luxury hotels, too.

Hiking, mountains & youth culture

Northern Seoul (p176) From budget hostels around the university and theatre district of Daehangno to campgrounds, guesthouses and resorts near the hiking of Bukhansan, Northern Seoul's options are wide ranging.

Gwanghwamun & Jongno-gu

HANOK

Seochon Guesthouse ₩₩

MAP P53

Just south of Tongin Market, this charming *hanok* with mostly Korean-style rooms is run by kind hosts who offer a homemade breakfast and lots of neighbourhood tips.

Bukchon Maru ₩₩

MAP P63

The *ondol* rooms at this *hanok* guesthouse are basic, authentic and cosy, and the family running it couldn't be more hospitable. Only the family room has its own bathroom.

Butler.Lee ₩₩₩

MAP P63

Manages about 20 premium self-catering *hanok* of various sizes around Gyeongbokgung, some of them notable historic homes and all of them gorgeously decorated.

Rak-Ko-Jae ₩₩₩

MAP P63

Beautifully restored *hanok* with an enchanting garden and a mud-walled sauna. Northwest, there's a second branch with a culture lounge and cafe.

BOUTIQUE

Boan Stay ₩₩

MAP P53

In Seochon on the 3rd and 4th floors of Artspace Boan 1942, these bright minimalist rooms feature art and furniture by contemporary designers, with a view onto Gyeongbokgung.

Tongtong Hotel ₩₩

MAP P56

Conveniently close to Ikseon-dong, with small rooms styled in a spare aesthetic and a lovely rooftop overlooking a Buddhist temple next door.

Myeong-dong & Jung-gu

TOP-END SPLURGE

The Westin Josun Seoul ₩₩₩

MAP P84

Among the most luxurious stays in the area, the Westin Josun has a spa, a pool illuminated by a skylight and a lounge bar that looks out on a Joseon-era pagoda.

The Plaza Seoul ₩₩

MAP P84

This landmark hotel overlooks Seoul Plaza and some rooms have views of City Hall. There's a spa, pool, fitness centre and oyster bar in which to indulge.

BOUTIQUE

Hotel28 ₩₩

MAP P76

This classy boutique hotel in the heart of Myeong-dong has a cinema theme. Korean film stills decorate rooms and there's a library, gym and high-end Korean restaurant, Congdu, on site.

L'Escape ₩₩

MAP P84

The decor throughout this plush hotel channels *belle époque* Parisienne glamour. Secret rooms have striking deep-red walls, while suites feature exuberant floral wallpaper. Also has a spa, gym and tearoom.

CONTEMPORARY COOL

Small House Big Door ₩₩

MAP P76

Recently renovated, this place offers an excellent style-to-price ratio with modern furnishings and rooms decorated in *obangsaek*, Korea's traditional five primary colours.

Metro Hotel ₩₩

MAP P76

There are splashes of style at this small hotel with boutique aspirations. Rooms are tidy and it has a nice terrace and excellent Myeong-dong location, just steps from the subway.

BUDGET

Zaza Backpackers ₩

MAP P76

A top option in the enclave of hostels and guesthouses south of Myeongdong station, with nice design touches and friendly staff. Head up to the rooftop terrace for views of N Seoul Tower.

HOW MUCH FOR A NIGHT IN

Luxury five-star hotel
from ₩300,000

Boutique hotel
from ₩220,000

Guesthouse
from ₩150,000

Hostel dorm bed
from ₩40,000

Namsan Hostel Guest House ₩

MAP P76

Nice, no-frills place with some of the lowest rates you'll find this close to Myeong-dong. Has private rooms and a female-only dorm, plus free laundry and a rooftop terrace.

Western Seoul

TOP-END SPLURGE

RYSE ₩₩₩

MAP P102

Takes the surrounding Hongdae aesthetic and dresses it up with artsy rooms, a private cinema, on-site skate shop and 15th-floor bar, the terrace of which overlooks the neighbourhood.

Hongyugain ₩₩₩

MAP P102

This *hanok* guesthouse in **Eunpyeong Hanok Village** (p111) is far removed from most of Seoul's sites, but it's ideal for groups who want a traditional stay and to wake up to mountain views.

Conrad Seoul ₩₩₩

MAP P113

Luxurious rooms with sweeping Han River views, a spa and indoor pool. Its position right in the middle of Yeouido makes it a solid choice for anyone with business on the island.

BOUTIQUE

L7 Hongdae ₩₩

MAP P102

Just outside Hongik University station, L7 isn't short on style. Crisp rooms have bold colours, there's a good range of public areas and you can't beat its rooftop pool.

GLAD Mapo ₩₩

MAP P102

This sleek hotel offers good value, with modern rooms, a gym, a work lounge and a location just steps from the well-connected Gongdeok station.

BUDGET

Time Travelers Relax ₩

MAP P102

Quirky art, a library, lots of plants and a small courtyard make this hostel a great budget option. Has private rooms and mixed dorms and is a short walk to Hongdae.

Roi Guesthouse ₩

MAP P102

Budget-friendly place with larger rooms than most and an excellent location on a quiet, tree-lined street in hip Yeonnam, just a short stroll from Gyeongui Line Forest Park.

Itaewon & Yongsan-gu

BUDGET

H Hostel Itaewon ₩

MAP P122

Sleeping cubbies and private rooms at very reasonable prices, with luggage storage, free breakfast and a spacious common area. The rooftop is a highlight.

FIIPHOTO/SHUTTERSTOCK

Itaewon nightlife (p126)

G Guesthouse Itaewon ₩
MAP P122
Budget digs in the heart of Itaewon, ideal for meeting fellow travellers in the kitchen or on the rooftop. Friendly staff are exceedingly helpful, with loads of recommendations at the ready.

Seoul Cube Itaewon ₩
MAP P122
For people who like to party, this hostel at the doorstep of Itaewon's club scene is good value for the price, offering free breakfast and convenient communal facilities. Paid laundry service, too.

BOUTIQUE AND SPLURGE

Mondrian Seoul Itaewon ₩₩
MAP P122
Chic contemporary hotel with a Mediterranean touch. Swanky indoor and outdoor pools, lobby and rooftop bars, and a restaurant on the premises, along with yoga, a sauna and indoor virtual golf.

Imperial Palace Boutique Hotel ₩₩
MAP P132
With comfortable rooms in a prime location, about midway between Itaewon and Hangangjin stations, this boutique stay is easy to spot with its bright colour-block exterior.

Grand Hyatt Seoul ₩₩₩
MAP P132
Built in 1978, one of Seoul's original luxury hotels has flawless service and magnificent views of Namsan. On site is a spa, museum and several restaurants, including the Michelin-recommended Teppan.

TOP TIP
Remember to book accommodation in Seoul well in advance if you're planning to visit during the busy seasons of spring and autumn. This also applies if you want to stay in the most central and popular locations. See p22 for more information on when to go to Seoul.

Gangnam & Southern Seoul

TOP-END SPLURGE

Signiel Seoul ₩₩₩
MAP P157
The city's poshest, and loftiest, stay. Rooms occupy floors 87 to 101 of the Lotte World Tower. Facilities include a spa, a gym with personal trainers, guest lounge and rotating art displays.

Park Hyatt Seoul ₩₩₩
MAP P144
Has a dreamy infinity pool and spacious open-plan rooms with floor-to-ceiling windows and luxurious bathrooms.

On a gorgeous Zen-inspired property next to Starfield COEX Mall.

Josun Palace ₩₩₩
MAP P144
A glamorous hotel with mid-century-modern touches and rooms in soothing shades of white and cream. There are three on-site restaurants, plus a lounge, pool and sauna.

BOUTIQUE

Owall Hotel ₩₩
MAP P144
Six stunningly designed rooms that bring together Japanese and Scandinavian minimalism. Each room is unique, but all come with a private terrace; two have their own pools.

H Avenue Hotel Yeoksam ₩₩
MAP P144
Smartly furnished rooms in a high-rise. Two suites have access to small rooftop swimming pools, glamping tents and city views.

FAMILY-FRIENDLY

Seoul Olympic Parktel ₩₩
MAP P157
Within Olympic Park, this tower has tidy, basic rooms, some of which have lush views over the park's greenery. The lobby displays artworks from the SOMA collection.

Lotte Hotel World ₩₩₩
MAP P157
Some rooms look directly onto the Lotte World Adventure theme park's Magic Island, sure to fulfil every child's wildest dream. Also has cartoon character rooms they'll love.

Dongdaemun & Eastern Seoul

DONGDAEMUN & SINDANG

Mangrove Dongdaemun ₩
MAP P165
Co-working and living apartment block offering simple budget rooms (including dorms) with self-catering kitchens, canteen and rooftop terrace.

PIPE Hostel Dongdaemun ₩₩
MAP P165
Clean, simple and small private rooms with en-suite bathrooms. Common areas include a shared kitchen and laundry room.

ABP Sindang ₩₩₩
MAP P165
Standing for A Better Place, with four stylishly designed self-catering units; check in at **Manmool** (p170) cafe-bar.

Hotel Shilla ₩₩₩
MAP P165
Luxe digs on a hillside near Namsan. Highlights include an all-season outdoor pool and the Michelin-starred La Yeon Korean restaurant.

JW Marriott Dongdaemun Square ₩₩₩
MAP P165
Swish pad beside Dongdaemun's round-the-clock wholesale markets and malls. The best rooms offer views of the old city-wall gate **Heunginjimun** (p164).

SEONGSU & SEOUL FOREST

Seoul Forest Stay ₩
MAP P172
Dorms and private rooms at this hostel that's handy for Seongsu. Friendly English-speaking owner and rooftop chill-out area.

Hotel Poco ₩₩
MAP P172
Perfect base if you want to explore trendy Seongsu. Deluxe double rooms feature a dart board and mini ping-pong table.

Northern Seoul

DAEHANGNO & CHANGSIN-DONG

Original Backpackers ₩
MAP P179
Superior design hostel with lots of cool facilities, including an 'AI' laundry and rooftop kitchen where you can enjoy your breakfast, included in the rates.

Glue Hotel ₩₩
MAP P179
Orange pillows, house plants and art elevate this boutique hotel. Some rooms have views across to Ihwa Maeul and there's a sophisticated cafe-bar in the basement.

Mayplace ₩₩
MAP P179
Rainwater recycling and solar power boost the eco-credentials of this pleasant and handily located hotel. Also has a coin laundry and rooftop garden.

Nabijam ₩₩₩
MAP P179
With a name meaning 'sweet dreams', this century-old *hanok* has been artfully updated into a cosy and contemporary self-catering bolthole for two.

TOP TIP
Staying in a *hanok* is a beautiful experience, especially if you're a fan of unique architecture. See p55 for more information about *hanok* buildings.

BUAM-DONG & BUKHANSAN NATIONAL PARK

Guesthouse The Kims ₩₩
MAP P188
Stay in the swish home of a retired Korean couple, with several room configurations available, including one with a balcony offering glorious views of Bukaksan.

Ui-dong Family Camping Ground ₩₩
MAP P193
Pitch your own tent or sleep in a glamping tent with beds, air-con and cooking facilities. The tent's *ondol* (underfloor heating) makes it a year-round option.

Anto Resort ₩₩₩
MAP P193
Set in landscaped grounds on the national park's doorstep, the spacious, stylish rooms at this luxe resort feature wooden decor.

Day Trips from Seoul

INCHEON

Gyeongwonjae by Walkerhill ₩₩₩
Set within Songdo Central Park, this palatial *hanok*-style hotel cuts a regal figure against the surrounding skyscrapers. Has a lotus pond in the courtyard and luxurious rooms, some with private patios.

Harbor Park Hotel ₩₩
Plain but well-equipped rooms with views of the working harbour and Chinatown. Facilities include a fitness centre and 4th-floor restaurant that serves a weekend buffet.

DENIS KABANOV/SHUTTERSTOCK

Hwaseong (p206), Suwon

GANGHWADO

Hotel Everrich ₩₩
Offering expansive views towards the mainland from its hillside perch on the outskirts of Ganghwa's main town, this contemporary hotel has stylish rooms in a range of sizes.

Spoonbill Pension ₩₩
This south-coast pension provides nice views out to the ocean, and all rooms have enclosed verandas and picnic tables with built-in barbecue grills.

SUWON

Hotel Dono ₩₩
Decent modern rooms and a great location just a couple of blocks from both Hwaseong's main gate and the cafes and restaurants of the trendy Haengnidan-gil neighbourhood.

Novotel Ambassador Suwon ₩₩₩
Spacious and contemporary in design, with an ideal location next to Suwon's subway and train station. Has a restaurant, lobby bar and fitness centre.

YONGIN

Golden Tulip Ever Yongin ₩₩
A family-friendly hotel near the entrance to Everland, should you want to get an early start on your theme-park fun.

GAPYEONG

Leikki Puisto ₩₩₩
Fantastic family accommodation with super-king-size, four-person beds, separate self-catering kitchens, a big kid-friendly pool and charming children's play area.

TOOLKIT

The chapters in this section cover the most important topics you'll need to know about in Seoul. They're full of nuts-and-bolts information and valuable insights to help you understand and navigate Seoul and get the most out of your trip.

***Jjigae* with *banchan* (p224)**

BARECA MEDIA/SHUTTERSTOCK

Money

CURRENCY: KOREAN WON (₩)

Credit Cards

Major international cards such as Visa, Mastercard and American Express are widely accepted, with many places – even street stalls – set up for contactless payment. However, there will be times that your card isn't accepted or incurs a fee, so always carry some Korean paper money.

ATMs

ATMs that accept foreign cards are common: look for ones that have a 'Global' sign or the logo of your credit-card company. ATMs often operate from 7am to 11pm, but some are 24-hour. Restrictions on the amount you can withdraw in one transaction can vary, but are usually around ₩1,000,000 per day.

Exchanging Money

Money can be changed at banks and licensed moneychangers, which keep longer hours than banks and provide a faster service, but may only exchange certain currencies.

Tipping

Tipping is not a custom in Korean culture and is not required or expected, except at some high-end Western-style restaurants.

HOW MUCH FOR

Subway fare with/without Tmoney card
from ₩1550/1650

Museum entry
free, or from ₩1000

Taxi starting rate
₩4800

Public toilet
free

HOW TO… Save on Public Transport

Get a rechargeable Tmoney card, which gives adults ₩100 off each public-transport ride. Transfer within 30 minutes during the day (or an hour at night) for free (remember to tap your card when you exit or you'll be charged again). Board buses before 6.30am for a 20% discount.

Remember to get your remaining Tmoney balance refunded before you leave.

SUPERMARKET STEALS

Many Korean supermarkets offer discounts on ready meals and other perishables towards the end of the working day. Also look for convenience-store buy-one, get-one deals, in Korea called 1+1.

TAXES & REFUNDS

If you spend more than ₩30,000 at participating tax-free shops, you can receive a partial refund on some items (between 5% and 7%) of the 10% value-added tax (VAT).

Be sure to collect the special receipt, which can be used to obtain a tax refund at the airport or, increasingly, in locations in and around Seoul's shopping areas.

Seoul also has a growing number of shops and malls where goods are sold tax-free on the spot, but you'll need to show your passport.

Family Travel

Korean culture adores children and makes them the centre of attention, so travelling with your kids here is recommended. Expect locals to be helpful. Throughout Seoul are many kid-friendly parks, cinemas, video-game arcades, PC rooms, tenpin bowling alleys, *noraebang* (karaoke rooms), board-game cafes and mom cafes.

Getting Around

Kids under six can travel free on subways and buses, while youth under 18 are entitled to different levels of discounts depending on their age. When purchasing a Tmoney card for kids and teens, bring along their passport as proof of age so the card can be set up to take advantage of their discounted fares.

Facilities

Many toilet facilities have changing tables and some have lower sinks and family bathrooms. Nursing rooms can be found in subway stations, malls and airports, though you won't see anyone breastfeeding in public.

Restaurants

Many restaurants are specifically set up to serve meals family-style. Foods that may appeal to kids are Korean fried chicken, *tonkatsu* (breaded pork cutlets), *ramyeon* noodles, *gimbap* (seaweed-wrapped rice rolls), *mandu* (dumplings; pictured) and street snacks and sweets. Bakery cafes are another good option. Consider packing small forks for kids who may struggle with chopsticks. Few restaurants have high chairs.

KID-FRIENDLY ATTRACTIONS

Amusement Parks

Lotte World (p160) is Seoul's equivalent of Disneyland, with thrill rides, a sky walk and a castle, and **Everland** (p209) in Yongin is an easy day trip from Seoul.

Parks

Visit the deer that live in **Seoul Forest** (p173), or play at one of the city's other parks such as **Olympic Park** (p158) and **World Cup Park** (p108).

Baseball

Watching Korean fans supporting their teams (p161) can be just as enjoyable as following the game.

K-POP FUN

Thanks to the global appeal of K-Pop culture, it's likely that your kids will need little persuasion for the chance to scope out its beating heart.

Go shopping for K-Pop idol merch and *manhwa* (Korean comics and graphic novels), hunt down the locations of popular K-Drama, films and K-Pop videos, and make your own content at places such as **HiKR Ground** (p95). Meanwhile, keep an eye peeled for Haechi, Seoul's lovable big pink mascot inspired by the mythical lion-like creature that guarded palaces.

CLOCKWISE FROM TOP LEFT: GUITAR PHOTOGRAPHER/SHUTTERSTOCK, TYASINDAYANTI/SHUTTERSTOCK, KABARDINS PHOTO/SHUTTERSTOCK, ANDREY LOBACHEV/SHUTTERSTOCK

Food, Drink & Nightlife

When to Eat

Achim (breakfast, 7am to 10am) Koreans usually eat breakfast at home, or sometimes grab a pastry or *gimbap* from a bakery or shop. Brunch is popular on weekends.

Jeomsim (lunch, noon to 2pm) Make sure to eat lunch before most restaurants close for a break between around 2.30pm to 5pm.

Jeonyeok (dinner, 6pm to 9pm) Smaller places that don't serve alcohol close earlier, while resto-bars may stay open past 10pm.

Where to Eat

Restaurants Occasionally a restaurant may turn away solo diners because it only serves meals in portions for a minimum of two.

Cafes Bakery and dessert cafes are super popular and good places for breakfast or a light meal.

Bars Most bars serve good-quality *anju* (food to accompany drinks) made for sharing.

Street food Look for stalls in markets, pedestrian zones and areas with busy nightlife.

Pojangmacha These 'covered wagons' are outdoor food tents that act like mini-restaurants and bars.

MENU DECODER

Bap (밥) Cooked rice. Menu items with *bap* in their names include bibimbap, *bokkeumbap* and *gimbap*.

Banchan (반찬) Most Korean restaurants include free side dishes such as kimchi, bean sprouts or cooked vegetables with the ordered meal.

Guk (국) or **tang** (탕) Soup. Some varieties include *samgyetang* (ginseng chicken soup), *gamjatang* (meat and potato soup), *galbitang* (beef-rib soup) and *haejangguk* (hangover soup).

Jjigae (찌개) Stews, often spicy, starring ingredients such as kimchi, *doenjang* (fermented soybean paste) and *dubu* (tofu), along with vegetables, meat or seafood.

Mandu (만두) Filled dumplings.

Guksu (국수) or **myeon** (면) Noodles.

Hanjeongsik (한정식) Korean banquet spread of 12 or more dishes.

Chuga (추가) Extra or more, ie 'cheese *chuga*' (치즈추가) means a side of cheese melted atop your main dish.

HOW TO... Navigate a Korean Restaurant

Because Korean restaurants often specialise in one dish, their menus are usually short and simple. Sometimes the menu is posted on the wall; increasingly, tables will be equipped with touchscreen tablets on which you can place your order. If there's no tablet, summon a server, either by pushing the button that may be on your table, or by calling out *'yogiyo'*, which means 'here please'.

Metal chopsticks and spoons may be found in an oblong box on the table, or in a drawer hidden in the side of the table. (The spoon is for rice, soup and any dish with liquids; the chopsticks are for everything else.)

A carafe of water or tea, along with cups, will be provided, as will *banchan* (side dishes), or they may be located in a 'self-service' area of the restaurant for you to retrieve yourself.

NIIK LEUANGBORIBOON/SHUTTERSTOCK

HOW MUCH FOR A...

Gimbap from convenience store
₩2500

Bottled water
₩1000

Barbecue dinner
₩50,000

Kimchi jjigae
₩10,000

Instant ramyeon
₩900

Draught beer
₩4500

Bottle of soju at restaurant
₩5000

Americano
₩1500-6000

HOW TO... K-BBQ

Gogi jip, or barbecue 'meat houses', are popular restaurants in Korea and a common place to kick off *il-cha*, or the first round of a long night out. Their main selling point is the quality of the meat, including top-tier Korean beef *hanwoo*, and every table has its own small gas or charcoal grill set into it. Often boisterous establishments, you'll see servers whisk between tables with smouldering charcoal in tow, and tabletops littered with emptied soju and beer bottles.

Some meats, such as bulgogi (thinly sliced beef) and *galbi* (ribs), will come marinated in a sauce. Others, such as *chadolbagi* (thinly sliced brisket) or *samgyeopsal* (unsalted pork belly), won't. Diners typically cook their own meat on the grill, though servers will often swoop in to assist. Meat is cut into bite-sized pieces using *gawi* (scissors).

Once the meat is ready, it's time to assemble a wrap *(ssam)* using lettuce, perilla and other types of leafs. Take a leaf in your hand, place the meat on top and add any toppings you like, such as sliced garlic, kimchi, shredded green onion, *cheongyang gochu* (spicy green pepper) and a dollop of *ssamjang* (fermented soybean and red-pepper sauce), to your taste. Then wrap it all up and eat it in one bite.

Other dishes to order to eat alongside *gogi* include kimchi or tofu *jjigae* (stew), *gyeran-jjim* (steamed egg) and *gonggi-bap* (a bowl of rice).

Seating, Storage & Spills

Seats at *gogi jip* are often stools, sometimes with lids that come off to reveal storage for your bag and coat. Aprons are typically available to protect your clothing from errant spatters and spills.

DRINKING CULTURE & PRACTICALITIES

The legal drinking age in Korea is 19. Carry your passport or other ID for entry to clubs, which sometimes will not accept a photo of your identification.

Eating while drinking is a customary part of Korean socialising, and many *hof* (German-inspired pubs) and other bars in Seoul (though not all) will require you to buy *anju* (bar food) with your drinks, or be a little put off if you don't (though the more Americanised the establishment, the less likely this is to be the case).

Traditionally, *anju* include snacks such as dried squid and fruit platters. Often certain *anju* are specially paired with certain alcohols. Have fried chicken with beer (a combo called *chimaek*), pizza with beer (*pimaek*) and types of *jeon* (savoury pancakes) with *makgeolli* (particularly on rainy days).

Drinking, drinking a lot and drinking for a long time is a norm of Korean nightlife, with an evening out often comprising many *cha*, or rounds, as revellers hop from restaurant to bar to club to *noraebang* (private singing room). However, as in other countries, there's also a changing attitude toward excessive alcohol consumption, particularly among young people, and nonalcoholic beers, mocktails and other alcohol-free options are getting easier to find.

While drinking alcohol in public spaces such as parks was once commonly permitted, Seoul has been shifting to banning public consumption in more and more areas. You may still see people imbibing, but steer clear, as it can result in fines.

LGBTIQ+ Travellers

Korea has never outlawed homosexuality, but this shouldn't be taken as a sign of widespread tolerance or acceptance. This is a conservative society and sexuality in general is a taboo subject. LGBTIQ+ travellers who disclose their sexual orientation should be prepared for some less-than-positive reactions. Attitudes are changing, however, especially among young people, and LGBTIQ+ travellers should have few fears about visiting Seoul.

Seoul's Gaybourhoods

Seoul's two most famous locations for LGBTIQ+-friendly watering holes and gathering spaces are Itaewon and the Jongno 3-ga area around Nakwon-dong. It's not the most PC of names, but Itaewon's 'Homo Hill' is where international LGBTIQ+ visitors will feel most comfortable hanging out. The bars and clubs along the short alley tend to be tiny, so on warm nights the crowds often spill into the street.

The scene in Nakwon-dong is more discreet and centred on gay Korean men. A bar here that's welcoming to overseas gays is **Shortbus** (p54).

QUEER ROLE MODELS

Public LGBTIQ+ figures are rare in Korea. In 2022 Cha Hae-yeong became South Korea's first openly gay elected official. The then 35-year-old bisexual woman won in Mapo's 6th electoral district, one of Seoul's more liberal neighbourhoods. In 2020 singer Kwon Do-woon became the first major Korean celebrity to come out on his own terms since actor Hong Seok-cheon did so during a TV interview in 2000.

Chingusai

With its name meaning 'Between Friends', Chingusai *(chingusai.net)* has been campaigning for LGBTIQ+ human rights since 1994 and is one of Korea's oldest sexual-minority rights organisations. Its website outlines Korean attitudes to the gay community and provides strategies for South Korean members of the LGBTIQ+ community to successfully come out.

SEOUL QUEER CULTURE FESTIVAL

The high point of LGBTIQ+ visibility in Seoul is the annual **Seoul Queer Culture Festival** *(sqcf.org)*, usually held in June or July. It includes a well-attended gay-pride parade, some 60 booths where you can join in various creative and interactive activities, and the Seoul Queer Film Festival.

More Resources

@lesvos_itaewon Yoon Kim Myung-woo, aka Myeongwoo Hyeong, runs Lesvos as a community space for Seoul's queer community.

lgbtpride.or.kr Founded in 1997, Solidarity for LGBT Human Rights of Korea (HaengSeongIn) is one of Korea's oldest and most active LGBTIQ+ organisations.

DISCRIMINATION

Korean law provides no protection from discrimination based on sexual orientation or gender identity. Same-sex marriages and civil unions are illegal. Queer students face bullying at schools and same-sex couples cannot adopt.

There have been continued attempts to block Seoul's annual Pride festival, but in 2025 the 26th annual event still managed to draw a record number of participants.

Health & Safe Travel

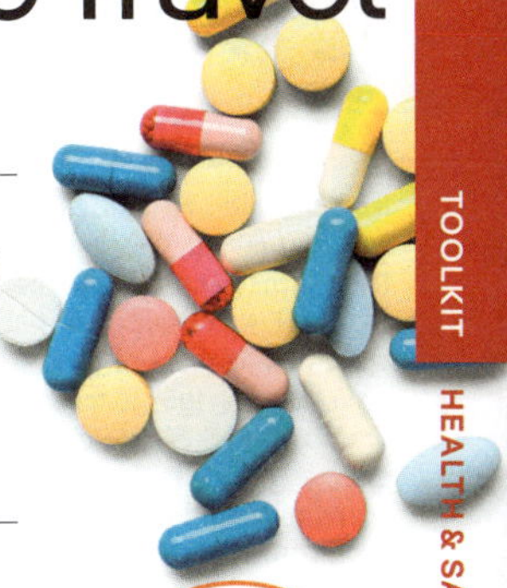

HOSPITALS & PHARMACIES

The quality of medical care in Seoul is high, and local clinics are easy to find. To buy most stronger medications, you need a doctor's prescription. Many common over-the-counter meds are available without a prescription at any *yak-guk*, or pharmacy. Pharmacists often speak English, but if you run into difficulties, dial 02-1330 to reach an interpreter.

Heavy Rains & Extreme Heat

Check weather forecasts regularly. In monsoon season, from late June through August, Seoul gets hit by typhoons and heavy rains, which can cause catastrophic floods and landslides. In July and August, temperatures above 30°C are common. Alongside the humidity, it can lead to heat exhaustion. Hydrate regularly, use sun protection and seek out air-conditioning.

Vaccinations & Preventable Disease

There are no special vaccination requirements for visiting Seoul, but you should consider vaccinations against hepatitis A, hepatitis B, COVID-19, typhoid, tetanus, measles-mumps-rubella and, if you plan to do a tonne of hiking during peak mosquito season, Japanese encephalitis.

TIPS

Motorists can be impatient with pedestrians, so take extra care when crossing the road.

Download the Emergency Ready App for support in English.

SEOUL AIR QUALITY

Seoul uses coloured lights on N Seoul Tower to indicate the level of air pollution. Also check digital signage and air-quality apps.

Blue
Good
0-15µg/m^3 of microdust

Green
Fair
16-35µg/m^3 of microdust

Yellow
Bad
36-75µg/m^3 of microdust

Red
Extremely Bad
76µg/m^3 or more of microdust

Tap Water

Seoul's tap water is safe to drink, but most locals don't – there's a perception that old metal pipes make it unsafe. Filtered, purified water is available free of charge in almost all restaurants, as well as in most public buildings and tourist attractions.

DEMONSTRATIONS

Police in full riot gear, carrying shields and batons, are not an uncommon sight in central Seoul, particularly near Gwanghwamun. Student, trade-union, environmental, anti-American and other protests can occasionally turn physical. Keep well out of the way of any confrontations that may occur.

FROM LEFT: NITO/SHUTTERSTOCK, PIXEL-SHOT/SHUTTERSTOCK

Responsible Travel

Climate Change & Travel

It's impossible to ignore the impact we have when travelling; Lonely Planet urges all travellers to engage with their travel carbon footprint, which will mainly come from air travel. While there often isn't an alternative, travellers can look to minimise the number of flights they take, opt for newer aircrafts and use cleaner ground transport, such as trains. One proposed solution – purchasing carbon offsets – unfortunately does not cancel out the impact of individual flights. While most destinations will depend on air travel for the foreseeable future, for now, pursuing ground-based travel where possible is the best course of action.

The **UN carbon footprint calculator** shows how flying impacts a household's emissions.

The **ICAO Carbon Emissions Calculator** allows visitors to analyse the CO_2 generated by point-to-point journeys.

Ride Public Transit

Seoul's public transport system is vast, convenient and efficient, so opting for subways and buses over taxis is usually an easy choice. Since 2018, the city has been replacing its gas-fuelled buses with electric ones.

Recycle Right

Koreans are serious about rubbish sorting and recycling. Follow suit when disposing of your own garbage at your accommodation: food waste, general rubbish and various recyclables are all binned separately.

Seoullo 7017 (p88) is an overpass trans-formed into a beautiful garden promenade. **Seonyudo Park** (p115) is crafted from an old water-filtration plant and **Oil Tank Culture Park** (p107) is made from abandoned oil tanks.

See rubbish turned into art at **Seoul Upcycling Plaza** *(seoulup.or.kr)*, the world's largest space dedicated to upcycling.

VOLUNTEER

Opportunities for volunteering can be found through the Seoul Global Center *(global.seoul.go.kr)*, the Seoul Volunteer Center *(volunteer.seoul.go.kr)* and the Seoul International Women's Association *(siwakorea.com)*.

TAKE A HIKE

Explore Seoul's green hills and mountains along many clearly marked hiking trails. Hire hiking boots and clothing from the Seoul Hiking Tourism Center (p195).

Shop Local

Visit traditional markets to support local farmers, fishers and craftspeople. Gwangjang, Namdaemun, Dongdaemun and Tongin are all great ones to peruse.

Bring Reusable

Seoul now charges for plastic shopping bags, so come prepared with your own reusable one. You might consider bringing your own travel chopsticks, napkin and drinking glass to avoid the single-use disposables handed out at convenience stores and cafes.

Avoid Packaged

Korea has introduced some regulation to curb excessive packaging, but it can still be hard to escape. There are plenty of greener options, though, such as choosing loose produce from a market over individually wrapped produce from a convenience store.

Buy Secondhand

Hunt for preloved items at secondhand markets such as **Seoul Folk Flea Market** (p167) and **Dongmyo Flea Market** (p167), and charitable enterprises such as Beautiful Store *(beautifulstore.org)*. The 2nd floor of **Gwangjang Market** (p72) specialises in vintage clothing.

Be Mindful of Overtourism

Signs posted throughout Bukchon Hanok Village read 'Please be quiet' and 'This place is a residential area' to remind visitors that it is a real neighbourhood of 6500 residents.

Ttareungi, Seoul's public bike-sharing service, is a seamless way to get around, with docking stations all across the city.

Koreans have taken to mountain plogging – picking up rubbish when they go hiking in national parks such as Bukhansan. Rubbish bags are available from the Bukhansan National Park Ui Ranger Station.

Food Waste

Seoul has achieved an impressive food-waste recycling rate of more than 97%. This success is largely due to a mandatory 'pay-as-you-throw' system and widespread use of technology like RFID bins that weigh waste and charge residents accordingly.

RESOURCES

seoulsolution.kr
Read about Seoul's urban-planning and sustainable-development policies.

wwfkorea.or.kr
Local branch of the World Wide Fund For Nature.

kfem.or.kr
Korean Federation for Environmental Movement.

FROM TOP: CATINSYRUP/SHUTTERSTOCK, PIXEL-SHOT/SHUTTERSTOCK

Accessible Travel

Seoul has taken big strides in catering for travellers with disabilities, but still has a long way to go to make it a truly accessible city.

Discounts

Many tourist attractions, especially those run by the government, offer generous discounts or even free entry for visitors with disabilities, along with a helper.

Airport

Incheon International Airport is equipped with electric vehicles to shuttle passengers with mobility and visual impairments to and from gates. Escort services are available before departure and wheelchairs are freely available, too.

City Paths

Seoul has been installing lower kerbs for greater accessibility, especially in high-pedestrian areas. Some old neighbourhoods, however, can be challenging to navigate, particularly if they're hilly. The paths along the Cheonggye-cheon and Seoullo 7017 are accessible by lifts.

RESOURCES

seouldanurim.net Centre run by the Seoul Tourism Organisation that aims to make the city accessible to everyone.

koreawheelchair tour.com Travel agency dedicated to those with restricted mobility.

english.visitseoul. net Information on accessibility across the city.

SUBWAYS

Most subway stations have elevators, stair lifts and ramps, accessible toilets and Braille tiles to help find directions. Gaps between subway platforms and carriages are minimal. Inside subway cars, there's always priority seating for those who need it.

Danurim Accessible Tourism Center

Danurim's website *(seouldanurim.net)* has lots of information, including suggested itineraries. You can also arrange an airport pick-up service with wheelchair-ramp-equipped vehicles, and rental of wheelchairs and shower wheelchairs for your time in the city.

Accommodation

Some accommodation options, mainly midrange and top-end hotels, offer adapted rooms for those with disabilities. You can also search rental sites for wheelchair-accessible units.

BUSES

Buses are equipped with low floors, ramps and designated spaces for wheelchair access. Occasional crowding issues, however, can make them difficult to use.

Sights

With elevator access, **N Seoul Tower** (p78) offers panoramic views of the city. The **National Museum of Korea** (p124) has barrier-free exhibits with adjustable kiosks where visitors can access voice commentary, use Braille keypads and ask questions in sign language. Palaces such as **Gyeongbokgung** (p50) have some ramps.

Nuts & Bolts

OPENING HOURS

Banks 9am-4pm Monday to Friday

Post offices 9am-6pm Monday to Friday

Restaurants typically 10am-10pm, with break time 2.30-5pm

Bars normally 6pm-1am, with extended hours Friday and Saturday

Cafes 8am-10pm

Museums 10am-6pm Tuesday to Sunday

Shops 10am-8pm

Toilets

There are plenty of clean and well-signed *hwajangsil* (toilets) in Seoul. They're easily found in subway stations, parks and other public places, and are free. While Seoul has mostly transitioned to seated toilets, there are still a few squat-style ones. Face the hooded end when you squat. Toilet paper is usually available, but it's wise to carry a stash just in case. Some sewage systems can't tolerate toilet paper being flushed and you'll be asked to dispose of it in the bin instead.

Measures

Korea uses the metric system. Some traditional measures still exist, such as *pyeong* for floorspace.

Smoking

It's forbidden to smoke in public enclosed spaces, parks, on train platforms and outside subway stations and bus stops.

GOOD TO KNOW

Time zone
GMT +9

Country calling code
+82

Emergency numbers
119 (fire & ambulance), 112 (police)

Population
9.6 million

PUBLIC HOLIDAYS

New Year's Day 1 January

Seollal (Lunar New Year) 6-8 February 2027, 26-29 January 2028

Independence Movement Day 1 March

Children's Day 5 May

Buddha's Birthday 13 May 2027, 2 May 2028

Memorial Day 6 June

Constitution Day 17 July

Liberation Day 15 August

Foundation Day 3 October

Hangeul Day 9 October

Chuseok (Autumn Harvest Festival) 14-16 September 2027, 2-4 October 2028

Christmas Day 25 December

Electricity

220V/60Hz

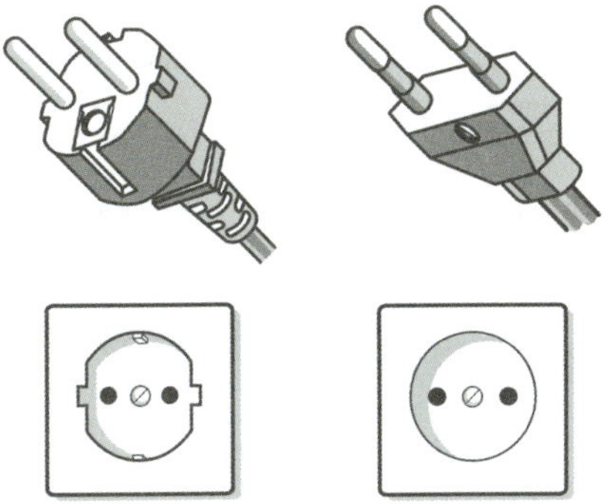

Language

Korean is spoken by around 80 million people. Its linguistic family is a matter of debate. Some scholars say it's an Ural-Altaic language; others place it with Jeju languages in their own family: Koreanic. Korean script, *hangeul*, is simple and accessible, as each character represents a sound of its own. There are a number of competing Romanisation systems in use today for *hangeul*. Since 2000, the government has been changing road signs to reflect the most recent Romanisation system, so you may encounter signs, maps and tourist literature with at least two different Romanisation systems.

Basics

Hello. 안녕하세요. *an·nyŏng ha·se·yo*

Goodbye. 안녕히 *an·nyŏng·hee*

(if leaving/staying) 계세요/가세요. *gye·se·yo/ga·se·yo*

Yes. 네/예. *né*/*yé* (Both of these mean 'yes' and they're used about equally.)

No. 아니요. *a·ni·yo*

Excuse me. 실례합니다. *shil·lé ham·ni·da*

Sorry. 죄송합니다/미안합니다. *choé·song ham·ni·da*/*mee·an·ham·ni·da* (Both expressions are used about equally.)

Thank you. 고맙습니다. *go·map·sŭm·ni·da/* 감사합니다*kam·sa·ham·ni·da*

You're welcome. 괜찮아요. *gwaen·cha·na·yo*

What is your name? 성함이 어떻게 되세요? *Sŏng-ha-mul ŏt-tŏ-ke dway-se-yo*

My name is ... 제 이름은 ...입니다. *je i·rŭ·mŭn ...·im·ni·da*

Do you speak English? 영어 할 줄 아세요? *yŏng·ŏ hal jul a·se·yo*

I don't understand. 못 알아 들었어요. *mot a·ra·dŭ·rŏss·ŏ·yo*

Directions

Where's a/the ...? ...어디예요? *ŏ·di·ye·yo*

What's the address? 주소가 뭐예요? *ju·so·ga mwŏ·ye·yo*

Could you please write it down? 적어 주시겠어요? *jŏ·gŏ ju·shi·gess·ŏ·yo*

Please show me (on the map). (지도에서) 어디인지 가르쳐 주세요. *(ji·do·e·sŏ) ŏ·di·in·ji ga·rŭ·ch'ŏ ju·se·yo*

Turn left/right. 좌회전/우회전하세요. *jwa·hoé·jŏn/u·hoé·jŏn ha·se·yo*

Time

What time is it? 몇 시예요? *myŏs·shi·ye·yo*

It's (two) o'clock. (두) 시요. *(du)·shi·yo*

Half past (two). (두) 시 반이요. *(du)·shi ba n yo*

At what time ...? 몇 시에 ...? *myŏs·shi·é ...*

At (five) o'clock. (다섯) 시에. *(da·sŏs)·shi·é*

morning 아침 *a·ch'im*

afternoon 오후 *o·hu*

evening 저녁 *jŏ·nyŏk*

yesterday 어제 *ŏ·jé*

today 오늘 *o·nŭl*

tomorrow 내일 *nae·il*

NUMBERS (KOREAN)

1 하나 *ha·na*

2 둘 *dul*

3 셋 *set*

4 넷 *net*

5 다섯 *da·sŏt*

6 여섯 *yŏ·sŏt*

7 일곱 *il·gop*

8 여덟 *yŏ·dŏl*

9 아홉 *a·hop*

10 열 *yŏl*

Know Your Numbers

Use pure Korean numbers for hours when telling the time, for counting objects and people, and for expressing your age.

Use Sino-Korean numbers for minutes when telling the time, for dates and months, and for addresses, phone numbers, money and floors of a building.

NUMBERS (SINO-KOREAN)

1 일 *il*

2 이 *yi*

3 삼 *sam*

4 사 *sa*

5 오 *o*

6 육 *yuk*

7 칠 *ch'il*

8 팔 *p'al*

9 구 *ku*

10 십 *ship*

DONATIONS TO ENGLISH

You'll find some Korean words are familiar to you, as they are often used in English. Words such as kimchi, ramyeon, soju, K-Pop, hallyu and taekwondo.

Signs

영업 중 Open

휴무 Closed

입구 Entrance

출구 Exit

금지 Prohibited

금연 (구역) No Smoking (Area)

화장실 Toilets

신사용 Men

숙녀용 Women

WORD STRESS

Korean pronunciation is pretty straight-forward for English speakers, as most sounds are also found in English or have a close approximation. Korean distinguishes between aspirated consonants (formed by making a puff of air as they're pronounced) and unaspirated ones (pronounced without a puff of air). Syllables are pronounced with fairly even emphasis in Korean.

Emergencies

Help! 도와주세요! *do·wa·ju·se·yo*

Go away! 저리 가세요!
jŏ·ri ga·se·yo

Call ...! ... 불러주세요!
... bul·lŏ·ju·se·yo

a doctor 의사 *ŭi·sa*

the police 경찰 *gyŏng·ch'al*

I'm lost.
길을 잃었어요. *gi·rŭl i·rŏss·ŏ·yo*

Where's the toilet?
화장실이 어디예요?
hwa·jang·shi·ri ŏ·di·ye·yo

I'm sick.
전 아파요. *jŏn a·p'a·yo*

It hurts here.
여기가 아파요. *yŏ·gi·ga a·p'a·yo*

I'm allergic to ...
전 ...에 알레르기가 있어요.
jŏn ...é al·le·rŭ·gi·ga iss·ŏ·yo

Eating & Drinking

Can we see the menu?
메뉴 볼 수 있나요?
me·nyu bol·su in·na·yo

What would you recommend?
추천 해 주시겠어요?
ch'u·ch'ŏn hae·ju·shi·gess·ŏ·yo

Do you have any vegetarian dishes?
채식주의 음식 있나요?
ch'ae·shik·ju·i ŭm·shik in·na·yo

I'd like ..., please. ... 주세요.
... ju·se·yo

Cheers! 건배! *gŏn·bae*

짠! *jjan!*

That was delicious! 맛있었어요!
ma·shiss·ŏss·ŏ·yo

Please bring the bill.
계산서 가져다 주세요.
gye·san·sŏ ga·jŏ·da ju·se·yo

Question Words

how 어떻게 *ŏt·tŏ·k'é*

what (object) 무엇을 *mu·ŏ·sŭl*

what (subject) 뭐가 *mwŏ·ga*

when 언제 *ŏn·jé*

where 어디 *ŏ·di*

which 어느 *ŏ·nŭ*

who (object) 누구를 *nu·gu·rŭl*

who (subject) 누가 *nu·ga*

why 왜 *wae*

浚明堂

THE SEOUL

STORYBOOK

Our writers delve deep into different aspects of Seoul life.

Deoksugung (p82) in autumn
SANGA PARK/GETTY IMAGES

A HISTORY OF SEOUL IN 15 PLACES

Empire, colonial subjugation, independence, civil war, authoritarianism, democracy, emergence as a global cultural power – and that was just the 20th century. Seoul's history is a dramatic one, and while it can sometimes feel forgotten amid the city's mad dash into the future, it remains stubbornly present, etched in soil and stone. By Charles Usher

SEOUL'S OUTSIZED IMPORTANCE in South Korea means the city's history is also the country's history. In the tumultuous Three Kingdoms era (57BCE–CE668), when Baekje, Goguryeo and Shilla vied for supremacy, control of the peninsula ultimately rested on control of this strategic Han River Valley location. Its status as the peninsula's power centre was cemented when the Joseon dynasty relocated its capital here in 1394; for the next 600 years, anything that happened in Seoul reverberated across the peninsula.

History flows in more than one direction, of course, and Korea's status as a small country surrounded by large powers has left Seoul practiced in absorbing outside influences, whether friendly or otherwise. Chinese Confucian beliefs, Western religions, Japanese colonial impositions and American military interventions have all left their mark.

Today's Seoul reflects both of these currents. It's increasingly cosmopolitan, hosting international cultures and a growing foreign population, while its importance within Korea is greater than ever. One in five South Koreans lives here, and the city is home to the country's most prominent companies, media and cultural institutions. If anything has changed, it's that, as the seat of one of the world's biggest economies and the source of a globe-conquering pop culture, Seoul now influences not just the rest of Korea, but the rest of the world.

1. Amsa-dong Prehistoric Site Museum

WHAT THE FLOOD FOUND

Seoul's earliest traces (so far) were unknown until a century ago. Even then, it took an act of nature to uncover them. In 1925, a flood exposed artefacts along the banks of the Han River. Archaeologists estimated them to be at least 6000 years old, making their creators the first known Seoulites. Beginning in 1967, excavations unearthed stone axes, arrowheads, weights for fishing nets, comb-pattern pottery and the remains of pit houses, offering clues to how these people lived. To date, this site in the Amsa-dong neighbourhood on the city's far east side remains the largest Neolithic settlement discovered in Korea.

For more on the Amsa-dong Prehistoric Site Museum, see page 156.

2. Pungnap-toseong

THE FIRST CITY

When the northern Gojoseon dynasty collapsed in the 2nd century BCE, Baekje was among the successors to rise from its ashes. The new kingdom established its capital, Wiryeseong, in what's now Seoul, and the 2.1km-long Pungnap-toseong earthen fortification is thought to have enclosed its royal palace. The site was a major centre of power, and its strategic location saw Baekje, Goguryeo and Shilla vie for control during the Three Kingdoms period. Shilla prevailed in 668 and, for several centuries, Seoul ceded the spotlight to the Shilla capital of Gyeongju and, later, the Goryeo capital of Gaegyeong (now Kaesong).

For more on Pungnap-toseong, see page 156.

3. Gyeongbokgung

A NEW DYNASTY PROSPERS

In 1392, General Yi Seong-gye overthrew the Goryeo kingdom in a coup, declared a new dynasty (Joseon) and named himself King Taejo. In 1394, he moved the capital to Seoul, an especially propitious location according to feng shui. Among the first structures Taejo constructed was his palace, which he named Gyeongbokgung, meaning 'the new dynasty shall prosper'. Seoul, or Hanyang, as it was then known, was once again the most important city on the peninsula. The Joseon dynasty would rule from Seoul for the next 500 years, developing Korea's own script, overseeing scientific advancements and shaping society around its Confucian philosophy.

For more on Gyeongbokgung, see page 50.

4. Gwanghwamun Square

THE CITY TAKES SHAPE

After establishing its capital, the Joseon dynasty set about shaping the city, and the modern metropolis still bears the imprint of this urban planning. Seoul's fortress walls still stand, and the roads approaching Gyeongbokgung from the south and east gates are still two of the city centre's main thoroughfares. Where those roads converged, the dynasty laid out a broad boulevard, the Street of Six Ministries, to create a grand approach to the palace. Today that's Gwanghwamun Sq, the city's most prominent plaza, which remains home to government offices and provides the same majestic view of the palace gate and Bugaksan.

For more on Gwanghwamun Square, see page 52.

Comb-pattern pottery, Amsa-dong Prehistoric Site Museum (p156)

DEA PICTURE LIBRARY/DE AGOSTINI VIA GETTY IMAGES

5. Jeong-dong

NEW IDEAS, NEW INFLUENCES

An 1876 treaty with Japan opened Korean ports to international trade, ending Joseon's long-standing policy of isolationism. Foreigners began making their way to Seoul, bringing with them ideas and practices that would transform modern Korea. Many of the new arrivals settled in Jeong-dong, and the neighbourhood retains traces of their influence. Chungdong First Methodist, the country's oldest existing Protestant church, stands here, as does part of Pai Chai Hak Dang, its first modern intermediate school. This period also saw the appearance of imported technologies such as railroads, streetcars and electricity that would dramatically alter the city in the years to come.

For more on Jeong-dong, see page 89.

6. Jungmyeongjeon

AN EMPIRE, BRIEFLY

The turn of the 20th century in Seoul was turbulent, even by Korean standards. In 1895, Japanese agents assassinated Empress Myeongseong, and King Gojong went into hiding at the Russian legation. After his emergence, Gojong declared that Joseon was now the Korean Empire, an attempt to place the country on equal footing with its powerful neighbours. The experiment was short-lived. Bolstered by victory in the Russo-Japanese War, Imperial Japan set its sights on Korea. In 1905, at Jungmyeongjeon, a minor building on the grounds of Deoksugung, it pressured Korea into signing the Eulsa Treaty, making the country a Japanese protectorate.

For more on Jungmyeongjeon, see page 83.

ATOSAN/SHUTTERSTOCK

7. Seodaemun Prison History Hall

THE COLONIAL ERA

Five years after the Eulsa Treaty, Japan formally annexed Korea, initiating decades of colonial rule. While certain modernisations took place, the era was defined by oppression. Sites of historic and cultural importance, including Gyeongbokgung, were damaged or destroyed. In later years, the Korean language was suppressed, and Koreans were forced to take Japanese names. Independence activists were dealt with harshly. Thousands were jailed in Seodaemun Prison, now Seodaemun Prison History Hall, where they were tortured and made to labour producing materials for Japan's WWII efforts. The end of the war brought Korean independence, but the accompanying joy wouldn't last.

For more on Seodaemun Prison History Hall, see page 189.

8. War Memorial of Korea

ONE BATTLE AFTER ANOTHER

The decision to divide Korea into Soviet and US occupation zones at the end of WWII set the stage for the Korean War. Seoul's importance and its location in the middle of the peninsula meant the city bore some of the worst of the fighting. When North Korean forces invaded on 25 June 1950, they captured Seoul in just three days, and the city would change hands three more times over the course of the war. By the conflict's end, Seoul lay in ruins. Barely a hint of that destruction is visible today, but its memory and remnants of the war's battles are preserved at the War Memorial of Korea.

For more on the War Memorial of Korea, see page 128.

9. Ihwa Maeul

A BOOMING POPULATION

Seoul's population more than doubled in the decade following the Korean War, reaching nearly 3 million. It continued to grow by the millions until the early 1990s, as people flocked to the capital in search of economic opportunity. Seoul struggled to absorb them, and many poor arrivals had no choice but to settle in *dal-dongnae*, or 'moon villages', improvised neighbourhoods with mountain-slope locations that were said to at least provide a better view of the moon. *Dal-dongnae* became a defining feature of Seoul's postwar landscape and many persist as vibrant communities, with Ihwa Maeul being perhaps the most well known.

For more on Ihwa Maeul, see page 178.

10. Mullae Arts Village

BUILDING ECONOMIC FOUNDATIONS

In the wake of the Korean War, South Korea was one of the world's poorest countries. A full decade after the end of hostilities, its GDP remained a paltry $4 billion. That began to change in the 1960s as the autocratic president, Park Chung-hee, set the country on a path of intense industrialisation. In Seoul, much of this was concentrated in the city's southwest, including what's now Mullae Arts Village. While most of the area's factories have long since decamped to smaller cities or abroad, many operations remain – vestiges of Korea's economic revival.

For more on Mullae Arts Village, see page 115.

11. Eunma Town Apartments

CROSSING THE RIVER

With a growing population and economy, Seoul found that it needed to expand beyond its traditional boundaries. To do so, it returned to its roots – to the land where Baekje established its first capital. In the 1970s, the government began developing Gangnam, the area south of the Han River, which had previously been mostly rice paddies and mulberry fields. It moved government offices and educational institutions across the river and encouraged the construction of hundreds of residential complexes, such as the Eunma Town Apartments, beginning a process that would eventually see Gangnam become the city's wealthiest district.

For more on the Eunma Town Apartments, see page 154.

12. MMCA Seoul

A COUP AND MILITARY RULE

It's odd to associate Seoul's premier art museum with military dictatorship, but what's now the MMCA Seoul was once the headquarters of the notorious Defense Security Command (DSC). After Park's assassination by his intelligence director in 1979, any door to democracy was slammed

Seodaemun Prison History Hall (p189)

shut when General Chun Doo-hwan staged a coup, beginning a period of military rule that lasted until 1987. Under Chun's regime, the DSC regularly detained, interrogated and tortured political dissidents and suspected communists. The decision to establish the MMCA here in 2013 was met with controversy, given the site's history, but there's something poetic about the transformation.

For more on the MMCA Seoul, see page 62.

13. Olympic Park

SEOUL'S COMING-OUT PARTY

When Seoul was awarded the 1988 Summer Olympics, it was seen as an acknowledgement of the city's economic progress. Though preparation for the event put some of the Chun regime's worst tendencies on display – many residents were forcibly removed from areas marked for development – it also resulted in things such as an expanded subway system and the creation of the sprawling Olympic Park. Most importantly, the increased international attention breathed new life into the pro-democracy movement and, in December 1987, the country held free, fair and direct presidential elections. Dictatorship was over, the Games were on and Seoul had arrived.

For more on Olympic Park, see page 158.

14. Cheonggye-cheon

URBAN REGENERATION

Seoul's modern history is reflected in the Cheonggye-cheon. The stream became the site of a shantytown in the impoverished post–Korean War years, only to be paved over and covered with an elevated highway during the following decades' developmental rush. By the early 2000s, the now-prosperous Seoul had turned its focus from development to livability, and Mayor Lee Myung-bak led a project to restore the stream. Completed in 2005, the renovated Cheonggye-cheon became one of Seoul's most popular urban retreats. It's only the most visible of many efforts across the city to turn old industrial sites into welcoming public spaces.

For more on the Cheonggye-cheon, see page 94.

15. National Assembly Building

BACK FROM THE BRINK

On 3 December 2024, South Korea was nearly plunged back into dictatorship. Parroting conspiracy theories about election fraud and accusing his opponents of engaging in anti-state activities, President Yoon Suk-yeol declared martial law and ordered the military to blockade the National Assembly Building. With protestors impeding the forces' arrival, legislators scaled walls to make their way inside, where they voted 190-0 to overturn the declaration, forcing Yoon to rescind his decree. Following mass protests, the Assembly impeached Yoon on 14 December. The following April, the Constitutional Court upheld his removal from office.

For more on the National Assembly Building, see page 112.

MEET THE SEOULITES

Seoul is a multifaceted megacity that dances to a rhythm, fusing tradition and modernity, innovation and inspiration. Jennifer Chang introduces the people of this dynamic, cultural hotspot.

BEHIND K-POP, K-BEAUTY, K-Food and everything else that follows the K-prefix trend are the people who breathe life into these realms. Seoulites may seem guarded or standoffish on the surface, but approaching one will reveal that just beneath that surface is a fountain of *jeong* – a sense of connectedness or a deep bond formed between people, even among strangers. Displayed in myriad forms, *jeong* can be a bus driver going out of his way to help a tourist get off at the right stop, or a landlord who eagerly offers steamed corn to a tenant living below as she heads out to meet her friends.

Having been the nation's capital for more than 600 years, Seoul is the place that attracts the nation's brightest minds and success-driven talents. People from all over the country have flocked to this city for centuries, carrying their hopes and dreams for a more prosperous future.

Even now, people 'move up' to Seoul, both geographically and metaphorically, to put down roots in the place that drives the nation's political, cultural and economic activity. Thanks to the popularity of Korean culture, a growing number of people from around the world are also making the move to be a part of this vibrant city, stretching the homogeneous fabric of Korean society and enriching the city's culture.

The people of Seoul are almost always in a hurry. As a nation that leapt from war-time poverty to economic powerhouse in a single generation, speed was one of the core ingredients for rapid success. In what's known as the *ppalli ppalli* (hurry hurry) culture, high-speed internet is the expected norm and, rather than waiting in line to purchase groceries, Seoulites head to the self-service kiosks where transactions are made at lightning speed.

Seoul has one of the world's best metro systems, with nine lines servicing more than seven million users daily. The frenetic energy of the crowds is most palpable here. Even on weekends it's common to see the left side of the subway escalators reserved for those in a rush to get somewhere, while those with more time on their hands stand on the right.

This go-go-go mentality seems to be embedded in the DNA of Seoulites, who are constantly competing to climb the social ladder. Perhaps this is why trends come and go in a flash in the competitive capital. K-Beauty and K-Fashion are prime examples of this tendency. What's in style today could be out of fashion in a matter of weeks. With a strong presence of FOMO in the background and social media blasting out the latest trends in the foreground, Seoulites are known for being ultra-fashionable and well-groomed, early adopters and global tastemakers.

Who & How Many

Seoul's population stands at nearly 10 million, with around 400,000 foreign nationals residing in the metropolis. In recent years, the number of single-person households has increased due to demographic, economic and cultural factors, now accounting for about 40% of the city's four million households.

Pictured clockwise from top left: Performers, Lotus Lantern Festival (p70); Korean man; Driving in Seoul; Korean woman at Gyeongbokgung (p50)

CLOCKWISE FROM TOP LEFT: IYOCHIKA PHOTOGRAPHER/SHUTTERSTOCK, LEOPATRIZI/GETTY IMAGES, RUNSTUDIO/GETTY IMAGES, SUNWOO JUNG/GETTY IMAGES

THE WORLD OF SEOUL

As a Korean-American living in Seoul for nearly two decades, I've seen the country and its capital change at breakneck speed, transforming into the global cultural powerhouse it is today.

In the first few years after my return, speaking English in public places still turned heads. To satisfy a craving for non-Korean food, I had the option of seeking out fast-food chains or trekking out to Itaewon, a hub for the city's international community.

Now it's not uncommon to hop on a bus and overhear conversations unfold in multiple languages simultaneously – an elderly Korean man chatting it up with an American mother and daughter in English, while a group of Spanish-speaking tourists discovers fellow Spanish speakers aboard.

Seoul has earned the reputation of being one of the world's most exciting culinary destinations, with international cuisines available all over the city, and while I've recently become a resident of Itaewon, I often head to other neighbourhoods to seek out the best burgers or authentic Mexican flavours.

CITY OF CONVENIENCE

Living in South Korea's tech-forward capital means access to an uber-convenient lifestyle. By Jennifer Chang

IN A CULTURE that demands speed and efficiency, convenience and comfort come aplenty for those who live in Seoul, one of the world's leading smart cities. Underpinning this culture of convenience is the nation's status as a technology powerhouse. Korea has one of the world's most advanced digital infrastructures, and the hyper-connected nation was named the world's fourth most innovative country by the World Intellectual Property Organization's Global Innovation Index (GII) in 2025.

The Powered Commute

Imagine a typical morning commute. Mobile-transit apps provide real-time schedules for buses and trains, making it possible to gauge exactly when to leave the house. While you wait at an intersection, anxiously refreshing the bus app to check the arrival time, the in-ground LED traffic-signal light glows green. Installed as a pedestrian safety measure for smartphone zombies, the flashing LED strips give you the go ahead to dart through the crowded crosswalk and hop on one of over 7000 city buses equipped with free wi-fi.

For millions of residents who use the city's public transport network daily, inclement weather is no obstacle. During cold waves, commuters can snag a seat on a heated bench while waiting for the bus. Amid sweltering summer heat, bus riders can pop into so-called smart shelters. Introduced in 2020 in Seongdong-gu, Seoul now has over 200 of these high-tech shelters generating ecofriendly energy, offering commuters a place to rest and recharge both their bodies and their devices in a climate-controlled space.

Next-Level Delivery Service

In a country where the online penetration rate surpasses 97%, and over 95% of the population own smartphones, creature comforts are just a scroll away. Out of coffee

CLOCKWISE FROM TOP LEFT: MOOMUSICIAN/GETTY IMAGES, ARNAUD EECKHOUT/GETTY IMAGES.

Clockwise from top left: LED traffic-signal lights; 7-Eleven store; Market Kurly app; Coupang Eats delivery

beans for your morning cup of joe? Open a delivery app and place an order while getting ready for work. By the time you're out of the shower, your caffeine fix will be at your doorstep. Need a new sofa after a move? Coupang, the country's e-commerce giant, has the solution. Through its 'rocket delivery' service, it's possible to have it delivered the next day. The company also offers 'dawn delivery' for fresh food items. The life-changing service, first offered by the online grocery-delivery startup Market Kurly, became increasingly popular during the COVID-19 pandemic. For many, it's hard to imagine life before the programme.

Perfected through cutting-edge technology and consumer demand, Korea's fast and efficient delivery culture is awe-inspiring. But history shows that Korea was a 'delivery nation' long before the arrival of technology. Records from the late Joseon era indicate that the scholar Hwang Yun-seok (1729–91) travelled to Hanyang, the Joseon-dynasty capital and the historic name for Seoul, to take the state examination. In his diary, he noted that he enjoyed a delivery of *naengmyeon* (cold buckwheat noodles served in a savoury broth) with friends as a celebratory meal after the exam. At the time, food delivery meant people trekking on foot overnight, hauling food-filled earthenware strapped to their shoulders using carrying frames. Centuries on, delivery riders zip through the city on scooters, still dropping off orders of cold buckwheat noodles. Delivery times are typically under an hour, and consumers have access to a wide selection of global cuisine and drinks, which can be ordered through apps such as Coupang Eats, Yogiyo, Baemin or Baedal Minjok, which translates to 'Delivery Nation' or 'Delivery People'.

With a few clicks, office workers burning the midnight oil can relieve stress with an order of sweat-inducing spicy food, while those waking up with the midnight munchies can indulge in belt-busting bites with a dash of regret. For those who prefer to eat alfresco, popular picnic foods like fried chicken and pizza can be delivered to designated 'delivery zones' along the Hangang River. Last summer, the government launched the 'K-drone delivery' service so residents in remote areas can receive shipments of food and daily necessities. In a culture accustomed to breakneck change, it won't be long until drone delivery becomes the new normal for receiving a meal or snack.

Seoul's One-Stop Wonders

South Korea's first convenience store opened in the early 1980s. As of 2024, there were nearly 55,000 convenience stores across the nation, with around 9000 retail outlets in Seoul. With major chains like GS25, CU, 7-Eleven and Emart24 operating 24-hour stores in urban areas, those living within a few minutes' walk of a convenience store are seen as enjoying a coveted advantage known as *pyeonsegwon*. A play on the words *yeoksegwon* (a Korean real-estate term that means an area near a subway or train station) and *pyeonuijeom* (convenience store), these one-stop shops offer everything from banking and delivery services to daily necessities. Some offer drop-off services for laundry and dry cleaning. Within 48 hours of drop-off, your clothing will be delivered to your doorstep. Many of the bigger stores offer seating for customers so they can prepare ready-to-eat meals and snacks in the microwave and sit down for a quick bite. With a growing number of single-person households, the city's convenience stores almost function as an extension of the local resident's fridge, stocked with fresh fruit and veg as well as wine, whisky and beer.

Korean convenience stores have become must-visit destinations for K-Food and culture lovers. Korean dramas and films often feature these neighbourhood stores as the place where lead characters grab a meal or drown their sorrows over a bottle of soju, as portrayed in the Netflix hit series *Squid Game*. YouTubers and social-media influencers showcasing their *mukbang* (live-streamed eating shows) skills are pushing out viral videos sharing the latest food trends at convenience stores. Embracing the global popularity of Korean cultural content, some retail branches have opened themed stores ranging from K-Pop and Korean instant noodles to sports to attract more customers. Over the past four decades, K-convenience stores have evolved to become hip hangouts that stay on trend, while meeting everyday needs for the residents navigating life in this fast-paced metropolis.

Seoul Queer Culture Festival (p226)
CHUNG SUNG-JUN/GETTY IMAGES

EVERYDAY QUEER LIFE IN SEOUL

In hiking clubs, Pride marches and group chats, queer communities in Seoul are building lives that last. By Phillip Tang

SOMETHING IS EMERGING in Seoul's queer life – not sudden liberation, but steady, accumulated visibility. It shows up on dating apps, in basement bars, in group chats planning weekend hikes, or across a cafe table where two women linger longer than friends usually do – unreadable to the wider world, yet unmistakable to one another.

Making the Invisible Visible

Out on the streets of Seoul, same-sex couples rarely hold hands or show affection, and their relationships remain largely unrecognised by law. But look closer and traces of change are emerging. For much of South Korea's recent history, queer lives were not just marginalised but statistically invisible. That began to shift in October 2025, when the national Population and Housing Census finally allowed same-sex partners to register as 'spouse' or 'cohabiting partner'. Previously, anyone who selected 'spouse' was flagged as an error and erased from the data. Advocates called the update modest but historic – queer relationships were no longer automatically written out of the numbers.

Legal Baby Steps

Legal recognition has arrived in similarly incremental ways. In 2024 a Seoul court ruled that same-sex partners could access benefits through the National Health Insurance Service, acknowledging shared finances and caregiving responsibilities. The decision did not legalise marriage, nor did it resolve broader inequalities, but it addressed a practical reality for couples navigating illness, work and family obligations. Change in South Korea often moves through narrow rulings rather than sweeping reform, and queer rights have followed that pattern.

Pride & Public Life

The most visible expression of a slow forward shift arrives each summer at the Seoul Queer Culture Festival (Seoul Pride to most people). What began as a small, heavily contested gathering has grown steadily over the past decade. Organisers estimate that attendance has expanded from a few thousand people in the early 2010s to well over 100,000 in recent years. The crowd is noticeably broader now – not just long-time activists, but couples, families, allies and curious first-timers. The atmosphere is celebratory rather than confrontational, marked by music, banners and a sense of collective ease.

Conservative Christian groups still line nearby streets, placards raised, preaching through loudspeakers. Their presence is noticeable, but it no longer defines the event. For most participants, they register as background noise rather than a reason to stay away. Today, Pride in Seoul feels less like a provocation and more like a familiar, affirming fixture on the city's calendar.

Networks & Everyday Spaces

Away from these public moments, queer life in Seoul is organised through continuity rather than spectacle. 'Homo Hill',

a block of clubs once at the heart of Itaewon's gay nightlife, is now just one part of a scene spreading across Itaewon and Jongno, where bars bring gay men together and Jongno venues host trans meet-ups. These places are not just places to drink or dance but spaces of recognition – familiar faces return, conversations resume and newcomers learn which spaces feel welcoming. The emphasis is less on visibility and more on belonging.

Lesbian and queer women's networks have developed differently. Instead of clustering around nightlife with unsustainable rents, they often gather through smaller, dispersed communities – book clubs in Hongdae and Hapjeong, shared dinners coordinated through group chats, and weekend hiking or walking groups. People return because they know who will be there and that the setting allows them to relax into themselves.

Trans communities also maintain networks that prioritise safety and mutual support. Informal social meet-ups, peer-led health-information exchanges and creative projects circulate largely by word of mouth. Across queer life in Seoul, the unifying principle is ordinariness – these spaces are not framed as statements, but as ways to make daily life more liveable.

Online Life

Digital platforms are a key part of holding these networks together. Private messaging threads, invite-only forums and dating apps act as the glue, especially for those who aren't out at work or at home. Profiles often include hints of identity – a carefully chosen rainbow emoji, a nod to queer cinema, or references only those in the community might recognise – signalling to others in the know while keeping some privacy. For younger queer Koreans, these spaces are a lifeline – somewhere to feel seen, swap stories and figure out who they are, especially if offline life still feels tricky.

K-Drama

Cultural representation has shifted in parallel. Streaming series such as *His Man* and *Merry Queer* portray queer relationships without sensationalism, focusing instead on everyday intimacy. Since 2021, more than a dozen Korean BL dramas ('Boys' Love', an industry term for adult male-male romance series, with roots in Japanese manga) have also appeared on streaming platforms, reflecting a growing appetite for these stories. Audiences remain relatively small, but what makes this real progress is that these shows are on screen at all – unthinkable a decade previous and largely free of major backlash.

Public figures within South Korea have also helped shift perceptions, especially in music and online media. When idols, web-series creators or influencers speak openly about queer identity or include LGBTIQ+ storylines, fan responses now tend to be supportive, especially among younger audiences. These moments rarely provoke major controversy, signalling a subtle normalisation – queerness is increasingly treated as part of contemporary culture rather than as scandal.

Lasting Change

Queer life in Seoul isn't all easy. Laws protecting LGBTIQ+ folk are still far off and most people juggle what they reveal and to whom. Family expectations are strong and keeping quiet can feel safer. Coming out? It isn't always the goal here.

And slowly, you can see progress. More queer Koreans are choosing to stay in the city, building life and community rather than moving away from prying eyes. Spaces endure, relationships are being named and recognised, and everyday gestures of belonging keep accumulating. Being part of these communities isn't about discovering something hidden, but recognising what has always been there. Familiar routines, trusted faces and repeated connections add up to a presence that can't be overlooked. Queer life in Seoul is incremental, sometimes fragile, yet resilient. And for those who know where to look, it's quietly energising – proof that ordinary acts of belonging can add up to something lasting.

THE PAST MEETS PIXEL: HOW SEOUL REINVENTED ITS ART IDENTITY

Ancient traditions and state-of-the-art tech collide in a new global art hot spot. By Esther Carlstone

AN EVENING STROLL through the streets of Seoul can transport you back centuries in minutes. A traditional Korean house *(hanok)*, with its wooden lattice doors, may sit steps away from an ultramodern glass-and-steel structure featuring vibrant digital visuals projected onto it. You'll find this kind of past-future collision everywhere: pop-up installations splashed across building walls, striking architecture just kilometres from 600-year-old palaces, modern media folding centuries of tradition into digital forms. This juxtaposition of past and present lies at the heart of Seoul's art identity and has allowed it to evolve into one of the world's most experimental creative capitals.

From Minimalism to Megabytes

For centuries, Korean art was all about balance and quiet elegance. Joseon-era paintings employed spare brushwork, white porcelain was decidedly minimal and calligraphy was an exercise in negative space. Then the 1990s hit and everything changed.

Seoul's transformation into a digital mecca seemingly happened overnight. PC bangs (internet cafes) were in every neighbourhood and an entire generation grew up playing *StarCraft* and scrolling through manga-inspired webtoons. Basically, young Koreans became digitally fluent while most of the world was still trying to figure out the internet.

Artists in the late 1990s started asking: what if screens could be canvases? Traditionally trained painter Lee Lee Nam began digitally animating classical Korean artworks. All of a sudden, cranes were flying off ancient silk scrolls and butterflies were dancing through historic landscapes. Tradition was being brought back to life in a fresh way.

By the early 2000s, spaces such as Art Center Nabi gave Seoul its first real home for media art. While others were dismissing gaming as mindless fun, Korean artists saw it as legitimate art. The webtoon revolution happened around the same time – platforms such as Daum and Naver let anyone publish comics, and artists proved that visual stories you scroll through on your phone could be just as moving as print art.

The K-Pop Revolution

If you want to understand Seoul's modern art scene, you have to talk about K-Pop. Groups such as Big Bang, 2NE1 and, later, BTS weren't just making music; they were giving fans complete visual experiences. Their music videos cost as much as independent films and employed entire teams

RICH
os angeles

2NE1 (p247)

HAN MYUNG-GU/WIREIMAGE VIA GETTY IMAGES

of visual artists and designers who often crossed over to other visual mediums.

The K-Pop frenzy created jobs for hundreds of digital artists and multimedia creators. Galleries began hosting exhibitions on K-Pop visual culture. Production companies hired fine artists for album concepts. K-Pop turned years of restraint on its head and told the country it was more than okay to be loud, colourful, and unabashedly alive. That cultural shift moved artists to experiment with scale and creativity in ways that might have felt too flashy just a generation earlier.

Today's Scene: No Boundaries

Walk into any contemporary Seoul gallery and you'll see what happens when artists stop choosing between old and new. Art duo Kimchi and Chips create large-scale installations where light, sound and space blur together until you can't tell where one ends and another begins. In their 2022 work *Halo*, they projected light onto water vapour, creating 3D drawings that formed and dissolved in midair – high-tech art that channeled those misty Korean landscape paintings from centuries past.

Artist Yang Hae-gue builds grand installations from Venetian blinds and fluorescent lights, with clear connections to Korean shamanic traditions and folk craft. His grids and lines nod to the banners and symbols of shamanic ceremonies, making light and ordinary materials feel almost magical. Local collective D'strict created viral installations like *Wave* at Coex K-Pop Square, where a massive, seemingly 3D wave crashes above the streets over and over again.

The city's architecture tells its own story. Zaha Hadid's Dongdaemun Design Plaza rises from the urban landscape like an elegant spaceship. Its silvery curves house galleries and design studios. At night, LED installations glow across its surfaces, transforming into light art.

At the Leeum Museum of Art, three famous architects – Mario Botta, Jean Nouvel and Rem Koolhaas – each designed a building, and somehow they all work together. The MMCA Seoul sits on a former Defense Security Command site, mixing restored Art Deco buildings with modern galleries where AI-generated paintings sit alongside centuries-old ceramics, spanning time like the city itself. With a lineup like this, Seoul shows it's a city where the world comes to build, and where global ideas meet local stories.

Neighborhood Art Crawls

There's art to be found practically around every corner in Seoul. Head to Seongsu-dong, once a gritty industrial area, now home to studios where artists 3D-print ceramics using algorithms derived from Joseon pottery databases. In Itaewon, galleries such as Space Willing N Dealing showcase VR works in intimate spaces. Over in Bukchon, traditional *hanok* contain projections that make 500-year-old wooden beams come to life.

Samcheong-dong's streets are lined with contemporary galleries, while Hongdae is where you're likely to find experimental installations. It's not uncommon to stumble upon a hot new artist by following a line snaking around the block filled with fashionable youth.

Amid all the tech, traditional craft is still around, albeit in an evolved form. Young artists use laser cutters to create intricate *hanji* (Korean paper) works. Others use AI to generate patterns based on traditional *dancheong* temple decorations. At Insa-dong's craft shops, you'll find centuries-old techniques applied to contemporary designs.

A New Global Art Capital

Seoul's art scene has gone global thanks to major fairs such as KIAF and Frieze, government backing and international buzz, but it only keeps growing. Korean artists tap into worldwide trends while staying rooted in local history and memory. With the world's third-highest number of private galleries (approximately 831 as of 2022) and many of them in Seoul, there's no shortage of visual snacks to explore. That's the appeal for art lovers. Seoul isn't about museum-hopping – it's about stepping into creative energy where tradition, technology and pop culture meld into each other daily, often in the most unlikely of places.

INDEX

Map Pages **000**

D

E

F

G

H

Map Pages **000**

N

O

P

Y

Z

"Catching my breath at the summit of Inwangsan (p190), only to gasp again at the splendour of the city panorama."

SIMON RICHMOND

"Stepping into the botanical wonderland that is Changdeokgung's Secret Garden (p61)."

ANN BABE

"Enjoying the elevated perspective from the lawn-covered, aluminium roof of Dongdaemun Design Plaza (p166)."

SIMON RICHMOND

FROM LEFT: TWENTY47STUDIO/GETTY IMAGES, EFIRED/SHUTTERSTOCK

Mapping data sources:
© Lonely Planet
© OpenStreetMap http://openstreetmap.org/copyright

THIS BOOK

Destination Editor
Selena Hoy

Production Editor
Sarah Farrell

Image Researcher
Ania Lenihan

Cartographer
Rachel Imeson

Coordinating Editor
Andrew Bain

Assisting Editor
Maja Vatrić

Cover Researcher
Daisy Korpics

Thanks
Michelle Bennett, Soyi Kim, Darren O'Connell, Thomas O'Malley, Charlotte Orr, Vicky Smith

MIX
Paper | Supporting responsible forestry
FSC™ C021741
www.fsc.org

Paper in this book is certified against the Forest Stewardship Council™ standards. FSC™ promotes environmentally responsible, socially beneficial and economically viable management of the world's forests.

Published by Lonely Planet Global Limited
CRN 554153
11th edition – Oct 2026
ISBN 978 1 83758 413 0

10 9 8 7 6 5 4 3 2 1
Printed in Malaysia